LIBRARY

Tel: 01244 375444   Ext: 3301

This book is to be returned on or before the
last date stamped below. Overdue charges
will be incurred by the late return of books.

CHESTER COLLEGE

JOURNAL FOR THE STUDY OF THE NEW TESTAMENT
SUPPLEMENT SERIES
125

Executive Editor
Stanley E. Porter

Sheffield Academic Press

Her Testimony is True

Women as Witnesses
according to John

Robert Gordon Maccini

Journal for the Study of the New Testament
Supplement Series 125

In honour of my parents

Published by Sheffield Academic Press Ltd
Mansion House
19 Kingfield Road
Sheffield, S11 9AS
England

Printed on acid-free paper in Great Britain
by Bookcraft Ltd
Midsomer Norton, Bath

British Library Cataloguing in Publication Data

A catalogue record for this book is available
from the British Library

ISBN 1-85075-588-4

CONTENTS

Biblical scholars can either confess or conceal their prejudices, but they cannot pretend to have none. Because my wife, Rebecca, and I are both ordained pastors, I have more than an academic interest in the issues of women in the Bible and the church. I am committed, to the best of my understanding and ability, to the equality of women and men in all aspects of church life. I think that I stand somewhere between the 'far left' and the 'far right' on these matters, and I hope that this shows circumspection rather than irresolution on my part.

Because of my vested interest in the advancement of women in the church, I am predisposed to want the New Testament to be favourable toward women. That predisposition cannot be removed, and so I have tried to keep it in view if not in check by playing the devil's advocate against myself throughout the research. Readers will judge for themselves whether or not this gambit was desirable, successful, or even possible.

I once submitted an article to a feminist theological journal. The editors informed me that the article was excellent but unsuitable because it was not written from a feminist perspective. The editors urged me to submit the article to a New Testament publication, or to rewrite it from a feminist perspective and resubmit it to them. I did the former because I am incompetent to do the latter. My interest in biblical issues about women does not qualify me as a feminist. Still, I hope to offer something of worth to New Testament studies about women, and I am encouraged by the opinion of I.M. Lindboe: 'Within New Testament research it is not possible to erase the contributions of male scholars, even if they apply only traditional methods, without losing valuable and interesting studies'.[1]

Shortly after I arrived for three years of study in Scotland, Brian Keenan was released after more than four years of imprisonment in

1. I.M. Lindboe, 'Recent Literature: Development and Perspectives in New Testament Research on Women', *ST* 43 (1989), p. 153.

Lebanon at the hands of fundamentalist militants. Keenan authored a book about his experience, and writes in the first chapter,

> I think of the opening lines of the Bible: 'In the beginning was the Word, and the Word was with God'. Somehow those lines kept ringing back to me in the long captive silences, with a head full of words, a confusion of images, a mind not sane enough to find a rational perspective from which I could understand what was happening to me. Again I recall that ancient prologue to try to convey to you something of that imprisoned time and hopefully to explain something of what it meant and how it continues to have meaning.[2]

The biblical scholar notices immediately that Keenan has failed to get it right, that he has confused the opening words of John with those of Genesis. No matter. Brian Keenan knows, in a way that very few of us—including biblical scholars—ever do, the power that John's words have to shine the light of Christ into even the most abysmal darkness. My hope is that this book will be more than just a scholarly exercise in trying to get things right, that in some way it will reflect the light which still shines in the darkness. If that happens, this book will have been worth the effort that I and those who support me have poured into it.

---

2.   B. Keenan, *An Evil Cradling* (London: Arrow, 1993), p. 1.

ACKNOWLEDGMENTS

Her Testimony Is True represents the substance of my PhD dissertation accepted at the University of Aberdeen in 1994. I am grateful to many individuals and groups who helped to make possible that dissertation and therefore this book.

Grants were provided by Clan Donald Trust, by the American Baptist Churches Board of Educational Ministries, and by the Committee of Vice-Chancellors and Principals of the Universities of the United Kingdom. Professor I. Howard Marshall and Professor Ruth B. Edwards gave me the opportunity to teach the Gospel of John to undergraduate classes, providing me with invaluable experience and financial assistance.

It was my pleasure to work under the supervision of Ruth Edwards. Her superb scholarship, candid criticism, and warm spirit served to guide, challenge, and sustain me.

The staff of the Queen Mother Library at the University of Aberdeen set the standards for efficiency, cordiality, and patience.

I cannot adequately thank the congregation of Crown Terrace Baptist Church in Aberdeen for all they have done, especially their pastor, James M. Gordon, and secretary, Nancy Manning. Likewise, the congregation of Queen's Cross Church of Scotland in Aberdeen and their pastor, Robert F. Brown, gave incalculable support.

Among many other generous friends in the United States, I am indebted to Bessie Ewen, Eunice Strobel, Roland Regnier, Felicia Desmarais, and Ken and Kate Downes.

This book reflects only one portion of the loving support I have received from my family. For them—especially my wife Rebecca—I am grateful beyond measure.

Above all, thanks be to God.

ABBREVIATIONS

Abbreviations for the canonical (protocanonical) and apocryphal (deuterocanonical) books of the Bible will be apparent to the reader, and unless otherwise noted, citations in English are from the text of the NRSV. Text-critical abbreviations and sigla for the Greek text of the New Testament follow those of NA^{26}.

AASF	Annales academiae rerum scientiarum fennicae
AB	Anchor Bible
AGJU	Arbeiten zur Geschichte des antiken Judentums und des Urchristentums
AnBib	Analecta biblica
BAGD	W. Bauer, W.F. Arndt, F.W. Gingrich, and F.W. Danker, *Greek–English Lexicon of the New Testament*
BDB	F. Brown, S.R. Driver, and C.A. Briggs, *Hebrew and English Lexicon of the Old Testament*
BDF	F. Blass, A. Debrunner, and R.W. Funk, *A Greek Grammar of the New Testament and Other Early Christian Literature*
BETL	Bibliotheca ephemeridum theologicarum lovaniensium
Bib	*Biblica*
BibOr	Biblica et orientalia
BJRL	*Bulletin of the John Rylands University Library of Manchester*
BJS	Brown Judaic Studies
BSac	*Bibliotheca Sacra*
BTB	*Biblical Theology Bulletin*
BU	Biblische Untersuchungen
BZAW	Beihefte zur *ZAW*
BZNW	Beihefte zur *ZNW*
CBQ	*Catholic Biblical Quarterly*
CBQMS	*Catholic Biblical Quarterly*, Monograph Series
ConBNT	Coniectanea biblica, New Testament
DRev	*Downside Review*
EDNT	H. Balz and G. Schneider (eds.), *Exegetical Dictionary of the New Testament*
EgTh	*Eglise et Théologie*
EncJud	*Encyclopaedia Judaica*
EvQ	*Evangelical Quarterly*
ExpTim	*Expository Times*

FFNT	Foundations and Facets, New Testament
FTS	Frankfurter theologische Studien
GBT	Gender and the Biblical Tradition
HeyJ	*Heythrop Journal*
HTR	*Harvard Theological Review*
ICC	International Critical Commentary
Int	*Interpretation*
IR	Iconography of Religions
ISBE	G.W. Bromiley (ed.), *The International Standard Bible Encyclopedia*, rev. edn
JBL	*Journal of Biblical Literature*
JSNT	*Journal for the Study of the New Testament*
JSNTSup	*Journal for the Study of the New Testament*, Supplement Series
JSOTSup	*Journal for the Study of the Old Testament*, Supplement Series
JSPSup	*Journal for the Study of the Pseudepigrapha*, Supplement Series
JTS	*Journal of Theological Studies*
JTSA	*Journal of Theology for Southern Africa*
LD	Lectio divina
LJLE	Library of Jewish Law and Ethics
LS	*Louvain Studies*
LSJ	Liddell–Scott–Jones, *Greek–English Lexicon*
MM	J.H. Moulton and G. Milligan, *The Vocabulary of the Greek Testament*
NCB	New Century Bible
NEB	New English Bible
NGTT	*Nederuits gereformeerde teologiese Tydskrif*
NIDNTI	C. Brown (ed.), *The New International Dictionary of New Testament Theology*
NIGTC	New International Greek Testament Commentary
NIV	New International Version
NovT	*Novum Testamentum*
NovTSup	*Novum Testamentum*, Supplements
NRSV	New Revised Standard Version
NTOA	Novum testamentum et orbis antiquus
NTS	*New Testament Studies*
NTTS	New Testament Tools and Studies
NumenSup	*Numen*, Supplement Series
OBO	Orbis biblicus et orientalis
OCP	Oxford Centre Papers
PJL	M. Elon (ed.), *The Principles of Jewish Law*
POTTS	Pittsburgh Original Texts and Translations Series
SANT	Studien zum Alten und Neuen Testament
SBLCP	SBL Centennial Publications

SBLDS	SBL Dissertation Series
SBLEJL	SBL Early Judaism and its Literature
SBLMS	SBL Monograph Series
SBS	Stuttgarter Bibelstudien
SBT	Studies in Biblical Theology
SJLA	Studies in Judaism in Late Antiquity
SJT	*Scottish Journal of Theology*
SKK	Stuttgart kleiner Kommentar
SNTSMS	Society for New Testament Studies Monograph Series
SPB	Studia postbiblica
SPIB	Scripta Pontificii Instituti Biblici
SR	*Studies in Religion /Sciences religieuses*
ST	*Studia theologica*
Str–B	[H. Strack and] P. Billerbeck, *Kommentar zum Neuen Testament aus Talmud und Midrasch*
SWR	Studies in Women and Religion
TA	*Theology Annual*
TCGNT	B.M. Metzger, *A Textual Commentary on the Greek New Testament*
TDNT	G. Kittel and G. Friedrich (eds.), *Theological Dictionary of the New Testament*
TEV	Today's English Version
TS	*Theological Studies*
TU	Texte und Untersuchungen
TW	Theologie und Wirklichkeit
TNTC	Tyndale New Testament Commentaries
VT	*Vetus Testamentum*
VTSup	*Vetus Testamentum*, Supplements
WBC	Word Biblical Commentary
WMANT	Wissenschaftliche Monographien zum Alten und Neuen Testament
WUNT	Wissenschaftliche Untersuchungen zum Neuen Testament
ZNW	*Zeitschrift für die neutestamentliche Wissenschaft*
ZSNT	Zacchaeus Studies, New Testament

Chapter 1

INTRODUCTION

1. *Rationale*

The subtitle of this study mentions three topics—women, witness, and the Gospel of John—each of which has received considerable attention from New Testament scholars.

John's Gospel continues to inspire widespread interest and intense study. The ever-growing mountain of secondary literature is a living monument to the abiding richness and relevance of this short and ancient book. E. Malatesta's Johannine bibliography, spanning 1920–65, exceeds two hundred pages to feature more than three thousand entries; G. Van Belle picks up where Malatesta left off, covering 1966–85, and stretching his bibliography to some five hundred pages to encompass more than six thousand entries.[1] These numbers are formidable in light of the fact that just two compilers (there are others) are dealing with a single book. The figures seem almost staggering when viewed against other factors: the brief time period canvassed, the limited number of entries, and the continuing proliferation of works in the years following Van Belle's collection. The assertion in Jn 21.25 about Jesus' unrecorded activities seems to be true also of the secondary literature on John's Gospel: 'The world itself could not contain the books that would be written.'

The topic of witness, never ignored by New Testament scholars, saw a flurry of studies in the 1960s–70s. The standard treatment is that of A.A. Trites, in which he devotes separate chapters to the Gospel of John,

---

1.   E. Malatesta, *St John's Gospel 1920–1965: A Cumulative and Classified Bibliography of Books and Periodical Literature on the Fourth Gospel* (AnBib, 32; Rome: Biblical Institute Press, 1967); G. Van Belle, *Johannine Bibliography 1966– 1985: A Cumulative Bibliography on the Fourth Gospel* (BETL, 82; Leuven: Leuven University Press, 1988).

the Johannine Epistles and Revelation.[2] The topic of witness has received particular attention in John's Gospel because of its emphasis there. The preeminent studies are those of J.M. Boice and J. Beutler.[3] Among the books and articles there have also appeared several dissertations, most recently one by M.R. Wilton.[4]

The phenomenon of women's studies is, except perhaps for that of literary approaches to exegesis, the most conspicuous and vigorous of the past twenty years in biblical studies. Work in this area flows on with no signs of ebbing: 'The work of feminist scholars, both individually and collectively, has been greeted in some quarters with impatience, irritation, dismissiveness, even contempt. But it has also established women's studies as a permanent focus of biblical studies.'[5] Two of the four canonical Gospels, Luke and John, have proved especially fertile ground for women's studies. Van Belle's bibliography on the Gospel of John features a short but separate section on women, a section that Malatesta's earlier volume did not need and that future compendia must expand. As of this writing, however, I am aware of no published monograph on women in the Gospel of John, although several books and articles (to be encountered in the course of this study) do deal with the subject, some of them at length.[6]

Since each of these—women, witness, John—has received considerable attention, how can I justify the present study? The rationale lies in the weaving together of those three topics in order to address a specific question: How might the testimonies of women as presented in John's Gospel have been perceived by a first-century Jewish readership?

2.   A.A. Trites, *The New Testament Concept of Witness* (SNTSMS, 31; Cambridge: Cambridge University Press, 1977).

3.   J.M. Boice, *Witness and Revelation in the Gospel of John* (Exeter: Paternoster Press, 1970); J. Beutler, *Martyria: Traditionsgeschichtliche Untersuchungen zum Zeugnisthema bei Johannes* (FTS, 10; Frankfurt: Joseph Knecht, 1972).

4.   M.R. Wilton, 'Witness as a Theme in the Fourth Gospel' (PhD dissertation, New Orleans Baptist Theological Seminary, 1992).

5.   C. Murphy, 'Women and the Bible', *The Atlantic Monthly* (August, 1993), p. 41.

6.   There is at least one relevant dissertation, that of S.E. Dollar, 'The Significance of Women in the Fourth Gospel' (ThD dissertation, New Orleans Baptist Theological Seminary, 1983).

2. *Method*

Just as the three strands of women, witness, and John's Gospel are woven together in my topic, so three factors are considered in my method: metatext, context, and text.

First, metatext is the approach to the text. Metatext involves the recognition that a gap exists between the ancient author and the modern reader, and therefore, that the latter comes to the text from beyond, to one degree or another, as an outsider. Thus, the reader must be deliberate in choosing an approach and be mindful of what that approach can and cannot do. I reject having to choose between the historical-critical method that has dominated Johannine study for so long and the narrative-critical method that over the last decade has given many indications that it may soon eclipse its predecessor. The two methods should not and need not compete, but rather, can complement each other well.

> While the two methods understand authors and readers in different ways, both methods actually use the same author-text-reader model of communication; for this reason, the results of narrative-critical exercises can be fruitfully incorporated into a historical-critical agenda. Reconstructive exercises associated with historical criticism... are not necessarily antithetical to the aim of interpreting the final, finished form of the Gospel, but may serve precisely that aim.[7]

The historical critic must remember that the proper object of exegesis is the text in its final form. The narrative critic must remember that often the final form of the text is uncertain and, in any event, that it did not come into existence in a vacuum.

The matter of method, then, becomes one of emphasis. I have chosen to emphasize a narrative approach, believing that it best suits my goals. Because I seek to understand how readers in John's culture might have responded to his presentation of women as witnesses, I am interested, although not exclusively so, much more in where the text is going than where it comes from, in its direction rather than its derivation.[8] I am conscious, nevertheless, of two caveats issued by J. Ashton.

---

7. M.C. de Boer, 'Narrative Criticism, Historical Criticism, and the Gospel of John', *JSNT* 47 (1992), p. 48.

8. I owe this last phrase to N.T. Wright, who used it in an address to the British New Testament Conference at St Andrews University on 16 September 1993.

In the first place, we cannot exclude a priori the possibility that some passages may not be fully intelligible without a knowledge of their history; from time to time it may be necessary to supplement the broad synchronic approach favoured by many exegetes with rigorous diachronic analysis. Secondly, the message of the Gospel is conditioned by the environment in which it was composed. It reflects, that is to say, the circumstances of the people for whom it was written and of the Johannine prophet who wrote it.[9]

Ashton's second caveat points to my second methodological strand, context, which involves the recognition that a text is conditioned by and reflects the elements that comprise the culture in which it took shape. The one element I have chosen to provide a basic context for this study is Jewish Law in first-century Palestine. This choice provides a specific focus while at the same time enjoying a comprehensiveness unattainable through narrower lenses. This is because the Law was not simply an important aspect, not even the most important aspect, of Jewish life, but rather, constituted what it meant to be Jewish. Since John's Gospel stems from an environment that was essentially Jewish (however heterogeneous or syncretistic that may have been), the Law is much more than a canvas upon which John paints his portrait of Jesus' life; it is part and parcel of the portrait itself. Of that, John's first-century readers would have been keenly aware. D. Nörr comments,

> The stories and parables of the Gospels are shot through with legal problems far more than the modern reader of the Gospels would imagine. They crop up in contexts which appear as far removed from the law as the last words of Jesus from the cross in John's Gospel (19.26f.), the parable of the Good Shepherd (Jn 10.11f.), and the passages about the forgiveness of sins (for instance, Mt. 6.12; 18.23ff.), to give only a few examples. Behind them lies not only the close connection of law and religion, so characteristic of Judaism, which makes the individual's relationship with God a legal relationship; they also indicate the almost intimate familiarity which men in the ancient world had with the legal system which applied to them, a familiarity which is characteristic of comparatively simple legal systems but would be utopian for us today.[10]

More specifically, the Jewish laws for evidence will be in view, particularly as they apply to women. It might appear peculiar to the modern

---

9. J. Ashton, *Understanding the Fourth Gospel* (Oxford: Clarendon Press, 1991), p. 382.

10. D. Nörr, 'Problems of Legal History in the Gospels', in H.J. Schultz (ed.), *Jesus in his Time* (Philadelphia: Fortress Press, 1971), p. 118.

reader that rules applicable to testimony given in courts of law should also apply to testimony given in the pages of a book, the Gospel of John. But once the modern reader comes to appreciate what Nörr has explained, the notion that it is odd for John and his readers to show concern for the Jewish laws of evidence vanishes.

Thirdly, there is the text itself. Just as I have rejected the 'historical versus narrative' dilemma as false, I also shun that of 'historicity versus symbolism'. While no one can prove for another that the events told in John's Gospel actually occurred, neither can anyone disprove them. So the only way forward for me is to state my presuppositions. I assume that the incidents John records are based upon real events from Jesus' life, and that John reports them in such a way as to highlight his own understanding of their significance.

> It is important to reject a false contrast, unfortunately all too common, which opposes the 'historical' and the 'symbolic' as if bringing out the symbolic dimension of a narrative or of a saying would thereby diminish its historical reality. Sometimes, when commenting on an event reported in some narrative, we say without scruple: 'Oh, it's only something symbolic', as if the insistence on the symbolic took something away from the importance of the historical event and eventually destroyed it. In fact, however, it is possible to state as a general proposition: History is in itself run through with symbolism according to the measure of whoever reads it.[11]

It is legitimate for someone to say, 'I don't believe that the events John narrates really happened'. But it is a misreading of John's Gospel to say, 'John didn't believe that the events he narrates really happened'. As B. Lindars remarks, 'When all allowance is made for John's free exercise of his imagination in reproducing traditional material, we must still recognise that he himself thought that he was describing something that actually happened and meant the story to be taken at face value'.[12]

My first assumption also has implications for what has come to be known as 'the Johannine community'. Because I assume that the events John reports are real, even if theologically and narratologically contoured, I also assume that his Gospel is more of a window on the life of Jesus than it is a mirror on the Johannine community. Again, this

11. X. Leon-Dúfour, 'Towards a Symbolic Reading of the Fourth Gospel', *NTS* 27 (1981), p. 439.

12. B. Lindars, *The Gospel of John* (NCB; London: Marshall, Morgan & Scott, 1972), p. 180.

assumption does not deny that John moulded narratives to speak to the needs of those in his congregation and beyond, but it does reject that he fabricated events for that purpose. On the basis of this second assumption, I will touch now and then upon the matter of what statuses and functions women might have had in the Johannine community, but I will not make proposals on that matter in my conclusions.

A final issue bridges metatext, context and text. Rhetoric as a tool for biblical criticism has been rediscovered, and during the last decade or so has come into its own as an individual discipline under the umbrella of literary criticism. Rhetoric—people speaking and writing to persuade others—is common to all times and places, to John's culture and to ours. T. Okure writes,

> It is indeed most curious that while the importance of rhetoric has been particularly emphasized in recent years, little or no attempt has been made to apply this category in any systematic way in the interpretation of John's Gospel. Yet this Gospel, more so than any other book in the NT canon openly declares itself in rhetorical terms (20.30-31).[13]

So along with Jewish Law, rhetoric will also factor into or, better, overarch my methodology, and if Okure is correct, justifiably so.

13. T. Okure, *The Johannine Approach to Mission: A Contextual Study of John 4.1-42* (WUNT, 2.31; Tübingen: Mohr [Paul Siebeck], 1988), p. 308.

Chapter 2

THE GOSPEL OF JOHN AS TRIAL

1. *The Rhetorical Purpose*

Matthew, Mark, Luke, and John are Evangelists not simply because they tell about Jesus Christ, but because they intend to evoke belief in him. They write Christian propaganda. In current usage the word propaganda usually implies pernicious goals, spurious contents and insidious tactics—implications contrary to the nature of the Gospels. Still, strictly speaking, the Gospels are propaganda because they intend to propagate faith in Jesus Christ. Even a cursory reading of the texts confirms this without the authors having to spell out their motives and goals. But two Evangelists do articulate their incentives and objectives, Luke at the beginning (Lk. 1.1-4) and John toward the ending (Jn 20.30-31).

Luke is responding to others who 'have undertaken to set down an orderly account of the events that have been fulfilled among us' (Lk. 1.1). Luke tells Theophilus that he seeks to set the record straight, since his information derives from 'those who from the beginning were eyewitnesses' (Lk. 1.2) to the matters being committed to pen and ink. John informs his readers that he presents some of what Jesus said and did in the presence of his disciples so that 'you may come to believe that Jesus is the Messiah, the Son of God, and that through believing you may have life in his name' (Jn 20.31). The appeals by Luke and John to eyewitness authority show their concerns to convince readers that their accounts of Jesus are trustworthy. John takes the further step of confessing the hope that readers will accept not only the truth of his report about Jesus' words and deeds, but also that they will embrace the truth of his claim about Jesus' identity: he is the messiah, the Son of God.

There is disagreement regarding the literary genre(s) of the Gospels, but all are by nature rhetorical documents because they seek to persuade. Each of the Gospels has a particular strategy for addressing the major rhetorical problems confronting them. G.A. Kennedy lists these problems as (1) convincing people that Jesus is the expected messiah of the Jewish faith, (2) dealing with the failure of the end of the age to materialize quickly in the terms in which Jesus seemed to describe it, (3) providing historical verification for what is narrated about Jesus, (4) establishing that Jesus is not a son of God, but the Son of God.[1] Interpreting the Gospels as rhetoric is a burgeoning practice but not a new one. As early as the first half of the second century, Papias and Justin Martyr interpreted the Gospels and their traditions in terms of Hellenistic rhetorical categories, and within two generations after the appearance of the Gospels, educated Christians understood them within ancient rhetorical canons.[2] Later, others such as Origen and Augustine would apprehend the Gospels as rhetorical works.

There is no consensus as to how precise a match exists between Christian and Classical rhetoric. A.N. Wilder and G.A. Kennedy tend to draw firm lines between Christian and Classical modes of persuasive discourse, contrasting the revelatory authority of Christian preachers against the rational persuasion of Graeco–Roman rhetors. For Wilder, the Gospel is essentially 'revelation, not persuasion', and for Kennedy, Christian preaching is 'not persuasion, but proclamation, and is based on authority and grace, not on proof'.[3] These modern views of Wilder and Kennedy parallel the ancient perspective of Eusebius (*E.H.* 3.24) that the first Christian preachers, the apostles, 'were common in their language, relying upon the divine and wonderful energy granted them, they neither knew how, nor attempted to propound the doctrines of their master, with the art and refinement of composition', and that they 'bestowed but little care upon the study of style'. That Gospel proclamation is not couched in compelling or artistic language does not mean, however, that Christian preachers had no persuasive designs or skills, but rather, that the persuasive power of Christian preaching resides in divine *fiat* versus human *ratio* (see 1 Cor. 1.17), and further, that the material of the New Testament, especially the Gospels, as written

---

1. G.A. Kennedy, *New Testament Interpretation through Rhetorical Criticism* (Chapel Hill: University of North Carolina Press, 1984), pp. 98-101.

2. D.E. Aune, *The New Testament in its Literary Environment* (Philadelphia: Westminster Press, 1987), pp. 66-67.

3. A.N. Wilder, *Early Christian Rhetoric* (Cambridge, MA: Harvard University Press, 1971), p. 21; G.A. Kennedy, *Classical Rhetoric and its Christian and Secular Tradition from Ancient to Modern Times* (London: Croom Helm, 1980), p. 127.

rhetoric does not fit with anything like precision into the literary canons of Classical rhetoric.

The distinctions made by Wilder and Kennedy remain essentially valid but have been refined. Kennedy refines his own position by drawing a line between a 'radical Christian rhetoric' that relies solely upon authoritative proclamation and rhetoric that does appropriate in some measure the persuasive tools of Classical rhetoric.[4] J.R. Levison thinks that Kennedy provides incomplete criteria for distinguishing between his radical category and its refinement, and that the category of radical Christian rhetoric wrongly isolates Christian preaching as proclamation, thus erroneously disqualifying Christian preaching as persuasion. Erasing some of the lines drawn between the Christian preacher who is a passive mouthpiece for the Spirit and the Classical rhetor who relies on the persuasive tools of human reason, Levison offers another model in which the Christian preacher, diligently seeking God, receives from the Spirit gifts of persuasive discourse and consciously develops and uses them.[5] By heeding the individuality of each author and situation, Levison's work serves to correct the rigid dichotomy between authoritative proclamation and rational persuasion. For example, John and Paul both make authoritative proclamations, but their individual rhetorical strategies proceed quite differently. John's rhetoric better aligns with Kennedy's radical mode in that John requires his audience to accept his Spirit-led revelation of Jesus' God-given signs and words without benefit of extended rational persuasion.[6] Paul's rhetoric fits better with Levison's alternative mode in that Paul, also under the guidance of the Spirit, employs his formidable rhetorical skills in lengthy argumentation

---

4.   Kennedy, *New Testament Interpretation*, p. 7.

5.   J.R. Levison, 'Did the Spirit Inspire Rhetoric? An Exploration of George Kennedy's Definition of Early Christian Rhetoric', in D.F. Watson (ed.), *Persuasive Artistry* (JSOTSup, 50; Sheffield: JSOT Press, 1991), pp. 25-40.

6.   M. Warner notes that John's persuasive art has propositional and intellectual elements, but only at the level of rhetorical *logos*, which in John's case is juridical: the scandal of the supreme Jewish court convicting the Messiah on the capital charge of blasphemy ('The Fourth Gospel's Art of Rational Persuasion', in *idem* [ed.], *The Bible as Rhetoric* [London: Routledge & Kegan Paul, 1990], p. 163). P. Riga equates the Johannine σημεῖα with the Synoptic παραβολαί, and notes that rhetorically, both signs and parables are media not for making doctrine more intelligible but for divine revelation ('Signs of Glory: The Use of "Semeion" in St John's Gospel', *Int* 17 [1963], pp. 403-405).

to convince his readers of the eminent soundness of his case.[7]

The rhetorical cast of John's Gospel is increasingly recognized. R.G. Hall observes that John chooses 'prophetic history—an inspired chronicle of the past—as the vehicle for his ideas'.[8] Being a 'revealed history' based upon eyewitness testimony and God's inspiration, John's chronicle and interpretation of events are endowed with prophetic authority in accordance with ideals for the writing of Jewish history in the first century. Hall further observes that 'revealed history' was a rhetorical technique used by Jews and Christians alike for persuasive purposes: 'Because the past could only be understood by revelation, revelation of the past was a powerful tool in the hand of those who wielded it. It gave them an ethos so powerful and an argument so unassailable that, could they pull it off, their point was gained.'[9] Rhetorical traits in John's Gospel have been noticed before, but the rediscovery that the entire book is cast in a rhetorical mould needs more emphasis, especially because recent rhetorical studies of the New Testament books focus predominantly on the Pauline Epistles.

Warner sees persuasion as John's main purpose and writes, 'If we follow the classic Aristotelian definition of "rhetoric" in terms of the available means of persuasion...we may say that the complex art [John's Gospel] undoubtedly displays may properly be considered in the first instance in terms of rhetorical artifice—an art of persuasion'.[10] Similarly, Okure finds the most important methodological outcome of her work to be the discovery that the character of John's Gospel is essentially rhetorical. She finds the entire Gospel 'seething with formal rhetorical traits', convincing her that 'rhetoric is an all-embracing characteristic of the Evangelist's method'.[11]

While the narrative approaches of M.W.G. Stibbe and R.A. Culpepper differ, both highlight John's rhetorical nature. Stibbe says of John 18–19, for example, 'Every narrative technique is employed with the rhetorical purpose of persuasion in mind'.[12] Unlike Stibbe, Culpepper is

7.   Eusebius (*E.H.* 3.24) esteems Paul as the most powerful of all in the preparation of argument.

8.   R.G. Hall, *Revealed Histories: Techniques for Ancient Jewish and Christian Historiography* (JSPSup, 6; Sheffield: JSOT Press, 1991), p. 235.

9.   Hall, *Revealed Histories*, p. 247.

10.   Warner, 'Rational Persuasion', p. 153.

11.   Okure, *Approach to Mission*, pp. 306-307.

12.   M.W.G. Stibbe, *John as Storyteller: Narrative Criticism and the Fourth Gospel* (SNTSMS, 73; Cambridge: Cambridge University Press, 1992), p. 120.

unconcerned about the identity and credibility of historical personalities behind the text, but is very much interested in those matters in regard to the literary personalities in the text. Culpepper notes John's use of self-authenticating literary strategies.

> The gospel makes use of virtually all of the devices available for heightening the credibility and authority of a narrative: appeal to tradition, a reliable narrator, inspiration (the Paraclete), eyewitness testimony, the authority of an esteemed figure (the Beloved Disciple), and the approval of a community. Internally, the provision of historical, geographical, and descriptive detail which is either demonstrably true or verisimilar serves to confirm the claims the narrative makes for itself.[13]

Culpepper further notes that John's plot 'is controlled by thematic development and a strategy for wooing readers to accept its interpretation of Jesus'.[14] Strictly a literary critic, Culpepper is careful to state that John courts readers to accept his interpretation of Jesus. To that I would add that John's more fundamental hope was that his interpretation of Jesus would move readers to accept Jesus himself. In any case, Culpepper's work highlights how John wields a panoply of literary weapons in the battle to persuade, and he perhaps makes a muted acknowledgment that literature and history are partners in persuasion when he remarks, 'Confession ultimately depends upon story for its credibility'.[15]

The rhetorical model neither exhausts nor limits the literary character of John, but it is a useful interpretative tool. John's rhetoric fits Kennedy's radical category while still exhibiting certain elements of Classical rhetoric. Every rhetorical situation, including John's, has an author whose credibility must be established (*ethos*), an audience whose favour must be secured (*pathos*) and a discourse whose methods must be convincing (*logos*). *Ethos* undertakes to establish the integrity and reliability of the author's character. John twice claims that his reports are true and stand upon eyewitness authority (Jn 19.35; 21.24). *Pathos* seeks to put the audience in a frame of mind sympathetic to the author. John accomplishes this in several ways, for example, by echoing in his prologue both Genesis and the Wisdom tradition. *Logos* aims to convince readers of the author's case by means of proofs. John's text

---

13. R.A. Culpepper, *Anatomy of the Fourth Gospel: A Study in Literary Design* (FFNT, 1; Philadelphia: Fortress Press, 1983), pp. 48-49.

14. Culpepper, *Anatomy*, p. 98.

15. Culpepper, *Anatomy*, p. 89.

abounds with the words Jesus spoke, the signs he performed, and numerous witnesses to both.

But is it right to identify John as a rhetor? How could he (or any of the Evangelists) be so versed in the conventions of Classical rhetoric that his work abounds with formal rhetorical traits? The latter question begs several other questions of authorship, but it also overlooks that John may have used rhetorical styles and devices unconsciously and instinctively, especially under divine inspiration.

> The Greeks merely became intellectually conscious of an impulse which is part of our repertoire as symbol users. As the Greeks applied that impulse to the art of political discourse, the Hebrews applied it to narrative, but they did not conceptualize it, for such conceptualizing was foreign to the modes of discourse in which they were engaged.[16]

Levison recalls the strong Jewish tradition of Spirit-inspired rhetoric (Wisdom, Sirach, Susanna) in which 'the Spirit equips a person to be intelligent in thought and, consequently, persuasive in speech'.[17] It is hard to imagine a New Testament writing to which this concept of rhetoric is more applicable than the Gospel of John, given its marked emphasis on Spirit-inspired teaching, remembrance, revelation, and truth (Jn 14.26; 15.26; 16.12-13). Thus, the fact that conventions of Classical rhetoric apply to John's Gospel does not mean that John must have been schooled in them or must have written with pen in one hand and rhetoric primer in the other.

The existence of formal rhetorical traits in John's Gospel can be understood in a different light: 'What we might call the "rhetoric" of early Christianity is not, then, rhetoric in the technical sense; rather, the word is used in the wider sense, denoting the manner and circumstances that promote persuasion.'[18] Furthermore, Palestine and Syria were hardly in rhetorical quarantine, and so the Gospel writers 'would have been hard put to escape an awareness of rhetoric as practiced in the culture around them, for the rhetorical theory of the schools found its immediate application in almost every form of oral and written communication'.[19] Thus, in a culture whose communication was saturated with

---

16. D. Patrick and A. Scult, *Rhetoric and Biblical Interpretation* (JSOTSup, 82; Sheffield: Almond Press, 1990), p. 31.

17. Levison, 'Did the Spirit Inspire Rhetoric?', p. 31.

18. A. Cameron, *Christianity and the Rhetoric of Empire: The Development of Christian Discourse* (Berkeley: University of California Press, 1991), p. 26.

19. Kennedy, *New Testament Interpretation*, p. 10.

rhetoric, John would recognize, without necessarily having been schooled in the finer points of Classical rhetoric, the need to establish his credibility, win readers' affections and provide persuasive evidence. *Ethos, pathos* and *logos* are in many ways as much a matter of common sense and exposure to the conventions of cultural discourse as they are of formal training.

Wilder is well aware of the literary gap between Christian and Classical rhetoric, and thus perceives that 'Greek and traditional human-ist categories are inadequate as measuring rods' for the Gospels, because the Gospels do not fit precisely into the literary moulds of Classical rhetoric.[20] Yet, persuasion of any audience does presuppose some com-monality of 'attitudinizing conventions, precepts that condition (both the writer's *and* the reader's) stance toward experience, knowledge, tradi-tion, language, and other people'.[21] To persuade someone of something unknown requires something that is known, some common ground on which the appeal can be based. It is therefore mistaken to seat Christian and Classical rhetoric in two different theatres or to view Graeco–Roman culture merely as the backdrop for New Testament literature. Rather, a syncretistic culture was the soil into which the seeds of the Christian message were sown. Early Christian literature 'should be viewed as rooted in the attempt to attract and convince persons of the Hellenistic world, be they already Christians, Jews, or pagans'.[22]

A distinctive early Christian rhetoric meshes with that commonly practised in the Roman Empire because persuasion is best accomplished through what is already known, and the intermingling of the Christian, Jewish, Hellenistic and Roman facilitated Christian persuasion of non-Christians.[23] For example, Paul's persuasive strategies can appeal variously to his Jewish roots (Rom. 11.1; Phil. 3.5), his Christian experience (1 Cor. 9.1; 1 Tim. 2.7) and even to Greek poets (Acts 17.28; 1 Cor. 15.33) as the circumstances warrant. This situation is analogous to that where some scholars once thought that the Greek of the New Testament was a uniquely 'Christian Greek', a notion long since banished by (among other things) the Papyri. The Christian message was

---

20. Wilder, *Early Christian Rhetoric*, p. 36.

21. T.O. Sloan, cited by W. Wuellner, 'Where Is Rhetorical Criticism Taking Us?', *CBQ* 49 (1987), p. 450.

22. E. Schüssler Fiorenza (ed.), *Aspects of Religious Propaganda in Judaism and Early Christianity* (South Bend: University of Notre Dame Press, 1976), p. 2.

23. Cameron, *Rhetoric of Empire*, pp. 29-39.

unique, but the Greek that voiced it was the *lingua franca* of the culture. Likewise, Christian rhetoric adopted and adapted the rhetorical *lingua franca* of its milieu. The result was a Christian rhetoric related to but not identical with Classical rhetoric. 'The challenge for early Christians', remarks B. Mack, 'was to (mis)use conventional modes of conviction in the attempt to articulate a new and distinctive ethos.'[24]

The understanding of John's rhetorical agenda is controlled by Jn 20.30-31. These verses evoke the image of a lawyer selecting the most compelling pieces of evidence for a summation to a jury. Viewed in the light of Hellenistic and rabbinic literature, these verses may be recognized as 'a formal rhetorical statement which provides the key as to how material in the Gospel is to be read'.[25] D.A. Carson notes that recent discussions of purpose have tended to ignore Jn 20.30-31: 'The purpose of the Fourth Gospel has been delineated largely on premises other than and broader than this explicit contribution to the theme within the canonical text.'[26] The Gospel as a whole will manifest the purpose stated in Jn 20.30-31, but if those verses provide a blueprint for that purpose, there is no need to reconstruct one from the nuts and bolts of the text. Following on the heels of Jesus' blessing on those who believe without having seen, Jn 20.30-31 is aimed directly at the readers and surely holds the key to John's rhetorical framework.

Even if John's blueprint of purpose sits in plain view on the table of Jn 20.30-31, how it should be read is not so obvious. Two exegetical issues arise.

First, Jn 20.30-31 states that some of Jesus' many σημεῖα (signs) are recorded for persuasive purposes. John 7.31 shows that Jesus' miracles are intended to convince Jews of his messiahship: 'When the Messiah comes, will he do more signs than this man has done?' But J.L. Martyn sees a conflict: 'John presupposes that his use of Jesus' miracles as evidence pointing to his messiahship will make sense to *Jews*, whereas Jewish sources seem to give us no reason to view this presupposition as

---

24. B. Mack, *Rhetoric and the New Testament* (Minneapolis: Fortress Press, 1990), p. 38.

25. Okure, *Approach to Mission*, p. 39. W.J. Bittner likens the form of Jn 20.30-31 to the *pauca e multis* device of Classical rhetoric (W.J. Bittner, *Jesu Zeichen im Johannesevangelium: Die Messias-Erkenntnis im Johannesevangelium vor ihrem jüdischen Hintergrund* [WUNT, 2.26; Tübingen: Mohr [Paul Siebeck], 1987], pp. 202-205).

26. D.A. Carson, 'The Purpose of the Fourth Gospel: John 20.31 Reconsidered', *JBL* 106 (1987), p. 639.

a realistic one.'[27] Martyn resolves the perceived tension by explaining that Jesus absorbed the miraculous expectations placed upon other eschatological figures, notably prophets like Moses and Elijah. However, Martyn's reading of Jewish sources and messianic expectations is open to question. W.J. Bittner remarks,

> The ancient Jewish sources speak clearly about the miracles of the messianic era. But curiously, they leave open the standing of the messiah in relation to these miracles. Will he perform them himself, or will he usher in an era of miracles? Because of this uncertainty, the conclusion has often been drawn in New Testament research that the messiah was not expected to perform miracles.[28]

Indeed, other scholars, contrary to Martyn, think that it was common among first-century Jews to expect the Messiah to reveal his identity through miraculous deeds.[29] Regardless of which side in this dispute is taken, Jesus' signs clearly are offered as an integral part of the testimony to his origins, identity and authority, although John makes it equally clear that faith begun in miracles should not end in them.

R.T. Fortna is convinced that John's Gospel is built upon a Signs Source whose intent is stated in Jn 20.30-31: 'Undoubtedly both author and reader would have been confronted with many other theological issues; but as a textbook for potential Jewish converts the Gospel of Signs sought to prove one thing only: that Jesus was the Messiah in whom men should believe.'[30] But if Jn 20.30-31 does perorate a Signs Source, then perhaps the purpose statement applies only to the Signs Source material and not to John's Gospel as a whole. Fortna thinks not, maintaining that John shared in the purpose of his Signs Source.[31]

Apart from the issue of sources, perhaps John intends only the recorded signs, not the Gospel as a whole, to be what persuades the reader. English translations tend to render ταῦτα in Jn 20.31 as 'these'

27. J.L. Martyn, *History and Theology in the Fourth Gospel* (New York: Harper & Row, 1968), p. 87.

28. Bittner, *Jesu Zeichen*, p. 136.

29. For example, R. Kysar, *John, the Maverick Gospel* (Atlanta: John Knox Press, 1976), p. 68.

30. R.T. Fortna, *The Gospel of Signs: A Reconstruction of the Narrative Source Underlying the Fourth Gospel* (SNTSMS, 11; Cambridge: Cambridge University Press, 1970), p. 234. The Signs Source theory, first proposed by A. Fauré and later popularized by R. Bultmann, remains unproven.

31. Fortna, *Gospel of Signs*, p. 234 n. 1.

rather than 'these things', meaning that ταῦτα refers only to the σημεῖα and not to the entire Gospel. John uses the plural of τοῦτο some sixty-five times. With only one exception (Jn 10.21), the use is substantival rather than adjectival, with 'these things' as the referent, and never modifying a specific nominal subject. This overwhelmingly consistent usage suggests that ταῦτα in Jn 20.31 should be understood as referring to the entire contents of the Gospel and not just to the signs. In any event, as P.J. Judge observes, John 'has placed his entire gospel under the rubric of σημεῖα'.[32]

The conclusion of John's Gospel refers to ὁ μαθητὴς ὁ μαρτυρῶν περὶ τούτων καὶ ὁ γράψας ταῦτα (Jn 21.24), affirming that the author writes about 'these things' and not just 'these signs', because the σημεῖα are not specifically in view there. Moreover, the ἄλλα πολλά of Jn 21.25 shows that 'these things' in Jn 21.24 are part of 'many other things', not just signs, that Jesus did. Against this interpretation, C. Roberts argues that ταῦτα in Jn 20.31 and τούτων and ταῦτα in Jn 21.24 refer grammatically only to their immediate antecedents, that is, the signs of the Gospel (Jn 20.31) and the events of John 21 (Jn 21.24). However, Roberts then says of Jn 20.31, 'In effect ταῦτα refers to the previous twenty chapters'.[33] But that is precisely the point I am arguing here. Roberts appears to be making an ungainly attempt to distinguish between what ταῦτα says (grammar) and what it means (effect). Also, Roberts's study is inconsistent because it does not allow for the same 'effect' in Jn 21.24-25. Most exegetes rightly conclude that τούτων and ταῦτα in Jn 21.24 refer to the entire Gospel, and it is clear that John offers not part but all of his Gospel as persuasive evidence.[34]

Secondly, a question over the variant readings at Jn 20.31 is often framed in terms of whether the author wrote a *Gemeinde-Evangelium* to reinforce the faith of believers (πιστεύητε, present subjunctive) or a *Missionsschrift* to inculcate faith in unbelievers (πιστεύσητε, aorist subjunctive). E.A. Abbott maintains that John uses ἵνα with the present

---

32. P.J. Judge, 'A Note on Jn 20,29', in F. van Segbroeck *et al.* (eds.), *The Four Gospels 1992* (BETL, 100; 3 vols.; Leuven: Leuven University Press, 1992), III, p. 2191. R. Nicol contends that ποιεῖν σημεῖα includes all that John's Gospel proclaims about Jesus, both his works and words (R. Nicol, *The Sēmeia in the Fourth Gospel: Tradition and Redaction* [NovTSup, 32; Leiden: Brill, 1972], p. 115).

33. C. Roberts, 'John 20.30-31 and 21.24-25', *JTS* 38 (1987), p. 409.

34. For example, R. Schnackenburg, *The Gospel according to St John* (repr.; 3 vols.; New York: Crossroad, 1990 [1979]), III, p. 373.

subjunctive of πιστεύω to denote continuous faith and with the a<
subjunctive to denote initial faith, and on that basis he concludes t,
John's purpose was to confirm believers not to convert unbelievers.[35] If
Abbott's premise is correct then his conclusion is too, because the present subjunctive is to be preferred.[36] But the argument in this form tries
to prove too much. The tense of one verb in a single verse cannot
suffice to identify John's audience as believers or unbelievers. All that
can be said with certainty about ἵνα πιστεύ[σ]ητε in Jn 20.31 from the
grammar alone is that the author aims to persuade more than one reader
in the matter of faith.[37]

The purpose statements of John and 1 John are similar but hardly
identical. Unmistakably, 1 John is written to assure believers of the fruits
of their faith: 'I write these things to you who believe in the name of the
Son of God, so that you may know that you have eternal life' (1 Jn
5.13). By comparison, Jn 20.31 sounds more like the author urging
readers to take a first step of faith: 'But these are written so that you
may come to believe that Jesus is the Messiah, the Son of God, and that
through believing you may have life in his name.' For John, knowledge
follows and completes belief.[38] Unlike 1 Jn 5.13, Jn 20.31 is not directed
'to you who believe', nor does it contain 'that you may know'. Thus,
Jn 20.31 seems much more concerned with instigating faith in unbelievers than with moving present believers to knowledge (even though

35. E.A. Abbott, *Johannine Grammar* (London: A. & C. Black, 1906), §§2524-
29; *idem*, *Johannine Vocabulary* (London: A. & C. Black, 1905), §1553.
H. Riesenfeld sees the ἵνα-sentences as a characteristic mode of expression within
the Johannine community, and maintains that an analysis of Jn 20.31 on that basis
shows John's Gospel not to be a *Missionsschrift* (H. Riesenfeld, 'Zu den
johanneischen ἵνα-Sätzen', *ST* 19 [1965], pp. 213-20).

36. G.D. Fee details the superiority of the witnesses for πιστεύητε, in particular
𝔓[66] whose *videtur*, he argues, is unwarranted. Fee proposes that the copyist(s)
changed πιστεύητε to πιστεύσητε either to suggest the idea of coming to faith or to
bring it into line with a more common idiom ('On the Text and Meaning of John
20,30-31', in van Segbroeck *et al.* (eds.), *Four Gospels*, III, pp. 2193-205).

37. J. Painter sees the debate over the tenses in Jn 20.31 as irrelevant, but not
because the textual problem is intractable: 'Jn was concerned that faith should be
authentic, perceive the true nature of Jesus and thus lead on to real decision and obedience. Clearly Jn is written on the assumption that readers have not attained this perception' (J. Painter, *The Quest for the Messiah: The History, Literature and Theology
of the Johannine Community* [Edinburgh: T. & T. Clark, 1991], p. 332 n. 20).

38. J. Gaffney, 'Believing and Knowing in the Fourth Gospel', *TS* 26 (1965),
pp. 215-41.

John surely covets knowledge for new converts as well).[39]

Carson translates Jn 20.31 in a different way, arguing that the syntax requires the crucial clause be rendered, 'that you may believe that the Christ, the Son of God, is Jesus'.[40] Thus, ὁ χριστὸς ὁ υἱὸς τοῦ θεοῦ is the subject of ἐστιν while 'Ιησοῦς is the predicate—precisely the reverse of the English translations.[41] This syntactical point bears on the 'confirming versus converting' question in regard to John's intended audience. According to Carson, translating Jn 20.31 as 'Jesus is the messiah' answers the question 'Who is Jesus?' while the translation 'The messiah is Jesus' answers the question 'Who is the messiah?' The former intends to predicate Jesus and the latter to identify the messiah. If this is correct, it follows that the question 'Who is the messiah?' is more likely to be pondered by those holding (or at least familiar with or inquisitive about) Jewish messianic expectations than by Christians who already know that the messiah is Jesus.[42] Carson concludes that John

39. Because seventy-four of the ninety-eight occurrences of πιστεύω are found in Jn 1–12, R.E. Brown (*The Gospel according to John* [2 vols.; AB 29, 29a; New York: Doubleday, 1966], I, p. 513) suggests that the 'Book of Signs' (Jn 1–12) is directed at unbelievers and the 'Book of Glory' (Jn 13–21) at believers. But Brown does not factor οἶδα and γινώσκω into these statistics.

40. Carson, 'John 20.31 Reconsidered', p. 643. Fortna supports Carson, but only in terms of Fortna's hypothetical pre-Johannine source: 'The purpose of the present Gospel is too complex to be stated in this [evangelistic versus Christological] way or based so heavily on a single verse'. For Fortna, the verse 'asserts both that *Jesus* is the Christ and that Jesus is the *Christ*' (R.T. Fortna, *The Fourth Gospel and its Predecessor: From Narrative Source to Present Gospel* [Philadelphia: Fortress Press, 1988], p. 323). Fee ('Text and Meaning', p. 2205) opposes Carson, arguing that while 'Ιησοῦς could be the predicate, that cannot be shown through the means Carson uses. Fee believes that Johannine usage on the whole suggests that 'Ιησοῦς functions as the subject of the clause.

41. In this discussion I assume that ὁ υἱὸς τοῦ θεοῦ is an appositive to ὁ χριστός. V.H. Neufeld sees no significant differences in John's use of the titles: ὁ υἱὸς τοῦ θεοῦ, while expressing ideas not contained in the basic Johannine *homologia* ὁ χριστός, also refers to the Christ of Jewish messianic hopes (V.H. Neufeld, *The Earliest Christian Confessions* [NTTS, 5; Leiden: Brill, 1963], pp. 73-74, 97, 105). M. de Jonge views ὁ υἱὸς τοῦ θεοῦ as a title that interprets ὁ χριστός (M. de Jonge, 'Jewish Expectations about the "Messiah" according to the Fourth Gospel', *NTS* 19 [1972–73], p. 252). Notice that Jesus links the messiah with the Son of God when answering the demand to state explicitly whether or not he is the messiah (Jn 10.22-39).

42. Jewish (and Samaritan) messianic expectations in Jesus' time were diverse, with no one model as the norm (see S. Mowinckel, *He That Cometh* [Oxford: Basil

sought to identify Jesus with first-century Jewish messianic expectations, that his Gospel is evangelistic and that his target audience was most probably non-Christian Jews who had sufficient exposure to Christianity to look toward it for an answer to the question, 'Who is the messiah?'[43] Modern readers familiar with John's text but unfamiliar with its context will miss how absurd the assertion appeared to ancient readers holding prevailing Jewish messianic expectations that the messiah was in fact an obscure Nazarene, convicted of and condemned for blasphemy by the supreme Jewish court, and subjected to the ignominy of Roman crucifixion. Convincing such ancient readers of Jesus' messiahship required that John be uncommonly persuasive.[44]

What must not be lost from sight is this: whether John's primary goal was to induce faith in unbelievers or to deepen the faith of believers, experience shows that his Gospel does both. In the course of events, John's Gospel undoubtedly came into the hands of Diaspora Jews, God-fearers, Samaritans and Christians of various backgrounds, all of whom read it with profit, even as widely diverse audiences do today. The 'church or mission' dilemma is a false one that should be abandoned. John himself had no interest in categorizing his audience in that fashion.

Blackwell, 1956], especially Part II; similarly, M. de Jonge, 'Jewish Expectations', pp. 246-47). Virtually all twenty-three references in John to the χριστός or the μεσσίας (a term found nowhere in the New Testament besides Jn 1.41; 4.25) occur in a context of messianic expectation or identity, the two exceptions being where 'Christ' forms part of the title 'Jesus Christ' (Jn 1.17; 17.3).

43. Carson ('John 20:31 Reconsidered', pp. 645-46) perceives Proselytes and God-fearers in John's target audience as well as Diaspora Jews. Neufeld (*Christian Confessions*, pp. 69-107), after studying Johannine confessional language, also concludes that John's readership was basically Jewish. The notion that John's less than amicable attitude towards oἱ 'Ιουδαῖοι means that he could not have intended to convert Jewish readers (so, for example, Ashton, *Fourth Gospel*, p. 105), overlooks the fact that prophetic preaching and evangelistic literature, both ancient and modern, routinely criticize the beliefs and behaviours of the people they seek to change.

44. W.A. Meeks argues that John, as a 'book for insiders' already belonging to the Johannine community, can scarcely be a missionary tract ('The Man from Heaven in Johannine Sectarianism', *JBL* 91 [1972], p. 70). I find Meeks's view curious because although some gap surely exists between the ancient and modern contexts, John's is probably the most popular Gospel for distribution as an evangelistic tract. Meeks (p. 71) himself appears to attenuate his position when he allows that John might be addressing not just insiders within the community but also those 'in some ambivalent relationship between it and the larger society'.

So far as the Evangelist is concerned it is irrelevant whether the possible
readers are already 'Christians', or are not yet such; for to him the faith of
'Christians' is not a conviction that is present once for all, but it must per-
petually make sure of itself anew, and therefore must continually hear the
word anew.[45]

To summarize: (1) the basic Classical rhetorical categories of *ethos*,
pathos and *logos* are reflected in John's Gospel; (2) the controlling text
for discerning John's purpose is Jn 20.30-31; (3) John's entire Gospel,
not just the σημεῖα, is advanced as evidence; (4) the tense of πιστεύω
in Jn 20.31 does not provide sufficient grounds to identify John's audience as believers or unbelievers; (5) Ἰησοῦς ἐστιν ὁ χριστὸς ὁ υἱὸς
τοῦ θεοῦ is best read as intending to answer the question 'Who is the
messiah?' with 'The messiah is Jesus', although this does not mean that
John wrote only for Jewish unbelievers. These five strands may be
woven together into this conclusion: John's narrative uses common cultural conventions of rhetorical discourse to persuade people familiar with
and curious about the identity of the messiah that the messiah is none
other than Jesus of Nazareth.

2. *The Juridical Character*

A central feature of all the Gospel passion narratives is Jesus' trial before
the Jewish and Roman authorities, to which the four Evangelists assign
roughly the same amount of material. But although the four Evangelists
allot equal time to Jesus' civil trial, the entire sweep of John's narrative
drama takes the form of a cosmic trial between God and the world, with
Jesus at the centre.

Seeing John's Gospel as a trial requires seeing the central place that
legal contests occupy in Old Testament thought. Trites believes that the
Fourth Gospel presents a controversy very similar to the one found in
Isaiah 40–55, although Beutler rejects the notion that any direct con-
nexion exists between John's presentation of witnesses and the Old
Testament legal disputes involving God and Israel or God and the gods

---

45. R. Bultmann, *The Gospel of John: A Commentary* (Philadelphia:
Westminster Press, 1971), pp. 698-99. Okure (*Approach to Mission*, p. 292)
asserts, 'The modern distinction between *Missionsschrift* and *Gemeinde-
Evangelium*, or the view that missionary activity applies only in respect of non-
believers is simply alien to the Gospel'.

of the nations.[46] In spite of Beutler's reluctance, Trites's view has much to commend it, especially since the 'frequency and diversity of the application of the *rîb*-phraseology in the Old Testament reveals a frame of mind, and not only a way and means of expression', and since justice is 'the dominant conception in Israel's religious and ethical way of thinking'.[47] The use of the ריב (dispute) in legal codes (for example, Exod. 23.2, 3, 6; Deut. 17.8; 25.1) establishes its legal content, but the predominant use of the ריב is juridical metaphor. By the time of the eighth-century prophets, the ריב metaphor assumes cosmic proportions, with both major and minor prophets (Amos, Isaiah, Micah, Jeremiah, Ezekiel, Malachi) featuring it in disputes between God and Israel or between God and Gentiles.

Gemser describes how the juridical mindset contributes to the Jewish dramatic view of world history and how the prophetic theme of controversy between God and people was the vehicle used to express the belief of Jewish spiritual leaders that the religious and ethical conduct of their nation was amiss.[48] This same understanding of world and nation is conspicuous in John's Gospel. The Word of God (note the prophetic tone) comes to his own people but they do not accept him (Jn 1.11), because although he comes to save the world, he also comes to condemn lack of belief, to chide preference for darkness and to expose evil behaviour (Jn 3.17-21). These Johannine themes rehearse the message of the prophets who brought God's judging word and light to bear upon the unbelief and injustice rampant among God's people.

John therefore pursues his rhetorical purpose by framing the historical trial of Jesus within a narrative-length literary and theological trial akin to the metaphor of the ריב controversy. In that sense, John devotes all his material to Jesus' trial. To support such an assertion requires a departure from the approach that deals only with how Jesus' trial corresponds historically to first-century Roman and Jewish jurisprudence. Jesus' trial in John's Gospel is not a singular event within the passion narrative but something woven into the whole literary and theological fabric.

---

46. Trites, *Concept of Witness*, p. 79; Beutler, *Martyria*, p. 306.
47. B. Gemser, 'The *RÎB* or Controversy-Pattern in Hebrew Mentality', in M. Noth and D.W. Thomas (eds.), *Wisdom in Israel and in the Ancient Near East* (VTSup, 3; Leiden: Brill, 1955), p. 136.
48. Gemser, 'Controversy-Pattern', p. 133.

a. *The Entire Gospel*

In John's conclusion are these words: 'This is the disciple who is testifying (μαρτυρέω) to these things and has written them down, and we know that his testimony (μαρτυρία) is true' (Jn 21.24). Even though clearly within the Gospel genre, John's account of the life, death and resurrection of Jesus defines itself more as a Testimony (μαρτυρία) than a Gospel (εὐαγγέλιον—a word never appearing in John). The juridical mould is apparent, and emphasizing it is not new. Some seventy-five years ago, W. Heitmüller observed that the copious use of witness terminology in John's Gospel makes it seem almost like a trial; a few years later, H.C. Townsend perceived sufficient juridical traits in John's Gospel to characterize it as 'The Gospel of evidence'; J. Painter echoes this notion by calling John's Gospel a 'book of witness'; more recently, J.A. du Rand has designated John's Gospel a 'witnessing narrative'.[49]

Over the years, scholars have paid ever-increasing attention to juridical traits in John's structure.[50] Aided by John's repetitive use of themes, exegetes have offered many various blueprints for John's literary structure—no fewer than twenty-four by G. Mlakuzhyil's reckoning.[51] Whatever structure(s) might be perceived, Mlakuzhyil affirms that Jesus commands literary and theological centre-stage in the Johannine drama. Mlakuzhyil interprets the body of John's Gospel as a drama in five acts

49. Heitmüller is cited by J. Beutler, *Martyria*, p. 26; H.C. Townsend, 'The Gospel of Evidence', *Expositor* 8 (1923), pp. 312-20; J. Painter, *John: Witness and Theologian* (London: SPCK, 1975), pp. 9-11; J.A. du Rand, 'Die Evangelie van Johannes as getuigende vertelling', *NGTT* 24 (1983), pp. 383-97. I am grateful to Michael Coumans who translated du Rand's article from the Afrikaans for me.

50. Along with works already mentioned: T. Preiss, *Life in Christ* (London: SCM Press, 1954), pp. 9-31; R. Leivestad, *Christ the Conqueror* (London: SPCK, 1954), pp. 202-206, 259-60; I. de la Potterie, 'Jésus roi et juge d'après Jn 19,13', *Bib* 41 (1960), pp. 217-47; N. Brox, *Zeuge und Märtyrer: Untersuchungen zur frühchristliche Zeugnis-Terminologie* (SANT, 5; München: Kösel, 1961), pp. 70-109; N.A. Dahl, 'The Johannine Church and History', in W. Klassen and G.F. Snyder (eds.), *Current Issues in New Testament Interpretation* (London: SCM Press, 1962), pp.139-41; W.A. Meeks, *The Prophet King: Moses Traditions and the Johannine Christology* (NovTSup, 14; Leiden: Brill, 1967), pp. 65-66, 305-307; S. Pancaro, *The Law in the Fourth Gospel: The Torah and the Gospel, Moses and Jesus, Judaism and Christianity according to John* (NovTSup, 42; Leiden: Brill, 1975).

51. G. Mlakuzhyil, *The Christocentric Literary Structure of the Fourth Gospel* (AnBib, 117; Rome: Biblical Institute Press, 1987), pp. 17-85.

(John 2–4; 5–10; 11–12; 13–17; 18–20), framed by an introduction (Jn 1.1–2.11, with 2.1-11 bridging the introduction and the first act), a conclusion (Jn 20.30-31) and an appendix (Jn 21.1-25).[52] He shows that each section of this drama points to the Father by revealing an aspect of who Jesus is. To Mlakuzhyil's observations I would add that the medium for this drama is the forensic confrontation, the lawsuit, between God and the world in the person of Jesus Christ. Thus, the trial motif in John's Gospel is not just one theological theme among others, but rather, 'It is judgement in action, judgement *as story* or *drama*'.[53]

This monumental lawsuit—'"the great trial" that seems to engage the life of Jesus'[54]—is played out again and again in smaller scale legal disputes throughout the drama. John uses vignettes to encapsulate the overall narrative: 'The story is repeated over and over. No one can miss it. Individual episodes can almost convey the message of the whole.'[55] It might even be argued that the uniqueness of John's episodes and the lack of typical Synoptic material (for example, kingdom parables) are due to John's overriding concern to present material that bears witness that the messiah is Jesus.[56]

The lawsuit scheme runs through the overarching frame of John's story. John's narrative compares favourably to the Old Testament 'forensic narratives' in which the facts of the story are presented to the readers in such a way as to move them to render the judgment desired by the author. This type of discourse was familiar in Jewish culture, where historians adapted it as a tool to persuade readers as to the guilt or innocence of the subjects of their writings.[57] John's Gospel can be compared and contrasted with the book of Job, for example, which also presents the drama of an extended trial. After a brief introduction, Job's drama begins in God's heavenly court and moves to earth; John's first scene opens in God's heavenly presence and shifts to earth. In Job,

---

52. Mlakuzhyil, *Literary Structure*, p. 349.

53. Ashton, *Fourth Gospel*, p. 226. W.R. Domeris advances the forensic setting of John's Gospel as partial evidence that it is cast in the mould of a Greek drama ('The Johannine Drama', *JTSA* 42 [1983], pp. 29-35).

54. I. de la Potterie, *La vérité dans saint Jean* (2 vols.; AnBib, 73, 74; Rome: Biblical Institute Press, 1977), I, p. 81.

55. Culpepper, *Anatomy*, p. 89.

56. Painter (*Quest*, p. 347) thinks that because the Gospel of John is written eyewitness testimony, it concentrates on witness terminology and lacks the Gospel and preaching terminology found in the Synoptics, Acts and Paul.

57. Patrick and Scult, *Rhetoric*, pp. 57-67.

Satan roams the earth, ascends to the heavenly court and descends to earth to engage in a trial; in John, the Word dwells in heaven, descends to earth to engage in a trial and ascends to heaven.

Once the Word is made flesh in Jesus, the lawsuit between God and the world commences on the earthly plane. God sends his Son as agent and witness into the world to enlighten it, take away its sin, save it and give it life. Yet he is not of the world, and those who are of the world reject his witness, bringing God's anger and judgment upon themselves through their unbelief. Those who have been given to Jesus by the Father accept his witness, escape judgment, become God's children and pass from death to eternal life through their belief. John plays this main theme repeatedly with minor variations by way of encounter after encounter in which people either escape judgment by accepting Jesus' witness or incur judgment by rejecting it. Throughout these encounters various witnesses certify Jesus' status while others accuse, judge, condemn and execute him. By his crucifixion, resurrection and ascension, Jesus at last overcomes the world, his status is vindicated and God's case is won. Even though the verdict continues to be applied to individual cases, God's lawsuit with the world is a *res judicata*.

Clement of Alexandria distinguished John from the Synoptics as a 'spiritual gospel' (πνευματικὸν...εὐαγγέλιον).[58] Using Clement's famous phrase as a rationale, some interpreters have sought to dislodge John's Gospel from its earthly plane and confine it to the celestial. Preiss, thinking John's reputation as supreme mystic to be over-systematized, pulls excessively ethereal understandings back to earth by showing that what makes John's Gospel 'spiritual' is its 'juridical mysticism'.[59]

> There is one aspect of Johannine thought which, while not being divorced from the whole, seems to me to afford a more coherent system of ideas. The reason for that is doubtless its less 'mystical' character. This aspect has been strangely neglected by exegetes and still more so, if that is possible, by those who have tried to give a bird's eye view of Johannine thought: I mean the juridical aspect.[60]

Preiss assays Jesus' career as a 'giant juridical contest', a contest that 'constitutes the structural ensemble of Johannine thought'.[61]

58. According to Eusebius, *E.H.* 6.14.
59. Preiss, *Life in Christ*, p. 25.
60. Preiss, *Life in Christ*, p. 11.
61. Preiss, *Life in Christ*, pp. 17, 22.

A second proponent of John's forensic nature is A.E. Harvey, and reading his *Jesus on Trial* alongside of Preiss's *Life in Christ* makes it doubly convincing that a 'giant juridical contest' does in fact control the broad sweep of John's literary structure. Harvey eschews a strictly historical investigation of Jesus' trial, without disregard for historical issues, by steering a course between the literary and historical approaches. Harvey employs historical data to inform his literary analysis of John's presentation of Jesus' trial.

> It is possible to understand the Fourth Gospel as a presentation of the claims of Jesus in the form of an extended 'trial'. In part, this may be seen as a literary device: it was by rehearsing the arguments of the claimant against his adversaries before an imaginary court that Hebrew writers had deepened their readers' understanding of the 'righteous case' of God against his people or of an innocent man such as Job against his calumniators; similarly the evangelist could take the claims to be made for Jesus as an opportunity to focus attention on the witnesses and the arguments which were relevant. But in this case the device was by no means artificial. Jesus had, as a matter of historical fact, been tried before a competent court, and had in addition committed acts and spoken words which were fraught with legal consequences. In devoting so much of his Gospel to these incidents, the writer may have been doing no more than selecting such material from the traditions about Jesus as would enable him to present the case for Jesus Christ to his readers and challenge them—as the world has been challenged ever since—to reach their own verdict.[62]

Harvey's work lends support to the claim that John's purpose was persuasion and that rhetoric was the controlling literary principle when John selected material and shaped his narrative. Although Harvey does not invoke the category of rhetoric specifically, he does stress that persuasion guides John's literary agenda, and accordingly, that John 'appears to have cast much of his material in the form of a long-drawn-out trial'.[63] According to Harvey, John does three things in order to 'retry' Jesus before the reader: (1) presents witnesses who had no voice in the original trial, (2) reargues the case bringing out points lost upon the original judges, (3) introduces witnesses who have given evidence subsequently to the original trial.[64] Readers thereby are asked to render

---

62. A.E. Harvey, *Jesus on Trial* (London: SPCK, 1976), p. 17.

63. Harvey, *Jesus on Trial*, p. 123. Stibbe (*John as Storyteller*, pp. 88, 111) senses that the 'whole of John's story feels like a courtroom scene', and could be described as an 'extended trial narrative'.

64. Harvey, *Jesus on Trial*, p. 104.

their own verdicts, but unlike the participants in the original trial, to do so relying upon a different complement of witnesses and corpus of evidence.

A third advocate for John's Gospel being an extended literary litigation is Trites, who sees in John's pages strong connections with Old Testament lawsuit imagery, particularly Isaiah 40–55. Trites discerns both God's cosmic lawsuit with the world and the sustained use of juridical metaphor in John's Gospel: 'John, like his Old Testament counterpart [Isaiah], has a case to present, and for this reason he advances his arguments, challenges his opponents and presents his witnesses after the fashion of the Old Testament legal assembly.'[65]

b. *The Smaller Units*

The opening section of John's Gospel (Jn 1.1-18) is customarily called the 'prologue', but is more fittingly heard as an 'overture' because the latter term better suits a drama while also highlighting the thematic bonds between Jn 1.1-18 and the body of the Gospel obscured by the term prologue. This dramatic overture, the '*Logos* Hymn', is divided into three parts (Jn 1.1-5, 9-14, 16-18) by two references to John the Baptist's testimony (Jn 1.6-8, 15). This immediately establishes a forensic tone to the Gospel, while a third reference to the Baptist's testimony (Jn 1.19) links that tone with the initial earthly action in the main body of the book beginning at Jn 1.19. Some exegetes view the references to the Baptist as editorial intrusions upon the integrity of the *Logos* Hymn, while others hold Jn 1.1-18 to be a unit composed by the author. In either case, what links together the three parts of the *Logos* Hymn itself as well as the *Logos* Hymn to the main body of the Gospel is a prominent witness, reinforcing how definitive the theme of testimony is and will be. Further forensic themes that later will be prominent throughout the Gospel are introduced in the *Logos* Hymn itself: the legitimacy and authority of Jesus as God's agent, the conflict between accepting and rejecting him, the contest between light and darkness, the right of believers to become God's children, and Jesus' relationship to Moses and the Law.

Ashton supports Harvey's thesis of an extended literary trial, except that he fails to see any trial motifs in John 1–4.[66] I find this curious because at Jn 1.19-51 the earthly action of John's drama commences

---

65. Trites, *Concept of Witness*, pp. 79-80.
66. Ashton, *Fourth Gospel*, p. 228.

with Jesus' eventual antagonists, the Jewish authorities, confronting Jesus' first witness, John the Baptist, by cross-examining him in a duly delegated official investigation. Right on the heels of that confrontation more witnesses to Jesus appear: the Holy Spirit, the first disciples and Jesus himself.

At Jn 2.1-11, the wedding at Cana, Jesus performs the first of many signs/works that will reveal his identity as God's agent and lead people to accept him as such. The contest between Jesus and his adversaries heats up quickly at Jn 2.13-22 as he directly challenges them by clearing the temple. The Jewish authorities demand evidence of his credentials to justify such an action, and they want it in the form of a sign. Jesus provides this proof proleptically by alluding to his resurrection, even though they typically misinterpret the figurative nature of his response about raising the temple in three days.

The encounter between Jesus and Nicodemus in Jn 3.1-21 presents the entire scheme of the lawsuit in miniature. As a Pharisee, leader and teacher, Nicodemus represents Jesus' worldly adversaries who misunderstand and refuse to accept the truth of his status and testimony. Whether viewed as Jesus' words or John's comments, Jn 3.16-21 follows this confrontation with the theme of the cosmic lawsuit whereby God intends to save the world through the agency of his Son but judges and condemns those who reject him. Trites comments that in the Nicodemus episode, 'The Evangelist has introduced a theme which is of importance to his courtroom imagery. Jesus is on trial and evidence is being brought to support his case; men must make up their minds.'[67]

Before John the Baptist fades from the scene, he reappears in Jn 3.22-36, once again within the context of dispute with a Jew (v. l. 'some Jews'), to recapitulate and expand his testimony. Paralleling the way in which Jn 3.16-21 comments upon the encounter between Jesus and Nicodemus, Jn 3.31-36 certifies Jesus' credentials and testimony and underscores the theme of the lawsuit between heaven and earth, the verdict of which brings eternal life to the faithful and God's wrath upon the disobedient.

John 4.1-42 finds Jesus persuading Samaritans of his case, and they believe in and testify to the fact that he is God's messiah and the saviour of the world. When read in conjunction with the Nicodemus story, this pericope rehearses a motif established at the outset in John 1: Jesus' own people reject him while others accept him. The sense of courtroom

67. Trites, *Concept of Witness*, p. 96.

drama is heightened here as the Samaritans, the traditional rivals of the Jews, become advocates for Jesus. When the Galileans welcome Jesus (Jn 4.43-45) and he heals the royal official's son (Jn 4.46-54), that theme sounds again in the tension between those who receive Jesus through the testimony of his signs (represented by οἱ Γαλιλαῖοι) and those who do not (represented by οἱ Ἰουδαῖοι). The healing of the royal official's son, the second of Jesus' signs, has the official briefly investigating the circumstances of the healing by questioning his servants. Later, the Jewish authorities, with greater thoroughness and vigour, will inquire about the healing of the paralytic (Jn 5.9-18) and investigate the healing of the man born blind (Jn 9.8-34). Such investigation into Jesus' miracles is lacking in the Synoptics.[68]

In Jn 5.1-47, when Jesus heals the man at the pool of Beth-zatha, the first full-blown legal dispute between Jesus and his adversaries occurs. The Jewish authorities thrust accusations of sabbath breaking and blasphemy at Jesus who, alluding to the legal mandate for corroborating testimony, parries with a panoply of defence witnesses and counter-accusers: John the Baptist, his (Jesus') works, the Father, the scriptures and Moses. This episode functions as a forensic paradigm that sets up a legal divide between those who accept and those who reject the Father's testimony to Jesus: 'Just as the disciples had become for the Fourth Evangelist perfect models for the total response to the witness of the Father, so the Jews and the world represent those who meet and utterly reject such witness.'[69]

John 6.1-71 widens the dispute over Jesus beyond the Jewish leaders to the crowds and even to his own disciples. The crowd witnesses Jesus multiplying the loaves and fishes while his disciples witness him walking upon the lake. When the crowd verifies the feeding miracle but fails to grasp its significance, they place Jesus in the dock, demanding a sign as substantiating evidence for his claims. The Jewish leaders join in as the debate intensifies in step with Jesus' claim to be the bread from heaven. They dispute his case based on his homely credentials, and Jesus appeals to the Father and the scriptures for support. When Jesus then pushes his case too far in the call to eat his flesh and drink his blood, even his own

---

68. Notice that in the Synoptic parallels to the healing of the royal official's son (Mt. 8.5-13; Lk. 7.1-10), the centurion does not conduct an investigation into the circumstances of the healing.

69. U.C. von Wahlde, 'The Witnesses to Jesus in John 5.31-40 and Belief in the Fourth Gospel', *CBQ* 43 (1981), p. 404.

disciples enter the controversy, many of them changing their verdict and deserting him. Jesus then challenges the Twelve, and Simon Peter offers a corporate confession of Jesus as the Holy One of God, while Jesus insists that one in their midst is a devil who will betray him. This episode and its poignant conclusion provide a précis of the cosmic lawsuit. God presents evidence for the case in Jesus' words and works, and the jury splits into two factions: those who believe, accept and follow, and those who disbelieve, reject and betray.

John 7 opens with Jesus in Galilee trying to avoid (or postpone) death at the hands of his foes, while his brothers urge him to widen his witness into Judea. Jesus declares that his testimony against the world's evil works has earned him the world's hatred, and his words portend that the controversy is close to the boiling point. After hesitating, Jesus does go to Jerusalem, and the lawsuit resumes with his status and credentials once again at issue. The forensic tone becomes pronounced as each side buttresses its case by advancing evidence. Jesus adduces God, Moses, and scripture, while his opponents likewise cite scripture and the Law. The crowd is a hung jury, some of them convinced that Jesus is the messiah, others that he is not. The scene concludes with Nicodemus advocating an official hearing as required by law, but the Pharisees scorn him.[70]

The dispute begun in John 7 continues into John 8, as does the forensic atmosphere, which increasingly thickens. Jesus claims to be the light of the world, the Pharisees impugn his testimony, and he contends for its validity, citing the law of evidence and its imperative for two (or three) witnesses (Deut. 19.15). Jesus defends the legitimacy of his judgment based on his origins, counterclaims bankruptcy for his adversaries' judgment, and the argument then returns to credentials. After a break, the argument extends from Jn 8.21 to the end of the chapter. Jesus' antagonists finally play what they believe is their trump card when they call Abraham as their witness, but in fact Abraham is Jesus' witness and, like Moses (Jn 5.45), accuses them. When Jesus claims precedence over Abraham, they are ready to forego any further debate and execute the death sentence at once even though none of them can convict Jesus of sin.

---

70. The juridical tenor of Jn 7.53–8.11, the incident of the woman caught in adultery, is more than conspicuous. The pericope is almost certainly a later addition to John's Gospel, but because it is thematically relevant, I will discuss it in the Excursus.

As if to prove his contention that he is the light of the world, Jesus restates it in John 9 and leads a beggar from darkness into light, from blindness to vision. This touches off another manifestly juridical confrontation. The Pharisees launch a thorough inquiry, interrogating the man and his parents about the circumstances of the healing. In the process, the man becomes a witness and a believer as he moves through the stages of seeing Jesus as a man, a prophet, the Son of Man and Lord. Jesus summarizes the events of Jn 9.1-41 with a forensic theme, stating that he has come into the world for judgment.

Again, now in John 10, claims for Jesus' status kindle opposition and division among his opponents. Rather than seeing Jesus as a good shepherd, they charge him with demon possession and demand that he affirm or deny being the messiah. Trites perceives juridical colour in that demand: 'After the fashion of the Old Testament lawsuit Christ's opponents now summon him to state his case (10.24).'[71] Jesus' response is that he has already done so in word and deed, and when he goes on to equate himself with God, they prepare to follow the legal imperative to put blasphemers to death (Lev. 24.16). Jesus' rejoinder likewise cites the law, and the debate ends with him eluding arrest.

In John 11 the raising of Lazarus dramatically climaxes Jesus' signs. John makes it clear that this miracle has evidential value for Jesus' status, and indeed it does evoke belief and confession among Jesus' followers and others. Jesus' own enemies must acknowledge the miracle even while missing its significance and expressing hostility toward it. At this point Jesus' adversaries have had enough, so they call a meeting (Jn 11.47, συνήγαγον) and plan to put him to death (Jn 11.53, ἐβουλεύσαντο [v. l. συνεβουλεύσαντο]). J.A.T. Robinson sees special significance in the words συνήγαγον and ἐβουλεύσαντο. Jesus having fled, a legally convened council formally indicts him and in essence issues a warrant by asking the public to divulge his whereabouts so that he might be arrested. Jesus now is an officially proscribed criminal awaiting arrest and trial.[72]

John 12 brings together at supper in Bethany the principal figures and witnesses in the raising of Lazarus. Here the anointing of Jesus advances tacit evidence of his messiahship. Jesus' public entrance to Jerusalem furnishes similar evidence by way of the scripture being fulfilled. Trites

---

71. Trites, *Concept of Witness*, p. 108.

72. J.A.T. Robinson, *The Priority of John* (London: SCM Press, 1985), pp. 223-29. Robinson also points out other quasi-legal terms in Jn 11.45-53.

compares this fulfillment motif with the lawsuit in Isaiah 40–55, where prediction and fulfillment establish God's case just as in John, where Jesus' fulfilled predictions are meant to evoke belief.[73] When the ῞Ελληνες look for Jesus, he recognizes that the cosmic lawsuit is drawing close to its crucial point because the time now has come for the Son of Man to be glorified, for the world to be judged and for the ruler of the world to be cast out. Once again the crowd cites the Law to challenge or clarify Jesus' enigmatic statement about being lifted up. Jesus provides no clarification, but in essence insists that all the evidence is in and his audience must now decide for or against him. Two Old Testament quotations from Isaiah supply evidence that unbelief was to be the response to the messiah's coming, and John shows the audience divided over Jesus, some of them fearing the legal penalty for confessing faith in Jesus.

John 12.44-50 merits special attention because it is Jesus' final public speech.[74] Jesus restates his case, credentials and testimony. He does this by calling aloud (ἔκραξεν) in a way strongly reminiscent of Wisdom as she calls out in public for people to heed her and live, or reject her and be judged (Prov. 1.20-33; 8.1-36; 9.1-12). Jesus' recapitulation of his ministry brings to mind a lawyer's closing argument and judge's summation before a jury deliberates its verdict.

Most commentators see a clear bipartite arrangement in the Gospel of John, with the second section commencing at John 13. With his public ministry concluded, Jesus' time of glorification has arrived. Since Jesus must now depart to the Father, he focuses upon preparing the disciples to carry on his ministry. At this point the strident tone of the lawsuit yields to an aura of loving intimacy as Jesus provides care and instruction for his friends. Yet the dispute between God and the world is never very far from sight as Satan the accuser and his agent Judas Iscariot are lurking about during the supper and footwashing, plotting the demise of God's agent Jesus.

John 14–16 continues Jesus' preparation of his disciples who even at this late stage have their doubts and confusion. Jesus must yet again testify even to them about his identity as God's agent, and darken the for-or-against line drawn between belief and unbelief. Just as Jesus' time has

---

73. Trites, *Concept of Witness*, pp. 110-11.

74. John gives no context for these verses, but they clearly belong with Jesus' public proclamation and not with the private instructions his disciples will receive in John 13–16.

now come, so too has that of the Holy Spirit (see Jn 7.39). This is a crucial turn in the course of the lawsuit. With God's agent Jesus returned to his heavenly home, those chosen to carry on that agency on earth will require the help of the Holy Spirit as they encounter the same opposition as did Jesus. This advocate (παράκλητος) now comes to earth as God's agent to assist the followers of Jesus, testify to him and plead his case, while standing in opposition to the accuser (διάβολος) who is legally defeated by Jesus' death and ejected from the heavenly court (see Jn 12.31).

As with the footwashing of John 13, Jesus' prayer in John 17 records his loving care for his followers, this time as he asks his Father to protect them. Again, the contentious atmosphere of the lawsuit thins but never evaporates. Running through Jesus' petitions are the tensions between those who belong to God and those who belong to the world: belief and unbelief, truth and falsehood, love and hatred, good and evil.

In John 18–19 comes the sequence of Jesus' arrest, civil trial and crucifixion. Identifying forensic themes there is superfluous, but some of John's personal touches in contrast to the Synoptists merit attention. John makes an effort to show that the arresting party contains deputies of both the Roman and Jewish authorities, and that the identity of the person they seek to arrest is beyond dispute. This touch adds the flavour of a formal legal proceeding, as does John's note that Jesus is bound while being taken into custody. In John (and Luke) no false witnesses appear before the high priest (cf. Mk 14.55-60, and par.), and John recounts Jesus suggesting to the high priest that he call as witnesses those who heard him speak, that is, true witnesses. Jesus even calls to witness the officer who strikes him for making that suggestion.

John records that in the initial meeting, Pilate immediately asks for a formal declaration of the charges against Jesus, and John also makes his audience privy to details of Pilate's examination of Jesus, which the Synoptics do not contain. John enhances the legal atmosphere by recording Pilate's mandate to Jesus' accusers that they try him by Jewish Law, their insistence that their Law requires his death, and the squabble between Pilate and the Jewish authorities over the charges against Jesus even as he hangs on the cross.

Jesus' cry, 'It is finished', brings the contest between God and the world to its dramatic conclusion. In Jesus' trial and death those who judged him are themselves judged. John shows how Jesus' opponents are concerned to persevere in their hollow legality to the very end as they seek to remove the bodies from the crosses before the arrival of the high sabbath day.

In John 20, John seems to be accumulating evidence by reporting not only Jesus' empty tomb but also his empty grave clothes, the presence of two angels (compare the δύο ἄνδρες of Lk. 24.4) and four separate resurrection appearances where Matthew and Luke have two each and Mark none.[75]

Previously, I mentioned that even though the cosmic litigation between God and the world culminates in the death, resurrection and ascension of Jesus, and is thus a *res judicata*, the verdict continues to be applied to individual cases. John's eschatology therefore needs to be noted briefly. Trites applies the forensic metaphor 'lawsuit of the last day' to John's eschatology.[76] John's 'realized eschatology', whereby people incur present judgment through disbelief (Jn 3.18), does not exclude the return of Christ (Jn 14.3; 21.22) and the resurrection and final judgment of the dead (Jn 5.28-29; 6.39-40, 44, 54; 12.48). John's eschatology therefore spans the present and the future in regard to judgment. As Trites says, 'The Last Day is not thought to bring a new and independent act of judgment; rather, it will reveal the final outcome of the lawsuit that has been in progress over the claims of Jesus Christ'.[77] Jesus succinctly sets the eschatological tone of John's Gospel when speaking of the hour that is both approaching and has already arrived (Jn 4.23; 5.25; 16.32).

c. *The Vocabulary*

I. de la Potterie remarks, 'Throughout John's Gospel there is a vocabulary borrowed from legal parlance'.[78] Although the conspicuous cases of John's juridical vocabulary (μαρτυρία is a good example) have been well documented, its more pervasive juridical colour has not. De la Potterie deals with several words mostly limited to the theme of testimony while Trites expands that number but also focuses mainly on that

---

75. The conclusion of Mark is problematic. The shorter ending assumes one appearance while the longer one looks like a compilation of appearances garnered from the other Gospels.

76. Trites, *Concept of Witness*, pp. 123-24.

77. Trites, *Concept of Witness*, pp. 123-24.

78. De la Potterie, *Vérité*, I, p. 81. Similarly, R.F. Collins observes, 'The language of the courtroom runs throughout the story, which contains a fairly large dose of blatantly legal terminology' (R.F. Collins, *John and his Witness* [ZSNT; Collegeville, MN: Liturgical Press, 1991], pp. 14-15).

one theme.[79] In what follows I will attempt to explore John's vocabulary more thoroughly, dealing with more words plus a few phrases.

I noted previously how the Old Testament reflects juridical disputes (ריבים) in ancient Jewish life. The ongoing strife and debate in John's narrative create a forensic climate consistent with that of the numerous Old Testament ריבים. This cultural phenomenon of the ריבים provides the backdrop which, along with John's literary lawsuit, must be kept in view if the unnoticed or underemphasized juridical connotations of some words are to emerge. I have created ten lexical fields representing several aspects of the judicial process in order to expose the more comprehensive forensic complexion of John's vocabulary. These fields neither exhaust nor restrict the meanings of the words they contain, nor do I propose that every word discussed is a legal *terminus technicus*. When taken *en masse*, however, these words thicken the juridical atmosphere, and support de la Potterie's insight that jurisprudential language permeates John's vocabulary.

Legal Commands. John uses words obviously belonging to the legal sphere, such as νόμος, δίκαιος, ἐξουσία, ἔξεστι. There is eminent concern for the giving and obeying of commandments that represent a new law coming directly to Jesus from the Father, supplanting old legal demands (Jn 13.34).[80] John insists that those who love Jesus will keep (τηρέω) his words (λόγος) and commands (ἐντολή) just as he has kept those of his Father (Jn 14.15, 21, 23, 24; 15.10; 17.6). The LXX likewise uses τηρέω for obeying God's words, commandments and laws (1 Kgs 15.11; Prov. 3.1; 31.2; Tob. 14.9; Sir. 29.1). Those who fail to keep (φυλάσσω) Jesus' words (ῥῆμα) are to be judged by his word (λόγος) on the last day (Jn 12.47-48). Like τηρέω, φυλάσσω appears in the LXX and the Pseudepigrapha, often within legal contexts to express obedience to legal ordinances and customs (Exodus, Leviticus, Deuteronomy, *Testament of the Twelve Patriarchs*).

The word λόγος calls for a brief note. Increasingly it is recognized that John's concept of λόγος can be traced, perhaps with more accuracy, to Jewish as well as Greek roots. It is reasonable, however, to suggest that the Hellenistic idea of λόγος as intelligible and recognizable

---

79. De la Potterie, *Vérité*, I, pp. 79-116; Trites, *Concept of Witness*, pp. 78-124.

80. Jesus neither rejects nor supplants Torah, but rather, its Pharisaic accretions (Pancaro, *Law*, pp. 514-34).

cosmic law would not be lost upon those reading John, where the cosmic λόγος quite literally does become intelligible and recognizable (Jn 1.14), and does so on the heels of the Law that came through Moses (Jn 1.17).[81] Rabbinic thought equated דבר not only with Wisdom but also with a pre-existent Torah, and R. Schnackenburg notes, 'Rabbinism speaks of the Torah as [John's] prologue does of the Logos'.[82]

Criminals. John speaks about thieves (λῃστής) and robbers (κλέπτης) in the passage about the sheep (Jn 10.1, 8, 10). All four Gospels acknowledge that Judas Iscariot betrayed Jesus, but only John marks him as a κλέπτης (Jn 12.6) and, likewise, only John brands Barabbas as a λῃστής (Jn 18.40), perhaps revealing how he supported himself as a political insurrectionist (cf. Mk 15.7; Lk. 23.19).

John alone identifies Judas Iscariot as ὁ υἱὸς τῆς ἀπωλείας (Jn 17.12). Here, John probably has uppermost in mind the gap between the chosen and the lost, yet a link between ὁ υἱὸς τῆς ἀπωλείας and lawlessness might be forged. A wise υἱός obeys his father while a disobedient one ends up ἐν ἀπωλείᾳ; the υἱός who keeps the commandment escapes ἀπώλεια (LXX Prov. 13.1; 29.27). Isaiah brands the lawless (υἱοὶ ἄνομοι) as τέκνα ἀπωλείας (LXX Isa. 57.3-4). The phrase ὁ υἱὸς τῆς ἀπωλείας appears only one other time in the New Testament, where Paul couples it (in the preferred reading) with lawlessness: ὁ ἄνθρωπος τῆς ἀνομίας (2 Thess. 2.3).

While all four Gospels record that Jesus was accused of breaking the Law, only John recounts Jesus actually being labeled as a criminal with the epithet κακὸν ποιῶν (Jn 18.30; cf. Lk. 23.32 where Jesus' criminal co-crucifixants are κακοῦργοι).[83] In John, Jesus is accused of breaching both Jewish Law (βλασφημία, Jn 10.33) and Roman law (ἀντιλέγει τῷ Καίσαρι, Jn 19.12).[84]

81. H. Kleinknecht, 'λέγω', *TDNT*, IV, p. 81. The λόγος statements in John's prologue perhaps are analogous to Palestinian Jewish Torah (O. Procksch, 'λέγω', *TDNT*, IV, p. 98; G. Kittel, 'λέγω', *TDNT*, IV, p. 132).

82. Schnackenburg, *John*, I, p. 484. E.K. Lees parallels rabbinic statements about the Torah with those about the Logos in John's prologue (*The Religious Thought of St John* [London: SPCK, 1950], p. 101).

83. Various MSS at Jn 18.30 have the similar terms, κακὸν ποιήσας or κακοποιῶν or κακοποιός.

84. In a courtroom scene, Josephus (*Ant.* 14.325) uses ἀντιλέγω for Messala's refutation of accusations from adversaries.

Informing, Arresting. Like the Synoptists, John employs παραδίδωμι for the handing over of Jesus to the authorities. But only John describes the act of informing the authorities of Jesus' whereabouts with ἡμνύω (Jn 11.57), which in this context implies a response to an official warrant for Jesus' arrest.[85] The legal connotation of μηνύω appears in *3 Macc.* 3.28, where Ptolemy issues a legal edict offering rewards to those who inform against Jews whom he seeks to put to death. Similarly, in referring to attempts to arrest Jesus, only John uses πιάζω (Jn 7.30, 32, 44; 8.20; 10.39; 11.57), a word that has the sense, 'to take a person into custody for alleged illegal activity'.[86]

Testing, Interrogation, Investigation. Like the other Gospels, John uses πειράζω in reference to testing, which is not a legal word per se but one commonly used in Gospel contexts where legal disputes occur (Mt. 22.35; Mk 10.2; 12.15; Jn 8.6) and even when used in the general sense of testing always connotes probation.[87] John alone shows Jesus testing one of his disciples (Jn 6.6), as well as his disciples' unwillingness to interrogate (ἐξεστάζω) him about his identity after his resurrection (Jn 21.12).[88]

The Johannine discourses are characterized by question and answer dialogues resembling legal inquiries. In fact, Johannine discourses are perhaps better construed as 'juridical debate'.[89] Thus, John often uses ζητέω and employs ἐρωτάω and ἀποκρίνομαι far more frequently than any other Gospel writer. John has two of the six New Testament occurrences of ἐραυνάω, and only he uses it to refer to a careful investigation of the scriptures (Jn 5.39; 7.52); both occurrences arise in contexts of accusations involving the Law: Jesus for breaking it (Jn 5.16) and the crowd for being ignorant of it (Jn 7.49). The Pharisees need to

---

85. Forensic connotations in Jn 11.57 are noted in J.H. Moulton and G. Milligan, *The Vocabulary of the Greek New Testament, Illustrated from the Papyri and Other Non-Literary Sources* (repr.; London: Hodder & Stoughton, 1949 [1930]), 'μηνύω', p. 410.

86. J.P. Louw and E.A. Nida (eds.), *Greek–English Lexicon of the New Testament according to Semantic Domains* (2 vols.; London: United Bible Society, 1988), I, 037.110.

87. Moulton and Milligan, *Vocabulary*, 'πειράζω', p. 501.

88. Compare the forensic uses of the substantive ἐξέτασις in Wis. 1.9 and *3 Macc.* 7.5. An interesting text to compare with Jn 21.12 is *T. Job* 31.1, in which Eliphas urges a careful questioning (ἐξε[σ]τάζω) of Job to verify his identity.

89. Trites, *Concept of Witness*, p. 79.

give an answer (ἀπόκρισις) to those who sent them to investigate John the Baptist (Jn 1.22), while Jesus, at one point during his trial, declines to give an ἀπόκρισις to his examiner (Jn 19.9).

Accusation, Advocation. Along with the Synoptists, John employs the juridical terms αἰτία, κατηγορέω and κατακρίνω. The Synoptists use κατακρίνω always to record Jesus as the object of accusation, while John alone uses it to record that Jesus' accusers themselves stand accused by no less a personage than Moses (Jn 5.45), the agent of God's Law (Jn 1.17). John alone records Pilate asking Jesus' accusers what κατηγορία—official legal charge—they lodge against him (Jn 18.29).[90]

The contrast between ὁ διάβολος and ὁ παράκλητος is one of the strongest forensic aspects in John. Although all four Evangelists use διάβολος for the devil, John alone explicitly states that Jesus' adversaries and accusers are agents of the διάβολος (Jn 8.44), who in Jewish and Christian thought is the arch-adversary and arch-accuser of God's people (LXX Zech. 3.1-5; Rev. 12.10). The forensic functioning of the Spirit is found beyond the borders of John's Gospel. However, the παράκλητος, God's agent who pleads Jesus' case and convicts the world, can be found only in John (Jn 14.16, 26; 15.26; 16.7-11) and once in 1 John (1 Jn 2.1), where the παράκλητος (there, Jesus Christ) is an advocate for believers who break God's Law by sinning (cf. 1 Jn 3.4).[91]

Witness. It is difficult to overemphasize the centrality of the witness words μαρτυρέω and μαρτυρία in John, and their statistical prominence is striking. John contains roughly 41 percent (47 of 114) of the New Testament occurrences of μαρτυρέω and μαρτυρία. Moreover,

90. Some MSS at Lk. 6.7 use κατηγορία with a similar meaning to tell of how the scribes and Pharisees look for a charge against Jesus.

91. John embraces both forensic and non-forensic connotations for παράκλητος (R.E. Brown, 'The Paraclete in the Fourth Gospel', *NTS* 13 [1966–67], pp. 113-32; G.M. Burge, *The Anointed Community: The Holy Spirit in the Johannine Tradition* [Grand Rapids: Eerdmans, 1987], pp. 3-41). Boice (*Witness and Revelation*, p. 145) finds it difficult to reconcile the comforting and judging aspects of the Spirit's witness, but C.H. Talbert (*Reading John: A Literary and Theological Commentary on the Fourth Gospel and the Johannine Epistles* [London: SPCK, 1992], p. 207) explains that the Paraclete serves as an abiding presence for 'insiders' while exposing and convicting the unbelief of 'outsiders'. L. Morris proposes 'friend at court' as a comprehensive translation for Paraclete (*Jesus Is the Christ: Studies in the Theology of John* [Grand Rapids: Eerdmans, 1989], p. 164).

those two words are scarce in the other Gospels (μαρτυρία: Matthew 0, Mark 3, Luke 1; μαρτυρέω: Matthew 1, Mark 0, Luke 1). It is fair to say that within the Gospels μαρτυρία and μαρτυρέω are very much John's words, comprising one element of a uniquely Johannine vocabulary.

But witness is not confined to μαρτυρέω and μαρτυρία. Central to the New Testament is that 'seeing and hearing together constitute the totality of sensual and spiritual perception which underlies eyewitness, personal experience and individual certainty'.[92] And indeed, John has significant numbers of verbs of hearing and seeing: ἀκούω, βλέπω, ἐμβλέπω, θεάομαι, θεωρέω, ὁράω. Witnesses also know what they have heard and seen, and John accordingly displays large numbers of words related to knowing. Especially prominent are γινώσκω and οἶδα, and in jurisprudence γινώσκω can indicate the giving of legal recognition (cf. Jn 1.10; 6.69; 7.49; 16.3; 17.23, 25).[93]

Witnesses or the accused stand in public, ἵστημι (the Baptist in Jn 1.35-36 and Jesus in Jn 7.37; compare the woman caught in adultery in Jn 8.3, 9); they confess, ὁμολογέω (Jn 1.20; 9.20), deny, ἀρνέομαι (Jn 1.20; 18.25, 27) and declare what they know, ἀναγγέλλω, ἀπαγγέλλω, γνωρίζω (especially Jn 17.26), δείκνυμι, ἐμφανίζω, φανερόω—all of which are significant in John.

A witness calling aloud (κράζω, Jn 1.15; 7.28; 12.44) is significant because κράζω has forensic usage in Classical Greek and the Papyri,[94] in the Pseudepigrapha (*1 En.* 103.14; 104.3; *T. Abr.* [B] 10.4), and the New Testament (Acts 23.6; Rom. 8.15). The testimony of witnesses is received or rejected (λαμβάνω, Jn 3.11, 32, 33; 5.34), perhaps similar to the juridical phrase δίκην λαμβάνειν.[95]

Jesus will send out his chosen disciples as witnesses (Jn 15.27; 20.21), and it is intriguing that John's one and only use of ἀπόστολος (Jn 13.16) has, as K.H. Rengstorf notes, a forensic sense.[96]

Truth, Falsehood. John's concern with truth is as intense as it is with witness. John has roughly 41 percent (75 of 181) of the New Testament occurrences of ἀλήθεια, ἀληθινός, ἀληθής, ἀληθῶς. The lone use of

92. W. Michaelis, 'ὁράω', *TDNT*, V, p. 341.
93. R. Bultmann, 'γινώσκω', *TDNT*, I, p. 691.
94. Harvey, *Jesus on Trial*, p. 23 n. 7.
95. G. Delling, 'λαμβάνω', *TDNT*, IV, p. 5.
96. K.H. Rengstorf, 'ἀποστέλλω', *TDNT*, I, p. 421.

ἀδικία (Jn 7.18) is intriguing because John contrasts it with truth (cf. Rom. 2.8; 1 Cor. 13.6) rather than making the usual contrast with righteousness or justice as found in the Synoptics and Acts. John often mentions speaking the truth or falsehood (verb of speaking plus καλῶς or κακῶς, Jn 4.17; 8.48; 13.13; 18.23), speaking frankly and openly (verb of speaking plus παρρησία, Jn 7.13, 26; 10.24; 11.14; 16.29; 18.20), lying (ψεῦδος or ψεύστης, Jn 8.44, 55), and deceit (δόλος, Jn 1.47 [cf. LXX Prov. 12.17: ὁ δὲ μάρτυς τῶν ἀδίκων δόλιος]; πλανάω, Jn 7.12, 47). All four Evangelists record Jesus prefacing statements with ἀμήν, but only in John does Jesus use the doubled ἀμήν (25 times), a phrase that solemnly affirms the truth of Jesus' words and well suits the context of a legal contest over his claims.[97]

Certification. As with witness and truth, John's concern for belief is consuming, with πιστεύω taking up some 40 percent (98 of 241) of the New Testament occurrences. The demand to believe Jesus colours this Gospel from start to finish, and P. Seidensticker remarks, 'John can secure the credibility of Jesus only through the utilization of juridical categories'.[98] Whoever rejects Jesus (ἀθετέω) will be judged by his word (Jn 12.48), and this use of ἀθετέω should be read in close relationship to the claim of the Law. To reject Jesus is to nullify the Law, and to nullify the Law is to reject God.[99]

John is eager to certify that Jesus is God's agent, a concept linked with the שליח institution in which one person is commissioned as the legal agent of another.[100] John uses ἀποστέλλω and πέμπω copiously, and he shows Jesus coming and working in the name of his sender (Jn 5.43; 10.25; 12.13). P. Borgen observes that the 'Johannine idea of

97. Trites, *Concept of Witness*, p. 90. Abbott (*Johannine Grammar*, §2611a) suggests that the Johannine formulas ἀμὴν ἀμήν and ἀπεκρίθη... καὶ εἶπεν could be symbolic allusions to Jewish canons of twofold witness.

98. P. Seidensticker, *Der Auferstehung Jesu in der Botschaft der Evangelisten: Ein traditionsgeschichtlicher Versuch zum Problem der Sicherung der Osterbotschaft in der apostolischen Zeit* (SBS, 26; Stuttgart: Katholisches Bibelwerk, 1967), p. 143.

99. M. Limbeck, 'ἀθετέω', *EDNT*, I, p. 35; LSJ, 'ἀθετέω', p. 31.

100. H. Lindner and E. von Eicken, 'ἀποστέλλω', *NIDNTT*, I, pp. 127-28; Rengstorf, 'ἀποστέλλω', *TDNT*, I, pp. 413-20. The link with שליח, however, must be made cautiously. The legal institution can be traced to post-Exilic times, but the noun שליח does not appear until rabbinic times. Also, unlike Jesus, the שליח does not subdelegate agents (Jn 20.21).

the mission of Christ as God's agent is seen within the context of a lawsuit'.[101]

Jesus is certified as God's agent because he always does the will of the one who sent him (Jn 4.34; 5.30; 6.38), and anyone who accepts Jesus' testimony certifies (σφραγίζω) that God is true (Jn 3.33; cf. 6.27). In the LXX, σφραγίζω occurs often in contexts of legal certification (for example, Est. 8.8; Jer. 39.10, 25, 44).[102] Jesus' signs (σημεῖον) and works (ἔργον) also authenticate his divine agency (Jn 3.2; 5.36; 7.31; 10.25, 37-38; 14.10-11; 17.4).[103]

The ἐγώ εἰμι formula is found often in John (26 of 29 times on Jesus' lips), and in its unpredicated form sometimes certifies Jesus as God's agent (Jn 8.24, 28, 58; 13.19). A juridical link arises in conjunction with Isaiah 40–55, where ἐγώ εἰμι serves to establish the Lord's identity and authority in a lawsuit against unbelievers and rivals (Isa. 43.10-12), even as Jesus insists upon his identity and authority as God's agent amidst unbelief and contention.[104] Further, the LXX employs a prefatory ἐγώ εἰμι to certify the Lord's legal pronouncements, as in the Decalogue and throughout the the legal codes of Leviticus.

Judgment. As with words of witness, truth and belief, John teems with words of judgment: κρίνω, κρίσις, κρίμα (31 occurrences between them). This speaks for itself except to highlight Jn 9.39, where Jesus explicitly says that he came into the world for judgment (κρίμα). This solitary use of κρίμα among the many uses of κρίνω and κρίσις underlines it and perhaps heightens the legal overtones of the λόγος coming into the world. John also has four of the six Gospel instances of ἐλέγχω, a manifestly legal word meaning to expose, convince or convict.

Jesus judges as sinful those who belong to the world, saying that they

---

101. P. Borgen, 'God's Agent in the Fourth Gospel', in J. Neusner (ed.), *Religions in Antiquity* (NumenSup, 14; Leiden: Brill, 1968), pp. 140-41. Ashton (*Fourth Gospel*, pp. 308-28) treats the juridical aspects of Jesus' mission, agency, and sonship.

102. C.K. Barrett (*The Gospel according to St John: An Introduction with Commentary and Notes on the Greek Text* [Philadelphia: Westminster Press, 2nd edn, 1978], p. 226) compares σφραγίζω with חתם, meaning 'to sign, subscribe (as a witness, judge etc.)'.

103. R. Heiligenthal, 'ἔργον', *EDNT*, II, p. 50.

104. Schnackenburg, *John*, II, p. 200; Bultmann, *John*, pp. 225-26 n. 3; Brown, *John*, I, p. 537; also Trites, *Concept of Witness*, p. 89.

are without excuse (πρόφασις, Jn 15.22). L. Morris remarks that πρόφασις denotes something put forth to justify an action or defend a position.[105] The word as used in Jn 15.22 smacks of a legal defence, especially given the reference to the Law in Jn 15.25 (compare the forensic settings of πρόφασις in *T. Jos.* 8.5 and *T. Job* 11.11).

Central to John is Jesus' ὥρα, his hour. Jesus' hour signifies both the judgment of the world and also the possibility of its salvation.[106] This tension between judgment and salvation is prominent in John (Jn 3.17; 12.47), and those verses make it worth noting that one of the several meanings which σῴζω bears is deliverance from judicial condemnation.[107]

Pilate has the legal power in civil crimes to acquit and release prisoners (ἀπολύω, Jn 18.39; 19.10, 12), but Jesus has the power to do so with the sin of the world (Jn 1.29), where the phrase ὁ αἴρων τὴν ἁμαρτίαν τοῦ κόσμου suggests judgment annulled and liability removed (cf. 1 Jn 3.4-5).[108] The παράκλητος also convicts and acquits, and the occurrence of δικαιοσύνη in Jn 16.10 may signify the justification or acquittal of those with faith in Christ.[109] Jesus also sets people free from sin (ἐλευθερόω, Jn 8.32, 36), a concept paralleled in Paul, who shows that the law of the Spirit of life in Christ Jesus sets people free (ἐλευθερόω) from the law of sin and death (Rom. 8.2).

In Jn 14.30 Jesus states that his adversary, ὁ τοῦ κόσμου ἄρχων, has no power over him. The phrase ἐν ἐμοὶ οὐκ ἔχει οὐδέν parallels the Hebrew idiom אֵין לוֹ עָלַי, which is found in legal contexts.[110] The NEB accordingly translates, 'He has no rights over me'.

A crucial verse in John's Gospel is Jn 16.33, where Jesus says, 'I have conquered (νικάω) the world'. This verse summarizes the results of the legal strife between God and the world in the coming of Jesus, and it does so using a word having a clearly legal connotation. Indeed, νικάω

---

105. L. Morris, *The Gospel according to John* (NICNT; Grand Rapids: Eerdmans, 1989), p. 681 n. 54.

106. H. Giesen, 'ὥρα', *EDNT*, III, p. 507.

107. W. Foerster, 'σῴζω', *TDNT*, VII, p. 966.

108. The precise Old Testament background of ὁ ἀμνὸς τοῦ θεοῦ is debated. If John is read as alluding to Isa. 53, it could be argued that the lamb bears rather than removes sin. But the close connexion between bearing sin and removing guilt not only permits but requires that the two understandings be held together (so Barrett, *John*, pp. 176-77; Bultmann, *John*, p. 96 n. 1).

109. Trites, *Concept of Witness*, p. 119 n. 3.

110. Barrett, *John*, p. 469; Schnackenburg, *John*, III, p. 87 n. 127.

can be understood in the juridical sense of winning a court case.[111] In Jesus' victory over the world, its advocate, ὁ ἄρχων τοῦ κόσμου τούτου, is sentenced to expulsion (ἐκβάλλω, Jn 12.31; compare the expulsion from the synagogue in Jn 9.34-35) and stands condemned (κρίνω, Jn 16.11). Thus, Jesus' crucifixion is in fact his victory in the cosmic lawsuit, and the accuser is banished from court.

A last word is ἕλκω, of which John has five of the eight New Testament occurrences. John speaks of God drawing people to Jesus (Jn 6.44) and of Jesus drawing all people to himself by his conquering crucifixion (Jn 12.32-33). Borgen relates ἕλκω to משׁך in the judicial context of *halakhah*, and marks Jn 12.31-32 as a courtroom scene in which Jesus, as God's agent, legally acquires title to and secures claim upon those transferred to him by the sender (cf. Jn 6.39; 17.2, 6-7).[112]

Sentencing, Punishment. Jesus warns his adversaries that they will die in their sins (ἀποθνήσκω, Jn 8.21, 24), while they seek to put him to death for his alleged lawbreaking (ἀποθνήσκω, Jn 19.7; ἀποκτείνω, Jn 5.16, 18; 7.1, 19, 20, 25; 8.37, 40, especially 18.31; and once of Jesus' disciples, 16.2). Only John links the attempts to kill Jesus with stoning (λιθάζω), a form of execution prescribed by Jewish Law (Jn 8.7 [cf. 8.59]; 10.31-33; 11.8).

Like the Synoptists, John uses σταυρόω for the Roman form of execution, and mentions that Jesus' name and the charges against him were affixed to the cross. However, only John notes that Pilate wrote the charges on a τίτλος (Jn 19.19, 20). The word τίτλος derives from the Latin loanword *titulus*, which is a public listing of criminal charges and the 'technical Roman designation for the board [or the inscription] bearing the name of the condemned or his crime, or both'.[113]

John alone reports that those who confess and follow Jesus are to suffer the penalty of expulsion from the synagogue (ἀποσυνάγωγος, Jn 9.22; 12.42; 16.2). On the other hand, those who disobey the Son are consigned to God's anger (ὀργή, Jn 3.36), and there is a legal slant to John's one and only use of that word in a very important summary

111. Bultmann (*John*, p. 564 n. 2) notes this juridical meaning; cf. Moulton and Milligan, *Vocabulary*, 'νικάω', p. 427; LSJ, 'νικάω', p. 1176.

112. Borgen, 'God's Agent', pp. 141-42. In two of its other three New Testament occurrences ἕλκω is used in a legal context, albeit the negative one of getting hauled into court (Jas 2.6; Acts 16.19; cf. 21.30).

113. Brown, *John*, II, p. 901.

(Jn 3.31-36). W. Pesch notes that in the New Testament ὀργή most often expresses God's judgment, and that John emphasizes the juridical aspect of God's eschatological anger: 'The saving mission of Jesus becomes a judgment for the one who does not believe in Jesus.'[114]

3. *Witnesses in the Gospel of John*

John surrounds readers with a great cloud of witnesses to Jesus. The Synoptists also advance such witnesses, but John's independence in witness themes is striking. Beutler locates John's uniqueness in the deliberate and systematic deployment of witnesses: 'The uniqueness of the Evangelist's work is first the arrangement of the individual witnesses for Jesus within his Gospel...into a consistent and connected argumentation from testimony.'[115]

Discussions of witness in John customarily isolate μαρτυρία and μαρτυρέω because their frequent occurrences make adequate treatment of the topic impossible without giving heed to them. All the major monographs rightly devote special attention to the words μαρτυρία and μαρτυρέω, but thereby force other pertinent words to travel second-class. Preferential treatment of New Testament μάρτυς cognates should not be allowed to give the impression that the locus of witness resides only in that word and its family, especially in John's case where μαρτυρία and μαρτυρέω figure so prominently. The concept of witness in John is not hermetically sealed within μαρτυρία and μαρτυρέω, and John's pages are replete with other words pertinent to witnessing—words concerning truth, belief, hearing, seeing, knowing, judging, writing, telling and showing. Although I recognize how essential μαρτυρία and μαρτυρέω are, my purpose and method are best served by not isolating those two words, because the idea of witness resides not in them alone but also in other words and phrases as well as in the events narrated in the larger literary structures.

The value of the monographs on witness in John by Boice, Beutler and Trites is by no means diminished by their focus on μαρτυρία and μαρτυρέω. On the contrary, those monographs are invaluable and their contributions must be appropriated. All three agree that John's concept of witness and, more specifically, his witness terminology take root in the language of jurisprudence, both Hellenistic and Semitic. Boice

---

114. W. Pesch, 'ὀργή', *EDNT*, II, p. 530.
115. Beutler, *Martyria*, p. 365.

observes that in μαρτυρία and μαρτυρέω John develops and recasts themes that are already suggested in the Old Testament, especially in Isaiah and in 'the application of the substantive (the "testimonies") to the written law of God'.[116] Trites traces New Testament witness language, specifically words of the μάρτυς family, to Hellenistic and Semitic origins. Like Boice, Trites believes that John presents a controversy very similar to the one found in Isaiah 40–55 and that the concept of witness is to be understood in terms of Old Testament legal language.[117]

J. Beutler is unwilling to confine the understanding of John's witness terminology to the parameters of Old Testament legal language, to the same degree as Boice and Trites. Beutler distinguishes in John two major *Textgruppe*—the various witnesses to Christ, and Christ as witness to divine revelation—and sees in them different linguistic formulations and backgrounds.[118] Three noteworthy conclusions of Beutler's work are: (1) witness terminology in John cannot be traced as a whole to any one background, either Hellenistic or Semitic; (2) when one of John's idioms can be traced to sources (such as μαρτυρέω [or μαρτυρία] περί τινος to the rabbis), John's stamp upon it is unique; (3) some idioms (like μαρτυρέω τῇ ἀληθείᾳ) are of John's creating.

Given the intermingling of Hellenistic and Semitic cultures in Jesus' milieu, it is reasonable to conclude that the forensic colour of John's witness terminology would be readily apparent to a wide range of readers even where John adopts, adapts or creates. Trites notes that 'John is definitely concerned to present legally admissible evidence'.[119] That would be clear to John's readers no matter what degree of Hellenistic-Semitic synthesis may have existed in their cultures.

John's witnesses are not limited to giving evidence of a forensic nature, important as such evidence is. Beutler makes it clear that in both the roots of John's witness terminology and in John's own usage as well, the elements of religious apologetic are evident. Likewise, Boice affirms that John's use of witness has a theological character; thus, 'Witness so considered is no mere witness in an original forensic sense but a religious witness, involving the presentation, verification, and

---

116. Boice, *Witness and Revelation*, p. 16.
117. Trites, *Concept of Witness*, pp. 79-80.
118. Beutler, *Martyria*, p. 42.
119. Trites, *Concept of Witness*, p. 81.

acknowledgment of the claims of Jesus Christ'.[120] Beutler and Boice both think that forensic witness, particularly human testimony, therefore defers to the testimony of God's self-revelation in Jesus Christ. Boice states,

> When testimony is described as revelation the forensic aspects of the word group fall away or at least retreat into the background, and the self-testimony of the sovereign God, pictured perhaps by the language of the court, but ultimately transcendent and independent of any human witness or support, remains.[121]

This concept is crucial for understanding that John has no intention of presenting witnesses only to verify certain facts about Jesus' words and actions. Witnesses play thoroughly rhetorical roles in John's attempt to persuade readers that the messiah is Jesus. Thus, John's witnesses do not simply stand in the dock, give evidence and stand down without taking sides one way or another concerning Jesus' identity and mission. For John it is insufficient merely to assent, for example, to the fact that Jesus performed a sign. John demands that assent to Jesus as the one who performs signs should progress to belief in Jesus as the one who comes from God.

Beutler duly notes the characteristic Johannine dynamic of moving from an external testimony that has seen to one that has believed.[122] John makes the distinction between assent and belief abundantly clear when showing that even though Jesus' arch-enemies acknowledge his signs (Jn 11.47), they still deny his origins (Jn 10.24-25; cf. 12.37). The forensic value of the evidence given by witnesses is not thereby dismissed, but a distinction is made between the evidence itself and the revelation to which it is meant to point; testimony given merely for its own sake is nowhere to be found in John's Gospel. Boice upholds both sides of this distinction by asserting that the persuasion provided through supplementary witnesses to Jesus 'is as far removed from mere legal evidence as a person is removed from a document, but it is a persuasion which utilizes evidence rather than rejecting it'.[123]

Beutler supports the notion that John presents his Gospel in the form of a great trial between Jesus and his opponents, and that John deploys his witnesses accordingly.

---

120. Boice, *Witness and Revelation*, pp. 28-29.
121. Boice, *Witness and Revelation*, pp. 22-23.
122. Beutler, *Martyria*, p. 365.
123. Boice, *Witness and Revelation*, p. 112.

> The uniqueness of the Evangelist's work lies finally in the arrangement of
> the various individual witnesses for Jesus into a 'great trial' that extends
> through the entire Gospel from the delegation of the Jews to John the
> Baptist at the Jordan... to the hour of judgment in Jesus, and in which
> Jesus and the Jews, belief and unbelief, are opposed.[124]

Categorizations of these witnesses are not in short supply and can
appear artificial (John must have the 'perfect number' of seven witnesses)
or blurred (John the Baptist's witness: divine, human or both?), when in
reality the pattern of witness in John is somewhat complex.[125] For the
most part, the major monographs examine these witnesses not so much
in isolation (although that is sometimes the case) but without looking at
how they function as a part of John's story. Thus, another limitation of
the monographs on witness in John involves the narrative role of the
witnesses, especially their rhetorical function vis-à-vis the readers. One
can choose not to follow the monographs on this course without faulting
them for failing to do what they have no intention of doing. Nevertheless,
it is one thing to categorize John's witnesses and another thing to perceive their individual and collective effect as John processes them before
the readers.

According to Boice's scheme, which is typical, the witnesses in John's
Gospel are seven: (1) John the Baptist, (2) the other human witnesses,
(3) the Father, (4) Jesus Christ, (5) Christ's works, (6) the scriptures,
(7) the Holy Spirit.[126] These seven are readily apparent even if, as
already noted, the categories given this way can be somewhat inadequate. Recalling an observation made by B.F. Westcott, Boice notes that
these seven types of witness 'cover the whole range of the possible
proof of religious truth—internal and external, personal and experiential'.[127] This would indicate John's concern that the testimony he
provides be comprehensive as well as true.

Customarily, the broader bifurcation for these seven witnesses is made

---

124. Beutler, *Martyria*, p. 365.

125. J.C. Hindley explicates the topic in 'Witness in the Fourth Gospel', *SJT* 18
(1965), pp. 319-37; see especially pp. 333-34.

126. Boice, *Witness and Revelation*, pp. 26-27; similarly, B.F. Westcott, *The
Gospel according to St John: The Greek Text with Introduction and Notes* (2 vols.;
London: John Murray, 1908), I, pp. xcii-xcvi; J.H. Bernard, *Critical and Exegetical
Commentary on the Gospel of John* (ICC; 2 vols.; Edinburgh: T. & T. Clark, 1928),
I, pp. xc-xciii; M.C. Tenney, 'The Meaning of "Witness" in John', *BSac* 132
(1975), pp. 229-41.

127. Boice, *Witness and Revelation*, p. 9.

between human and divine, the human witness being derivative and dependent in contrast to the authoritative autonomy of the divine. Boice recognizes the general legitimacy of this distinction but makes a major qualification in John's case where 'a division is indicated, not between the divine and the human testimony, however valid that distinction may be, but between the testimony of Jesus Christ and all other testimony, including that of the Father and the Holy Spirit'.[128] This means that all testimony points to Jesus, who is himself the witness par excellence and whose self-testimony and testimony to the Father are one and the same: 'The manifold testimony that the Father gives for Jesus is nothing other than that which Jesus gives for himself. They are not just identical in content; they are one and the same.'[129]

Jesus claims not to accept human testimony such as that of John the Baptist (Jn 5.34). In light of the divine origin and the positive influence of the Baptist's testimony (Jn 1.6-8, 19-51; 3.25-30), this seeming rejection of human testimony requires clarification. Jesus acknowledges how the Baptist attracts and steers others to him even though he has a greater testimony in the works given him by the Father (Jn 5.31-36; cf. 1 Jn 5.9). The thought expressed in Jn 5.34 is that human testimony is not given in order to secure Jesus in his own identity but to convince others of it, and that such testimony is useful even though the truth of Jesus' claims is independent of it.[130]

The superiority of divine testimony does not render human testimony worthless. Indeed, Jesus prays for those who will believe in him through the word of human witnesses (Jn 17.20). The proclamation of the eye-witnesses will give their contemporaries access to the words and deeds of Jesus, and the written records of what they witness will provide access to later generations. Human witnesses are essential to the process that enables readers to receive divine testimony after the earthly life of Jesus. The human witnesses in John's pages focus the readers' attention on the testimony of Jesus and the Father, calling readers to believe. Trying to persuade people that the messiah is Jesus on the basis of human testimonies alone, however reliable, is of course insufficient,

128. Boice, *Witness and Revelation*, pp. 27-28.

129. Beutler, *Martyria*, p. 366.

130. Pancaro (*Law*, pp. 211-12) stresses the lasting value of the Baptist's testimony even though Jesus does not stake his claims upon it. Cf. C.H. Dodd, *The Interpretation of the Fourth Gospel* (Cambridge: Cambridge University Press, 1953), p. 329; Beutler, *Martyria*, pp. 257-58.

because no one comes to Jesus without being drawn to him by the Father (Jn 6.44). Nonetheless, such testimonies are essential first steps leading the readers to an experiential confirmation of Jesus (Jn 7.17) under the guidance of the Paraclete (Jn 15.26-27).

John 20.29 offers a key to understanding the readers' response to John's witnesses. There, Jesus speaks directly to John's readers who, unlike Thomas, lack the advantage of laying eyes on the risen Christ: 'Blessed are those who have not seen and yet have believed.' How then do such people come to believe? The answer follows immediately in the next verses, which contain John's purpose statement (Jn 20.30-31). John intends to provide evidence that leads the readers from acknowledging Jesus' words and deeds to believing Jesus' identity as the messiah. Even given that divine witness is superior and human witness derivative, the human witnesses in John play a crucial role in providing that evidence which leads to faith.[131]

Boice thinks that among the human witnesses in John the apostles are unique. Assuming a late date for John requires Boice to hold that John's use of witnesses is partially guided by his understanding of the apostolic age.[132] But unlike the Synoptists, John never refers to anything resembling an apostolic office.[133] And while Acts depicts the establishment and primacy of the apostolic office, John sees witnesses other than the apostles as also being of primary importance. Boice's failure to grasp this is evident when he says that John structures his story so that 'the evidence for the resurrection rests, not primarily upon the women, although Mary Magdalene is a witness to the opened sepulcher, but upon the testimony of the two chief apostles, Peter and John, who are first to look into the grave. They verify that the tomb was empty.'[134]

131. I disagree with the view of M. Davies: 'The Gospel does not provide the kind of testimony which would convince outsiders looking for historical veracity' (*Rhetoric and Reference in the Fourth Gospel* [JSNTSup, 69; Sheffield: JSOT Press, 1992], p. 152). Davies's statement seems to be in tension if not conflict with another she makes when discussing the miracle at the Cana wedding. Referring to Jesus' mother, the steward, the bridegroom and the servants, Davies (p. 223) states, 'Only in so far as their actions confirm the miracle for the reader are they noticed'.

132. Boice, *Witness and Revelation*, p. 114.

133. John's one and only use of ἀπόστολος (Jn 13.16) is no exception. Schnackenburg (*John*, III, p. 25) explains that the term 'has no more than a functional significance... and does not point to the disciples as apostles in any specific sense'.

134. Boice, *Witness and Revelation*, p. 118.

Boice fails to mention the crucial fact that Mary Magdalene witnesses not just the opened sepulchre but the risen Christ. At that point in the story she, unlike Peter and John, verifies not just that the tomb is empty but that Jesus is alive. She has seen and heard what Peter and the Beloved Disciple have not, and when Jesus sends her to 'his brothers' (Jn 20.18) she becomes—in the venerable patristic term—the *apostola apostolorum*. This example shows that the testimony not just of some but of all the human witnesses to Jesus is important as John establishes his case for his readers.

As mentioned previously, Trites recognizes John's concern to present legally admissible evidence and thus sees, in accordance with the Jewish legal system, that 'the whole of John's Gospel conforms to the principle that everything must be confirmed by the testimony of two or three witnesses'.[135] Harvey also appreciates the importance of John conforming to the Jewish evidence rules and the importance of human witnesses to John's readers. Of interest are those witnesses who had no voice in Jesus' trial before the civil and religious authorities. Harvey explains that according to the Jewish legal system, Jesus' associates would have been excluded as witnesses, being seen as prejudiced due to their relationships with him. John then seeks to allow them to submit their testimony in a literary retrial before the reader. Thus, previously excluded witnesses such as John the Baptist, Andrew, Philip, Nathanael and Peter now give their evidence.

According to Jewish legal standards, what mattered was not just that a witness related facts but that the witness was a person of character and integrity. Harvey observes, 'A Jewish court was not much concerned (and indeed was not equipped) to investigate *facts*: the main question it had to decide was the admissibility and competence of the witnesses'.[136] A case in point is the narrative about Susanna. Her accusers' credibility resides not in their testimony per se but in their status: 'Because they were elders of the people and judges, the assembly believed them' (Sus. 41). Further, when Daniel comes to Susanna's defence, he can do so not because he personally witnessed any of the events under investigation (he did not) but because he is God's emissary (Sus. 45) and the elders, acknowledging him as such, grant him peer status (Sus. 50). This does not imply that the content of someone's testimony was irrelevant or that eyewitness status was unimportant. Eyewitnesses in fact carried

135. Trites, *Concept of Witness*, p. 121.
136. Harvey, *Jesus on Trial*, p. 47.

great weight in ancient Jewish and Hellenist courts just as they do in courts today. But Harvey's point is that since the factual content of testimony often was unprovable, the character of the witness frequently became tantamount to the facts themselves. It is therefore incumbent upon John to demonstrate that the additional witnesses are of that reliable type.

> The first Christian disciples were also men who presumably recognized Jesus for what he was, and whose evidence could be trusted, since they had become the actual founders of the church...They, like [John the Baptist], were witnesses. And it is important to show that they were the kind of witnesses who were to be trusted.[137]

Harvey encounters a stumbling block, however, in the person of Martha. Harvey excises her from his witness list and exiles her to this footnote in his text:

> We have left out of the account the confession of Martha before the raising of Lazarus... A woman's testimony would not have been accepted in a court of law, and this is the one formulation of Jesus' true identity which seems to have no evidential function.[138]

Because Harvey thinks that a woman's testimony was unacceptable in Jewish courts, he must say that Martha's witness has no evidential function in order to preserve his scheme that shows John offering further witnesses to Jesus who are credible.

But is it true that Martha's testimony does not function as evidence? Theologically and literarily it comes at a high point in John's narrative and rhetorical strategy, because the raising of Lazarus is the last and greatest of the signs Jesus performs before concluding his public ministry and preparing himself and his disciples for his passion. It would seem to be the most unlikely place for John to summon a witness whose testimony was inadmissible, irrelevant or suspect.

This look at the Gospel of John as a trial now comes to an end. In a literary retrial before readers, John seeks to use credible human witnesses to make the case that Jesus—quite contrary to the judgment of the authorities who tried, convicted and executed him as a blasphemer— is indeed the messiah, the Son of God. One of these witnesses who provides a crucial testimony is a woman, and this apparent anomaly calls for an investigation into the status of women as witnesses in biblical culture.

---

137. Harvey, *Jesus on Trial*, p. 33.
138. Harvey, *Jesus on Trial*, p. 45.

Chapter 3

WOMEN AS WITNESSES IN BIBLICAL CULTURE

The Gospel of John reflects life in a land ruled by Rome, but the laws germane to women as witnesses lie within that domain of religious self-governance toward which Rome adopted a laissez-faire attitude, except where that attitude led to disruption of the civil order.

> Essentially it is Jewish law which provides the background of the Gospels... In the Palestinian world from which the material of the Gospels may ultimately have originated, Jewish law was basically the law of the land despite Hellenistic influences and the Roman occupation.[1]

Looking at the laws pertaining to women's testimony in biblical culture therefore involves the Pentateuch and its rabbinic expansions.

Using rabbinic literature to reconstruct the situations of Jews and Christians in Jesus' time demands discretion because the processes and history of that literature's formation are not entirely clear, and rabbinic literature contains some retrojections from its own time onto earlier contexts. L.A. Archer's caution is noteworthy.

> There is no way of determining to what extent these rulings [of the Mishnah] reflect the reality of everyday life in Hellenistic Palestine. We have no means of knowing what proportion of the nation adhered to or were even aware of the intricate weave of Mishnaic law which only later came to be regarded as normative and orthodox... In the period under consideration we have to be constantly aware of the fact that there was no normative Judaism as such and therefore no one source may legitimately be taken as reflecting a broad and general social reality. In addition to the differences which existed between schools of thought, sects and individuals of the time, there would have been variation in custom consequent upon region, upon whether people were urban dwellers or village folk, upon the level of education, development and concern, and so on.[2]

1. Nörr, 'Legal History', p. 123.
2. A. Archer, *Her Price Is beyond Rubies: The Jewish Woman in Graeco–Roman Palestine* (JSOTSup, 60; Sheffield: JSOT Press, 1990), pp. 61-62. Barrett

Even with Archer's caveat in mind, it is hard to overstate the centrality of law to Jewish life. M. Meiselman makes this point most emphati-
cally: 'To the Jew, reality is ultimately law.'[3] Similarly, J.D.M. Derrett
comments, 'Law was important to the Jews, not merely as a means of
adjusting rights and duties and solving disputes, but also as a means of
communicating with divinity and discovering how men should live. In a
very special way knowing something about the law made one a Jew.'[4]
God's justice was the heartbeat of Israel's society and God's law
structured Israel's life.

Israel's jurisprudence relied heavily upon judges and the testimony of
witnesses. The Old Testament invokes a vast array of witnesses: God,
people, heaven, earth, the tabernacle, the altar, the ark, the book of the
law, songs and stones. Significantly, it is the Decalogue that provides the
first Old Testament reference to testimony in the forensic mode, where
false witness is forbidden (Exod. 20.16). That this should be embedded
in a God-given law code that proscribes such serious transgressions as
idolatry, murder, adultery and theft, underscores the gravity with which
Israel regarded legal proceedings, particularly the deposition of evidence.
This imperative for truthful testimony is reiterated and expanded to
include impartiality in testifying (Exod. 23.1-3, 6-7; Lev. 6.5), obligation
to testify (Lev. 5.1) and plurality of witnesses (Num. 35.30). These rules
are picked up in the codification of Israel's legal system, found in
Deuteronomy, which includes the rules for evidence. Incorporating older
tradition(s), Deut. 1.9-18 establishes a central judicial organization for
Israel that upholds the requirements of witness impartiality (Deut. 1.17),
veracity (Deut. 5.20) and plurality (Deut. 17.6; 19.15).[5]

Israel's legal code reckoned breaches of laws concerning social, religious and political matters to be more serious transgressions of God's

---

(*John*, p. 33) notes that even though John's Gospel predates the rabbinic literature,
'It remains very probable that John himself (or perhaps the authors of some of his
sources) was familiar with the oral teaching which at a later date was crystallized in
the Mishnah, Talmud, and the Midrashim'.

3. M. Meiselman, *Jewish Woman in Jewish Law* (LJLE, 6; New York: Ktav,
1978), p. 65.

4. J.D.M. Derrett, *Law in the New Testament* (London: Darton, Longman &
Todd, 1970), p. xxxiii.

5. Deprecation of false testimony is found in the New Testament: Mk 10.19 and
pars.; 14.56-57 and par.; Mt. 15.19; Rom. 13.9 (v.l.); 1 Cor. 15.15. Allusions to
the requirement of multiple witness are found in the New Testament: Mt. 18.16;
Jn 5.31-32; 8.17; 2 Cor. 13.1; 1 Tim. 5.19; Heb. 10.28; and in Josephus, *Life* 49.

will than those concerning the body and property of individuals. These violations therefore were considered to be crimes against the nation of Israel as a whole, and one of the most grievous of these was false testimony.[6] Accordingly, false testimony was a crime subject to the *lex talionis*: 'The judges must make a thorough investigation, and if the witness proves to be a liar, giving false testimony against his brother, then do to him as he intended to do to his brother' (Deut. 19.18-19 [NIV]).[7] Thus, as happens to the two false witnesses in the story of Susanna (Sus. 61-62), a perjurer might suffer capital punishment, which demonstrates again how seriously Israel regarded the laws of evidence: 'A false witness will not go unpunished, and the liar will perish' (Prov. 19.9).

While the Pentateuch records no instances of women giving legal testimony, neither does it record any explicit prohibition of such. This presumably reflects the actual practice in Israel in pre-Exilic times; that is, women's testimony was prohibited not *de jure* but *de facto*. For example, Num. 5.11-31 describes the ordeal intended to establish the guilt or innocence of a wife whose husband suspects her of adultery but has no witnesses. The wife does not testify to her own guilt or innocence, but rather, she assents to the oath administered by the priest to the effect that, if guilty, she will miscarry upon drinking the 'water of bitterness'. But this case is not decisive because rabbinic writings describe the suspect being brought before the great court where she does not testify but does plead guilty, 'I am unclean', or not guilty, 'I am clean' (*m. Sot.* 1.4-5). Further, although the rabbis clearly distinguish women from official witnesses, women are permitted to enter statements, taken into account, concerning the suspect's guilt or innocence: 'She was defiled', or, 'She was not defiled' (*m. Sot.* 6.4).

The *Protevangelium of James* reports this ritual in regard to the conception of Jesus. The high priest interrogates Mary and Joseph, and both declare their purity. But Mary's asseveration of innocence, which accords with the practice of *m. Sot.* 1.4-5 and is given with the oath, 'As the Lord my God lives', receives no response, while Joseph's deposition,

---

6.   H.E. Goldin, *Hebrew Criminal Law and Procedure* (New York: Twayne, 1952), pp. 14, 54.

7.   The NRSV translates, 'And the judges shall make a thorough inquiry. If the witness is a false witness, having testified falsely against another, then you shall do to the false witness just as the false witness had meant to do to the other.' In this case the NRSV's inclusive language obscures the Hebrew masculine words that for some people provided the rationale to disqualify women from witnessing.

given with a similar oath, moves the high priest to adjure him, 'Do not give false witness, but speak the truth' (*Prot. Jas* 15.2). Thus Mary's statement, although solicited and heard, does not appear to attain the level of witnessed testimony. The episode ends with the high priest dispensing the 'water of the conviction' to them both (*Prot. Jas* 16.1-2). That Joseph is required to drink the water renders the description of the ritual highly suspect, as nowhere in Jewish Law or literature is the husband so required.

Two cases in Deuteronomy involving the parent-child relationship controvert the idea that under no circumstances did women function as witnesses. The parents of a contumacious son are required to bring him before the elders at the town gate, where both father and mother must testify to the son's recalcitrance (Deut. 21.18-21).[8] Likewise, when a husband accuses his wife of not having been a virgin at marriage, her parents are obliged to appear before the elders at the town gate and display the 'tokens of virginity' (a blood-stained garment or bed covering) as evidence of their daughter's innocence, although in this case only the father testifies vocally (Deut. 22.13-21). The need for reliable witnesses in these two cases is underscored by the gravity of the penalty should the son or daughter be found guilty: death by stoning.[9]

For the second temple period, rabbinic laws regarding competent witnesses are relevant and prominent.[10] The terse Deuteronomic rules for evidence swell considerably at the hands of the rabbis. Since the basic

8.   Goldin (*Law and Procedure*, p. 172 n. 13) cites a *baraita* stating, 'His father and his mother must have the same kind of voice, the same appearance, and be of the same stature; otherwise he cannot be condemned to death'. P. Buis and J. Leclercq note that the rebellious son case diverges from the codes of Deut. 19.15-21 by assuming that parental witness is sufficient because it precludes the risk of false testimony from spiteful persons (*Le Deutéronome* [Paris: Gabalda, 1963], p. 149).

9.   No case is known of a conviction and execution under the rebellious son law. H.H. Cohn attributes this to jurists interpreting the law so narrowly as to render it impracticable ('Rebellious Son', *PJL*, col. 491). The situation implies a son of majority age—at least thirteen (G. von Rad, *Deuteronomy* [London: SCM Press, 1966], p. 138).

10.   This section of the discussion utilizes Z.W. Falk, *Introduction to Jewish Law of the Second Commonwealth* (AGJU, 11; 2 vols.; Leiden: Brill, 1972), I, pp. 113-43; L. Swidler, *Women in Judaism: The Status of Women in Formative Judaism* (Metuchen, NJ: Scarecrow Press, 1976), pp. 115-16; J.R. Wegner, *Chattel or Person? The Status of Women in the Mishnah* (New York: Oxford University Press, 1988), pp. 120-27; Meiselman, *Jewish Woman*, pp. 73-80; H.H. Cohn, 'Witness', *PJL*, cols. 605-612.

premise of witnessed testimony is that unimpeachable knowledge is a necessary but insufficient condition to convict, many technical refinements to the rules of evidence accrue. Two types of witnesses are recognized: constitutive and probative. Constitutive witnesses attest to legal acts and ritual matters (such as marriage contracts and food purity), while probative witnesses testify in court to things they have witnessed and to their previous constitutive testimony (such as criminal prosecutions and lawsuits). Similarly, witnesses are disqualified according to two criteria: lack of credibility (for example, perjurers) or technical grounds (for example, Gentiles).

Although the Pentateuch does not explicitly exclude women as witnesses, rabbinic opinion against women's testimony was overwhelming, and rabbinic practice normally debarred women from testifying in legal proceedings; that is, women did not function as probative witnesses: '[The law concerning] an oath of testimony applies to men but not to women' (*m. Šebu.* 4.1).[11] Further evidence comes in *m. Sanh.* 3.4, where the list of male kin ineligible to testify presupposes no need to catalogue female counterparts. It is very likely, however, that rabbinic opinion against women as witnesses was, although overwhelming, not monolithic. *Sifre Deut.* 190 opposes the opinion, 'One might perhaps hold that a woman also is fit to bear testimony', indicating that some rabbis must have held that opinion.[12]

The disqualification of women as probative witnesses is based on technical grounds rather than lack of credibility. The rabbis therefore acknowledge that women have inherent mental and moral capacities to testify accurately and honestly, and accordingly, the lists of intrinsically incompetent witnesses do not include women.[13] The inherent capacities

11. D. Daube notes that rabbis had difficulty in adducing scriptural support for excluding women from giving testimony: 'The mere silence of Scripture was, of course, not enough: positive authority had to be adduced. Several ways of obtaining it—highly forced constructions of Deuteronomic texts—are preserved' (*Witnesses in Bible and Talmud* [OCP; Oxford: Centre for Postgraduate Hebrew Studies, 1986], p. 15).

12. Daube (*Witnesses*, p. 15) notes that this 'one might hold' form of argument 'is normally used with reference to an idea which was once accepted or which circumstances suggest should now be accepted, but which, for decisive reasons, must be rejected'.

13. Meiselman (*Jewish Woman*, pp. 79-80) draws attention to the logical fallacy of 'like result implies like cause' in the thinking of those who equate women's status in Jewish courts with that of intrinsically incompetent witnesses such as gamblers,

of women for accuracy and honesty are acknowledged also in that women were eligible to take oaths, including oaths of judicial proof employed in cases lacking requisite witnessed testimony.[14]

In some circumstances the rules were relaxed to allow women to testify. For example, a woman could testify in these situations: (1) a lawsuit challenging her virginity prior to marriage, when no independent corroboration exists (*m. Ket.* 1.6-7; 2.5-6); (2) as sole witness to a man's death (*m. Yeb.* 15.1-2; 16.7); (3) certain cases involving property (*m. Šebu.* 5.1; 7.8; *m. Ket.* 9.4). A succinct statement of the principle under which exceptions were made is that usually, within areas of their special knowledge, women could depose credible statements but not witnessed testimony. Meiselman provides an example.

> The eating of certain types of fat called *helev* is a criminal act. The eating of other types of fat, called *shuman*, is not a criminal act. Thus, an accused person can be convicted if a woman testifies that the fat was *helev* and two witnesses testify that he ate it. The logic is simple. For purposes of identification, all that is required is a credible statement and hence a woman's statement is accepted. For purposes of accusation, witnessed testimony is required and hence two witnesses, free from all technical disqualifications, are required.[15]

B. Cohen thinks that the exclusion of women as witnesses became more stringent as time passed and that women previously may have been allowed to testify. Cohen's argument is not accepted by Daube,

usurers, pigeon-racers, minors, deaf mutes and fools. The compendium of incompetent witnesses expanded with the passage of time (cf. *m. Sanh.* 3.3; *m. Roš Haš.* 1.8; *t. Sanh.* 5.5; *b. Sanh.* 25b; *t. Bek.* 3.8; *t. Dem.* 5.2).

14. Jewish law recognizes five types of oaths: covenant, adjuration, promise, loyalty and judicial proof (H.H. Cohn, 'Oath', *PJL*, cols. 615-21). Also, Jewish women could litigate as plaintiff or defendant (*m. B. Qam.* 1.3). Josephus (*Ant.* 4.255) urges widows to protest to the council if their levir refuses marriage. Note also the parable in which a widow repeatedly appears before a judge demanding that he grant her justice against her opponent (Lk. 18.1-8), and the vision of Hermas in which Rhoda convicts him of his sins in front of the Lord in heaven (*Herm. Vis.* 1.1).

15. Meiselman, *Jewish Woman*, p. 76. Falk (*Jewish Law*, I, p. 123) notes that the sages allowed women to testify in cases 'where the testimony was such as women were qualified for' (*t. Ket.* 1.6; cf. *m. Roš Haš.* 1.8). Since women generally were excluded from the public arena, their testimony seems to have been taken informally and not in open court. Philo's list of public places where men are to be found includes lawcourts, suggesting that women did not ordinarily frequent them (*Spec. Leg.* 3.74).

who believes that the Jewish practice of excluding women from giving testimony must have been a well established one.[16] But the lack of a *de jure* exclusion of women witnesses in the Old Testament and the presence of one in the rabbinic writings suggests that Cohen may be correct. If so, then a sequence whereby exemption of women as witnesses led to exclusion of women as witnesses is plausible.

Why were women technically disqualified from witnessing? Many explanations have been offered, none of them definitive. The foregoing evidence rules out intrinsic incompetence, contrary to proposals along those lines—for example, Josephus' (*Ant.* 4.219) expansion of the Mosaic law that mandates multiple witnesses:

> But let not a single witness be credited; but three, or two at least, and those such whose testimony is confirmed by their good lives. But let not the testimony of women be admitted, on account of the levity and boldness of their sex.

Some Talmudic references likewise ascribe flightiness to the female mind (*b. Šab.* 33b; *b. Qid.* 80b), but R. Loewe maintains that Jewish law thereby assumes women to lack not veracity but maturity.[17]

A midrash from the second-century school of Rabbi Akiba links the disqualification of women with the law of witnesses, claiming that since Deut. 19.17 says 'two males' (שני האנשים), the 'witnesses' (עדים) of Deut. 19.15 likewise must be males (*Sifre Deut.* 190).[18]

A ninth-century midrash collection understands women's ineligibility

16. B. Cohen, *Jewish and Roman Law: A Comparative Study* (2 vols.; New York: Jewish Theological Seminary of America, 1966), I, pp. 128-29; Daube, *Witnesses*, p. 14.

17. R. Loewe, *The Position of Women in Judaism* (London: SPCK, 1966), pp. 23-24. One thirteenth-century midrash, citing Gen. 18.15, does maintain that the cause of womens' debarment from giving testimony is their propensity for prevarication: 'And then Sara denied it: I did not laugh. It is from this place that it is taught that women are unqualified to bear witness' (*Yalqut Shimoni* 1.82; see Str-B, III, p. 217).

18. See Str-B, III, p. 560; Daube, *Witnesses*, p. 7. The Pentateuch employs only the masculine form to speak of witnesses, and Cohn ('Witness', col. 606) explains, 'By the method of *gezerah shavah*, it is derived from Scripture that only men can be competent witnesses' (the *gezerah shavah* is 'a technique for equating two concepts, for the purpose of legal detail, based upon formal similarity of biblical terminology rather than similarity of concept' [Meiselman, *Jewish Woman*, p. 212]). Cohn notes that Maimonides used this argument but that it is disputed on the grounds that all of Torah uses the masculine form.

to witness as the result of the transgression of Adam and Eve: 'To the women he gave nine curses and death', one of the curses being, 'She is not to be believed as a witness' (*Pirqe Rabbi Eliezer* 14.7d, 7).[19]

Another explanation has it that women, like kings (who also were excluded from witnessing), should not be subjected to the indignity of interrogation, and that a woman's proper environment is the privacy of the home and not the publicity of the court (Ps. 45.13 was invoked as support: 'All glorious is the princess within her chamber' [NIV]). On this basis attempts have been made to portray the disqualification of women's testimony as altruistic: by exempting women from the legal compulsion to testify (Lev. 5.1), they are spared the trauma of public interrogation.

Finally, it is explained that God, exercising inscrutable divine preroga-tive, simply chose to exclude women from being witnesses through a *Gezerat HaKatuv*, a divine decree of Torah.[20]

1. *Legal Testimony*

The book of Susanna narrates an instance of a woman embroiled in legal proceedings.[21] Immediately after the presentation of the protagonist and her family, the legal context is set up by the introduction of two wicked elders, newly appointed as judges, who are hearing cases. The judges attempt to extort sexual relations from Susanna under the threat that they will bear witness against her that she had participated in such rela-tions with a man other than her husband. Susanna will not acquiesce, shouts for help and soon finds herself on trial for adultery.[22]

19. See Str-B, III, pp. 250-51.

20. M. Kaufman, *The Woman in Jewish Law and Tradition* (Northvale, NJ: Jason Aronson, 1993), pp. 198-200.

21. Susanna dates from near the beginning of the first century BCE to a Palestinian milieu and is based on a Semitic *Vorlage*. The recensions of the LXX and Theodotion differ markedly in some places, but not so as to affect the main concern here, which is how Susanna functions in the trial.

22. In Deut. 22.23-27 a betrothed woman's cry for help is construed as evidence that sexual intercourse with a man other than her husband occurred under duress. H.J. Boecker notes that the cry has a 'technical legal meaning' (*Law and the Admin-istration of Justice in the Old Testament and Ancient East*, [London: SPCK, 1980], pp. 50-51). Notice the bitter irony of Susanna's case in light of the mishnaic law which, in order to forestall lapses in sexual propriety, prohibits a man from being alone with two women, but allows a woman to be alone with two men

The LXX and Theodotion differ on the details of the trial but agree on who testifies. Susanna is placed in the midst of the assembly and her accusers lay their hands upon her head. At that point in the LXX, before they testify against her, she looks upward, weeps and protests her innocence to God in silent prayer (ἀνακύψασα ἔκλαυσεν ἐν ἑαυτῇ λέγουσα). Both the LXX and Theodotion record the testimony given against her, which the assembly accepts unchallenged because of the status of her accusers as elders and judges.[23] In contrast to the LXX, Theodotion locates Susanna's protestation of innocence at this point in the story.[24] Theodotion has Susanna petitioning God in a loud voice (ἀνεβόησε δὲ φωνῇ μεγάλῃ) and, unlike the LXX, explicitly labeling her antagonists' accusations as false testimony (ψευδῆ μου κατεμαρτύρησαν). As Susanna is led away for execution, God intervenes through Daniel who, in Theodotion, is granted elder status by the assembly, which recognizes that God has called him. Daniel's cross-examination of the two elder-judges exposes their false testimony, and then they are put to death in accordance with the *lex talionis*.

The crux of this matter is that during her trial Susanna is never questioned, nor does she ever protest her innocence to anyone other than God. Why does Susanna never testify? C.A. Moore's notion that the presiding elders did not deign to ask Susanna for her side of the story displays an uncritical stance toward the Jewish legal process.[25] Likewise, R.I. Pervo simply notes Susanna's silence at her trial and that there is no suggestion that her testimony was sought.[26] H. Engel sees Susanna's path blocked by the exigencies of her case: the judges who, according to Deut. 19.18, are mandated to investigate carefully the veracity of

---

(*m. Qid.* 4.12). Wegner (*Chattel or Person*, p. 160) observes, 'The rule permitting one woman to remain alone with two men but not one man with two women... assumes that two men will act responsibly in each other's presence rather than take advantage of a woman and that the presence of two will deter the woman from seducing either, as might otherwise happen'.

23. This breaches the requirement that a thorough inquiry be made into such testimony (Deut. 19.15-20).

24. One Syriac recension has Susanna's prayer in both places.

25. C.A. Moore, *Daniel, Esther, and Jeremiah: The Additions* (AB, 44; Garden City, NY: Doubleday, 1977), p. 77.

26. R.I. Pervo, 'Aseneth and Her Sisters: Women in Jewish Narrative and in the Greek Novels', in A.-J. Levine (ed.), *Women Like This: New Perspectives on Jewish Women in the Greco–Roman World* (SBLEJL, 1; Atlanta: Scholars Press, 1991), p. 148 n. 22.

accusing witnesses, are themselves those witnesses.[27] Also possible is that Susanna's testimony is either inadmissible or unreliable due to rabbinic proscriptions against self-testimony, or simply because she is female.[28] In any event, in the LXX Susanna protests her innocence silently to God, while in Theodotion her loudly vocalized protest is likewise directed to God but, although certainly audible to all concerned, goes unheeded by the assembly.[29]

The Qumran literature merits examination because the community behind it adhered strictly to the law and comprised not only the male sect dwelling by the Dead Sea but also family units of men, women, and children dwelling as enclaves in the camps and towns of greater Palestine (Josephus, *War* 2.120-24). True to the Deuteronomic code, the Qumran sect required that charges be sustained by a plurality of witnesses (1QS 6.1; CD 9.2-4) and that false witnesses be punished (1QS 7.17-18, although the *lex talionis* is not specifically indicated).[30] CD 9.16-10.3 briefly outlines some rules of evidence which, with variations, uphold the plurality requirements of the Deuteronomic code but also disqualify as witnesses both probationers (in capital cases) and those being disciplined for transgressing the community rule.

1QSa specifically mentions the presence of women in the assembly, and H.N. Richardson tries to show that in 1QSa, when a man aged twenty is newly admitted as a member of the community council, his

---

27. H. Engel, *Die Susanna-Erzählung: Einleitung, Übersetzung und Kommentar zum Septuaginta-Text und zur Theodotion-Bearbeitung* (OBO, 61; Göttingen: Vandenhoeck & Ruprecht, 1985), p. 109.

28. This matter is obscured somewhat by uncertainty about if and when self-testimony is permissible. Cohn ('Witness', cols. 607-608) comments, 'As relatives are incompetent to testify for or against the party to whom they are related, *a fortiori* the party himself is incompetent to testify for or against himself, for "a man is related to himself" (*Sanh.* 9b-10a; *Yeb.* 25b)'; furthermore, everything the self-witness says in court 'is properly classified as pleading'. Note the Pharisees' accusation that Jesus' testimony is invalid because he gives it on his own behalf (Jn 8.13; cf. 5.31-32); yet Annas the Jewish high priest and Pilate the Roman prefect both ask Jesus to testify at his own trial. Likewise, the high priest asks Stephen to testify before the council on his own behalf in response to (false) testimony brought against him (Acts 7.1). Compare all of this with Acts 25.16, where Roman law unequivocally gives accused persons the right to testify on their own behalf.

29. The story of Susanna has a Samaritan parallel that I will discuss in Chapter 5.

30. M.W. Weinfeld, *The Organizational Pattern and the Penal Code of the Qumran Sect* (NTOA, 2; Göttingen: Vandenhoeck & Ruprecht, 1986), pp. 38-41.

wife becomes eligible to witness and participate in judicial proceedings.[31] Richardson translates the text from which he argues, 'And at that time she will be received to bear witness of him (concerning) the judgments of the Law and to take (her) pl[a]ce in proclaiming the ordinances' (column 1, line 11).[32] Richardson's case rests on, among other things, the reading of תקבל (she will be received).

J.M. Baumgarten asserts that the scribe mistakenly wrote תקבל instead of יקבל (he will be received), apparently influenced by the immediately preceding reference to the woman (column 1, line 10).[33] Over Richardson's protests against emending the text, Baumgarten presents the following four arguments in favour of the scribal error. (1) A regulation for a wife to bring indictments against her husband is out of context with the passage, which deals with a man's initiation into the community, especially since it would fail to mention the husband's own status vis-à-vis judicial proceedings. (2) That the wife's eligibility to witness should be based on her husband's age is anomalous. (3) The Qumran sect is the most unlikely venue for women to be accorded the potent privileges of functioning in judicial proceedings and testifying against their husbands. (4) Other similar passages (CD 9.23-10.2; 10.6-7) suggest that the rule clearly refers to the time at which a young man qualified to witness in legal proceedings and to attend (not conduct) hearings in court.[34]

The exclusion of women as witnesses in the Qumran sect is congruent with the practice in other Jewish communities. This is a case in which a scribal error is virtually certain, as nothing could be more unlikely than women serving as witnesses against their husbands and as judges in legal proceedings by way of a 'feminist plank in the Qumran platform'.[35]

Turning to the writings of Josephus, there are cases of investigations and trials with women directly or indirectly involved. Herod formally places his son Antipater on trial for plotting parricide. No women appear among the witnesses at the trial, but Nicolaus the prosecutor enters hearsay evidence obtained from Antipater's mother (which Josephus disparages as 'whatsoever she had prattled like a woman') and from

31. H.N. Richardson, 'Some Notes on 1QSa', *JBL* 76 (1957), pp. 108-122.

32. Richardson, 'Notes on 1QSa', p. 111.

33. J.M. Baumgarten, *Studies in Qumran Law* (SJLA, 24; Leiden: Brill, 1977), p. 185 n. 7.

34. Baumgarten, *Qumran Law*, pp. 184-86.

35. This last phrase is Baumgarten's, *Qumran Law*, p. 183.

'Pheroras's women'—the wife, mother, and sister of Herod's deceased brother (*Ant.* 17.121).

In contrast to the courtroom context and hearsay evidence of the previous case, Josephus also shows women giving firsthand testimony in Herod's informal investigations. Salome denies that she framed a plot to murder Herod (*Ant.* 16.213-19), and Glaphyra denies that her husband Alexander plotted any treachery against Herod (*Ant.* 16.328-31).

Josephus reports two cases in which women swear oaths in response to questioning. Upon being asked by Herod if she has had criminal conversations with his uncle Joseph, Mariamne 'denied it with an oath' (*Ant.* 15.82-84). Before giving her statement concerning an alleged plot to kill Herod, the wife of his deceased brother Pheroras invokes God as a witness: 'Hear then, O King, and be thou, and God himself, who cannot be deceived, witnesses to the truth of what I am going to say' (*War* 1.595; cf. *Ant.* 17.68).

The New Testament provides no cases of women testifying in legal contexts. Paul excoriates Corinthian church members for bringing their legal disputes to pagan courts rather than settling them within the Christian community (1 Cor. 6.1). Paul never speaks about the witnesses but only of the judges and litigants. In 1 Cor. 6.1-8 Paul implores litigants (ἀδελφοί) to take such matters before the saints (ἅγιοι) and a wise judge (σοφός). Paul's vocabulary makes it difficult to tell if women were involved as litigants or judges because these three terms (with the possible exception of σοφός) could be used inclusively of men and women. If, as 1 Cor. 6.8 suggests, the lawsuits involved fraud, women may well have been witnesses in certain cases, at least according to Jewish Law. Given the context of 1 Corinthians 6, it is also possible that the lawsuits revolved around marriage, and therefore, involved dowries, divorce settlements and inheritances. If so, then under some conditions of Jewish Law, women could have participated as witnesses.[36] In the cases tried before pagan courts, women probably could have been witnesses as is provided by Roman law.[37]

Moving to other early Christian literature, *Acts of Paul* 20-43 records

36. B.W. Winter examines the relevant context in 'Civil Litigation in Secular Corinth and the Church: The Forensic Background to 1 Corinthians 6.1-8', *NTS* 37 (1991), pp. 559-72. Winter does not address the issue of women as witnesses, but does conclude that civil rather than criminal law is involved—meaning cases involving matters such as possession, breach of contract, damages, fraud and injury.

37. Cohen, *Jewish and Roman Law*, p. 128 n. 18.

the trial of Paul and Thecla before the governor Castellius in Iconium.[38] Castellius summons Thecla to stand before the judgment seat, hears the charges against her, and interrogates her about why she is breaking Iconian law by refusing to marry Thamyris, to whom she is betrothed. Thecla gives no answer, and her mother Theocleia cries out demanding that Thecla be executed as a warning to any other women who have followed Paul's teaching. Influenced by Theocleia's words, Castellius, after scourging and expelling Paul, condemns Thecla to be burned. She is spared from the flames by divine intervention.

Thecla accompanies Paul to Antioch, where she publicly rejects and humiliates an Antiochene named Alexander who had fallen in love with her and, having failed to dissuade her loyalty to Paul with money and gifts, tried to take her forcibly. For a second time Thecla is haled before a (this time nameless) governor, to whom she admits what she has done. This governor condemns her to death by wild animals, and a group of panic-stricken women protest before his judgment seat: 'An evil judgment! A godless judgment!' (*Acts of Paul* 27). Thecla is flung into the arena with the wild animals, but again she miraculously escapes death. The governor summons Thecla for questioning and she confesses herself to be God's handmaid, a believer in God's Son, and credits her miraculous deliverance to him. In response, the governor clothes and releases her, issuing a decree that accords with her confession. Finally, Paul commissions Thecla to teach the word of God which, after first returning to Iconium to bear witness to what has happened to her, she does: 'And when she had borne this witness she went away to Seleucia; and after enlightening many with the word of God she slept with a noble sleep' (*Acts of Paul* 43).

Thecla's story accentuates the gap between the Jewish and Graeco–Roman laws regarding women's legal testimony, as twice she is summoned to testify on her own behalf before the judgment seats of governors (compare the report by Josephus [*Ant.* 19.33] that Timidius used Quintilia as a witness against the Roman senator Pompedius).

The *Acts of Pilate* provides another instance of a woman connected with a trial.[39] The *Acts of Pilate* conflates and expands the Gospel accounts of Jesus' trial before Pilate (and the events following). The formal juridical setting is established by the petition of the Jewish authorities

38. The *Acts of Paul* most likely arose in Asia Minor and dates from about 185–95.
39. The extant *Acts of Pilate* was composed during the second–third century, but its *Grundschrift* probably is very early.

to Pilate: 'We beseech your excellency to place [Jesus] before your judgment-seat and to try him' (*Acts Pil.* 1.2). Pilate at first balks, but then he accedes and has Jesus brought in.

Therein commences a parade of witnesses, beginning with the messenger who lays down his kerchief for Jesus to walk upon as he enters the room, and then the soldiers' standards which, against the will of their bearers, bow in obeisance to Jesus. Twelve devout Jewish men rebut the charge that Jesus was born of fornication. The Jewish authorities press their accusations further, Pilate interrogates Jesus, and the two sides debate Jesus' guilt.

At this point several characters gleaned from the Gospels intervene to testify on Jesus' behalf. Nicodemus stands before Pilate to testify to Jesus' innocence, and the Jewish authorities try to impugn his testimony on the grounds that he is a disciple of Jesus. Next, the man whose illness had confined him to his mat for thirty-eight years steps forward to testify that Jesus healed him, and the Jewish authorities try to manipulate his testimony to their advantage by evincing that Jesus performed the healing on the sabbath and by attributing it to Jesus' sorcery. Then a man who had been born blind comes forward to testify that Jesus restored his sight. Then two more men, one of them having been a cripple and the other a leper, likewise come forward to testify to the healing they received from Jesus.

Now the final defence witness tries to testify of having been healed by Jesus. She is Bernice (Latin: Veronica), identified as the woman with a flow of blood (*Acts Pil.* 7.1; cf. Mk 5.25-29). But clearly her testimony is unwelcome, because unlike the males who step forward to witness, she testifies 'crying out from a distance' (ἀπὸ μακρόθεν κράζουσα). Also, the Jewish authorities retort, 'We have a law not to permit a woman to give testimony' (νόμον ἔχομεν γυναῖκα εἰς μαρτυρίαν μὴ ὑπάγειν [recension B: μαρτυρίαν γυναικὸς ὁ νόμος οὐ παραδέχεται]) (*Acts Pil.* 7.1).[40] Immediately a crowd of men and

40. The phrase νόμον ἔχομεν also appears in Jn 19.7 in regard to the charge that Jesus is a blasphemer. Since the law referred to in Jn 19.7 is probably Lev. 24.16, the use of νόμον ἔχομεν in *Acts Pil.* 7.1 might indicate that the *de facto* exclusion of women's testimony had reached *de jure* status as early as Jesus' time, but the late date for the final form of *Acts of Pilate* and its liberal borrowing from John militate against that idea. Better evidence comes from Josephus' appended citation of the Mosaic law concerning the plurality of witnesses: 'But let not a single witness be credited; but three, or two at least, and those such whose testimony is confirmed by their good lives. But let not the testimony of women be admitted, on

women cry aloud in Jesus' defence concerning his exorcisms and the raising of Lazarus, but by now the case is lost, and after further discussion during which the Jewish authorities sway Pilate to their opinion, Pilate orders Jesus scourged and crucified.

The *Acts of Pilate* seems to betray either an ignorance or a negligence of Roman trial procedures. The rejection of Bernice's testimony, however, demonstrates that such ignorance or negligence does not extend to the Jewish rules of evidence. This is confirmed in the council's examination of the rabbis Phineës, Adas and Angaeus, who claim to have seen the risen Jesus. The council adjures them by oath before God to tell the truth (*Acts Pil.* 14.2) and interrogates them separately in order to compare their accounts, citing the law of multiple witnesses (Deut. 19.15) in the process (*Acts Pil.* 16.5-6). Similarly, Joseph of Arimathaea is adjured by oath before God to confess, avoid perjury, and conceal nothing (*Acts Pil.* 15.5).

2. *Eyewitness Testimony*

Related to women's juridical testimony is their eyewitness testimony in other than strictly forensic contexts. Of particular interest are the women witnessing Jesus' crucifixion, burial and resurrection. All four Evangelists take note of a group of women who witness Jesus' crucifixion (Mk 15.40-41 and pars.).

The Synoptists place the women some distance from the cross and identify them as the group that followed Jesus from Galilee. The group includes Mary Magdalene (Matthew and Mark), Mary the mother of James (Matthew; Mark: James the younger) and Joseph (Matthew; Mark: Joses) and the mother of the sons of Zebedee (Matthew; = Mark's Salome?), but Luke specifies no one in the group. John locates them nearby Jesus' cross, identifying Jesus' mother and her sister, Mary the wife of Clopas, and Mary Magdalene (Jn 19.25-27).[41] The Synoptists recount that Joseph of Arimathea entombs Jesus and that some women witness the act. These women are Mary Magdalene (Matthew and Mark) and the other Mary (Matthew; = Mark's Mary the mother of Joses?), but Luke simply labels them as the group of women who had accompanied Jesus from Galilee, while John makes no mention of them whatsoever (Mk 15.42-47 and pars.). Summarizing, the four Evangelists

account of the levity and boldness of their sex' (*Ant.* 4.219).
    41. In Chapter 8 I will review alternative readings of John's list.

report that a group of women were eyewitnesses to Jesus' crucifixion and (except for John) his interment.

The Evangelists' record of the women's witness to Jesus' crucifixion and interment is stark in comparison to that of their witness to Jesus' resurrection.

In Mk 16.1-7, Mary Magdalene, Mary the mother of James, and Salome witness the empty tomb and an angelic young man who dispatches them with a message for Jesus' disciples and for Peter. In Mk 16.8, the shorter ending, they suppress the message out of fear, while in Mk 16.9-13, the longer ending, Mary Magdalene (and then two others, most likely alluding to the two men of Lk. 24.13-35) reports the message and is met with unbelief (Mk 16.9-13).

In Mt. 28.1-11, Mary Magdalene and the other Mary witness the empty tomb and the angel who sends them to tell Jesus' disciples. On the way, they encounter the risen Jesus, who commands them to inform his brothers, but Matthew does not relate the specifics of what happens to the two women and their mission.

In Lk. 24.1-11, the women who had accompanied Jesus from Galilee witness the empty tomb and two angelic men, who in this case do not send them to anyone but only remind them of Jesus' words concerning his resurrection. Having remembered Jesus' words, Mary Magdalene, Joanna, Mary the mother of James, and the other women with them report their experience to the apostles, who respond with disbelief, judging their words to be an idle tale.

In Jn 20.1-18, Mary Magdalene sees the tomb with the stone removed and reports this to Peter and the Beloved Disciple.[42] After Peter and the Beloved Disciple view the empty tomb and leave, Mary Magdalene looks in, sees the two angels and then, outside, Jesus himself. Jesus sends her to his brothers, to whom she announces that she has seen the Lord and then relays what Jesus has told her. John does not describe any reaction from the disciples.

Thus, four scenarios present themselves: (1) their testimony goes unreported (Mark's shorter ending); (2) their testimony is met with unbelief (Mark's longer ending and Luke); (3) the writer does not tell of their testimony (Matthew); (4) no reaction to their testimony is recorded (John). In the cases where the testimony is reported and met with

---

42. John's narrative is complicated by Mary Magdalene's use of 'we' and 'I' when voicing her ignorance of the whereabouts of Jesus' body (Jn 20.2, 13). I will address this complication in Chapter 9.

unbelief, the texts give no indication that such unbelief is due to the fact that women provide the testimony. In fact, Luke's account implies that what is incredible is not the messengers but the message itself: 'Now it was Mary Magdalene, Joanna, Mary the mother of James, and the other women with them who told these things to the apostles. But these (v. l. 'their') words seemed like nonsense to them, and they did not believe the women' (Lk. 24.10-11, my translation).

The Acts of the Apostles contains some instances of women's witness. The episode of Ananias and Sapphira (Acts 5.1-11) reflects the status of women in Jewish Law, including witness. The events of the story are congruent with rabbinic laws that grant to a woman of majority age the right to own and dispose of property, and to her husband the right of usufruct. Ananias and Sapphira jointly sell the land (Acts 5.1). This means quite probably that she owned it prior to marrying him and retained ownership through the marriage contract, because had she designated it as part of her dowry or acquired it after their marriage, he could have sold it on his own.[43] While the interrogation of Sapphira by no means takes place in a formal forensic context, note that women were allowed to testify in cases involving embezzlement, precisely the matter that Peter is investigating and of which Sapphira and Ananias are culpable.[44]

A second example involves the servant Rhoda in Acts 12.12-17, and is interesting in light of the way the women's resurrection report is received by the apostles in Lk. 24.10-11. Rhoda reports to those staying in the house of John Mark's mother that Peter, whom they know to be in prison, is in fact knocking at the door. Rhoda does not recognize Peter himself but rather his voice, and her statement is met with disdain. However, Rhoda's report is incredible not because she is female but because it is fantastic, and while those in the house question her sanity, they say nothing about her gender.

43. E. Haenchen, obviously assuming that the land belongs to Ananias, says that he 'sells his κτῆμα' (*The Acts of the Apostles* [Philadelphia: Westminster Press, 1971], p. 237). Derrett also seems to overlook the possibility that the land might have been Sapphira's property, saying only that Ananias could give away the profits from the sale of his land at the risk of forfeiting the bride price detailed in her *ketubah* and held in escrow should he divorce her or die (J.D.M. Derrett, 'Ananias, Sapphira, and the Right of Property', *DRev* 89 [1971], p. 227). For reviews of the pertinent codes see Loewe, *Position of Women*, pp. 34-35; Wegner, *Chattel or Person*, pp. 87-91; Archer, *Her Price*, pp. 171-88.

44. For the relevant regulations see Wegner, *Chattel or Person*, pp. 126-27.

A third instance, not precisely related to eyewitness, mirrors the gap between Jewish and Roman laws regarding women's roles in jurisprudence. Jewish women could not testify in court, much less act as jurists. Acts 25.23–26.32 recounts that at Paul's trial Bernice not only heard Paul's defence along with Agrippa, Festus, high-ranking officers and leading men of the city, but also appears to have participated in deliberating the verdict (Acts 26.30-31).[45]

The canonical Gospels and Acts prompt a look at the New Testament Apocrypha. In *Epistula Apostolorum* 7 begins the testimony of the eleven apostles concerning the events of the crucifixion and resurrection, which aims to counteract the corrupting influence of Cerinthus and Simon.[46] As the women approach the empty tomb, the Lord appears to them and commands that one of them go to his brothers with news of his resurrection.[47] Mary (Ethiopic) or Martha (Coptic) informs the eleven apostles, who react curtly with disbelief. She returns to the Lord with their response and he dispatches a second woman to do the same. Sarah (Ethiopic) or Mary (Coptic) does so, the former being met with accusations of lying, the latter with simple unbelief. This second woman returns to tell the Lord of the eleven's response, whereupon the Lord says to Mary and her sisters, 'Let us go to them' (*Epistula Apostolorum* 11). The eleven still react with unbelief until they finally touch the Lord's body. In this example, the eleven apostles encounter multiple witnesses in the form of women and refuse to accept their testimony, but the text nowhere indicates that such rejection is based on the messengers' gender.

The *Gospel of Mary* finds Peter questioning Mary (Magdalene) about revelations she has received privately from Jesus.[48] Mary's testimony to

45. Festus does not name Bernice in his exordium: Ἀγρίππα βασιλεῦ καὶ πάντες οἱ συμπαρόντες ἡμῖν ἄνδρες (Acts 25.24). This omission is understandable within the first-century Palestinian context and in view of the likelihood that Bernice was the only woman in a courtroom full of men. Josephus (*War* 2.344) relates how Agrippa strategically placed Bernice in the audience before trying to dissuade the Jews from waging war against the Romans.
46. The *Epistula Apostolorum* dates from the early to middle second century, probably from the milieu of Hellenistic-Jewish Christianity in Egypt, and is anti-Gnostic.
47. The women are Sarah, Martha, Mary Magdalene (Ethiopic text), or, Mary, she who belonged to Martha, Mary Magdalene (Coptic text).
48. The *Gospel of Mary* is a second-century Gnostic work existing in Greek and Coptic versions. The texts quoted here are from J.M. Robinson (ed.), *The Nag*

a vision of Jesus elicits unbelief from Andrew, who rejects her testimony on the basis of its content: 'I at least do not believe that the Saviour said this. For certainly these teachings are strange ideas' (*Gospel of Mary* 17). Peter disbelieves as well, rejecting Mary's testimony because he does not believe that Jesus would make such private revelations to a woman: 'Did he really speak with a woman without our knowledge (and) not openly? Are we to turn about and all listen to her? Did he prefer her to us?' (*Gospel of Mary* 17). Mary defends her integrity to Peter, and then Levi intervenes: 'Peter, you have always been hot-tempered. Now I see you contending against the woman like the adversaries. But if the Savior made her worthy, who are you indeed to reject her? Surely the Savior knows her very well. That is why he loved her more than us' (*Gospel of Mary* 18).

These texts from the *Gospel of Mary* encapsulate the ambivalence toward women's worthiness and ability to bear testimony. Andrew disbelieves Mary's testimony because of its content, while Peter's disbelief manifests a disparaging attitude toward her gender. It is not the case that Levi's defence balances or contradicts Peter's attitude, as he defends her because of the Saviour's aegis and not because women are inherently capable and qualified to receive such revelations and render valid testimony to them.

Although two of them are too late to have great relevance for the present discussion, three Gnostic texts merit a brief glance because each displays the persuasive use of a woman's eyewitness testimony.

In the *Acts of Andrew* Maximilla says that she 'was sent as an apostle by the Lord...not indeed to teach anyone, but to remind everyone who is akin to these words that they live in transient evils while they enjoy their harmful delusions' (*Acts of Andrew* 15).[49] She then urges her audience to stand fast in their faith, bolstering her exhortation by citing the evidence of her words and works which they have witnessed (*Acts of Andrew* 16).

In the *Gospel of Mani* the risen Jesus commissions Mariam as messenger to the eleven apostles, 'these wandering orphans' (cf. Jn 14.18).

> Say to them: 'Arise let us go, it is your brother that calls you.' If they scorn my brotherhood, say to them: 'It is your Master'. If they disregard

Hammadi Library in English (San Francisco: Harper & Row, 3rd edn, 1988).
    49. The *Acts of Andrew* dates from the mid-second century.

my mastership, say to them: 'It is your Lord.' Use all skill and advice until you have brought the sheep to the shepherd.[50]

Here the text indicates that Jesus anticipates reluctance on the part of the eleven apostles, but directed at himself rather than his female messenger. He also assumes that Mariam possesses the requisite persuasive abilities to finally convince the eleven.

The Sixth Act of the *Acts of Thomas* narrates the apostle Thomas bringing a murdered woman back to life and then asking her to tell of where she has been.[51] She describes the horrors of hell that she witnessed during her period of death. Thomas then uses her testimony to urge the listeners to repent: 'You have heard what this woman related... Believe therefore in Christ Jesus' (*Acts of Thomas* 58). The crowd duly responds to her testimony and Thomas' exhortation: 'So all the people believed, and yielded their souls obedient to the living God and to Christ Jesus' (*Acts of Thomas* 59).

In one case, rejection of the evidence for Jesus' resurrection is clearly based, at least in part, upon the witness of a woman. Celsus, in *The True Word* (c. 175), tells of a Jew challenging fellow citizens who believe in Jesus.

> But we must examine this question whether anyone who really died ever rose again with the same body... While [Jesus] was alive he did not help himself, but after death he rose again and showed the marks of his punishment and how his hands had been pierced. But who saw this? A hysterical female, as you say, and perhaps some other one of those who were deluded by the same sorcery.[52]

Writing some fifty years later, Origen responds to Celsus' assault on the veracity of Jesus' resurrection, insisting that Celsus' charge of hysteria is a fabrication for which there is no evidence in the scriptural account upon which he bases his criticism (*Contra Celsum* 2.60). Origen controverts Celsus' charge that Mary Magdalene was hysterical, but he does not even address the matter of her being a female. His rebuttal defends her composure not her gender.

---

50. The text of this third-century Manichean agraphon is from E. Hennecke and W. Schneemelcher, *New Testament Apocrypha*, I, p. 403. I have modernized the English.

51. The *Acts of Thomas* probably stems from a Christian Syrian milieu of the early third century.

52. According to Origen, *Contra Celsum* 2.55.

3. *Religious Testimony*

'Nowhere is the secondary status of women and their exclusion from the central institutions of Israelite society more apparent than in Exod. 19.15, where those who are preparing to enter the covenant with Yahweh are exhorted "do not go near a woman"'.[53] And indeed, it does appear that from the formal inception of Israelite society women were *déclassé*. Many of the practices and offices integral to Jewish religious life such as formal study of Torah, circumcision and priesthood were unavailable to women. A.C. Zuckoff observes, 'In essence, all the important ways in which Judaism defined what it meant to be a Jew were...either partially or completely closed to women'.[54] Meiselman, on the other hand, wants to emphasize how much of cultic observance was binding on women, and so he points out that women were exempt from only fourteen positive commandments.[55] However, Meiselman's list of exemptions includes circumcision and the learning, teaching and writing of Torah—things so fundamental to Jewish identity that it seems easier to construe Meiselman's list as evidence that supports rather than controverts Zuckoff and Setel. That women were sometimes exempted from laws that were always binding for men reflects the tension in the rabbinic view of a woman: she is man's spiritual-moral equal and at the same time his cultic-social inferior.[56]

As with witness, this circumscription of the cultic life of Jewish women seems to have come about through the progression from exemption to exclusion, and with a corresponding rationale behind it: releasing women from some legal obligations. One etiology in the case of witness has it that women were spared the indignity of public legal interrogation. Similarly, in cultic life the rationale was that women were unburdened from some public religious duties in deference to their physical nature and household duties. A mediaeval explanation held that

53. D.O. Setel, 'Exodus', in C.A. Newsom and S.H. Ringe (eds.), *The Women's Bible Commentary* (London: SPCK, 1992), p. 33.

54. Cited by Swidler, *Women in Judaism*, p. 85.

55. Meiselman, *Jewish Woman*, pp. 52-57.

56. According to R. Biale, the two creation accounts in Genesis reflect this same tension. In one account the woman is created with the man in God's image and in the other account created to meet the needs of the man (R. Biale, *Women and Jewish Law: An Exploration of Women's Issues in Halakhic Sources* [New York: Schocken Books, 1984], p. 14).

a woman sometimes finds herself in the dilemma of having to choose between her duty to obey God and her duty to obey her husband, in which case God defers to the husband to insure domestic tranquility.[57]

Thus, women were exempted by the rabbis from certain elements of mandatory cultic practice. Specifically, women were obliged to keep all but time-bound, positive ordinances.[58] Whether the intention was altruistic or otherwise, this release from the time-bound, positive statutes incumbent upon men had the effect of restricting women's participation in temple and synagogue. One exemption accorded women involved religious witness: women need not recite the *Shema*, which rabbinic law enjoined every Jew to recite twice daily (*m. Ber.* 3.3; *b. Qid.* 33b). Still, even if cases of women giving legal testimony are lacking in the Old Testament, such is not the case with religious witness. Despite the constraints on their cultic life, several women from the pages of the Old Testament and elsewhere utter prominent testimonies of faith.

On some occasions women conduct testimony to the Lord's greatness and mighty deeds. After the Israelites cross the Red Sea and are safely delivered from their Egyptian pursuers, Exodus 15 records first Moses then Miriam presiding over the Lord's praise, Moses leading the Israelites and Miriam the women. Miriam's song is but one couplet, 'Sing to the Lord, for he has triumphed gloriously; horse and rider he has thrown into the sea' (Exod. 15.21), while Moses' protracted version runs to eighteen verses (Exod. 15.1-18). This 'Song of the Sea' is one of the oldest pieces of Hebrew poetry. The longer song of Exod. 15.1-18 appears to be an expansion of Miriam's song (her couplet serving as an incipit), which was attributed to Moses and placed in the narrative. If so, this ancient song publicly confessing the greatness of the Lord was associated originally with Miriam.[59]

57. Biale, *Women and Jewish Law*, pp. 13-14.

58. Laws were either positive or negative, and either time-bound or perpetual. Thus, for example, women were not required to occupy shelters during Sukkoth (positive, time-bound), but they were required to abstain from unclean foods (negative, perpetual).

59. J.G. Janzen contends for the priority of Miriam's song at the level of textual narrative. Janzen perceives that Miriam's song and its introduction (Exod. 15.19-21) form an analepsis that repositions the reader back at Exod. 14.29 before Moses' song, which is sung as an antiphonal response (Exod. 15.1-18). Janzen maintains that the purpose for this somewhat jarring narrative device is to round off the Exodus saga with an inclusio highlighting women's strategic activities: women deliver Moses from the water and women celebrate the deliverance of Israel from the sea

A similar incident is found in Judges 5, the 'Song of Deborah', where Deborah the judge sings praises and thanks to the Lord for victory over the Canaanites. While the military commander Barak is also said to participate in the song (Judg. 5.1), the relevant verb is feminine singular (ותשר, 'and she sang'), the following verbs (Judg. 5.3) are singular (אשירה, 'I will sing', and אזמר, 'I will make music'), and it is Deborah who is called to sing while Barak is called to take captives (Judg. 5.12). Like the song of Miriam, Deborah's song is very early, dating perhaps from the twelfth century BCE.[60] According to Pseudo-Philo, Deborah's hymn will be 'a testimony' to the saving power of God (*Bib. Ant.* 32.17), and God's creation of Deborah herself 'will be a testimony of what the Lord has done for his people' (*Bib. Ant.* 32.15).

C.A. Brown notes that unlike Deborah's male counterparts who were military commanders only, she was a judge to whom the Israelites referred their legal disputes for adjudication (Judg. 4.5), and she is the only woman in the Bible having such a role.[61] Consistent with his preference that women be subjugate, Josephus fails to mention Deborah's station and activities as a judge (*Ant.* 5.202-209). However, one legend does underscore Deborah's status as an adjudicator of legal disputes: 'She dispensed judgment in the open air, for it was not becoming that men should visit a woman in her house.'[62]

(J.G. Janzen, 'Song of Moses, Song of Miriam: Who Is Seconding Whom?', *CBQ* 54 [1992], pp. 211-20).

60. For a discussion of Miriam and Deborah as the composers of their victory songs see A. Brenner, *The Israelite Woman: Social Role and Literary Type in Biblical Narrative* (Sheffield: JSOT Press, 1985), pp. 51-56.

61. C.A. Brown, *No Longer Be Silent: First Century Jewish Portraits of Biblical Women* (GBT; Louisville: Westminster/John Knox Press, 1992), p. 39. Brown (p. 89 n. 49) also notes that Deborah (*Bib. Ant.* 33.1-6) and Rebekah (*Jub.* 35.1-27) are the only two women who deliver testaments (in the manner of *Testament of the Twelve Patriarchs et al.*). J.C. Endes views Rebekah's testament as an 'exhortation to the Jewish community to bind together in unity and harmony, the genuine characteristics of covenantal love', and raises but does not answer the question of whether the readers of *Jubilees* would be surprised that the author deemed it appropriate for a woman to deliver such an exhortation to the Jewish community (J.C. Endes, *Biblical Interpretation in the Book of Jubilees* [CBQMS, 18; Washington: Catholic Biblical Association of America, 1987], pp. 175-76). R.D. Chesnutt thinks that Rebekah's role in *Jubilees* was both possible and desirable in the author's social world (R.D. Chesnutt, 'Revelatory Experiences Attributed to Biblical Women', in A.-J. Levine [ed.], *Women Like This*, p. 124).

62. L. Ginzberg, *The Legends of the Jews* (7 vols.; Philadelphia: Jewish

Another public proclamation of the Lord's greatness, found in the book of Judith, dates from the latter part of the second century and continues the tradition of women conducting testimonial songs.[63] Following the victory over Holofernes and the Assyrians, Judith receives the adulation of the people as they follow her, women dancing and men singing. Judith then initiates a public confession of thanksgiving (ἐξομολόγησις) to God before all Israel with all the people joining in a song of praise (Jdt. 16.1-17). Like the songs of Miriam and Deborah, Judith's song recites the mighty deeds of the Lord but also takes care to proclaim that the Lord has foiled the Assyrians by a feminine hand (ἐν χειρὶ θηλείας, Jdt. 16.6). The demise of Holofernes and the defeat of his forces at the hand of a woman humiliates them, and so this verse, presupposing that women are less than worthy opponents for men, cannot be construed as a veneration of women.

A last testimony, that of Hannah, mirrors the foregoing songs but is, strictly speaking, a prayer that witnesses to the person and works of the Lord.[64] Hannah, fulfilling a vow made to the Lord (1 Sam. 1.11), brings her newly weaned son Samuel for presentation at Shiloh along with an offering of a bull, flour and wine (1 Sam. 1.24). Some silences and variations in the MSS obscure the roles of Hannah, her husband Elkanah and the priest Eli, but in any case, following the presentation of Samuel, Hannah worships aloud in the Lord's house in a prayer of praise. As do the songs of Miriam, Deborah and Judith, Hannah's prayer celebrates the victory and uniqueness of the Lord: 'My heart exults in the Lord; my strength is exalted in my God. My mouth derides my enemies, because I rejoice in my victory. There is no Holy One like the Lord, no one besides you; there is no Rock like our God' (1 Sam. 2.1-2).

Hannah's vow in 1 Sam. 1.11 recalls that the Law enabled women to initiate religious vows.[65] Both men and women could take the vow of the *nazir* (Num. 6.2), and the Lord excoriates both husbands and wives for making vows to the queen of heaven (Jer. 44.24-25). The vows of

Publication Society of America, 1968), IV, pp. 35-36.

63. Notice that Deut. 31.19-21 designates Moses' song (Deut. 32.1-43) as a witness for God.

64. In Pseudo-Philo (*Bib. Ant.* 51.3-6) Hannah's prayer assumes the form of a hymn.

65. In light of Hannah's case, note that the rabbis quote 1 Samuel 11 as proof that Samuel was a *nazir* (*m. Naz.* 9.5), but decree that a mother cannot impose the vow of the *nazir* upon her son (*m. Naz.* 4.6).

men and autonomous women (unmarried majors, divorcees, widows) were automatically binding, while under certain circumstances the vows of dependent women (unmarried minors, marrieds, levirate widows) could be annulled. Again the situation arises in which men are irrevocably bound by law while women can be exempted. With vows, the rationale for exemptions need not be postulated as the preservation of a woman's dignity or deference to her domestic duties. Since women were most often economically dependent upon men, the onus for fulfilling the vow of a woman could sometimes fall upon her father or husband. The law seeks to protect men in that eventuality by making provisions under certain circumstances for them to annul a woman's vow, while at the same time protecting women from men capriciously exercising the right to annul their vows (cf. Num. 30.1-16).[66]

Not only could women make vows, but, as mentioned before, the Law judged women competent to swear oaths (see Num. 5.19-22)— excluding the oath of probative witness—and thereby acknowledged women to possess the intrinsic mental and moral capacities for accuracy and honesty.[67] Moses specifically includes women among those who seal the covenant renewal at Moab with an oath (Deut. 29.9-15; cf. Josephus, *Ant.* 4.309-10). In Song of Songs, the female lover four times imposes an oath on the daughters of Jerusalem, adjuring them to perform or abstain from certain actions (Song 2.7; 3.5; 5.8; 8.4). The context, of course, is poetic not legal, but the word used for adjuration (שׁבע) is the common one used for swearing someone to an oath, and the daughters of Jerusalem seem to acknowledge it as such (Song 5.9). In the first two instances she adjures them 'by the gazelles or the wild does'. R. Gordis understands this phrase as a euphemism for the Divine Name: 'The desire to avoid mentioning God's name would be particularly strongly

---

66. For rabbinic examples and clarifications of men revoking the vows of women, see *m. Ned.* 10.1-11.12; *m. Naz.* 4.1-6; 9.1. Philo, his subordinationist views of women notwithstanding, upheld the equal worth of the vows of all persons (*Spec. Leg.* 2.34), although D. Sly thinks that Philo's stance reflects his own philosophical and ethical interests more than actual Jewish legal praxis in Alexandria (D. Sly, *Philo's Perception of Women* [BJS, 209; Atlanta: Scholars Press, 1990], pp. 225-26).

67. The distinction between oath and vow is not always clear. Generally, an oath is a sworn asseveration to tell the truth or a sworn obligation to perform certain actions, and is made between people, invoking God as guarantor. A vow is the promise of a votive offering or service to God in return for God's fulfillment of a request.

felt in connection with an oath concerned with the physical aspects of love.'[68] The LXX renders the phrase as an adjuration 'by the powers and forces of the field' (ἐν [ταῖς] δυνάμεσι καὶ ἐν [ταῖς] ἰσχύσεσι τοῦ ἀγροῦ). Gordis believes this to be the LXX's recognition of the solemn oath contained in the Hebrew euphemism, and he points to the midrashic equation of the gazelles and wild does with 'the hosts of heaven and earth' (*Midrash Shir Hashirim Rabbah* 2.7).

An example of an oath coupled with a confession comes from Rahab. Despite her ignoble status as a Canaanite prostitute, Rahab has heard of the Lord's mighty deeds and confesses to the Israelite spies: 'The Lord your God is indeed God in heaven above and on earth below' (Josh. 2.11).[69] Rahab's confession closely resembles that of the Mosaic injunction, 'So acknowledge today and take to heart that the Lord is God in heaven above and on the earth beneath; there is no other' (Deut. 4.39).[70] In comparing the two texts it might appear that Rahab's confession does not necessarily express Israelite monotheism. She confesses that the Lord אלהים הוא while Moses enjoins that the Lord הוא האלהים. Also, Rahab does not say, 'There is no other'. However, the presence or absence of the article is insufficient to establish or disprove monotheism. The LXX renders both אלהים and האלהים with the anarthrous θεός, and the unquestionably monotheistic Psalm 100 states, דעו כי יהוה הוא אלהים (Ps. 100.3). Further, in this context Rahab's confession functions like the preamble of an Israelite covenant form and has the markings of a monotheistic creed from the Deuteronomistic mould.[71]

Rahab's case presents the apparent anomaly of a Canaanite prostitute confessing the Israelite Lord and administering an oath to men rather than taking one from them (Josh. 2.12). And yet the New Testament upholds this Canaanite prostitute as a paradigm of faith (Heb. 11.31) and

68. R. Gordis, *The Song of Songs and Lamentations: A Study, Modern Translation and Commentary* (New York: Ktav, rev. edn, 1974), p. 28.

69. In Josh. 2.1 Rahab is identified as אשה זונה, which can be understood as a prostitute (so the LXX) or an innkeeper (so Josephus, *Ant.* 5.5-15). But the two roles need not exclude one another.

70. It has been proposed that the Deuteronomic historian(s) added the Rahab material to Joshua; see M.A. O'Brien, *The Deuteronomic History Hypothesis: A Reassessment* (OBO, 92; Göttingen: Vandenhoeck & Ruprecht, 1989), pp. 68-71.

71. K.M. Campbell, 'Rahab's Covenant', *VT* 22 (1972), pp. 243-44; M. Weinfeld, *Deuteronomy and the Deuteronomic School* (Oxford: Clarendon Press, 1972), p. 331.

works (Jas 2.25), and locates her in Jesus' lineage (Mt. 1.5).[72] The Rahab saga plays a key role in Joshua by presaging both the incident with the Gibeonites (Joshua 9) and Joshua's peroration of the book (Joshua 24). 'The pagan prostitute is the first one to recite saving history in the final edition of the book.'[73]

An example of a religious oath sworn by a non-Jewish woman is that of the Moabite Ruth to her Israelite mother-in-law Naomi.

> Do not press me to leave you or to turn back from following you! Where you go, I will go; where you lodge, I will lodge; your people shall be my people, and your God my God. Where you die I will die—there will I be buried. May the Lord do thus and so to me, and more as well, if even death parts me from you! (Ruth 1.16-17).

No verbs of swearing are present here, and superficially this seems to be simply a solemn promise. However, Ruth's promise of behaviour and invocation of sanctions have the features of a formal oath and are so recognized by most authorities.[74] The formula, 'So may the Lord do... and more so', appears commonly in connection with oaths (for example, 1 Sam. 3.17; 14.44; 20.13).[75] Since Naomi's assent is implied only by her silence (Ruth 1.18), the oath may be a unilateral oath either of promise for future conduct or of loyalty. In either case, implicit in Ruth's oath is a confession of Israel's God as she invokes the name of the Lord (as required when swearing an oath) and transfers her allegiances from the Moabite people and gods to Israel and the Lord.[76]

---

72. It is not certain that Joshua's Rahab and Matthew's Rahab are the same person, but the presence of other foreign women (Tamar and Ruth) in Matthew's genealogy strongly points in that direction.

73. R.G. Boling and G.E. Wright, *Joshua* (AB, 6; Garden City, NY: Doubleday, 1982), p. 146.

74. For example, J.M. Sasson, *Ruth: A New Translation with a Philological Commentary and a Formalist-Folklorist Interpretation* (Sheffield: JSOT Press, 2nd edn, 1989), pp. 28-31, especially p. 30.

75. E.F. Campbell notes that of the twelve occurrences of this formula, only in Ruth 1.17 and 1 Sam. 20.13 is יהוה used rather than אלהים, reinforcing that the loyalty is to the God of the Israelites. Campbell reads Ruth's words as a 'solemn oath formula' (E.F. Campbell, *Ruth* [AB, 7; Garden City, NY: Doubleday, 1975], pp. 74-75).

76. Another foreign woman, the queen of Sheba, makes a confession of the Lord. Having confirmed for herself Solomon's reputation for wisdom, she bursts into a doxology: 'Praise be to the Lord your God, who has delighted in you and placed you on the throne of Israel. Because of the Lord's eternal love for Israel, he

A second foreign woman who swears an oath is the poor widow of Zarephath. When Elijah asks her for water and bread, she swears that she lacks sufficient provisions, using a conventional oath formula, 'As surely as the Lord your God lives' (1 Kgs 17.12; compare Elijah's oath to Ahab in 1 Kgs 17.1). The widow's statement bears the earmark of an oath and was understood as such by Josephus: 'she affirmed upon oath' (*Ant.* 8.322).

In the *Apocalypse of Moses* the devil, speaking through the serpent, entices Eve to eat the fruit and to swear on oath to give some to her husband. Eve says to the devil, 'I do not know what sort of oath I should swear to you; however that which I do know I tell you: By the throne of the Lord and the cherubim and the tree of life, I shall give (it) also to my husband to eat' (*Apoc. Mos.* 19.2). The devil receives Eve's oath which, of course, she later regrets (*Apoc. Mos.* 19.3; 20.3). Formally, Eve's oath is promissory and has a typical invocation of the Lord, in this case using the Lord's throne.[77]

From the Qumran literature, 1QapGen relates how Lamech fears that his wife Bitenosh had conceived Noah by angelic beings rather than by him. Lamech adjures Bitenosh to swear by the Most High, the Great Lord, the King of all Ages to tell the truth of how she conceived. At first she responds with an emotional promise to tell the truth but does not swear the desired oath. Bitenosh perceives that Lamech's countenance reflects his disapproval, and so she swears the solemn oath: 'I swear to you by the Great Holy One, by the King of the h[eavens...] that this seed is from you' (1QapGen 2.14-15).[78] Given the attitude in many quarters that women were unreliable, it is revealing that Lamech, even after hearing Bitenosh's oath, still entertains doubts and seeks confirmation, which he finally secures from from his grandfather Enoch. However, the text gives no explicit reasons for Lamech's doubts.

Another stream of religious witness flows from Israel's prophetic

---

has made you king, to maintain justice and righteousness' (1 Kgs 10.9). Jesus invokes the queen of the south (Sheba) as a witness who will rise up in judgment against the wicked and adulterous generation of sign-seekers (Mt. 12.42 and par.).

77. The provenance of the *Apocalypse of Moses* is hard to establish, but most likely it originates in Palestinian Judaism of the first century and is rooted in Pharisaic theology. If so, then doubly interesting is Jesus' comment to the scribes and Pharisees, 'Whoever swears by heaven swears by the throne of God and by him who sits upon it' (Mt. 23.22; cf. 5.34).

78. The text of 1QapGen is that of J.A. Fitzmeyer, *The Genesis Apocryphon of Qumran Cave 1: A Commentary* (BibOr, 18; Rome: Biblical Institute Press, 1966).

tradition. The range of prophetic milieux, roles and expressions in Israel defies simple categorization.[79] But clearly, several women of the Old Testament and the New Testament stand squarely in that broad prophetic stream. The designation 'prophet' (נביאה, προφῆτις) is accorded specifically to five women in the Old Testament: Miriam (Exod. 15.20), Deborah (Judg. 4.4), Huldah (2 Kgs 22.14; 2 Chron. 34.22), Noadiah (Neh. 6.14) and the wife of Isaiah (Isa. 8.3).[80]

Miriam, Deborah and Hannah have already been mentioned in connexion with songs and prayers of witness. Miriam and Deborah's musical prowess connects with their status as prophets. The lexical field for prophesying (נבא) can include musical expression, and several Old Testament incidents display prophetic activity involving music.[81] Both Miriam and Deborah also had leadership roles in Israel, Miriam being a member of the triad that led Israel in the Exodus (Mic. 6.4), and Deborah, who assumed the esteemed title 'Mother' (Judg. 5.7), judging Israel in the anarchical days after the occupation of Canaan.[82]

The prophet Huldah stands at a pivotal point in Israel's history. When the high priest Hilkiah discovers the lost book of the law, king Josiah directs him and other leaders to enquire of the Lord about the book. The deputation consults Huldah, whose prophecy triggers Josiah's reforms and the renewal of the covenant (2 Kgs 22.14-20; 2 Chron. 34.22-29). In the deputation was Ahikam, a supporter of the prophet Jeremiah (Jer. 26.24). This arouses speculation as to why the comparatively obscure woman Huldah was sought rather than the prominent man Jeremiah who was active at the time. That question vexed the rabbis: 'But if Jeremiah was there, how could she prophesy?' (*b. Meg.* 14b), and they offer possible answers: (1) Huldah was a close relative of

---

79. G.V. Smith sees prophets involved in six areas: temple worship, monarchy, wisdom, ecstatic behaviour, covenant law and apocalyptic (G.V. Smith, 'Prophet', *ISBE*, III, pp. 992-97).

80. Although both Hebrew and Greek have individual words for male and female prophets, I am avoiding the word 'prophetess' here because English words bearing suffixes like -ess, -ette, -enne and -trix tend to imply inferiority.

81. BDB, 'נבא', p. 612. Samuel and Saul associated with ecstatic musical prophets (1 Sam. 10.1-13; cf. 19.18-24). David, who used music to alleviate Saul's periods of spirit-induced torment (1 Sam. 16.23), set apart musical prophets (1 Chron. 25.1-6). Elisha summoned a musician to help him prophesy to the kings of Israel, Judah and Edom (2 Kgs 3.15).

82. Compare the use of the title 'Father' for priests and prophets (Judg. 17.10; 18.19; 2 Kgs 6.21; 13.14).

Jeremiah and so he did not object; (2) women are tender-hearted (and thus Huldah would pray for them); (3) Jeremiah was absent (*b. Meg.* 14b). The biblical text itself offers no clues, but certainly Huldah's prophetic credentials were creditable even redoubtable. Huldah's venerated status is manifested in the tradition that labels the southern gates to the temple mount as the 'Huldah Gates' (*m. Mid.* 1.3).

Two other prophets deserve mention, even if little can be said about them: Isaiah's wife, who was a prophet (Isa. 8.3), and Noadiah, whose attempt to intimidate Nehemiah in his efforts to rebuild the wall of Jerusalem (Neh. 6.14) blemishes the otherwise exemplary record of the other women prophets.

Rabbinic tradition acknowledges forty-eight male and seven female prophets. Along with Miriam, Deborah and Huldah, the rabbis include Sarah, Hannah, Abigail and Esther (*b. Meg.* 14a).[83] Sarah's discernment of the problem between her son Isaac and Hagar's son Ishmael was seen by the rabbis to have been led by the Holy Spirit, hence the Lord's command that Abraham do whatever Sarah tells him regarding the matter (Gen. 21.8-12). Similarly, the rabbis construed Esther's royal attire (Est. 5.1) to be clothing of the Holy Spirit. The rabbis saw the words and deeds of Abigail in 1 Sam. 25.20-35 as prophetic, and in rabbinic tradition Abigail debates with David the legalities of his intention to kill Nabal (*b. Meg.* 14a, b).

The New Testament continues the tradition of women's religious testimony in song, prayer and prophecy. Luke's birth narrative offers several relevant examples. Elizabeth, prompted by the Holy Spirit, pronounces blessings upon Mary and her unborn child, prophetically calling the child 'my Lord' (Lk. 1.39-45). Mary's canticle (Lk. 1.46-55) echoes Hannah's prayer (1 Sam. 2.1-10), and, like all the women's songs cited previously, exalts the person and works of the Lord, especially the Lord's abasement of the mighty and exaltation of the humble.[84] After the canticle of Zechariah (Lk. 1.68-79), Luke shows two aged prophets, Simeon and Anna, who are in attendance when Jesus' parents bring him to the temple in compliance with the law that required firstborn males to be presented and consecrated to the Lord (Exod. 13.2, 12). In this

---

83. According to *Gen. Rabbah* 67.9 and *Seder 'Olam Rabbah* 21, all the Biblical matriarchs were prophets (Ginzberg, *Legends*, I, p. 341).

84. The problem, introduced by some MSS, of whether the Magnificat is to be attributed to Mary or Elizabeth is irrelevant to the present discussion because in either case a woman is the speaker.

context of legal ceremony, Simeon and Anna testify to the identity of the baby as the one sent by God for salvation and redemption. I.H. Marshall points out that a surprising amount of detail is used to introduce Anna, the 'second witness'.[85] Luke emphasizes Anna's credentials: she is a prophet, of distinguished lineage, venerable and devout (Lk. 2.36-37). Unlike the speeches of Elizabeth, Mary, Zechariah and Simeon, Anna's specific words are not given, but her thanksgiving to God suggests public praise (ἀνθομολογέομαι, Lk. 2.38). Moreover, in contrast to Simeon's speech that addresses the fulfillment of one person's longing to see the consolation of Israel (Lk. 2.25-32), Anna acts as a witness who addresses the expectations of the wider audience by speaking about the child 'to all who were looking for the redemption of Jerusalem (v. l. 'Israel')' (Lk. 2.38).

The events of Pentecost in Acts 2.1-13 are interpreted by Peter as the fulfillment of a prophecy by Joel (Acts 2.16-21). Peter's confirmation of Joel 2.28-29, that both men and women will prophesy, picks up the tradition of women prophets in Israel and forecasts those who will carry that tradition into the Christian church. For example, Acts 21.9 reports that Philip the evangelist had four unmarried daughters who prophesied.[86]

Acts tells of a spirit-possessed slave girl who for several days in Philippi testifies in public that Paul and Silas are 'slaves of the Most High God, who proclaim to you a way of salvation' (Acts 16.17). When Paul finally exorcises the spirit from her, causing her owners to lose the revenue derived from her divinations, they haul Paul and Silas before the magistrates on a trumped-up charge. For whatever reasons, no account of a formal trial ensues, and since the slave girl is not mentioned as being among those who come before the magistrates, it is futile to speculate about what role she might have played had the trial been held.[87] The slave girl's proclamation is accurate, but in this case the

85. I.H. Marshall, *The Gospel of Luke: A Commentary on the Greek Text* (NIGTC; Grand Rapids: Eerdmans, 1978), p. 123.

86. Luke supplies no particulars of their words or actions. F.F. Bruce sees the mention of Philip's daughters as significant because of traditions that say Luke received from them much of the information for the earlier part of Acts as well as much of the material unique to his Gospel. Bruce also notes Papias' testimony that Philip's daughters were known as sources for early church history (F.F. Bruce, *The Acts of the Apostles: The Greek Text with Introduction and Commentary* [Grand Rapids: Eerdmans, 1953], p. 387).

87. The stripping, beating and imprisonment of Paul and Silas may have been preliminaries to an impending trial which, as it turns out, never occurred, or simply

prophecy in not inspired by the Holy Spirit but by a 'spirit of divination' (πνεῦμα πύθωνα, Acts 16.16). The value of this example is somewhat tarnished because the slave girl's utterance is reminiscent of cases where the demon-possessed acknowledge the identity of the exorcist, Jesus, as being from God (for example, Mk 1.24 and par.; 5.7 and pars.; Lk. 4.41).

Just as Peter had predicted at Pentecost through the prophecy of Joel, the church in Corinth saw prophetic activity from both men and women. Paul's first letter to the Corinthians singles out the women prophets for attention, but as with Philip's daughters in Acts 21.9, no details of their prophecies are given. In a reconstruction of the situation in Corinth, A.C. Wire proposes that the women prophets are at the centre of a conflict with Paul.[88] The women prophets are exercising extensive freedom in both personal and communal living in ways that do not meet with Paul's expectations. Due to the nature of the prophecies and glossolalia, leadership in the community is determined not by station but by function. Thus, those who use the gifts of prophecy and tongues have strong influence. The ethics being fostered in the community are 'release from external authorities' and 'communal expression of divine authority', leading Paul to regulate prophecy and glossolalia and to demand the women's silence.[89] Whether Wire's reconstruction is wholly accurate is not certain, but it correctly reads the strong sway held by the women prophets in the Corinthian church.

A last prophet named in the New Testament is Jezebel (Rev. 2.20). According to the author of Revelation, this woman imputes to herself the title of prophet, and the name Jezebel is probably a sobriquet applied by the author in disparaging comparison to the Jezebel who married king Ahab (1 Kgs 16.31). That she is an influential teacher in the church at Thyatira would indicate a woman of some charisma. No specifics of her prophecies are given, but only that her teaching originates in Satan and misleads some Christians into immorality and the consumption of

the assumption by the magistrates of Paul's and Silas' guilt with the intent to release and expel them next day (I.H. Marshall, *The Acts of the Apostles* [TNTC; Grand Rapids: Eerdmans, 1980], pp. 270-71).

88. A.C. Wire, *The Corinthian Women Prophets: A Reconstruction through Paul's Rhetoric* (Minneapolis: Fortress Press, 1990).

89. Wire, *Corinthian Women Prophets*, p. 184. J.M. Bassler sees the demand for women's silence as a non-Pauline gloss (J.M. Bassler, '1 Corinthians', in Newsom and Ringe, *Commentary*, p. 328).

food sacrificed to idols. As with Noadiah in the Old Testament, Jezebel is the one blotch upon the estimable record of women prophets in the New Testament.

The issue of women as teachers, deacons and evangelists arises in Paul's writings and elsewhere in the New Testament.[90] For example, Paul refers to Phoebe as a deacon (Rom. 16.1), Prisca as a co-worker (Rom. 16.3), Mary as one who labours (Rom. 16.6), Junia as compatriot, co-prisoner and prominent among the apostles (Rom. 16.7), Tryphaena and Tryphosa as workers in the Lord (Rom. 16.12), and to women who struggled alongside him in the work of the Gospel (Phil. 4.3). 1 Timothy forbids women from teaching or having authority over a man (1 Tim. 2.12), and this strongly suggests that some women actually did so or at least were trying to do so. Also in 1 Timothy, a bishop (1 Tim. 3.1) and deacon (1 Tim. 3.12) must be 'the husband of one wife', while the γυναῖκες of 1 Tim. 3.11 could be referring either to women who were themselves deacons or to the wives of male deacons.

These examples from Paul's letters are fraught with problems of text, grammar, context or interpretation. Because of those problems, and because no specific words or actions of women serving in these capacities are given, it is precarious to draw any precise conclusions in regard to their witness. Nevertheless, when all these examples are coupled with the explicit examples of the women prophets, and when that evidence is taken corporately, a rather strong picture emerges of women being actively involved in the religious testimony of the early Christian churches.

The texts gathered here support the view that, in general, Jewish women are 'believed in matters of immense religious significance'.[91]

4. Conclusion

1. *Legal Testimony*. Jewish women were excluded first *de facto* then *de jure* from being witnesses in most but not all circumstances. Some people believed that women were incompetent to testify because their nature is flawed by propensities for frivolousness and lying. But according to the rabbis, the *de jure* disqualification was based on technical grounds rather than a lack of credibility. Thus, women were permitted to testify in

90. I avoid 'deaconess' for the same reason as I did 'prophetess'.
91. Kaufman, *Woman in Jewish Law*, p. 202.

some instances regarding matters of which they had knowledge, and were competent to swear oaths in accordance with
Pentateuchal laws. Also, it was seen in certain texts that women
were allowed to testify in Graeco-Roman courts.

2. *Eyewitness Testimony.* In non-forensic contexts the testimony
of women was, of course, not legally banned, but the texts
show that such testimony received mixed reactions. In some
cases women's testimony was met with scepticism or disbelief
based on their gender, and this was not unexpected. In other
cases scepticism or disbelief was due simply to the nature of the
testimony itself. On other occasions women's testimony was
not only accepted but led others to belief.

3. *Religious Testimony.* Texts that supply evidence of women's
competence to testify in a religious vein are much more
numerous and consistently positive. The intrinsic ability of
women to give honest and accurate testimony is recognized in
their comparatively frequent religious prophecies, prayers,
songs, confessions, oaths and vows.[92]

What, then, can be concluded from an expanding and evolving code
of law, a small selection of texts and a large span of time? Sketching
trajectories from ancient Israel through rabbinic Judaism(s) and early
Christian literature is a very precarious business that cannot account for
local variations and should not assume that trends move consistently in
any direction. Using legal codes can be equally hazardous, and a word of
caution is in order in regard to how much weight can be placed upon
evidence obtained from them.

> Conjectures on the basis of data furnished by law codes can be only rela-
> tively true. Legal regulations are one thing, actual practice another.
> Women's legal status is one thing, her actual position another. Love,
> hatred, greed, ambition, and personal excellence have ever been powerful
> formative influences in individual lives and in human society. Life is
> never wholly determined by the letter of the law.[93]

92. The topic of women as martyrs is related to women as witnesses, but will not
be discussed because it will not help to elucidate the texts to be studied in John. For
the view that John prepared readers for martyrdom, see P.S. Minear, *John: The
Martyr's Gospel* (New York: Pilgrim Press, 1984).

93. E.M. MacDonald, *The Position of Women as Reflected in Semitic Codes of
Law* (Toronto: University of Toronto, 1931), p. 73.

That statement is confirmed by the exceptions that prove the rule— women like Athalia, the almost forgotten queen among the kings of Israel and Judah who ruled for six years; Salome Alexandra, the queen who sat upon the Hasmonean throne for eight years; Beruryah, the outstanding scholar and teacher of Torah whose halakhic opinions were taken seriously by her male contemporaries.

Yet the matter at hand in the following chapters involves but a single document, the Gospel of John, which I presume to have been written during the second half of the first century, primarily for a Jewish audience. Within those parameters it may be concluded with reasonable confidence that John's primary audience lived in a milieu in which Jewish women (1) were proscribed in most but not all instances from giving testimony in forensic contexts; (2) were competent to swear religious vows and oaths; (3) gave testimony in non-forensic contexts that was received sometimes positively, sometimes negatively, depending upon the circumstances; (4) were, under the influence of the Holy Spirit (or demonic spirits), widely recognized and accepted as prophets; (5) were viewed by some people as whimsical and deceitful by nature, and by others as stable and sincere.

Chapter 4

The Mother of Jesus Was There

The first woman to appear in John's Gospel does so at a wedding in the Galilean village of Cana. She is Jesus' mother, Mary.[1] The essential verses, Jn 2.3-5, being as enigmatic as they are brief, have generated an enormous amount of literature.[2] Those verses offer a narrow lens, while there are two wider lenses which afford a fuller view. One of these lenses looks at Mary's role within the context of Jesus' signs, and will be used in Chapter 7 to study her later appearance at Golgotha in conjunction with that at Cana. A second lens is provided by the literary unit Jn 2.1–4.54—the 'Cana to Cana' ministry tour—and will be used here to interpret Mary's function at the wedding against that of the royal official whose son Jesus' heals as the last act of that unit (Jn 4.46-54). These wider lenses enjoy the advantage of building on John's own peroration of the wine miracle as a 'sign' (Jn 2.11). But before moving to the interpretive frame of Jn 2.1–4.54, we must turn to the pertinent exegetical issues.

1. John 2.1-11 The Exegetical Issues

a. When Mary tells Jesus, 'They have no more wine' (Jn 2.3), interpreters understand her intentions in a variety of ways: informing, requesting, demanding, reproaching, praying. Since Mary's words divulge little on their own, the interpreter is practically forced to read her mind as well as

---

1. John never names Jesus' mother. I will use her Synoptic name for convenience and to avoid being pedantic.

2. For a history of interpretation, see R.F. Collins, 'Mary in the Fourth Gospel: A Decade of Johannine Studies', *LS* 3 (1970), pp. 99-142. For a survey of source and redaction theories, see W. Lütgehetmann, *Die Hochzeit von Kana (Joh 2,1-11): Zu Ursprung und Deutung einer Wundererzählung im Rahmen johanneischer Redaktionsgeschichte* (BU, 20; Regensburg: Friedrich Pustet, 1990), pp. 41-122.

her words. And yet Mary cannot be relaying information to Jesus with total disinterest. Certainly she expects something, but what?[3]

Derrett interprets the miracle within the legalities of reciprocal obligations for wedding gifts, and claims that Mary intervenes to preempt Jesus from becoming liable to a lawsuit for failing to provide the requisite wedding gift.[4] Derrett's theory reinforces the view that Mary has expectations of Jesus, but Derrett does not think that she anticipates a miracle: 'He intends to remedy the deficiency. She does not know how, but probably expects him to send out for some wine.'[5] At face value, Mary's words comprise only a request for Jesus to do something about the lack of wine. C.H. Giblin therefore argues, on the basis that prior to the wedding Jesus had performed no miraculous acts, that Mary expects help but not a miracle.[6]

However, Jesus himself appears to construe Mary's enigmatic words as a request for a miracle, since his response to her only makes sense if that is so. It is unlikely that Jesus would refuse a simple request to help remedy the wine shortage by some routine means with such a stern response and with a reference to his hour.[7] A comparison of Jesus' mother's words here with those of the sisters Martha and Mary in John 11 further suggests that she expects her request to be fulfilled in miraculous fashion. Martha and Mary simply inform Jesus that Lazarus is sick

3. It is often suggested that by calling Jesus' attention to the lack of wine, Mary gains the status of an intermediary between him and those in need. If so, then also deserving of that status in John's Gospel are the royal official (Jn 4.47) and Mary and Martha (Jn 11.3). Miracle narratives regularly feature individuals or groups bringing a need to Jesus' attention, and if Mary is an intermediary in that role, then many such intermediaries can be found in the Gospels.

4. Derrett, *Law*, pp. 228-46.

5. Derrett, *Law*, p. 242.

6. C.H. Giblin, 'Suggestion, Negative Response, and Positive Action in St John's Portrayal of Jesus (Jn 2.1-11.; 4.46-54.; 7.2-14.; 11.1-44.)', *NTS* 26 (1980), p. 202. M. Scott notes that Mary's words are, 'We have no wine', and not, 'We need a miracle' (M Scott, *Sophia and the Johannine Jesus* [JSNTSup, 71; Sheffield: JSOT Press, 1992], p. 181). This observation is true but of little help. Even if John does intend Mary's words to signify a request for a miracle, a phrase such as 'We need a miracle' would be out of character with his narrative art.

7. H. Räisänen comments, 'Jesus' solemn and dismissive answer is intelligible only if his mother has made a veiled request for a miraculous remedy' (H. Räisänen, *Die Mutter Jesu im Neuen Testament* [AASF, 47; Helsinki: Suomalainen Tiedeakatemia, 2nd edn, 1989], p. 160).

(Jn 11.3), but this unadorned report carries an implicit request for miraculous healing, as is shown by their insistence that if Jesus had responded promptly then Lazarus would not have died (Jn 11.21, 32).[8]

Thus, the most plausible reading is to see Mary at least implying if not requesting that Jesus should work a miracle. R. Schnackenburg, for example, construes Mary's words as a request that is 'imprecise, inspired by hope and confidence in Jesus, not excluding a miracle', while Bultmann is confident that she approaches Jesus 'with the aim of getting him to perform a miracle'.[9] How did Mary come to expect miraculous help from Jesus? That question has not been, perhaps cannot be, answered satisfactorily, but in any event is somewhat misguided: 'Such a question does not do justice to the literary genre or to the atmosphere of the Johannine narrative.'[10]

b. Modern ears recoil when Jesus addresses his mother, 'Woman' (γύναι), in Jn 2.4.[11] Exegetes routinely seek to soften the stridency with the perfunctory observation that Jesus customarily uses γύναι as a way of addressing women. But a careful look at the relevant texts shows that this is true only of women Jesus does not know. On eleven occasions in the Gospels, Jesus speaks to a woman using some term of address—twice a proper name (Μάρθα, Lk. 10.41; Μαριάμ, Jn 20.16), and nine times some other form. On six of the nine occasions when he uses some term of address other than a proper name, he is speaking to an

8.   The words spoken to Jesus by his mother in Jn 2.3 are prefaced by λέγει... πρὸς αὐτόν. J. McHugh contends that while John's use of λέγω with a dative object is common, his use of λέγω πρός τινα is sparse and usually occurs within contexts having 'a request to give considered thought to some matter, or to do some great favour' (J. McHugh, *The Mother of Jesus in the New Testament* [London: Darton, Longman & Todd, 1975], p. 391). Abbott (*Johannine Grammar*, §2366b), however, finds that John uses πρός τινα with verbs of speaking fairly often, and he sees nothing special in the pattern.

9.   Schnackenburg, *John*, I, p. 327; Bultmann, *John*, p. 116.

10.   R.E. Brown, *et al.* (eds.), *Mary in the New Testament* (Philadelphia: Fortress Press, 1978), p. 188; similarly, Bultmann, *John*, p. 116 n. 2.

11.   Attempts to forge symbolic links between Eve as 'Woman' and the mother of Jesus as 'Woman' are rife. Such symbolism may be a legitimate *sensus plenior*, but it is not at all clear that John intended it, and even less clear that Jesus had it in mind. Okure (*Approach to Mission*, p. 111 n. 63) notes that while John has persons functioning as examples (παραδείγματα), his symbolism is restricted to objects—light and darkness, for example.

unknown woman. Jesus calls the woman with the hemorrhage θύγατερ (Mt. 9.22 and pars., v. l. θυγάτηρ), Jairus' daughter ταλιθα (Mk 5.41),[12] or ἡ παῖς (Lk. 8.54); and four times he uses γύναι: the Samaritan (Jn 4.21), the woman caught in adultery (Jn 8.10), the Canaanite (Mt. 15.28), and the crippled woman (Lk. 13.12). Twice Jesus calls his mother γύναι, and on only one other occasion uses it to address a woman he knows, Mary Magdalene, whom he then calls by name (Jn 20.15-16).[13] This survey of Jesus' modes of personal address for women confirms how odd it is for him to call his mother γύναι because with only one specious exception, he never uses it to address women he knows.

This pattern is consistent with Jesus' pattern for addressing men. On fifteen occasions Jesus speaks to men using some term of address. Three times he addresses men he does not know: the widow of Nain's son (νεανίσκε, Lk. 7.14), the paralytic in Capernaum (τέκνον, Mt. 9.2; Mk 2.5; ἄνθρωπε, Lk. 5.20) and the man seeking his inheritance (ἄνθρωπε, Lk. 12.14). Twelve times Jesus addresses men he does know and on none of those occasions uses anything but proper names.[14]

Jesus' use of γύναι to address his mother may not sound as blunt in Koine Greek as it does in modern English or other modern languages, but attempts to mitigate the brusque tone of γύναι in this context are unsuccessful. It is precisely because Jesus is the last person most people would expect to treat his mother with formality or aloofness that his use of γύναι here is so pungent and prompts anxious explanations.[15] No

12. Greek: τὸ κοράσιον. The proper name Ταβιθά in some MSS is most likely corrupt (*TCGNT*, p. 87).

13. Jn 20.15 is no real exception because Jesus at first echoes the angels' address to Mary Magdalene (Jn 20.13), but then he removes the distance of γύναι and replaces it with the intimacy of Μαριάμ (Jn 20.16).

14. Two of these last instances are difficult to classify. Jesus hurls the epithet σατανᾶ at Peter (Mk 8.33 and par.); Jesus greets Judas Iscariot with ἑταῖρε according to Mt. 26.50 but with 'Ιούδα according to Lk. 22.48. With but two exceptions—Simon the Pharisee (Lk. 7.40) and Zacchaeus the chief tax collector (Lk. 19.5)—the only people Jesus ever addresses by name are members of the Twelve or his women followers. Also worth noting is that Peter uses γύναι and ἄνθρωπε to address three individuals he certainly does not know (Lk. 22.57, 58, 60; cf. Jn 18.15-16).

15. Derrett (*Law*, p. 238) writes, 'The correct explanation, namely that a religious devotee or ascetic will speak to a woman, if unavoidable, only in the most formal terms, seems not to have attracted attention'. The lack of attention is due

other instance of a son addressing his mother in this way has been found in Hebrew or Greek literature, and cases showing γύναι (or אשה) to convey respect or affection can be countered with cases showing it to manifest contempt (*T. Jos.* 5.2; *T. Job* 24.9). In any event, examples in which γύναι is used to address a woman other than a mother by her son are of questionable value for interpreting Jesus' use of it in Jn 2.4.

Jesus was capable of speaking harshly to allies as well as opponents (Mk 8.14-21; Mk 8.33 and par.; Lk. 24.25). Creating a Jesus who is nothing but gentle and polite toward friends and relatives may comfort scandalized readers but will misrepresent the Gospel texts. The desire to temper the tone of Jesus calling his mother γύναι apparently stems more from readers' discomfort with the text than from the text itself. The disquiet of readers and the palliatives of commentators notwithstanding, when Jesus calls his mother γύναι, he is creating a palpable barrier between her and himself.[16]

c. What does Jesus mean when asking τί ἐμοὶ καὶ σοί; of Mary?[17] The Greek idiom derives from a Hebrew one, and instances in both languages are well known.[18] Depending upon the context, various shades of meaning can be gleaned legitimately from the idiom, and options are rehearsed in the commentaries. It is sufficient here to assess the general tenor of the idiom in Jn 2.4 as one either of solidarity or of enmity.

---

perhaps to Derrett's failure to explain Jesus speaking to women in less than formal terms (Mk 5.34 and pars.; 5.41 and par.) or by name (Lk. 10.41; Jn 20.16).

16. Such distancing is consonant with the Synoptics. D.A. Carson (*The Gospel according to John* [Grand Rapids: Eerdmans, 1991], p. 171) finds it 'a remarkable fact that everywhere Mary appears during the course of Jesus' ministry, Jesus is at pains to establish distance between them'. B. Witherington considers it striking 'that all four Gospels to one degree or another indicate both that Jesus' mother failed at some point to completely understand or honour her Son... and that Jesus distanced Himself from her in the process of distinguishing His physical family from His spiritual one' (B. Witherington, *Women in the Ministry of Jesus* [SNTSMS, 51; Cambridge: Cambridge University Press, 1984], p. 99).

17. S. Ò'Cearbhalláin understands αὐτῇ in Jn 2.4 as a 'dative of instigation' (compare 'dative of cause' in BDF, §196). Thus, not 'to her' but 'because of her', Jesus says to himself: τί ἐμοὶ καὶ σοί κτλ (S. Ò'Cearbhalláin, 'What to me...?', *TA* 2 [1987-88], pp. 145-54). This idea is grammatically possible but contextually improbable. Nothing in the text indicates that Jesus speaks these words *sotto voce*.

18. Examples are provided by Abbott, *Johannine Grammar*, §2230; Schnackenburg, *John*, I, p. 328; Derrett, *Law*, pp. 238-43.

McHugh argues for the former: 'The mother of Jesus is here represented as standing with him, over against all others: Jesus addresses her
as one who already understands that his mission is to supply not material
but spiritual nourishment.'[19] On this reading, Jesus sees his mother as an
ally not an opponent, and in effect says to her, 'Why should you and I
be concerned?' But McHugh's reading is untenable because Jesus would
be imparting to τί ἐμοὶ καὶ σοί a meaning precisely opposite to that
which constitutes it as an idiom: τίἐμοὶ καὶ σοί always carries some
sense of 'you versus me' but never any sense of 'you and I versus
them'. No reason exists to see Jesus' use of it here as an exception to
that pattern.[20]

Beyond Jn 2.4, the idiom τί ἐμοὶ καὶ σοί occurs in the New
Testament only in the mouths of demons speaking to Jesus (Lk. 4.34
and par.; 8.28 and pars.). Discomforting parallels arise between demons
using the phrase to address Jesus and Jesus using it to address his
mother (recall the discomfort surrounding γύναι). In contrasting the
Synoptic occurrences of τί ἐμοὶ καὶ σοί with Jn 2.4, commentators
overlook one intriguing similarity. In Matthew's version of the Gadarene
demoniac episode, the demoniacs say, 'What have you to do with us,
Son of God? Have you come here to torment us before the time?' (πρὸ
καιροῦ, Mt. 8.29; cf. *Acts of Thomas* 45). This is provocative in light of
Jesus saying to Mary, 'What do you have to do with me, woman? My
hour has not yet come' (οὔπω ἥκει ἡ ὥρα μου).[21] The καιρός of
Mt. 8.29 refers to 'the great assize, when evil spirits, along with wicked
human beings, will receive recompense from Jesus, the Son of Man'.[22]
In John's Gospel, when Jesus announces that his hour has come
(Jn 12.23), he employs a similar eschatological theme: 'Now is the
judgment of this world; now the ruler of this world will be driven out'
(Jn 12.31). Just as Jesus comes to expel the demons before their time
(καιρός), it appears that Mary tries to force Jesus before his hour

19. McHugh, *Mother of Jesus*, p. 394.

20. Derrett (*Law*, p. 241) remarks, 'Whatever the tone, the meaning is a remon-
strance'. See also Abbott, *Johannine Grammar*, §2230; M. Zerwick, *Biblical Greek
Illustrated by Examples* (SPIB, 114; Rome: Biblical Institute Press, 1963), p. 70
n. 7.

21. My translation. The NRSV translates, incorrectly in my view, τί ἐμοὶ καὶ σοί
quite differently in Mt. 8.29 and Jn 2.4.

22. W.D. Davies and D.C. Allison, *A Critical and Exegetical Commentary on the
Gospel according to Saint Matthew* (ICC; 2 vols. [vol. 3 forthcoming]; Edinburgh:
T. & T. Clark, 1988–1991), II, p. 81.

(ὥρα).[23] This reinforces that τί ἐμοὶ καὶ σοί, γύναι; is much more of a stern reprimand than a mild distancing, and brings to mind how Peter's attempt to steer the course of Jesus' ministry drew the harshest possible reprimand: 'Get behind me, Satan! You are a stumbling block to me; for you are setting your mind not on divine things but on human things' (Mt. 16.23).

d. When Jesus speaks of his hour, does he refer to his revelation through ministry (this will be his first sign) or his glorification through death (the characteristic use of Jesus' ὥρα)?[24] Both views, as well as various ones in between, are defended.[25] Jesus' hour has a clear locus in his death, but is not literally confined there, and appears several times before the actual crucifixion (Jn 12.23; 13.1; 17.1). Nor is Jesus' hour chronologically confined to his death, because of John's 'telescopic' treatment of time. Even as Jesus points to the hour of resurrection for the dead that is yet to come and is already here (Jn 5.25; cf. 4.23), his signs point to the present and coming hour of his own death and resurrection. Thus, it is most probable that in Jn 2.4 Jesus is making an immediate reference to his death, which is the fulfillment of all the signs.

The context surrounding the wedding pericope further supports the ὥρα of Jn 2.4 being an evocation of Jesus' death. Immediately preceding the wedding story Jesus informs Nathanael and Philip, 'You will see heaven opened and the angels of God ascending and descending

---

23. Compare Jn 7.6-8, where Jesus' καιρός resembles his ὥρα. Brown (*John*, I, p. 306) sees καιρός as a 'Johannine alternate' for the ὥρα; Barrett (*John*, p. 312) states that in John's Gospel καιρός is 'not distinguishable from the more common ὥρα'; Schnackenburg (*John*, II, p. 140), however, sees the two as being distinct.

24. Οὔπω ἥκει ἡ ὥρα μου can be read as a question, thereby removing the apparent problem of Jesus rejecting Mary's prompting and then taking action anyway. But it creates another one, that is, how to explain Jn 2.4b as a positive response on the heels of the negative response in Jn 2.4a. In any event, such a reading struggles against both the narrative context and Johannine grammar.

25. For example, Beasley-Murray finds it most improbable that the ὥρα could be an immediate reference to the hour of Jesus' death (G.R. Beasley-Murray, *John* [WBC, 36; Waco, TX: Word Books, 1987], p. 35). Barrett (*John*, p. 191), on the other hand, finds it impossible that the ὥρα could refer to anything but Jesus' death. Schnackenburg (*John*, I, pp. 329-31) perceives that the hour of Jesus' death is remote, but that it might dwell in the background. Lindars (*John*, p. 126) understands the allusion to Jesus' death as too muted to be taken as the controlling factor in interpreting the pericope.

upon the Son of Man' (Jn 1.51). This can be heard not only as a reference to Jesus as the conduit between heaven and earth, but also as an adumbration of his dying and rising: 'The occasion to which the words of Jesus point is none other than his crucifixion.'[26] And it is in fact Philip and Andrew to whom Jesus eventually announces that the hour has come for the Son of Man to be glorified by dying and rising even as a grain of wheat (Jn 12.20-24); Jesus then prays, a voice from heaven answers, and some of the crowd interpret the (Father's) voice as that of an angel.[27]

The next event to follow the wedding at Cana, after the brief and undetailed respite in Capernaum, is the clearing of the temple. A comparison of John's temple clearing with the Synoptic versions is revealing (Jn 2.14-22 and pars.).[28] Upon being challenged to justify his action, Jesus responds in the Synoptics in terms of his authority (Mk 11.27-33 and pars.) but in John in terms of his death and resurrection, thus expressly linking the destruction of the temple with the destruction of his body (Jn 2.18-22).

After the temple incident another brief interlude follows (Jn 2.23-25), and then the encounter with Nicodemus (Jn 3.1-21). The meeting with Nicodemus also has Jesus' death in view, as Jesus punctuates the discussion about new birth by insisting that eternal life must be brought through the 'lifting up'—that is, the crucifixion and resurrection—of the Son of Man (Jn 3.14-15).[29]

The wedding at Cana therefore sits in a wider context in which Jesus' death is never far from sight. And so shadows of his death are cast even—and typically of John's penchant for double entendre and irony—upon a wedding celebration: 'Through John 2.4, the figure of the

26. F.F. Bruce, *The Gospel of John: Introduction, Exposition and Notes* (Grand Rapids: Eerdmans, 1983), p. 62.

27. It is perhaps significant that except for the glosses describing angelic activity at the pool of Beth-zatha (Jn 5.4), the only other mention of angels in John is at Jesus' tomb (Jn 20.12).

28. It is often argued that John relocated the temple clearing in order to emphasize the fulfillment and/or replacement of Judaism. The debates over whether the Johannine or Synoptic chronology for the temple clearing is correct or if Jesus cleared the temple twice do not affect the present issue, that is, the contrast between Johannine and Synoptic themes within the incident itself.

29. In Jn 16.16-25 Jesus uses the metaphor of the pain and joy of giving birth to describe his departure and return through death and resurrection.

miracle is placed with all certainty in the shadow of the cross.'[30]

A link between the Cana wedding and Jesus' death is not at all strange given that many ancient (and modern) cultures, including those of Palestine, routinely juxtapose marriage and death. For example, *m. Šab.* 23.4 states, 'They may await nightfall at the Sabbath limit to see to the business of [the reception of] a bride or of [the burial of] a corpse' (cf. *m. Ter.* 11.10; *m. Meg.* 4.3).[31] Also significant in light of the events at the Cana wedding is the fact that wine, as the symbol of eternal life, was at home not only in rites of marriage but also of circumcision and death.[32]

John's own peroration of the wedding episode holds the strongest hint that Jesus is alluding to the hour of his death: 'Jesus did this, the first of his signs, in Cana of Galilee, and revealed his glory (δόξα)' (Jn 2.11). Indeed, Jesus supremely reveals his glory in his death: 'The δόξα becomes apparent precisely in the cross.'[33]

A summary of the exegetical issues shows that Jesus' mother requests or at least strongly implies that he should remedy the shortage of wine in miraculous fashion. In response, Jesus calls his mother 'woman' (γύναι), which indicates that he is creating an appreciable distance between them. Jesus' question to Mary, 'What do you have to do with me?' (τί ἐμοὶ καὶ σοί;) is a further indication of distancing and also signals his disapproval of her attempt to influence the course of his ministry by pressing him to perform public miracles that will hasten his hour (ἡ ὥρα μου)—the hour of his death.

---

30. K. Barth, *Erklärung des Johannes-Evangeliums: Kapitel 1–8* (Zürich: Theologischer Verlag, 1976), p. 197. P.R. Duke marks the irony of the wine in light of Jesus' death (P.R. Duke, *Irony in the Fourth Gospel* [Atlanta: John Knox Press, 1985], p. 113).

31. E. Feldman cites rabbinic writings manifesting this paradoxical combination of celebration and lamentation, particularly the proximity of wedding and funeral, of bridegroom and mourner, and the use of wine for both wedding and funeral rites (E. Feldman, *Biblical and Post-Biblical Defilement and Mourning: Law as Theology* [New York: Yeshiva University, 1977], pp. 100-101).

32. E.R. Goodenough, *Jewish Symbols in the Greco-Roman Period* (12 vols.; New York: Bollingen, 1953–65), VI, p. 220; XII, p. 125. There is no consensus regarding sacramental allusions in John's Gospel, but the bread, vine, water and wine are universally acknowledged to be symbols of Jesus' body and blood.

33. Bultmann, *John*, p. 524. Lütgehetmann (*Hochzeit von Kana*, p. 336) notes that a connection between the wedding pericope and the events of Jesus' passion is prepared by the mention of Jesus' hour in Jn 2.4 and his glory in Jn 2.11.

2. *John 2.1–4.54: An Interpretative Frame*[34]

The changing of water into wine and the healing of the dying son bracket a section of Jesus' ministry that begins and ends in Cana of Galilee. John connects these two incidents in several ways, two of which are the most conspicuous. First, John prefaces the healing of the dying son by referring directly to the changing of water into wine at Cana (Jn 4.46). Secondly, John concludes the healing by identifying it as the 'second sign' (Jn 4.54), just as he had labeled the wine miracle the 'first sign' (Jn 2.11). No matter how the signs are defined and categorized, the changing of water into wine and the healing of the dying son are the only signs that John numbers, thus accentuating their connection.

At issue throughout this 'Cana to Cana' tour is whether people respond with belief or unbelief to Jesus' revelation in signs (and in words). The disciples believe after Jesus changes water into wine (Jn 2.1-12) and, proleptically, after he clears the temple (Jn 2.13-22). Many people believe after seeing Jesus' signs at the Passover festival, although John intimates that their belief is inadequate (Jn 2.23-25). Nicodemus is attracted to Jesus by signs but is chided for unbelief (Jn 3.1-21). Many inhabitants of Sychar believe following a chain of events begun when Jesus displays extraordinary knowledge of a woman from their town (Jn 4.1-42). The royal official and his household believe when Jesus heals his dying son (Jn 4.46-54).

The mother of Jesus and the royal official are involved in two different events that are parallel in form, as the following outline shows.

a. incident introduced (2.1-2//4.46)
b. request made (2.3//4.47)
c. action withheld (2.4//4.48)
d. request reasserted (2.5//4.49)
e. action taken (2.6-8//4.50a)
f. response to action (2.9-10//4.50b-53a)
g. incident summarized (2.11//4.53b-54)

---

34. My approach here resembles that of F.J. Moloney, 'From Cana to Cana (John 2.1–4.54) and the Fourth Evangelist's Concept of Correct (and Incorrect) Faith', in E.A. Livingstone (ed.), *Studia Biblica 1978 II: Papers on the Gospels* (JSNTSup, 2; Sheffield: JSOT Press, 1980), pp. 185-213, but is done in more detail and arrives at different conclusions.

a. *Incident Introduced* (Jn 2.1-2//4.46)

Again, notice the links between the two incidents made by way of geography (Cana of Galilee) and by direct reference to the wine miracle in that of the dying son.

b. *Request Made* (Jn 2.3//4.47)

Mary, as shown before, seeks something miraculous. That the royal official also desires a miracle is clear. His son has no chance of recovering from his illness (ἤμελλεν γὰρ ἀποθνῄσκειν), and Jesus brands the father's plea as one for signs and wonders (Jn 4.48, σημεῖα καὶ τέρατα).

Are the petitions of Mary and the royal official to be evaluated positively or negatively? Although both Mary and the royal official seek a miracle, neither actually demands a sign. Contrast the appeals of Mary and the royal official with, for example, that of the Jewish authorities, 'What sign can you show us for doing this?' (Jn 2.18), or that of the crowd, 'What sign are you going to give to us then, so that we may see it and believe you?' (Jn 6.30). Mary and the royal official seek help while those others demand credentials, but they all manifest some degree of belief at the miracle level. It would contradict Jn 20.30-31 to conclude that miraculous signs are not given as evidence meant to instil faith. Still, John shuns any faith which, instigated by the evidence of signs, fails to apprehend their true meaning: 'The Johannine critique of miracles is directed against neither the request for credentials nor against the miracle itself, but against a worldly interpretation of the miracle and the one who works it.'[35] Thus, the appeals made by Mary and the royal official for miraculous aid are not intrinsically inappropriate, and the evaluation of their appeals must hinge on Jesus' reaction and their counterreaction.

c. *Action Withheld* (Jn 2.4//4.48)

Jesus replies differently to Mary and the royal official, although superficially both replies look like censures. To the royal official Jesus responds, 'Unless you see signs and wonders you will not believe' Jn 4.48). Bittner characterizes Jesus' response as the declaration of a fixed principle concerning the nature of belief.[36] And yet, Jesus is not so

---

35. L. Schottroff, *Der Glaubende und die feindliche Welt: Beobachtungen zum gnostischen Dualismus und seiner Bedeutung für Paulus und das Johannesevangelium* (WMANT, 37; Neukirchener Verlag [Neukirchen–Vluyn], 1970), p. 256.

36. Bittner, *Jesu Zeichen*, p. 133. Bittner (p. 169) maintains that Jesus' words in

much castigating the royal official as he is confirming, albeit with frustration, a simple fact: for some people, miraculous signs are the necessary but insufficient condition for true faith.[37] Jesus' reply to his mother, as shown previously, is a reprimand based upon the timing of his hour. Because Jesus does not refuse to give signs, the point of contention is not the miracle itself, but rather, its timing. His hour has not come yet. Adhering strictly to the will of the one who sent him, Jesus assiduously resists any outside influence on the course of his ministry, and M. Hengel notes how Mary 'embodies the family of Jesus, which at the wrong time makes inappropriate demands of Jesus or does not understand him at all'[38] (cf. Jn 7.1-10). Jesus intends to retain control over the signs, and even though he complies with Mary's request, he works the miracle of the wine, as it were, in private.[39] Eventually, the signs will trigger the plot to put Jesus to death (Jn 11.45-53), but the timing of that hour must accord with the will of his heavenly Father rather than that of his earthly mother.

d. *Request Reasserted* (Jn 2.5//4.49)

Mary tells the servants to follow Jesus' orders, and so in one sense she does not revoice her petition. But in another sense hers is the most forceful reassertion possible because by ordering the servants to obey Jesus, she treats his compliance to her initial request as a foregone conclusion. The royal official reasserts his plea almost as if ignoring or even contradicting Jesus' reply. His first request was not for a sign but for help, and his second is the same: 'Sir, come down before my little boy

Jn 4.48 accord with the programme of Jn 20.30-31 and thus cannot be read as resistance to the demand for a sign.

37. Notice that in response to the demands in Jn 2.18; 6.30, Jesus has not refused to provide the sign (even though both audiences miss the significance). He will resurrect the razed temple, and he had already multiplied the loaves and fishes. Compare the Synoptic ambivalence about Jesus' attitude toward the demand for a sign (Mk 8.11-13 and pars.).

38. M. Hengel, 'The Interpretation of the Wine Miracle at Cana: John 2.1-11', in L.D. Hurst and N.T. Wright (eds.), *The Glory of Christ in the New Testament* (Oxford: Clarendon Press 1987), p. 102.

39. So Barrett, *John*, p. 189. The healing of the royal official's son is also somewhat of a private miracle. Starting with the healing at the pool of Beth-zatha in John 5, Jesus' miracles become fully public and instigate increasing opposition from his antagonists. On the Synoptic 'Messianic secret' and the Johannine 'hidden Messiah', see Barrett, *John*, p. 71; Schnackenburg, *John*, I, p. 322; S.S. Smalley, *John: Evangelist and Interpreter* (Exeter: Paternoster Press, 1978), pp. 28-29.

dies.' Again, both Mary and the royal official exhibit firm belief in the ability of Jesus to do something miraculous.

e. *Action Taken* (Jn 2.6-8//4.50a)

Jesus now acts, but again, if such action is a concession, it is nevertheless taken on his terms, which always are in accordance with the will of his Father.[40] Jesus orders the servants to fill the jars with water and take some to the banquet master, while he sends the royal official on his way with a promise that his son will live. At this point the two miracles take place, but also at this point the two stories part ways. Mary has left the stage not to reappear and other characters replace her, while the royal official will remain on the stage until the conclusion of the episode.

f. *Response to Action* (Jn 2.9-10//4.50b-53a)

In both stories the witnesses to the actual miracle are the servants. The wedding servants know where the water came from, how they filled the jars to the brim with water and where the wine came from. Although the banquet master remains ignorant of where the wine came from, he provides a crucial testimony by confirming that what the servants brought to him is in fact wine of the highest quality. Westcott comments, 'The independent witness of the two parts of the miracle establishes its reality. The ruler of the feast declares what the element *is*, the servants knew what it *was*.'[41] Similarly, the servants of the royal official know that his son is healed and they know precisely when that healing takes place.

John also declares the royal official's faith: 'The man believed the word that Jesus spoke to him and started on his way' (Jn 4.50). Although belief in Jesus through his miracles is not rejected, belief through his word is preferred: 'Faith should live not by miracles but by the word.'[42] Thus, the royal official models true faith because he takes Jesus at his word. By departing for home, without Jesus, in the belief that his request has been fulfilled, he moves from 'miracle faith' to 'word faith'.

---

40. Giblin ('Suggestion', p. 210) observes that the pattern of Jesus' behaviour in Jn 2.1-11; 4.46-54 also occurs in Jn 7.2-14; 11.1-44, and that in none of these cases does Jesus act inconsistently or change his mind: 'He never fails to attend to the situation presented to him, but in so doing he acts radically on his own terms.'

41. Westcott, *John*, I, p. 85. John's use of these two witnesses brings to mind the Deuteronomic requirement for two or three witnesses (cf. Jn 5.31-40; 8.17-18).

42. Nicol, *Sēmeia*, pp. 105-106.

g. *Incident Summarized* (Jn 2.11//4.53b-54)

Jesus had promised his followers an experience of things even greater than his uncanny knowledge (Jn 1.50). The fulfillment of that promise is not slow in coming for all the disciples, who celebrate with Jesus at the Cana wedding and see his miraculous power as he changes water into wine. Even more important than seeing a miracle, however, the disciples see Jesus' glory. To see Jesus' glory in the miracle is to see the sign, and thus, to believe truly in Jesus. The disciples' faith is not thereby perfected (Jn 11.14-15), and Jesus later will impugn it (Jn 16.31-32), but in their experience at the wedding they truly catch a glimpse of the glory that discloses Jesus' origin and identity (Jn 1.14). As R.H. Lightfoot puts it, 'The disciples were enabled to penetrate beyond their Master's outward action, and to grasp its significance in respect of His work and Person'.[43]

On the other hand, John offers no hint that Mary grasps the significance of the miracle. Räisänen thinks that because John typically makes misunderstandings of Jesus explicit, but makes no such indication about Mary, she possibly did understand the miracle as a sign.[44] This idea amounts to an argument from silence; but also, it falters because John expressly states that the sign is seen not by Jesus' mother but by his disciples (Jn 2.11). And surely, Mary cannot be numbered among Jesus' disciples here, as John twice distinguishes between her and them (Jn 2.1-2, 12). Jesus' mother has a miracle faith, and such faith is not disparaged per se. But John says nothing of her witnessing Jesus' glory, and hence, nothing about her seeing the sign.

John, in summarizing the healing of the royal official's son, couples it with the wedding by enumerating it as the second sign and by reiterating the geographical connection. John reaffirms the royal official's faith and adds to that a statement that his household also came to believe.

In comparing the sign of the wine miracle with that of the healed son, it can be seen from the requests of Mary and the royal official that both believe in Jesus' power to work miracles, but that the royal official moves beyond such belief to a faith that trusts in the power of Jesus' word. In both incidents, it is the servants (and at Cana, the banquet master) who act as witnesses to the actual miracle. The reaffirmation of

---

43. R.H. Lightfoot, *St John's Gospel: A Commentary* (Oxford: Clarendon Press, 1956), p. 102. Painter (*Quest*, p. 154) sees that the disciples' faith in Jn 2.11 signals a shift from 'a miracle worker christology' to an 'exalted Son of Man christology'.

44. Räisänen, *Mutter Jesu*, pp. 171-72.

the royal official's faith at the end of the healing miracle parallels the declaration of the disciples' faith and vision of Jesus' glory at the end of the wine miracle.

3. *The Mother of Jesus as a Witness*

Jesus' signs are evidence meant to evoke an acknowledgment of his origin, identity and authority (Jn 5.36; 10.31-39; 14.11; 20:30-31).

> That [the signs] actually took place, that they can be attested and that they are beyond doubt is of the same decisive importance to the evangelist as their symbolic force. They too (as 'works') are to be 'testimonies' whereby faith is proclaimed and unbelief convicted, and thus they have a sort of juridical validity.[45]

Thus, it is incumbent upon John to document supporting details, and indeed, his narratives often provide time, location, participants, circumstances and other information of evidential value.

In the *mise-en-scène* for the wedding, John lists when (the third day), what (a wedding) and where (Cana in Galilee). The terse presentation of these details indicates that they are not John's main concern, but their presence and placement stress their importance as evidence that buttresses the credibility of the story. John underlines that the lack of wine was real (Jn 2.3; cf. variant readings), that the jars were at first empty and then filled to the brim with water (Jn 2.6-7), that the water was changed to wine (Jn 2.9), that witnesses were present and that Jesus was the person responsible for what occurred (Jn 2.7, 8, 11).

Beyond proving the fact of the miracle, John seeks to elicit its significance. People can witness miracles without seeing signs: 'You are looking for me, not because you saw signs, but because you ate your fill of the loaves' (Jn 6.26). People can witness the miracles of Jesus without believing in the person of Jesus: 'Although he had performed so many signs in their presence, they did not believe in him' (Jn 12.37). Seeing the miracles while missing the signs amounts to recognizing Jesus as a worker of wonders but not as the messiah of God. John therefore has two distinct but connected concerns: first, to validate the fact of the miracle (*what* happened); secondly, to elicit the sign in the miracle (what *happened*). Thus, John describes how Jesus transformed water into wine and declares that Jesus revealed his glory. It is from this twofold perspective that the role of Mary as a witness should be evaluated. Does she

45. Schnackenburg, *John*, I, p. 525.

attest to the fact that Jesus works a miracle and/or to his identity as the messiah?

Mary, as the first woman to appear in John's Gospel, and as the first person to be named in the wedding narrative, is doubly prominent at that point. But to award her pride of place at the wedding on that basis would be incorrect. After speaking to the servants, Mary leaves the stage, and when John summarizes the miracle and identifies its significance, only Jesus remains standing at centre stage along with his disciples.

> John does not put primary emphasis on Mary and her intercession, nor on why she pursued her request, nor on the reaction of the headwaiter or of the groom. The primary focus is, as in all Johannine stories, on Jesus... What shines through is *his glory*, and the only reaction that is emphasized is the *belief* of the disciples.[46]

In evaluating Mary's faith, McHugh makes two statements that at first glance appear to be identical but are not: Mary (1) 'is represented as believing in her son *before* the first miracle'; (2) 'is there at Cana, fully believing, before Jesus has worked a single sign'.[47] For John, there is a vast difference between believing and fully (or truly) believing. Some people see Jesus' miraculous signs and believe, but he regards their faith as untrustworthy (Jn 2.23-25). Jesus' brothers believe in his miracles but not in him (Jn 7.3-5). John shows that faith can and does grow in stages.[48] Maturation of faith was seen in the royal official, and John treats growing faith as a paradigm in the healing of the blind man (John 9), which John presents as a 'dramatization of the full scale of the development of faith, beginning with a miracle and ending with a complete confession'.[49] Clearly, Mary believes in Jesus' miraculous abilities, but since John gives no indication that she, like the royal official, moves beyond miracle faith, or that she, like the disciples, sees Jesus' glory, McHugh is wrong to characterize Mary as fully believing.

Even more untenable, therefore, is McHugh's claim that John depicts Jesus' mother as 'the prototype and exemplar of faith'.[50] Jesus' rebuke

---

46. Brown, *John*, I, pp. 103-104.

47. McHugh, *Mother of Jesus*, pp. 399, 403.

48. Against Schottroff (*Glaubende*, pp. 254, 266), who insists that John never suggests any stages or gradations of belief. On the signs in relation to stages of belief, see Brown, *John*, I, pp. 527-28; Kysar, *Maverick Gospel*, pp. 67-73.

49. Nicol, *Sēmeia*, p. 102.

50. McHugh, *Mother of Jesus*, p. 403. McHugh reaches these conclusions

of Mary indicates that she misunderstands the timing if not the nature of his ministry. Only at his crucifixion is Jesus' mother inducted into the faith community (Jn 19.25-27), and, if evidence from Acts may be entered, only after his resurrection are Jesus' mother and brothers rooted in the faith community (Acts 1.14), strongly suggesting that what finally brought them to true belief was Jesus' death and resurrection rather than the signs he performed.

According to B. Olsson, Mary's action 'resembles most closely that of the many witnesses in John, such as John the Baptist, Moses and the OT scriptures... She points to Jesus.'[51] But it is most unlikely that John's first readers would have perceived Mary's words to Jesus and to the servants as a testimony resembling that of Moses and the Old Testament scriptures, especially when faced with explicit testimonies from those sources (Jn 1.45; 3.14; 5.39, 46). Mary could be likened to John the Baptist on a figurative level inasmuch as she directs others to Jesus and then fades away, and Olsson pushes that comparison: 'The role of Jesus' mother approaches that of John the Baptist: they both bear witness to, and point to, him who God sent to baptize ἐν πνεύματι.'[52] But Mary is hardly a congener of John the Baptist, who is expressly designated as God's chosen witness to Jesus (Jn 1.6-7) and whose testimony receives substantial attention and endorsement (Jn 1.15, 19-35; 3.22-30; 5.33-36; 10.40-42). Further, Mary gives no testimony in the form of confessional statements as does John the Baptist in calling Jesus 'the Lamb of God' (Jn 1.29, 36) and 'the Son of God' (Jn 1.34). Mary's words at the wedding reveal her belief in Jesus' miraculous abilities but cannot support the notion that her role there is somehow commensurate with the witness of John the Baptist, who is sent by God to testify to Jesus' origin and identity.

In accordance with Jn 20.30-31 (cf. 17.20), Jn 2.11 validates the disciples' witness: Jesus does the sign in the presence of his disciples so that

believing that the Evangelist redacted his sources in order to present Mary in a favourable light. Buck, however, arrives at exactly the opposite conclusion, that the redactor's work reflects an anti-Marian polemic meant to combat a burgeoning veneration of Mary that threatened the primacy of Jesus (H.M. Buck, 'Redactions of the Fourth Gospel and the Mother of Jesus', in D.E. Aune [ed.], *Studies in the New Testament and Early Christian Literature* [NovTSup, 33; Leiden: Brill, 1972], pp. 170-80).

51. B. Olsson, *Structure and Meaning in the Fourth Gospel: A Text-Linguistic Analysis of John 2.1-11 and 4.1-42* (ConBNT, 6; Lund: Gleerup, 1974), p. 46.

52. Olsson, *Structure and Meaning*, p. 112.

they can become witnesses. Even if Mary (unlike the disciples) does not testify to the sign that reveals Jesus' glory, is she (like the servants) a witness to the actual miracle?

Derrett argues that both Mary and the servants are incompetent as witnesses, she being female and they probably being slaves, and that readers would find such testimony suspect.[53] Schnackenburg and Bultmann, on the other hand, perceive that the servants are deliberately advanced for the purpose of testifying to the miracle, Bultmann seeing that they are depicted as 'impeccable witnesses'.[54] Olsson thinks that both the servants and Mary act as witnesses, but Mary only in that she informs the servants that Jesus is the one to be obeyed.[55] The text itself makes only one statement regarding knowledge of where the wine came from: the servants knew and the banquet master did not. Since Mary sought the miracle, it is likely that she knew as well, but if so, John chose not to spell that out.

Thus, Mary's value as a witness is diminished for two reasons: (1) unlike the servants, she is not named as one who has knowledge of how the wine was obtained; (2) unlike the disciples, she is not named as a believing witness to Jesus' glory revealed in the miracle.

Why does Mary play a conspicuous but non-witnessing role in the wine miracle? One obvious answer is that John is reporting an actual historical reminiscence more or less as it happened. At Jewish wedding feasts men and women tended to celebrate in separate groups, and so Mary's presence among the men and her interaction with Jesus and the servants would constitute a 'breach of etiquette' in which she disturbs the male guests.[56] This explanation, though plausible, nevertheless fails to account for John's literary and theological shaping of the story. Even though Mary has miracle faith, John remains silent in regard to her knowledge of where the wine came from, to her seeing Jesus' glory and to her believing in him. By this silence, John in effect excludes her as a

---

53. Derrett, *Law*, p. 244. Slaves, not being free Jewish citizens, cannot qualify as witnesses. However, the servants at the Cana wedding are διάκονοι not δοῦλοι, and John uses the two words differently (Abbott, *Johannine Vocabulary*, §§1784-92).

54. Schnackenburg, *John*, I, p. 333; Bultmann, *John*, p. 118 n. 5.

55. Olsson, *Structure and Meaning*, pp. 59-60.

56. So Derrett, *Law*, p. 238. Nevertheless, the practice of male–female segregation at wedding feasts cannot be posed as an inviolable rule (see also Archer, *Her Price*, pp. 243-44).

witness to the miracle and sign of Jesus and therefore, to the true identity of Jesus.

Perhaps John does not advance Mary as a witness simply because she is female; but other texts militate against that idea (as will be seen in following chapters).

Perhaps John is sensitive to the fact that as a close relative of Jesus, Mary is under most circumstances an incompetent witness (*m. Sanh.* 3.4) who therefore would make an inadequate or unfavourable impact upon readers.[57] Jesus' brothers also fall into that category and do not serve as witnesses (of course, John later brands them as unbelievers [Jn 7.5]). Jn 2.12 narrates that following the wedding celebrations, Jesus' mother and brothers and the disciples accompanied him to Capernaum, meaning either that he picked up his brothers en route or that they were at the wedding and John chose not to mention them. One apocryphal tradition has it that Jesus was invited to the wedding 'with his mother and his brothers' (*Epistula Apostolorum* 5), and the omission of the phrase 'and his disciples' from Jn 2.12 by Codex A has prompted the theory that Jesus' disciples were not at the wedding but that John substituted them for Jesus' brothers who were there.[58] If the bridegroom were one of Jesus' brothers, that could explain why John might want to leave the bridegroom anonymous rather than risk reinforcing the banquet master's perception that the bridegroom, that is, one of Jesus' brothers, and not Jesus, produced the good wine. It might also explain why Mary gives orders to the servants and expects help from Jesus. All of this is speculative, but in any event, if John did in fact substitute Jesus' disciples for his brothers, that could buttress the argument that for John, the ability of Jesus' immediate family to witness was inadequate if not suspect.[59]

The mother of Jesus was there. John's modest portrait of Mary at the Cana wedding has not deterred interpreters from lavishing exalted statuses upon her. Olsson inventories the stations that exegetes using Jn 2.1-11 have imparted to the mother of Jesus: partner in God's work

57. Notice that the servants, banquet master and disciples cannot be identified as relatives of Jesus.

58. For example, Lindars, *John*, pp. 127-28, 132-33.

59. The lack of Jesus' disciples at Jn 2.12 in Codex A can be understood in other ways. The term 'brothers' may have referred to Jesus' disciples (see Jn 20.17), and a scribe, unaware of this, added the disciples to Jn 2.12. Or, the disciples may have been added to Jn 2.12 to prevent the misapprehension that Jesus left Capernaum without them (Jn 2.13), which would make their presence at the temple awkward (Jn 2.17).

and salvation, mediator, intercessor, prototype Christian, representative of Judaism, or the Jewish Christian church, or simply the church.[60] Any or all of those interpretations may well be valid as a *sensus plenior* in the hermeneutical and homiletical arenas, but they do not fare very well exegetically. Above all, John is concerned with witnesses to Jesus, and the mother of Jesus does not serve as such in Jn 2.1-11. She exhibits a miracle faith, but she testifies neither to the fact of the miracle (Jesus changed water into wine) nor to the content of the sign (Jesus revealed his glory). For now, the mother of Jesus fades from the scene; but she will reappear under very different circumstances: when Jesus' hour has come.

60. Olsson, *Structure and Meaning*, p. 20.

Chapter 5

A SAMARITAN WOMAN CAME TO DRAW WATER

Whether or not the text of the Samaritan episode in Jn 4.4-42 stems from one author, its final form possesses narrative unity and literary art. This well-crafted story deserves its many painstaking analyses.[1] However, Bultmann's succinct scheme best suits the task of studying the Samaritan woman as a witness: 'The rather complex edifice created by the Evangelist can be divided up quite simply: vv. 1-30 Jesus' witness to himself, vv. 31-42 the relation of the believer's witness to Jesus' self-witness.'[2]

At first glance, the task of evaluating the Samaritan woman as a witness seems facile if not superfluous because John explicitly says that she testifies: διὰ τὸν λόγον τῆς γυναικὸς μαρτυρούσης (Jn 4.39). Yet, a closer look will reveal that the nature of her testimony is not nearly so obvious as the fact of it. Neither is gauging the effect of her testimony upon the Samaritan villagers and upon John's readers without difficulties.

This pericope lies within the frame of Jn 2.1–4.54, the outer edges of which were used in Chapter 4 to discuss the ways in which Jesus' mother functions at the Cana wedding. The larger issue accentuated by that frame—positive or negative response to Jesus' self-revelation in words and signs—remains in the forefront in Jesus' encounter with the Samaritans. The story is bound to other material in the 'Cana to Cana'

---

1. Among many others: Okure, *Approach to Mission*; Olsson, *Structure and Meaning*; E. Leidig, *Jesu Gespräch mit der Samaritanerin und weitere Gespräche im Johannesevangelium* (Basel: Friedrich Reinhardt, 1981); G.R. O'Day, *Revelation in the Fourth Gospel: Narrative Mode and Theological Claim* (Philadelphia: Fortress Press, 1986); H. Boers, *Neither on This Mountain nor in Jerusalem: A Study of John 4* (SBLMS, 35; Atlanta: Scholars Press, 1988); J.E. Botha, *Jesus and the Samaritan Woman: A Speech Act Reading of John 4.1-42* (NovTSup, 65; Leiden: Brill, 1991).

2. Bultmann, *John*, p. 176.

tour not only by that larger issue but in other ways as well.

Commentators rightly attend to the differences between Nicodemus and the Samaritan woman. Also worth comparing are the wedding at Cana and the encounter at Sychar—these for similarities. Both happen in small towns beyond Judea (Cana in Galilee; Sychar in Samaria), at specified times (third day; sixth hour), and feature Jesus, his disciples, a woman (mother of Jesus; Samaritan woman), and others (servants, bridegroom, chief steward; villagers). The wedding at Cana is echoed at Sychar by the Samaritan's husbands and by the well itself, a common Old Testament setting for meetings between men and women involving marriage (Genesis 24; 29; Exodus 2). Water is central to both incidents, as are the drawing of it and the vessels employed. Jesus addresses both nameless women as γύναι, and although each woman plays a significant part, both episodes culminate by shifting the focus away from them and onto others (Jesus' disciples; the villagers). Both stories manifest the purpose outlined in Jn 20.30-31: a sign reveals that the messiah is Jesus, and people then attain some level of belief in him.[3]

1. *John 4.4-42: The Exegetical Issues*

a. To evaluate the woman's status as a witness, her understanding about Jesus' true identity must be ascertained. The woman undergoes a process in which she moves from a shallower to a deeper understanding of who Jesus is.[4] As the conversation opens, she initially recognizes him simply as a Jew (Jn 4.9). The discourse continues, and when Jesus unveils preternatural knowledge of her personal life, she concludes that he is a prophet (Jn 4.19). After further dialogue, she begins to ponder if Jesus might be something more than a prophet, and when she mentions the messiah, Jesus openly claims the office, if not much more: ἐγώ εἰμι, ὁ λαλῶν σοι (Jn 4.26).[5] It is not, however, this frank admission by

3. Jesus' signs are intended to evoke recognition of his origin and identity, and so his extraordinary knowledge of the Samaritan woman (Jn 4.17-18; cf. 1.47-51) is sign-like in its effect even though John does not call it a σημεῖον. Of the sundry topics touched upon during their conversation, the woman isolates Jesus' uncanny knowledge as the source of her inkling that she may have met the messiah (Jn 4.29), and her report of his exceptional knowledge is what prompts the initial belief of the villagers (Jn 4.39).

4. This process is characteristic of Jesus' conversations in John's Gospel. See Leidig, *Jesu Gespräch*, pp. 162-74.

5. Jesus' intent in this verse is debated. Is he simply admitting to being the

Jesus but his uncanny knowledge that causes her to see him as no ordinary prophet and which she chooses to attract the villagers: 'Come and see a man who told me everything I have ever done! He cannot be the Messiah, can he?' (Jn 4.29). Her words indicate that if Jesus did intend the sublime 'I AM' that marks him as the one who eclipses messianic expectations—Samaritan or Jewish—she has missed it and still thinks of him as the messiah of her expectations, that is, one delimited by extraordinary prophetic knowledge.[6] This conclusion, however, needs further support, which follows in the next exegetical point.

b. In Jn 4.29 the woman says to the villagers: μήτι οὗτός ἐστιν ὁ χριστός; What do these words reveal of the woman's own convictions about Jesus? Is she denying, affirming or simply questioning Jesus' messiahship? Her words form a *crux interpretum* whose resolution must stem from the context. But however the negative force of μήτι may be nuanced, it cannot be obliterated. It remains a negative particle. Botha notes, 'The last part of her utterance has the grammatical form of an interrogative, and a rather weak one at that, and although it is not a *denial*, it is also not a strong *affirmative*'.[7]

Thus, on strictly grammatical grounds, some ambiguity remains. But contextually, can she, so to speak, say no and mean yes? Okure reads the verse as 'a veiled confession couched in the form of a question in order to appeal to the personal judgment of the Samaritans, get them to reflect, and so arouse their interest in Jesus'.[8] Can it be, then, that her

person she has in mind? Is he making a more specific messianic claim? Is he taking for himself the name of יהוה in an 'I AM' statement? John's penchant for polysemy often permits readers to embrace rather than reject alternatives.

6.   It is mistaken to impose on the woman any one putative Samaritan messianic concept. Although the predominant Samaritan messianic model was the *Taheb*, the returning prophet like Moses, this model was not understood uniformly, and in fact, 'The coming of an eschatological prophet like Moses was not a *sine qua non* of early Samaritan Mosaism' (J.D. Purvis, 'The Fourth Gospel and the Samaritans', *NovT* 17 [1975], p. 189). Furthermore, as Purvis also notes, early Samaritanism was 'a complex religious system embracing a variety of theological positions' (J.D. Purvis, 'The Samaritans and Judaism', in R.A. Kraft and G.W.E. Nickelsburg [eds.], *Early Judaism and its Modern Interpreters* [SBLCP; Philadelphia: Fortress Press; Atlanta: Scholars Press, 1986], p. 81).

7.   Botha, *Speech Act Reading*, p. 164; similarly, O'Day, *Revelation*, p. 76.

8.   Okure, *Approach to Mission*, p. 174. Lindars (*John*, p. 193) maintains that while μήτι implies no, 'The implications of v. 42 hardly allow this. John means it to be an expression of cautious faith.'

words reflect strategy rather than doubt? Perhaps she anticipates that the villagers would greet an assertion that Jesus is the messiah with scorn or indifference. Perhaps she contemplates a negative response from the villagers because she is female, or because her claim is so astonishing, or both: 'The urging of the woman is intended to induce the townspeople to investigate this man for themselves... [She] is careful not to state the incredible outright.'[9]

That line of argument cannot be ruled out, but whether or not her gender would require her to adopt such a strategy is a matter to be addressed later. For now, it may be said that the verse on its own is vague enough to allow disparate interpretations. Nevertheless, when she concludes that Jesus is a prophet (Jn 4.19), she makes her only unambiguous formulation of belief in Jesus. The fact that μήτι οὗτός ἐστιν ὁ χριστός appears to obscure more than clarify the state of her belief urges the conclusion that if John had wanted to present her as firmly believing in Jesus as the messiah, he would have stated it as unequivocally as he did her belief in Jesus as a prophet.

c. At Jn 4.39 many Samaritans believe on account of the woman's report: πολλοὶ ἐπίστευσαν εἰς αὐτὸν τῶν Σαμαριτῶν διὰ τὸν λόγον τῆς γυναικὸς μαρτυρούσης κτλ. The verse brims with Johannine locutions to be examined (πιστεύω, λόγος, μαρτυρέω), and also has a textual variant needing attention (εἰς αὐτόν).

The verbal similarities between Jn 4.39 and Jn 17.20, where Jesus prays περὶ τῶν πιστευ[σ]όντων διὰ τοῦ λόγου αὐτῶν εἰς ἐμέ, should not be forced as a close theological parallel between the witness of Jesus' disciples and that of the Samaritan woman.[10] The immediate referents of Jesus' prayer in Jn 17.20 are the disciples in attendance at the last supper, where Jesus tells them that their witnessing will follow their reception of the Paraclete, the Spirit of truth, and that they will witness because they have been with him from the beginning (Jn 15.26-27). The Samaritan woman fits neither of those categories. Further, she testifies not to Jesus as the messiah but to part of her brief experience with him. Her testimony is a report of fact but not a confession of faith.

---

9. Botha, *Speech Act Reading*, p. 167. A.T. Robertson suggests that the formulation in Jn 4.29 preempts opposition and arouses curiosity (*A Grammar of the Greek New Testament in the Light of Historical Research* [London: Hodder & Stoughton, 1914], p. 1175).

10. Against, for example, Scott, *Sophia*, pp. 193-94.

John's use of μαρτυρέω to describe her words does not perforce lend a forensic quality to her testimony or qualify it as a Johannine faith statement (compare the ways μαρτυρέω is used in Jn 2.25; 4.44; 7.7; 13.21; 18.23).

> The combination of μαρτυρεῖν with ὅτι does not occur often in John and cannot be regarded as typical. Jn 4.39 places a ὅτι-recitation after μαρτυρεῖν that most translators render with a colon followed by the testimony of the Samaritan woman in direct speech: 'He has told me everything that I have done.' The subject of the testimony is therefore a matter of fact: the experience that the woman has had of Jesus' knowledge. The 'testimony' is given to the townspeople and bears no legal stamp. The woman acknowledges only what she has heard and experienced.[11]

Despite her lengthy dialogue with Jesus, the several topics discussed, her recognition of him as a prophet and her inkling that he might be the messiah, what she finally tells the villagers is that he displayed extraordinary knowledge of her. As with the μήτι κτλ. of Jn 4.29, it might be argued that this reflects her strategy to interest the unreceptive villagers. But this argument is unconvincing because Jn 4.39 reiterates the content of her testimony, underscoring that this particular content is the foundation of their belief. This careful restatement of her testimony shows that 'the witness which she gives to the townspeople is her own seemingly limited conception of Jesus' identity and function. The reader is momentarily left to ponder in which Jesus the Samaritans believe.'[12] Most striking is that Jesus' direct call for the woman to believe him: πίστευέ μοι, γύναι (Jn 4.21), followed by a disclosure to her of his identity: ἐγώ εἰμι, ὁ λαλῶν σοι (Jn 4.26), receives only a tentative response.[13]

John 4.39 speaks of the villagers' faith in Jesus, which at this point is miracle faith: 'The woman's report about Jesus the "miracle man" leads many to belief in him.'[14] John says of the villagers that πολλοὶ ἐπίστευσαν εἰς αὐτόν, and πιστεύω εἰς [αὐτόν] is a key Johannine

---

11. Beutler, *Martyria*, p. 215. Similarly, Brox (*Zeuge und Märtyrer*, p. 70) sees that in Jn 4.39 μαρτυρέω is used in a neutral sense.

12. O'Day, *Revelation*, p. 87.

13. In one sense, then, Davies (*Rhetoric and Reference*, p. 227) may be correct to regard the Samaritan woman as a 'half-hearted missionary'.

14. E. Haenchen, *Das Johannesevangelium: Ein Kommentar* (Tübingen: Mohr [Paul Siebeck], 1980), p. 248. A common Samaritan expectation was that the eschatological Mosaic prophet would work miracles (S.J. Isser, *The Dositheans: A Samaritan Sect in Late Antiquity* [SJLA, 17; Leiden: Brill, 1976], p. 131).

faith formulation.[15] Thus, it might be argued that at that point the villagers' faith is complete:

> For John, this faith on account of the woman's word is not second-rank, not of lesser worth, not merely a first step towards faith based on the word of Jesus. Nowhere in John is there greater and deeper faith than that depicted with the phrase, 'They believed in him'.[16]

However, that the villagers are marked by ἐπίστευσαν εἰς αὐτόν means nothing by itself. Another group marked by ἐπίστευσαν εἰς αὐτόν soon sought to stone Jesus (Jn 8.30-59). Nicol observes that John sometimes uses πιστεύω loosely, that he 'intends to denote nothing more than an initial interest in Jesus with it', and that he 'applies the word πιστεύω to their curiosity in v. 39 before they had even seen Jesus'.[17] Since the story is about unfolding revelation and deepening faith, the notion that the Samaritans' belief had climaxed before the story's dénouement is anomalous. Jn 4.30 recounted of the villagers, ἤρχοντο πρὸς αὐτόν, and since ἔρχομαι πρός can act as a synonym for πιστεύω in John, the imperfect tense probably underlines that their faith is in process.[18] The villagers' belief remains in process in Jn 4.40 when they ask Jesus to stay (μένω) with them, and continues in process until their confession in Jn 4.42, echoing the course of discovery that the first disciples underwent in Jn 1.35-42 (compare μένω in Jn 1.38, 39). Thus, the first hand of Codex A perhaps displays a better grasp of the story by using ἐπίστευσαν without εἰς αὐτόν to describe the state of the villagers' faith, as this 'absolute' use of πιστεύω is less precise, requiring clarification of its object from the context.[19]

15. Schnackenburg, *John*, I, p. 560.

16. R. Walker, 'Jüngerwort und Herrenwort: Zur Auslegung von Joh 4.39-42', *ZNW* 57 (1966), pp. 49-50.

17. Nicol, *Sēmeia*, pp. 42, 100. Abbott (*Johannine Vocabulary*, §1523) notes that John takes pains to show that 'believe' might represent a transient emotion or have a non-moral significance.

18. See Schnackenburg, *John*, I, p. 564. Too much should not be made of this symbolic sense of the imperfect of ἔρχομαι. The imperfect tense in Jn 4.30 is required by the chronology of the narrative, and later, the villagers 'came' to Jesus (ἦλθον πρὸς αὐτὸν οἱ Σαμαρῖται, Jn 4.40) before his two day sojourn with them and their subsequent confession. Regarding the other three instances of the imperfect of ἔρχομαι in John: Jn 8.2 belongs to the non-original material of Jn 7.53–8.11; Jn 11.29 will be discussed in Chapter 6; Jn 19.3 is clearly iterative.

19. With the absolute use of πιστεύω John can indicate either superficial or

d. Jn 4.41 forms another *crux interpretum*. Either a second group of villagers came to faith in Jesus: πολλῷ πλείους ἐπίστευσαν (*plur.*), or a single group deepened their faith in him: πολλῷ πλεῖον ἐπίστευσαν ($\mathfrak{P}^{75}$ e r[1]). In essence, the two variants pose this question: More believers or deeper belief?

G.D. Kilpatrick holds that $\mathfrak{P}^{75}$ is the correct text, πλεῖον rather than πλείους. Kilpatrick argues that πλείους, a contracted form, was introduced by Atticists to eliminate what was (to them) the objectionable combination of πολλῷ πλεῖον found in $\mathfrak{P}^{75}$, and that this is borne out both by the lack of the contracted form of πολύς elsewhere in John and by the omission in *f*[1] of πλέ[ῖ]ον τούτων from Jn 21.15.[20]

Haplography might be able to explain how πλεῖον got into $\mathfrak{P}^{75}$ (ΠΛΕΙΟΝΕΣΕΠΙΣΤΕΥΣΑΝ becomes ΠΛΕΙΟΝΕΠΙΣΤΕΥΣΑΝ). But πλεῖον is easily understood as something written deliberately rather than by error, as it makes as good if not better sense of the narrative than the πλείους reading. It makes good sense that a single group of Samaritans who had heard first the woman and then Jesus would say to her, 'It is no longer because of what you said that we believe' (Jn 4.42), while it makes less sense for that remark to come from a second group that had not heard her. Perhaps the first group of villagers who heard the woman relayed her testimony to the second group, but the story says nothing of this. Or perhaps the speakers in Jn 4.42 are the first group of believers, not the 'many more' who believe because of Jesus' word in Jn 4.41. This, however, demands a good deal of verbal and mental gymnastics to be construed as the plain sense of the text, as Abbott demonstrates.

authentic faith (Painter, *Quest*, p. 331; see also Schnackenburg, *John*, I, p. 561; Dodd, *Interpretation*, p. 185).

20. 'John iv 41 ΠΛΕΙΟΝ or ΠΛΕΙΟΥΣ', *NovT* 18 (1976), pp. 31-32, supported by J.K. Elliott: 'In John there is no example of the contracted forms [of πλείων] and so πλεῖον should be read at iv 41' (J.K. Elliott, 'The Two Forms of the Third Declension Comparative Adjectives in the New Testament', *NovT* 19 [1977], p. 237). Jn 4.1 has πλείονας not πλείους, Jn 7.31 πλείονα not πλείω, Jn 15.2 πλείονα not πλείω. The alternate spelling πλέον at Jn 21.15 may stem from a different hand than that of Jn 4.41 (unfortunately, $\mathfrak{P}^{75}$ ends at Jn 15.8). It should be noted that the two instances of contracted forms of μείζων have variants using regular forms (Jn 1.50; 5.36), while there are four instances of regular forms of μείζων where there is a contracted form available but no variants (Jn 5.20; 14.12; 15.13; 19.11). The contracted form ἐλάσσω appears at Jn 2.10, but it too has variants (see Elliott, 'Two Forms', p. 238; also *TCGNT*, pp. 210-11, 232).

Some (say, fifty) believed because of the woman's word; but many more (say, a hundred) believed for the first time, *or (as regards the fifty) had their belief strengthened*, because of Christ's word: and all these came to the woman saying, 'The beginning of our belief came from you: but now we have heard Him for ourselves and we believe because of His word'.[21]

Although πλεῖον gives a literarily and logically smoother reading than πλείους, it must be acknowledged that the latter makes sufficient sense to have survived in the vast majority of manuscripts and translations.

That 𝔓[75] enjoys support from only two Old Latin witnesses must be balanced against the great antiquity and exceptional quality of its own witness. But in any event, the text cannot be established by the external evidence, nor does the internal evidence of transcriptional probabilities lean decisively in either direction. Instead, John's witness-belief environment must serve as the final arbiter, and this environment is to be found in texts where one party instigates some initial interest or belief in Jesus for a second party who then meets Jesus personally.

In Jn 1.35-51 John the Baptist turns the attention of two of his disciples toward Jesus, 'Look, here is the Lamb of God'. The disciples' interest is piqued and they follow Jesus, who asks them what (or whom) they are seeking, and they respond by asking him where he is staying. Accepting Jesus' invitation to come and see, they stay the day with him. One of the two, Andrew, then finds his brother Simon and informs him that they have found the messiah. In this case, the Baptist instigates an initial level of interest and belief: the disciples follow Jesus and call him 'Teacher'. Then, after having spent time with Jesus, the two disciples of John become disciples of Jesus. They come to believe that Jesus is the messiah. Their final level of belief therefore is superior to that prompted

---

21. Abbott, *Johannine Vocabulary*, §1504. Walker ('Jüngerwort und Herrenwort', p. 51) seems to defy logic by arguing that the 'many more' who come to believe because of Jesus (Jn 4.41) are identical with those who believed because of the woman (Jn 4.39). M.C. de Boer recognizes that 'πολλῷ πλεῖον may capture the sense contextually intended or demanded by πολλῷ πλείους', but he wants to keep both options open: 'Perhaps both greater numbers *and* greater faith are involved' ('John 4.27—Women (and Men) in the Gospel and Community of John', in G.J. Brooke (ed.), *Women in the Biblical Tradition* [SWR, 31; Lampeter: Edwin Mellen, 1992], p. 216 n. 25). O'Day (*Revelation*, p. 88) suggests that the inconsistency can be explained by the exigencies of the narrative: 'John intends the confession of v. 42 to be the confession of all the Samaritans and therefore must bring both groups of believers together.' This solution is possible but unnecessary if πολλῷ πλεῖον is admitted.

by John although still owing its start to his witness.

In Jn 20.19-29 the cowering disciples, minus Thomas, are met by the risen Jesus, who blesses them and shows them his pierced hands and side as evidence that he is the same one who was crucified. The disciples recognize him as the Lord, and Jesus blesses them again, commissions them to share in his mission, and endows them with the Holy Spirit. They tell Thomas of their encounter with the Lord, but he refuses to believe without benefit of the same evidence they had received. One week later Thomas' demand is met when Jesus appears in similar fashion and invites Thomas to touch and see his wounds. This experience moves Thomas to confess, 'My Lord and my God'. In this case, the disciples awaken in Thomas enough belief for him not to reject categorically the possibility of a risen Jesus, but not enough for him to embrace it without personally experiencing the risen Jesus. So, as in Jn 1.35-51, the final state of his faith is superior to that provoked by the others but still owes its start to their witness.

The witness-belief environment found in these two incidents supports $\mathfrak{P}^{75}$ inasmuch as the faith that the villagers exhibit in Jn 4.39 cannot be the same faith that they confess in Jn 4.42. There is a qualitative difference in their faith.[22] It is tempting to construe the case of the villagers as the one example in John's Gospel where mature faith is attained solely through a human witness to Jesus, and that what changed for them was only the basis for and not the quality of their faith. But if the text is determined by $\mathfrak{P}^{75}$ and the witness-belief environment of John, this cannot be done. Nowhere in John's Gospel does anyone arrive at a mature faith in Jesus without personal experience of him or based only upon the testimony of another.[23]

---

22. Against Olsson, *Structure and Meaning*, p. 159.

23. This does not castigate those who must see to believe, for Jesus recognizes, albeit with frustration, that for his contemporaries visual evidence is the necessary precondition for faith (Jn 4.48). Nonetheless, Jn 20.29, coming as it does right before John states his purpose for writing (Jn 20.30-31), establishes that for his readers the witness of the Gospel itself is the basis for faith, and that for them faith comes by hearing not by sight. The historical events that reveal Jesus in John's Gospel are not thereby diminished, relativized or even mediated, but rather, by the Holy Spirit, are experienced in the hearing of the text. Nowhere is it more true than in the Gospel of John that the medium is the message (see Ashton, *Fourth Gospel*, pp. 515-53).

e. Like Jn 4.39, Jn 4.42 abounds with Johannine locutions (πιστεύω, ἀκούω, οἶδα, ἀληθῶς, κόσμος), and contains a textual variant (σὴν μαρτυρίαν).

After two days with Jesus, the villagers have made two significant steps. First, the ground of their faith has shifted from the woman's testimony of Jesus' miraculous knowledge to their personal experience of him. Secondly, the level of their faith has matured from belief in an unknown, miracle-working prophet-cum-messiah to belief in Jesus as the saviour of the world. Johannine vernacular stresses the maturation of the villagers' belief under Jesus' tutelage. 'Hearing' (ἀκηκόαμεν) represents a deeper faith, 'knowing' (οἴδαμεν) clarifies and completes faith, and Johannine faith is centred in the confession of it.[24] Therefore, Barrett errs in saying, 'Through the woman's testimony the Samaritans *believed*; they could do no more when they heard Jesus' own word'.[25] The Samaritans could and did do more than believe: they knew.

Once again, the villagers are contrasted with the woman in that she knows neither the gift of God (Jn 4.10) nor what she worships (Jn 4.22), but only that the messiah will come (Jn 4.25). The distinction between miracle faith and word faith applies to the Samaritans.

> The faith of the people of Sychar rests at first on the woman's report of how Jesus had revealed to her all that she had done. But faith which rests on miracles is of uncertain value and strength (cf. 2:23-25). Their faith becomes stronger and more reliable when they have heard Jesus' word. They recognize it as a message from God, no longer on the external evidence of miracles, but on the internal evidence of the words itself.[26]

Whether or not the villagers are deprecating her testimony will be addressed later (along with the textual variant). But in any case, it is clear that as far as they are concerned, the testimony of the woman has been superceded by what Jesus has told them during his two day sojourn, and that their faith now stands on superior ground.[27]

---

24. Schnackenburg, *John*, I, pp. 564-66; Brown, *John*, I, p. 513. Gaffney ('Believing and Knowing') notes that in John's Gospel knowledge is superior to belief, although the two are intimately related.

25. Barrett, *John*, p. 243.

26. J. Bligh, 'Jesus in Samaria', *HeyJ* 3 (October 1962), p. 345.

27. Contrasts made between 'Glaube aus zweiter hand' and 'Glaube aus erster Hand', or between 'Jüngerwort' and 'Herrenwort' (Bultmann, *John*, pp. 201-203; Walker, 'Jüngerwort und Herrenwort') are somewhat misguided. More accurately, the contrast is between the word of witnesses (*Zeugenwort*) and the word of Jesus (*Jesuswort*) (Olsson, *Structure and Meaning*, p. 159).

The villagers' confession in Jn 4.42 sparks debate. Is ὁ σωτὴρ τοῦ κόσμου a formula Samaritans would use, or did John place it on their lips? C.R. Koester is one of those who claim that the title was associated with neither Samaritan nor Jewish messianic hopes, and that John uses it here to counter claims that the Roman emperor is ὁ σωτὴρ τοῦ κόσμου.[28] A.T. Hanson also sees the use of ὁ σωτὴρ τοῦ κόσμου as anti-emperor polemic, but believes that John need not have obtained the title from Roman emperor parlance, and in fact was likely to have gotten it from Isaiah (Isa. 45.21-22).[29] Neufeld maintains that σωτήρ is used in both the Hellenistic and Jewish worlds, and the important fact is that in Johannine thought the title is messianic.[30] J. Macdonald contends that even if the formula 'the saviour of the world' is not found in Samaritan literature, the idea it represents is typical of Samaritan eschatological thought.[31]

Surprisingly, what often is overlooked in this debate is the content of John's narrative. Both the Evangelist and Jesus himself understand his mission to be the salvation of the world (Jn 3.17; 12.47). Unless John's understanding of Jesus was out of touch with Jesus' self-understanding, and unless a highly cynical view of John's historicity is taken, it is not surprising that the villagers arrive at the confession of Jn 4.42 after two days of hearing Jesus' own teaching, regardless of the nature of Samaritan messianic expectations. As Okure says, 'Jn 4.22 and the Gospel as a whole provide sufficient grounds for the use of the title'.[32]

A summary of the exegetical issues shows that the woman's miracle faith in Jesus as a prophet, based upon his preternatural knowledge, never matures to word faith, although she does ponder the possibility that he might be something even greater—the messiah. Upon the basis

28. C.R. Koester, '"The Saviour of the World" (John 4.42)', *JBL* 109 (1990), pp. 665-80.

29. A.T. Hanson, *The Prophetic Gospel: A Study of John and the Old Testament* (Edinburgh: T. & T. Clark, 1991), pp. 65-68.

30. Neufeld, *Christian Confessions*, pp. 75-76.

31. J. Macdonald, *The Theology of the Samaritans* (London: SCM Press, 1964), p. 367. J. Bowman finds it significant that 'the Samaritans when they acknowledge Christ hail him as the Saviour of the world... the title which they give to Moses in their liturgy' ('Samaritan Studies', *BJRL* 40 [1958], p. 313). G. Reim, however, questions the age of the material that Bowman cites (*Studien zum Alttestamentlichen Hintergrund des Johannesevangeliums* [SNSTMS, 22; Cambridge: Cambridge University Press, 1974], p. 121).

32. Okure, *Approach to Mission*, p. 176.

of her testimony to Jesus' miraculous knowledge, the villagers attain a similar miracle faith which then, founded upon their own experience of Jesus, matures to word faith in him as the saviour of the world.

2. *John 1.43-51: An Interpretative Frame*

The testimonies of the Samaritan woman and Philip lead others to Jesus, and a comparison will help to appraise her as a witness. This comparison is sometimes made in an unsystematic fashion via incidental cross references, but has been done in outline form by Scott, which I will follow and critique. Scott's outline appears as follows.[33]

	Philip		*Samaritan Woman*
1.43	Jesus calls Philip	4.7-26	Jesus calls the woman
1.45	Philip seeks Nathanael	4.28	Woman seeks the townspeople
1.46	Nathanael doubts Philip	4.39	(*In contrast*) Many believe her
1.46	Philip calls Nathanael to 'come and see'	4.29	Woman calls the townspeople to 'come and see'
1.47-48	Leads to an encounter with Jesus	4.40-41	Leads to an encounter with Jesus
1.49	Nathanael believes	4.41	More people believe
1.49	Confession of faith	4.42	Confession of faith

John 1.43//4.7-26

Is it accurate to say that Jesus 'calls' both Philip and the woman? Jesus issues a terse command to Philip, 'Follow me!' (ἀκολούθει μοι), to which Philip responds promptly and decisively. For John, ἀκολουθέω can mean both to follow physically and to follow as a disciple; characteristically, John intimates both meanings here. On the other hand, Jesus engages the woman in a protracted dialogue in which he tries, with only limited success, to get her to grasp who he is, and in which he never calls her to follow him.

John 1.45//4.28

Both Philip and the woman seek others, but what they say to their addressees shows that their purposes differ. Philip tells Nathanael of definitely having found that Jesus of Nazareth is the one written about by Moses and the prophets, whereas the woman seeks the villagers' help to investigate the possibility that a nameless stranger with wondrous knowledge might be the messiah (Jn 4.29).

---

33. Scott, *Sophia*, pp. 194-95.

John 1.46//4.39; 1.46//4.29

Scott contrasts Nathanael's doubt of Philip with the villagers' belief of
the woman, but fails to contrast what Nathanael and the villagers are
asked to come and see. Nathanael faces a much more astounding claim
than do the villagers. Philip does not claim, as does the woman, to have
met a stranger having wondrous knowledge who might be the messiah,
but to have found in Jesus of Nazareth the one about whom Moses and
the prophets wrote. Furthermore, Nathanael's words, 'Can anything
good come out of Nazareth?' may be understood to indicate surprise as
much as doubt, because when Philip says to him, 'Come and see', he
does so without hesitation, which is not the response of a serious sceptic.

Also, Scott disorders the events in the Samaritan story in order to
maintain parallels with that of Philip. By reversing the sequence of
Jn 4.39 and Jn 4.29, Scott obscures the crucial fact that the villagers
believe first in the stranger with the wondrous knowledge because of the
woman's testimony, but then, in Jesus as the saviour of the world
because of his own testimony. In contrast to my exegesis of Jn 4.41,
Scott sees two separate groups of believing villagers. Even so, whether
one group or two, Scott fails to distinguish between the initial and final
causes of their faith as well as between its initial and final levels.

John 1.47-48//4.40-41

Scott says nothing about the substance of Nathanael's encounter with
Jesus and of how it resembles yet contrasts with that of Jesus and the
Samaritan woman. Jesus reveals miraculous knowledge of Nathanael,
evoking from him the confession, 'Rabbi, you are the Son of God! You
are the King of Israel!' (Jn 1.49), whereas Jesus' miraculous knowledge
of the woman moves her to declare, 'Sir, I see that you are a prophet'
(Jn 4.16-19). Although both Nathanael and the woman believe because
of Jesus' miraculous knowledge, Nathanael's confession far surpasses
calling Jesus 'a prophet'.

All that John tells of Jesus' two day sojourn with the villagers is that
they emerged believing because of his word. Again, two levels of faith
are contrasted. The villagers at first believe in the woman's testimony to
the stranger who has amazing knowledge, but then in Jesus as the
saviour of the world because of his own word.

John 1.49//4.41; 1.49//4.42

Nathanael believes and pronounces a confession of faith, as do the villagers. Jesus tells Nathanael that his faith, built upon an experience of

miraculous knowledge, will find a superior foundation, namely, a vision of the Son of Man that will confirm Jesus as the one whom God sent from heaven (Jn 1.50-51). The villagers themselves proclaim that the foundation of their belief has already undergone a similar shift, that they have moved from miracle faith to word faith. Nathanael's confession of Jesus as the Son of God (cf. Jn 1.34; 20.31) and the villagers' confession of Jesus as the saviour of the world (cf. Jn 3.17; 12.47) disclose that both rightly understand his identity.

The testimonies of Philip and the Samaritan woman match well in the broad contours of their stories. After first encountering Jesus personally, Philip and the woman issue invitations by testifying about Jesus to others who then go on to believe in Jesus themselves. However, the details of those encounters and testimonies are hardly parallel, much less equivalent. Jesus issues a brief, unequivocal call of discipleship to Philip that he obeys, while Jesus engages in a protracted process of revelation with the Samaritan woman that she never fully apprehends. Philip testifies by making an unqualified faith statement about Jesus' identity, while the woman testifies by recounting Jesus' miraculous knowledge and by offering a diffident suggestion about his identity.

The foregoing analysis shows that Scott's comparison in outline form fails to attend to important details, and that it reorders events of the Samaritan narrative. Thus, the following conclusion by Scott is, in my opinion, mistaken: 'That there is no qualitative difference between the witness of the woman and that of men in the Fourth Gospel can be seen through a brief comparison of... Philip's witness and that of the woman herself.'[34] I have shown that the testimonies of the Samaritan and Philip are of quite different quality. Whether or not the Samaritan's testimony is therefore second-rate or even to be disparaged is a matter for the next section.

3. *The Samaritan Woman as a Witness*

John states that the Samaritan woman testifies (Jn 4.39), and it must be asked, 'What is the nature, range and effect of her testimony?' Answering this question requires attention to the cultural contexts.

---

34. Scott, *Sophia*, p. 194. Compare the remark of O'Day: 'The Samaritan woman is thus a witness and disciple like John the Baptist, Andrew, and Philip' (G.R. O'Day, 'John', in Newsom and Ringe [eds.], *Commentary*, p. 296). Scott also includes the Baptist in his comparison. Because this comparison is so common, I will address it in the next section.

Various proposals have been made that the author of John was a Samaritan, or employed Samaritan sources and theology, or directed the Gospel to a Samaritan audience. The theory of Samaritan influence in John has gained ground but remains unproven, and, although vital, is too complex to rehearse here.[35] Still, whatever John's background(s) and target audience(s) may have been, his Gospel was read by both Jews and Samaritans. Bultmann points out that the Samaritan episode of John 4 'evidently assumes local knowledge in its hearers'.[36] Both Jewish and Samaritan readers therefore must be considered. Furthermore, the beliefs, customs, and laws of Samaritans must be distinguished from those of Jews; the two are not identical. The Samaritans comprise a Jewish sect, but one which nevertheless retains its own distinctive theologies and praxes. A. Loewenstamm explains,

> The Samaritans have developed their code of religious practice by direct interpretation of biblical laws. A *halakhah* came into being, though not in the same way as Judaism. It often differs from the rabbinical *halakhah* by its stricter adherence to the letter of the law, as in the laws of the Sabbath and festivals or marriage between close relatives. In other cases it is based on different interpretation, as in the law concerning the levirate marriage (Deut. 25.5-10) or fixing the date of Pentecost, etc. There was no systematic codification of the law, and the few extant Samaritan halakhic compendia are arranged very loosely.[37]

Citing rabbinic opposition to public discourse with all women and rabbinic contempt for Samaritan women (for example, *Pirqe Aboth* 1.5; *b. ʿErub.* 53b; *m. Nid.* 4.1), commentators often assert that Jesus violates Jewish conventions if not laws by interacting with the Samaritan woman. Yet, in the realities of everyday life, especially in rural villages, such mores and codes are neither ironclad nor comprehensive, but vary according to locale, class, education and so forth (contrast Jn 4.8 with Jn 4.9).[38]

---

35. For a review and critique of the major proponents and theories, see M. Pamment, 'Is There Convincing Evidence of Samaritan Influence on the Fourth Gospel?', *ZNW* 73 (1982), pp. 221-30.

36. Bultmann, *John*, p. 177.

37. A. Loewenstamm, 'Samaritans', *EncJud*, XIV, cols. 740-41; see also M. Gaster, *The Samaritans: Their History, Doctrines and Literature* (London: Milford and Oxford University Press, 1925), p. 150; S. Lowy, *The Principles of Samaritan Bible Exegesis* (SPB, 28; Leiden: Brill, 1977), pp. 202-203; R. Pummer, *The Samaritans* (IR, 23.5; Leiden: Brill, 1987), p. 3.

38. See Archer, *Her Price*, pp. 61-62. Bowman ('Samaritan Studies', pp. 298-99)

One of the most frequently cited parallels to the meeting at the well between Jesus and the Samaritan woman in John 4 is Genesis 24. And yet, it goes unmentioned that the public conversation at the well between Abraham's servant and Rebekah transpires with no hint whatsoever that their actions are unusual, much less taboo. Is there another explanation for why the disciples are nonplussed because Jesus converses with a woman (Jn 4.27)? M.C. de Boer asks, 'Are they depicted as amazed because a (Jewish) *man* is talking with a woman or because *Jesus* is talking with a woman?'[39] Until this point, Jesus has spoken only with men, except for the curt exchange with his mother at the Cana wedding (Jn 2.3-4). Further, Jn 4.9 shows that the Samaritan woman's astonishment stems from Jesus' violation not of gender barriers but of religious/ethnic ones: 'How is it that you, a Jew, ask a drink of me, a woman of Samaria? Jews do not share things in common with Samaritans.'[40] As de Boer says, 'Prior to v. 27, the emphasis falls not on the character's gender, her womanhood, but on her ethnic identity: she is a *Samaritan* (vv. 7-9). A similar point applies to Jesus. His Jewishness, not his gender, matters.'[41] What dominates this narrative, then, is not the relationships between men and women but between Jews and Samaritans. In this particular context, the public dialogue between a man and a woman could well be nothing out of the ordinary.[42]

The customary absence of women from the public sphere in ancient Palestine may have been less rigid among Samaritans than among Jews. One reason for keeping Jewish women out of public was so that Jewish men might avoid accidentally contracting the ritual uncleanness from a menstruating woman that rendered a man unable to participate in the cultic activities. The dictum, 'The daughters of the Samaritans are

notes that Jewish attitudes toward Samaritans varied and that this is reflected in the differing attitudes of the four Gospels toward Samaritans (see also Purvis, 'Samaritans and Judaism', p. 87; Morris, *John*, p. 259 n. 25). Likewise, Samaritan attitudes about Jews display both criticism and solidarity, for example, 'The Jews are children of the Jewish people who have deviated from the right path but will return to it' (cited by Loewenstamm, 'Samaritans', col. 746).

39. De Boer, 'John 4.27', p. 224.

40. The NRSV parenthesizes Jn 4.9b, but my point is valid whether Jn 4.9b is understood as a comment made by the woman or by the author.

41. De Boer, 'John 4.27', p. 213.

42. The conclusion that among Samaritans public discourse between men and women was neither proscribed nor unusual has been supported in my personal correspondence with Samaritan scholar J.D. Purvis.

[deemed unclean as] menstruants from the cradle' (*m. Nid.* 4.1), is
habitually cited in regard to John 4. But this Jewish precept cannot be
projected automatically onto everyone in a story that takes place in
Samaria. The Samaritans undoubtedly observed the Pentateuchal codes
concerning ritual uncleanness, as they did all Pentateuchal laws, but
there is no reason to suppose that their observance was identical with
that of Jewish rabbis. Pharisaic reckoning deemed some menstruants
unclean at times when Samaritan reckoning did not.[43] Even among the
Samaritans themselves, customs regarding menstruants were not uniform. For example, Sakta, a first-century Samaritan leader, is said even
to have eliminated the mandatory purification for anyone who touches a
woman during her menstruation.[44]

Scott writes of the Samaritan woman, 'Contrary, then, to the conclusions of later Rabbinic writers, that women should neither be taught
theology nor engage in discussion of it with men, this woman is seen to
know something and to be prepared to discuss it openly, with a *male
Jew*'.[45] But can the conclusions of Jewish rabbis be applied to a Samaritan woman in Samaria? In general, Samaritans were hostile to Pharisaic
traditions, rejecting their oral tradition and their 'fences around the law'.
Samaritan splinter groups that adopted Pharisaic ways were
stigmatized.[46]

The reading and hearing of the law was the heart of Samaritan liturgy,
and Deut. 31.12 specifies that women, children and resident aliens be
present with the men. Unlike Jews, 'Samaritans would seem to have
made it incumbent upon women to attend the synagogue service, and

---

43. Isser, *Dositheans*, p. 86; Lowy, *Samaritan Bible Exegesis*, pp. 291-93.
J.D.M. Derrett cites Jewish customs and laws but fails to mention Samaritan ones in
'The Samaritan Woman's Purity (John 4.4-52)', *EvQ* 60 (1988), pp. 291-98.

44. J. Fossum, 'Sects and Movements', in A.D. Crown (ed.), *The Samaritans*
(Tübingen: Mohr [Paul Siebeck], 1989), p. 349; see in the same volume R. Pummer,
'Samaritan Rituals and Customs', pp. 665-68. Samaritan theology and praxis were
fairly but not absolutely uniform (Lowy, *Samaritan Bible Exegesis*, p. 298).

45. Scott, *Sophia*, p. 188. Compare the comment of T.K. Seim, 'Apart from the
fact that the conversation between Jesus and the Samaritan woman in itself represents
an offence against public decency and rules of purity, it develops into a theological
discourse supposed to surpass the mental capacity of women' (T.K. Seim, 'Roles of
Women in the Gospel of John', in L. Hartmann and B. Olsson (eds.), *Aspects on
the Johannine Literature* [ConBNT, 18; Uppsala: Uppsala University Press, 1987],
p. 68).

46. Isser, *Dositheans*, pp. 86, 109.

Sakta even had the women read together with the men'.[47] The Samaritan *Chronicle of Abul Fath* tells of a Jewish plot to kill a Samaritan priest being foiled by two women—one a Jew, the other a Samaritan. At one point the Jew asks the Samaritan not to enter the synagogue on the sabbath, making plain that it was her custom to do so. Generally, 'The Samaritans—in contrast to the Rabbinic Law exempting women from certain observances—do not make any distinction between the sexes in reference to their common obligation to carry out the Law'.[48] Because Samaritans interpreted the Pentateuch strictly, the injunction of Deut. 31.12 indicates that their practice of educating children of both sexes in the law and Samaritan traditions is not an innovation but probably dates back to their origins.[49] In fact, it appears that Samaritan dispositions toward women became increasingly subordinationist only with time, particularly under Muslim influence.[50]

I will present the following material to suggest that the routine application of rabbinic teachings to the Samaritan woman is inappropriate.[51] Three examples come from the *Chronicle of Abul Fath*.[52]

47. Fossum, 'Sects and Movements', p. 347.

48. Lowy, *Samaritan Bible Exegesis*, p. 135.

49. Bowman, 'Samaritan Studies', p. 309; Loewenstamm, 'Samaritans', col. 744. In the *Chronicle of Abul Fath*, Baba Rabbah mandates that men, women and children be taught the law.

50. Fossum, 'Sects and Movements', p. 347 n. 221.

51. The most common example is scholars misapplying rabbinic teachings on divorce to the Samaritan woman even though marriage and divorce praxes among Samaritans and Jews were not the same. See Pummer, 'Rituals and Customs', pp. 660-65; Gaster, *Samaritans*, p. 72.

52. Regarding Samaritan literature: (1) most literary and liturgical texts postdate the fourth century; (2) the earliest texts are preserved in mediaeval and modern manuscripts; (3) the textual tradition features free adaptation and editing (Purvis, 'Fourth Gospel', pp. 164-65). However, because of Samaritan rigor and conservatism, the traditions incorporated into their literature predate the fourth century and 'remain virtually unchanged for many centuries' (Lowy, *Samaritan Bible Exegesis*, pp. 59-60, cf. p. 503). The text of *Abul Fath* dates from the fourteenth century but probably contains 'the best and most extensive traditions derived ultimately from the first centuries A.D.' (Isser, *Dositheans*, p. 108), and therefore is 'rightly regarded as a "key" to unlocking Samaritan self-understanding in areas of social history, theology, sectarianism, and chronology' (P. Stenhouse, 'Samaritan Chronicles', in Crown [ed.], *Samaritans*, p. 221). The text of *Abul Fath* used here is from J. Bowman, *Samaritan Documents Relating to their History, Religion and Life* (POTTS, 2; Pittsburgh: Pickwick Press, 1977), pp. 114-213.

1. The servant girl Sul becomes enamoured with her master Yaham. Angered because Yaham will not respond to her, Sul convinces Simon the wizard that Yaham's father, the high priest Nathanael, has sent her with an order for Simon to kill Yaham secretly. Simon carries out the murder, but eventually Sul's plot is exposed. Simon then resuscitates Yaham, and Sul is tortured, forced to confess and executed. At one point Simon says to Nathanael, 'I see you in this great grief, and yet you sent your serving girl to me in order to have [Yaham] killed'. In this episode, Simon believes that the high priest commissioned a servant girl as his messenger and entrusted her with a crucial dispatch.

2. Dositheus, leader of a first-century Samaritan group, hires a prostitute to accuse falsely the revered scholar-elder Yahdu of fornication with her, giving her Yahdu's stolen mantle as evidence (compare Judah and Tamar in Genesis 38). She ascends Hargerizim and levels the accusation against Yahdu before the high priest Akbon and the congregation. Upon hearing her testimony, Akbon sets out to burn Yahdu. Yahdu avers his innocence, and the prostitute is interrogated under the threat of death should she be lying. She then confesses the plot. In this story, the testimony of a woman prostitute is heard and initially accepted by the high priest.

3. The high priest Akbon is accused by certain men of nepotism in his judging duties. To substantiate the accusation, the men lodge a false fornication charge against Akbon's daughter Maryam, expecting that he will not judge his own daughter's case impartially. The man accused of complicity with Maryam flees Akbon's subpoena, and Akbon, taking this as an admission of guilt, burns Maryam (cf. Lev. 21.9). Later that night, Akbon sees Maryam in a dream during which she avows her innocence. After twice more having the same dream, Akbon challenges the accusers, who admit their fraud and are burned (cf. Deut. 19.19). In this story, a woman's testimony eventually prevails over that of the men, but of course this is mitigated by the fact that it is only in a dream and not at a trial that Akbon hears and accepts her testimony.

A fourth example, comparable to the story of Akbon and Maryam, is found in the *Daughter of Amram*, which dates from between 100 BCE and 100 CE and is the Samaritan parallel to the Jewish story of Susanna.[53] In the Samaritan version, the woman's status and function

---

53. For the text of the *Daughter of Amram* and a discussion of its provenance see M. Gaster, *Studies and Texts in Folklore, Magic, Mediaeval Romance, Hebrew Apocrypha, and Samaritan Archaeology* (2 vols.; New York: Ktav, 1971), I,

differ strikingly from those of Susanna. The (unnamed) Samaritan protagonist is the daughter of the high priest as well as an unsurpassed student, scribe and teacher of Torah. She has taken the vow of a *nazir*, and it is two male Nazirites under her tutelage who perpetrate the fraud against her. As in Susanna, the two villains eventually are exposed by being interrogated separately, but in stark contrast to Susanna, Amram's daughter gives her testimony prior to being exonerated.

> And the Rabban commanded and they brought his daughter. And when she came, all the people came out to see her, her father asked her about everything that had happened to her. And she told him the whole truth of the thing. And all the men recognised the truth of her words and the purity of her actions and that the hermits had been telling falsehoods (*Daughter of Amram* 70–73).

Since Samaritans adhered strictly to the Pentateuch alone, which contains no *de jure* exclusion of women as witnesses, it is quite possible that Samaritan women were competent to testify under many circumstances, whereas Jewish women were excluded as witnesses by rabbinic codes in many (but not all) cases. This would account for the absence of any testimony from the protagonist in the Jewish Susanna and its presence in the Samaritan *Daughter of Amram*.

These several incidents from the *Chronicle of Abul Fath* and the *Daughter of Amram*, even with their folk tale quality, urge that Jewish rabbinic codes regarding the place of women in the public, religious and legal spheres should not be applied routinely to Samaritans. In the texts cited, Samaritan women appear as messengers and witnesses who are heard and believed, and the activities of these Samaritan women may help to illuminate the events of Jn 4.4-42.

The Samaritan woman of John 4 reports to the villagers that a man has told her everything about herself. She invites them to meet him for themselves, and she asks them to consider that he might be the messiah. The villagers respond to her without question or hesitation, indicating that she has sufficient credibility for them to act in that way. This militates against the argument that she firmly believes Jesus to be the messiah but must couch her belief in question form in order to forestall the anticipated doubt or scorn of the villagers. The villagers' response, 'They left the city and were on their way to him' (Jn 4.30), shows that

pp. 199-210. Gaster (p. 207) thinks that the Jewish and Samaritan versions stem from a single source that both groups adopted and adjusted for their purposes, but that the Samaritan version is the older.

her testimony of personal experience merits their action. Their statement, 'It is no longer because of what you said that we believe'
(Jn 4.42), reveals that in fact her testimony was accepted at face value
before they acted to confirm it. This accords with the response to
women's testimony seen in the *Chronicle of Abul Fath* and the
Daughter of Amram.

Samaritan readers of John probably could accept her testimony in the
same way as the villagers. But what about Jewish readers? Given the
relatively unfavourable view of women as witnesses in Jewish life, and
that Jewish-Samaritan relations were often less than genial, could Jewish
readers have seen the Samaritan woman as a credible witness?

First, Jewish attitudes toward Samaritans were not unswervingly
antagonistic, even though the first century was a period of strained relationships between the two groups. Secondly, Samaritan-Jewish hostili-
ties were internecine and, despite their mutual cultic exclusions, neither
group placed the other in the same class with Gentiles. Samaritan,
Jewish and Christian writings show that the two groups did in fact
intermingle. Therefore, in Jn 4.9 (οὐ γὰρ συγχρῶνται Ἰουδαῖοι
Σαμαρίταις), whether οὐ...συγχρῶνται is translated as 'do not have
dealings' or 'do not share vessels', the statement should not be taken as
categorical but as characteristic of Samaritan-Jewish antagonism.[54]

Two examples will illustrate this. R. Eliezer decrees, 'He that eats the
bread of the Samaritans is like one that eats the flesh of swine'
(*m. Šebu.* 8.10), and yet, Jews did dine with Samaritans, even counting
them among the quorum for saying the common grace (*m. Ber.* 7.1)
and allowing them to deliver the benediction (*m. Ber.* 8.8). The
previously mentioned story of the plot to kill Baba Rabbah treats the
friendship of the Jewish woman and the Samaritan woman with no hint
whatsoever that such a friendship is unwonted, and it is the Jewish
woman who thwarts the plot to murder the Samaritan priest.[55]

---

54. J.A. Montgomery contends that Jn 4.9b is either an inexact expression of the
author, or a gloss reflecting the actual conditions of a later time, or a phrase requiring
a translation other than 'have no dealings' (*The Samaritans, the Earliest Jewish Sect:
Their History, Theology and Literature* [1907; New York: Ktav, repr., 1968], pp. 158-
59). Montgomery (p. 176) explains that from the Jewish viewpoint, Samaritans were
not guilty of heresy but of schism. Daube believes that the 'Jews' of Jn 4.9b probably refers only to a group of Pharisees rather than to Jews in general (D. Daube,
The New Testament and Rabbinic Judaism [London: Athlone, 1956], pp. 373-82).

55. *Masseket Kutim (De Samaritanis)* 1.11 allows a Samaritan woman to deliver
and suckle the son of a Jewish woman. This talmudic legal tract encapsulates the

Jewish ambivalence about Samaritans is reflected in the rabbinic writings concerning Samaritans as witnesses:

> No writ is valid which has a Samaritan witness excepting a writ of divorce or a writ of emancipation. They once brought a bill of divorce before Rabban Gamaliel at Kefar Othnai, and its witnesses were Samaritans; and he pronounced it valid. Any writ is valid that is drawn up in the registries of the gentiles, even if they that signed it were gentiles, excepting a writ of divorce or a writ of emancipation. R. Simeon says: These, too, are valid; they are mentioned [as invalid] only if they were prepared by such as were not [authorized] judges (*m. Git.* 1.5).[56]

Samaritans were excluded as witnesses in certain cases probably not because of their race/religion but because of their variant legal praxis in those cases.[57] The fact that exceptions were made to the general disqualification of Samaritans as witnesses indicates that they were not considered to be intrinsically incompetent as witnesses, and *Masseket Kutim* 1.16 lists cases where Samaritans are reliable to testify. Thus, it may be argued with some confidence that a Samaritan woman, however ignoble she may have been in the eyes of some Jews, was not an intrinsically incompetent witness.[58]

As in the case of the mother of Jesus, many commentators liken the witness of the Samaritan woman to that of John the Baptist. This comparison receives perhaps its strongest formulation from H. Boers: 'She is Jesus' co-worker in an unprecedented way, more concretely even than John the Baptist'.[59] The analogy is not unfounded: like the Baptist, the Samaritan woman points others to Jesus and then gives way to his self-witness and the personal experience of the people she has attracted. The

---

ambiguity of Jewish attitudes toward Samaritans. Montgomery (*Samaritans*, pp. 154-95) offers further evidence of such ambiguity. Montgomery (p. 168) writes, 'The Talmudic opinions and decisions, far more than the popular tradition and vulgar brawls, bear witness to the actual historical relations originally existing between Jews and Samaritans. When we find the doctors of the IId Century wrestling over this problem, we have good evidence, otherwise almost wholly absent, that in the preceding centuries the Samaritans had a *quasi*-standing within the Jewish Church, which only the widening of the breach and the slow development of law could at last annul.'

56. Notice that Samaritans are distinguished from Gentiles.

57. Montgomery, *Samaritans*, p. 185.

58. The rabbinic treatment of Samaritan women as pariahs was largely confined to sexual matters, and was probably motivated by the desire to forestall Jewish men from marrying Samaritan women (Montgomery, *Samaritans*, pp. 179-81).

59. Boers, *This Mountain*, p. 185.

error of the analogy, as in the case of its use with Jesus' mother, is more in degree than in kind. The apex of the Samaritan woman's knowledge is, 'I know that Messiah is coming. When he comes, he will proclaim all things to us' (Jn 4.25), and the content of her testimony is, 'Come and see a man who told me everything I have ever done! He cannot be the Messiah, can he?' (Jn 4.29). John the Baptist, on the other hand, can declare of Jesus, 'I myself have seen and have testified that this is the Son of God' (Jn 1.34).

> [John the Baptist], like Jesus, is sent from God. More than any other figure in the Gospel story John stands wholly with Jesus. He is the primordial witness through whom all come to believe. He is the first believer to whom God reveals his Messiah by a prearranged sign. He is the ideal witness who bears testimony to Jesus in terms that echo Jesus' own self-witness. No character in the Gospel story itself, apart from Jesus himself, understands the nature of Jesus' messiahship as clearly and fully as John. Indeed John's perception ranks alongside that of Jesus himself and of the narrator who has the benefit of understanding the beginning from the perspective of the end.[60]

It has also been proposed that the 'witness which the woman bears is quite clearly apostolic in the Johannine perspective... In John's perspective the witness of the believing disciple brings a person to Jesus but then the disciple fades away as the prospective disciple encounters Jesus himself.'[61] This proposal is nearly identical to the comparison of the Samaritan woman and the Baptist, but suffers from the same flaw, namely, that her knowledge and faith remain inchoate. She is hardly a 'believing disciple', but rather, 'she remains within her partial categories', and thus is more accurately compared to Nicodemus than John the Baptist.[62]

M. Scott picks up on this apostolic category, suggesting that the Samaritan's witness 'is preceded by a typically apostolic reaction to the encounter and call of Jesus: she leaves her present mundane task to take up the role as witness'.[63] Scott compares the woman's call and response to the fishermen in the Synoptics: she leaves her water jar just as they

---

60. Painter, *Quest*, p. 401.

61. S.M. Schneiders, 'Women in the Fourth Gospel and the Role of Women in the Contemporary Church', *BTB* 12 (1982), p. 40; similarly, E. Schüssler Fiorenza, *In Memory of Her: A Feminist Theological Construction of Christian Origins* (London: SCM Press, 1983), p. 327.

62. Moloney, 'Cana to Cana', p. 198.

63. Scott, *Sophia*, p. 192.

leave their nets (Jn 4.28; cf. Mk 1.18 and pars.). Again, this comparison errs more in degree than kind, but it also fails at several key points. The significance of her leaving the water jar is ambiguous, and can sustain several interpretations (she forgets it in her haste; she intends to return for it; she no longer sees a need for it; she leaves it for Jesus to use). In contrast, the Synoptic fishermen abandon their nets—their former vocations—to follow Jesus' summons to fish for people. The woman receives no such call and leaves her jar to seek the villagers' help in identifying the strange prophet who has such amazing knowledge. Further, the Synoptic call of the disciples differs from the Johannine one, which makes no mention of the disciples abandoning their current vocations. As Talbert notes of the Johannine Jesus' disciples, 'So far, their commission has been "to be" the community (chs. 13–17); it has not been to leave their occupations and "to go" make disciples. Only in 21.3-14 will they learn of their task to be Jesus' fishermen.'[64] The label 'apostolic' outruns what the Samaritan woman actually says and does. Her activities are perhaps better classified as 'quasi-apostolic'.[65] But even that may be an overstatement.

Something must be said of Jn 4.31-38, the interlude during which Jesus instructs his disciples. E. Schüssler Fiorenza thinks that the ἄλλοι of Jn 4.38 refers to the Samaritan woman, that the verb κοπιάω describes her missionary work, and therefore, that 'the woman is characterized as the representative of the Samaritan mission'.[66] Of the many possible referents for the ἄλλοι of Jn 4.38, the woman is not a good candidate, if for no other reason than the fact that ἄλλοι is plural. If the narrative flow and context of John's Gospel form, as they should, the primary interpretative grid, then the theory of J.A.T. Robinson is the most sensible, namely, that the ἄλλοι refers to John the Baptist and his followers.[67] In any case, only a highly symbolic reading of her actions coupled with a putative Samaritan mission launched by the Johannine community allows her to be cast as a representative Johannine missionary.

64. Talbert, *John*, p. 259.

65. So R.E. Brown, *The Community of the Beloved Disciple: The Lives, Loves, and Hates of an Individual Church in New Testament Times* (London: Geoffrey Chapman, 1979), p. 189.

66. Schüssler Fiorenza, *Memory of Her*, p. 327.

67. J.A.T. Robinson, 'The "Others" of John 4.38: A Test of Exegetical Method', in *Twelve New Testament Studies* (SBT, 34; London: SCM Press, 1962), pp. 61-66. Based on a structural-theological grid, Okure (*Approach to Mission*, p. 163) identifies the ἄλλοι as the Father and Jesus.

The Samaritan woman testifies to her personal experience of an unknown Jewish man whom, because of the miraculous knowledge he shows, she construes to be a prophet, and possibly, the messiah. Her testimony is somewhat of a *Mittelding*. She is much more of a witness than Jesus' mother, much less of a witness than John the Baptist. She invites others to Jesus with the startling results that they come to know his true identity, of which she herself is ignorant: 'It is an ironic invitation in the mouth of the Samaritan woman, because she was able to see so little in the course of her conversation with Jesus. It is the correct invitation, but she offers it unknowingly.'[68]

That the Samaritan woman's knowledge of and witness to Jesus are limited in no way denigrates them. After the villagers attain a new level of faith based upon their personal experience of Jesus, they say to the woman, 'It is no longer because of what you said that we believe, for we have heard for ourselves, and we know that this is truly the Savior of the world' (Jn 4.42). The villagers do not malign but confirm her testimony. What she told them was true, but now they know and believe much more because of what Jesus has told them. This is typical of the witness/belief pattern in John's Gospel.[69]

John marks what the woman tells the villagers as the λόγος of the woman testifying (Jn 4.39), while the villagers designate her words as λαλιά (Jn 4.42). Both λόγος and λαλιά are used of Jesus' own proclamation (Jn 8.43), and so although the term λαλιά can sometimes mean 'idle chatter', its use in Jn 4.42 does not necessarily connote anything negative about the woman's testimony. In any case, as O'Day points out,

> The Samaria narrative presents at least three different perceptions of what the woman says and does: her own, the townpeople's, and the evangelist's. The reader therefore is given the responsibility to unravel the tension among these views and judge the value of the woman's words.[70]

Often overlooked are the variant readings for τὴν σὴν λαλιάν (Jn 4.42): τὴν λαλιάν σου (𝔓[75] B; Or); τὴν σὴν μαρτυρίαν (ℵ D b l r[1]).

---

68. O'Day, *Revelation*, p. 76. Brox (*Zeuge und Märtyrer*, p. 85) also perceives that the woman is unaware of the significance of her testimony.

69. Thus, in my view, J.L. Staley is quite wrong to say that John turns the woman's witness into 'a parody of authentic witness' (J.L. Staley, *The Print's First Kiss: A Rhetorical Investigation of the Implied Reader in the Fourth Gospel* [SBLDS, 82; Atlanta: Scholars Press, 1988], p. 101 n. 34).

70. O'Day, *Revelation*, p. 88.

The reading supported by 𝔓[75] and Codex B could well be the original, as it enjoys the sanction of two superb witnesses and can help to explain the other variants. The accepted reading uses the article before a possessive adjective (rare in John), thus taking the emphasis off of λαλιά and placing it on τὴν σὴν, making the contrast between her speaking and their hearing.[71] The text of Codex ℵ *al.* looks like an attempt to stave off any misperception that the woman's λαλιά is idle chatter; rather, it is μαρτυρία.[72] Any misconstruing of what the woman told the villagers as prattle was most likely to have been built upon the τὴν λαλιάν σου of 𝔓[75] and Codex B, and other MSS appear keen to prevent such a mistaken notion.

If the content of the Samaritan woman's testimony is not suspect, what about the woman herself? Okure writes, 'Because of her sex, nationality and deplorable marital history...the woman represents the lowest grade of humanity'.[73] But Okure also thinks that the story gains persuasive force through the rhetorical device of argument from *imparia* (unlikes); that is, the woman's witness is all the more effective when her background is contrasted with that, say, of Nicodemus.[74] In effect, Okure is arguing that the Samaritan woman's testimony is convincing precisely because she has an abject social status and a reprehensible personal life. But the last thing such a social status and personal life would do is qualify her as a persuasive and trustworthy witness in the eyes of readers holding to the Jewish standards for evidence and qualifications for witnesses. In any event, the notion that the Samaritan woman is a pariah to anyone and everyone is, as I have shown, untenable. That the foundation of the villagers' belief shifts from her witness to Jesus' word 'is scarcely because of an inferiority she might have as a woman—it is the inferiority of any human witness compared to encountering Jesus himself'.[75]

Schneiders remarks, 'In all probability, the scene recounted in John 4 has its real context not in the ministry of the historical Jesus but in the

71. Abbott, *Johannine Grammar*, §1989.

72. Barrett (*John*, p. 243) theorizes that τὴν σὴν μαρτυρίαν in Codex ℵ *al.* may have come about by assimilation from μαρτυρούσης in Jn 4.39. If so, this would lend support to the notion that these MSS are clarifying that her report is testimony not chatter.

73. Okure, *Approach to Mission*, p. 184.

74. Okure, *Approach to Mission*, pp. 112, 126-29.

75. Brown, *Community*, p. 188.

history of the Johannine community'.[76] That John has shaped the story for theological purposes cannot be disputed. But Schneiders cannot offer any proof that the Samaritan episode is not based on an actual event from the ministry of Jesus, and more importantly, the Evangelist gives no hint whatsoever that the story is to be taken otherwise. Given John's rhetorical goal and his emphasis on the truth of the Gospel's testimony, Okure is, in my view, correct to maintain that a 'fictitious account of a faith-response to Jesus by the woman and the Samaritans would hardly persuade the living audience of the Gospel to make a true faith-response to him'.[77]

But as always in John, the focus of the story is Jesus. Just as John shifted the focus from Jesus' mother to his disciples at the Cana wedding, John shifts the focus from the Samaritan woman to the villagers. When John closes the narrative, it is Jesus and the Samaritan villagers who stand at centre stage. Like the mother of Jesus, the Samaritan woman fades into the background, but unlike Jesus' mother, never to reappear. Still, it is an overstatement to say that John has no special interest in the figure of the woman.[78] John allots her far too much time and she plays much too central a part for that to be so.

A Samaritan woman came to draw water. But she did so much more. She encountered at the well a stranger having miraculous knowledge whom she recognized as a prophet and perhaps more than a prophet. On the strength of her testimony, her fellow villagers made their first steps toward what eventually would become their recognition of Jesus as the saviour of the world. To cast the Samaritan woman as Johannine disciple, apostle or missionary is to read a great deal more into her words and deeds than the text can bear. Nevertheless, in contrast to the mother of Jesus in Jn 2.1-11, the Samaritan woman does testify, and is in fact a prominent witness to what she knows. Her testimony, as far as it goes, is true. Samaritan, Jewish or other, it is not difficult to imagine John's readers, like the villagers, accepting her testimony and coming out to meet Jesus for themselves.

---

76. Schneiders, 'Women', p. 39.
77. Okure, *Approach to Mission*, pp. 188-89.
78. As does Bultmann, *John*, p. 193.

Chapter 6

THE SISTERS SENT WORD TO JESUS

'John 11 is not only the highpoint of integration of style, composition, and narrative in the Fourth Gospel, but also of history, theology, and spirituality.'[1] When Jesus calls Lazarus from death to life, John's Gospel reaches a peak and, perhaps, its interpretative centre.[2] The episode crowns Jesus' signs, initiates the transition between his ministry and passion, precipitates the events leading to his trial and death, and prefigures his resurrection. The death and resurrection of Lazarus afford the most graphic expression of John's promise that believers have life. J. Kremer therefore sees the raising of Lazarus as the cardinal sign for fulfilling John's stated purpose, and thus, for understanding the narrative itself: 'Even more than Jesus' other signs, this one should lead to faith in the Son of God (20.30f.), and so the Lazarus episode should be read primarily in light of that.'[3]

1. S.M. Schneiders, 'Death in the Community of Eternal Life: History, Theology, and Spirituality in John 11', *Int* 41 (1987), pp. 45-46. Lindars (*John*, p. 381) thinks that John, in order to impact the readers' emotions, displaced the temple clearing with the Lazarus story in a second edition. For composition and tradition theories, see G. Rochais, *Les récits de résurrection des morts dans le Nouveau Testament* (SNTSMS, 40; Cambridge: Cambridge University Press, 1981), pp. 113-46; J. Kremer, *Lazarus, die Geschichte einer Auferstehung: Text, Wirkungsgeschichte und Botschaft von Joh 11,1-46* (Stuttgart: Katholisches Bibelwerk, 1985), pp. 82-108; A. Marchadour, *Lazare: Histoire d'un récit, récits d'une histoire* (LD, 132; Paris: Cerf, 1988), pp. 33-63; Fortna, *Gospel of Signs*, pp. 74-87, and *Fourth Gospel*, pp. 94-109.

2. It has been suggested that the Lazarus narrative is the centre of a chiasm that envelops the entire Gospel of John. Marchadour (*Lazare*, pp. 94-99) reviews and rejects this theory.

3. Kremer, *Lazarus*, p. 21. On the persuasive intent of the Lazarus story, see W. Wuellner, 'Putting Life Back into the Lazarus Story and its Reading: The Narrative Rhetoric of John 11 as the Narration of Faith', *Semeia* 53 (1991), pp. 113-32.

1. *John 11.1-46: The Exegetical Issues*

a. The information furnished by Jn 11.1-2 raises the possibility that Mary and Martha were known to readers, and therefore, that the sisters might gain credibility as witnesses with readers by virtue of such knowledge.[4] Kremer observes that with the exception of the relationship between Mary and Martha, the opening verses of John 11 offer no other particulars about them in regard to their age, marital status or social rank. Kremer concludes from this that the narrator seems to assume that Mary and Martha are somehow known to the readers.[5] Kremer's conclusion is plausible, particularly because the opening verses of John 11 seem to show that it was Lazarus rather than Mary and Martha who had to be identified for the reader.

Jn 11.1 introduces Lazarus thus: ἦν δέ τις ἀσθενῶν Λάζαρος κτλ. The introductory formula using τις is common enough in John, but would seem to be an odd way to introduce someone familiar to readers. Note the lack of τις in introductions of other people who are named: John the Baptist (ἐγένετο ἄνθρωπος, Jn 1.6), Nicodemus (ἦν δὲ ἄνθρωπος, Jn 3.1), and in 𝔓⁶⁶, Caiaphas (εἷς δὲ ἐξ αὐτῶν, Jn 11.49). Also note the presence of τις in introductions of people not named: the Samaritan woman (ἔρχεταί τις γυνή, Codex ℵ *al.*, Jn 4.7), the royal official (καὶ ἦν τις βασιλικός, Jn 4.46), the sick man (ἦν δέ τις ἄνθρωπος, Jn 5.5) and some Greeks (ἦσαν δὲ Ἕλληνές τινες, Jn 12.20).

4. Out of roughly thirty references to some type of healing in the Gospels and Acts, identification of the subject is comparatively rare: Bartimaeus (Mk 10.46, unnamed in the parallels), Mary Magdalene (Lk. 8.2; cf. Mk 16.9), Aeneas (Acts 9.33), Tabitha (Acts 9.36), Eutychus (Acts 20.9). The subject's relatives are named even less frequently: Simon Peter (Mk 1.30 and pars.), Jairus (Mk 5.22; Lk. 8.41; unnamed in Mt. 9.18). The resurrection of Lazarus is the only New Testament healing story in which both subject and relatives are identified by name. In the other three healing stories in John, such parties remain anonymous: the royal official and his son (John 4), the crippled man at the pool (John 5), the man born blind and his parents (John 9). Jn 18.10-11 identifies the servant whose ear is severed as Malchus but makes no mention of his healing, while Lk. 22.49-51 reports the healing but leaves the servant anonymous.

5. Kremer, *Lazarus*, p. 53. Compare Davies's observation (*Rhetoric and Reference*, p. 334), 'The Evangelist uses these named characters, Martha, Mary, Lazarus, for dramatic effect and as witnesses of Jesus' activity, but shows no other interest in their biography'.

Further, Jn 11.1 speaks of Lazarus from Bethany, 'the village of Mary and her sister Martha', or in the Syriac tradition (*exc.* sy^p) of Lazarus from Bethany, 'the brother of Mary and Martha', both readings apparently assuming that readers are familiar with the sisters but not with Lazarus.

Finally, Jn 11.2 labels Mary as 'the one who anointed the Lord with perfume and wiped his feet with her hair', as if she is known to readers even before the actual anointing is recounted in John 12.[6]

It can be countered in all these cases that the opening verses of John 11 are providing rather than assuming information about the family. But in any event, the final form of John's Gospel is not consistent in regard to the audience's familiarity with people, places, customs and so forth, some of which are elucidated for readers while others are not. Additional credibility as witnesses would accrue to Martha and Mary among readers acquainted with them, but ascertaining the scope of such readership is impossible. While it is probable that many readers knew of the family from Bethany, it is equally probable that many did not, including those distanced by time and space from the events recounted, and especially those outside Christian circles.[7]

b. As with Jesus' mother at Cana, the attempt must be made to understand what the participants in the narrative expect of Jesus. In Martha's case, several verses are involved, but of particular interest here is the remark in which she voices to Jesus her confidence in him (Jn 11.21-22). Is Martha articulating her anticipation that Jesus will revive Lazarus or is she just expressing continuing confidence in Jesus in spite of her perception that Lazarus' death is, until the resurrection at the last day, final (Jn 11.24)?

The text of Jn 11.22 in NA^26 reads: [ἀλλὰ] καὶ νῦν οἶδα ὅτι ὅσα ἂν αἰτήσῃ τὸν θεὸν δώσει σοι ὁ θεός. The strong adversative ἀλλά

---

6. Jn 11.2 is often regarded as a gloss, which could be so, but no extant MSS lack it. If Jn 11.2 is a gloss, perhaps the editor is simply identifying the Mary in Jn 11.1 as the woman known to readers from the anointing tradition.

7. R. Bauckham regards it as 'a good general rule—not without exceptions—that where the early Gospel tradition preserves the names of characters in the Gospel story (other than those of public figures such as Pilate and Caiaphas), these named people were Christians well known in the early church' (R. Bauckham, *Jude and the Relatives of Jesus in the Early Church* [Edinburgh: T. & T. Clark, 1990], p. 9 n. 14). Some exegetes cite Jn 11.2 as evidence that John's target audience was Christian. Carson (*John*, pp. 405-406) offers a rebuttal.

is lacking in several MSS (notably 𝔓[75] ℵ B), and being of questionable authenticity, is bracketed by NA[26]. The text of 𝔓[75] ℵ B *al.* is to be preferred (so NA[25]) because of their quality, and because that reading helps to explain ἀλλά as an interpolation aimed at clarifying καὶ νῦν, the meaning of which is equivocal, as Abbott explains.

> There is ambiguity in xi.22 'If thou hadst been here my brother had not died; *and now* (καὶ νῦν) [?in spite of his death] I know that whatsoever thou shalt ask of God, God will give thee.' In classical Gk καὶ νῦν would naturally mean '*even* now': but it could hardly be used in this sense at the beginning of a sentence; because in that position, καὶ would naturally be taken as '*and*.' The question is complicated by the use of καὶ νῦν in LXX, where νῦν represents more than a dozen Heb. words.[8]

After sifting through the usages of καὶ νῦν in classical Greek and the LXX in comparison with those of John, 1 John and the remainder of the New Testament, Abbott opts for a Hebraic reading, interpreting Martha's words in Jn 11.21-22 this way.

> Lord, if thou hadst been here, my brother had not died. [But it pleased thee to be absent although we sent unto thee.] *And now* [Lord, what am I to say? *My hope is still in thee.*] I know that whatsoever thou shalt ask God, God will give it to thee.[9]

Abbott is well aware that 'καὶ νῦν, especially in an author like John, prone to transposition and asyndeton, will depend, for its meaning, on its context'.[10] Thus, the question of Martha's expectations must wait to be addressed within the fuller contexts of the pericope and entire Gospel. For now, it may be said that the reading of 𝔓[75] ℵ B *al.* is probably the original and that it portrays Martha's words as a vaguely expressed but confident expectation of help from Jesus, while the insertion of ἀλλά by other MSS might lend support to the idea that her words intimate that Jesus can revive Lazarus (compare the words of Jesus' mother in Jn 2.3).

c. Unmentioned in the commentaries and monographs is the variant reading of 𝔓[66] at Jn 11.27. The text of Jn 11.27 in NA[26] reads: λέγει αὐτῷ· ναὶ κύριε, ἐγὼ πεπίστευκα ὅτι κτλ, whereas 𝔓[66] reads: λέγει αὐτῷ· ναὶ κύριε, πιστεύω, ἐγὼ πεπίστευκα ὅτι κτλ. Although 𝔓[66] is alone in this reading, the age and quality of its witness

---

8.   Abbott, *Johannine Vocabulary*, §1719(e).
9.   Abbott, *Johannine Grammar*, §1915(v).
10. Abbott, *Johannine Grammar*, §1915(iii).

require that this variant receive attention. Also, the reading of 𝔓⁶⁶ might shed light on the interpretation of the text as NA²⁶ has it.

The question involves the content of Martha's faith confession.[11] Is Martha concurring with Jesus' claim and question in Jn 11.25-26 and then demonstrating that she truly understands what he has said? Or, is she stating her understanding of Jesus' identity, inattentive, in a sense, to his self-declaration? The difference is subtle but important, because Martha's confession is the most comprehensive in John's Gospel and most closely resembles that faith which John covets for readers (Jn 20.31).

At issue is not simply the range of Martha's titles for Jesus but the depth of her understanding of who he really is. For example, Nicodemus can call Jesus 'a teacher come from God' (Jn 3.2) without really understanding him (as the ensuing dialogue shows). In 𝔓⁶⁶ (ναὶ κύριε, πιστεύω, ἐγὼ πεπίστευκα ὅτι κτλ), the πιστεύω absolute finds its content most naturally in Jesus' self-proclamation in Jn 11.25-26 and thus would give Martha's words in Jn 11.27 the sense, 'Yes, Lord, I believe what you have just said about yourself, I have come to believe that you are...' (compare Jn 9.35-38, where the content of the πιστεύω absolute used by the man cured of blindness is clearly Jesus' claim to be the Son of Man). This interpretation suggests that Martha's confession is not an unwittingly compiled roster of titles for Jesus, but rather, a thoughtful expression of her understanding of his identity that is mindful of what he has just told her about himself.

d. I stated previously that because the phrase ἔρχομαι πρός can be a synonym for πιστεύω in John's Gospel, its use in Jn 4.30 is noteworthy. When the Samaritan villagers who are making their way to Jesus are said to be 'coming to him' (ἤρχοντο πρὸς αὐτόν), this use of the imperfect tense of ἔρχομαι perhaps underlines that their faith is in process. Similarly, Jn 11.29 recounts that Mary, after learning that Jesus is present and calling for her, arose and 'was coming to him' (ἤρχετο πρὸς αὐτόν). Is this phrase meant to symbolize that Mary is in the process of coming to faith to Jesus?

11. Previously, I mentioned Johannine πιστεύω formulas. Of the several used, the πιστεύω absolute is by nature the most nebulous. Whereas other πιστεύω constructions are clarified by objects, phrases and clauses, the πιστεύω absolute relies entirely on its larger context for clarification, including whether a particular usage indicates authentic or superficial faith.

Some MSS (notably 𝔓⁴⁵·⁶⁶) use present tenses to describe how Mary gets up and comes to Jesus (ἐγείρεται ταχὺ καὶ ἔρχεται πρὸς αὐτόν). Morris suggests that these present tenses could be original, and that past tenses (ἠγέρθη and ἤρχετο) might have been substituted for them in order to take into account the preceding ἤκουσεν.[12] If Morris is correct, then ἐγείρεται and ἔρχεται should be read in the Johannine 'historical present', producing the translation, 'She arose quickly and came to him', and thus attenuating any symbolic force of Mary being in the process of coming to faith in Jesus.

As with Jn 4.30, too much symbolism should not be heaped upon the imperfect of ἔρχομαι, especially here, where the narrative chronology requires that Mary be in the process of making her way toward Jesus. In any event, whether Mary 'came' or 'was coming' to Jesus, an attempt to gauge her faith from this one verb and verse is bound to fail because Mary's thoughts and hopes are not spelled out.

e. Typically of John's Gospel, the response to the revelation of Jesus' identity is integral to the Lazarus story: people believe or disbelieve. John 11.45-46 recounts that many of the Jews who had come to Mary believed in Jesus and that some of them informed the Pharisees of what Jesus had done. Textual variants complicate the verses, prompting two questions. First, are the informers some of those who witness Lazarus' resurrection, or are they some other group that had not witnessed Lazarus' resurrection personally? Secondly, did these people respond just to the raising of Lazarus, or to several things that Jesus did? Such questions must be addressed because along with Martha and Mary, these people are the significant witnesses.

Did the entire group or just part of the group that had come to Mary see what Jesus did and believe in him? At Jn 11.45, Codex D attempts to clarify the matter by reading τῶν ἐλθόντων, which agrees with τῶν Ἰουδαίων rather than οἱ ἐλθόντες, which agrees with πολλοί. Codex D thus gives the sense, 'Some people, a large number of them out of that group of Jews who had come to Mary, saw what he did and believed in him', in contrast to, 'A large number of people, namely, that entire group of Jews who had come to Mary, saw what he did and believed in him'.[13] This distinction depends upon the assumption of

---

12. Morris, *John*, p. 553 n. 60.

13. Bernard (*John*, II, pp. 401-402) and Marsh prefer this latter sense, seeing just one group of Jews that came to Mary, saw what Jesus did, and believed in him

strict agreement between participle and antecedent, which may be too demanding of John's Greek.[14] The larger context favours the interpretation advanced by Codex D. The τινὲς δὲ ἐξ αὐτῶν who inform the Pharisees (Jn 11.46) must be from the group that saw what Jesus did, for as is typical in John, the raising of Lazarus results in those who see the sign and those who see only the miracle; it exposes those with vision and those with blindness, belief and unbelief: 'The effect of the miracle is to divide the beholders into two groups.'[15]

In Jn 11.45, did those who believed in Jesus see one thing which he did (ὃ ἐποίησεν, 𝔓[66*] A[c] B *al.* [so NA[25]]) or more than one thing (ἃ ἐποίησεν, 𝔓[6.45] ℵ A *al.* [so NA[26]])? Likewise, in Jn 11.46, did those who go to the Pharisees report one thing that Jesus did (ὃ ἐποίησεν, C D *pc* it) or more than one thing (ἃ ἐποίησεν, *plur.*)?[16] Textual evidence for the plural in Jn 11.46 is overwhelming and may explain the presence of the plural in Jn 11.45, where the textual evidence is good for both the singular and the plural. In any event, too much cannot be made of the singular versus the plural usage of the relative pronoun here. When no immediate referent is supplied, it is not always apparent whether a given relative pronoun in the neuter singular used with ποιέω refers to one thing, more than one thing, or several things collectively (for example, Jn 2.5; 14.13; cf. 15.7, 16). And often, some MSS have the plural where others have the singular (for example, Jn 6.14; 8.38; 15.14; cf. 17.24, where many good MSS employ ὅ as the antecedent to κἀκεῖνοι).

The foregoing evidence yields the following interpretation. Many Jews

(J. Marsh, *The Gospel of St John* [Philadelphia: Westminster Press, 1968], pp. 440-42). Bernard therefore must suppose that those who informed the Pharisees did so without wanting to get Jesus into trouble, while Marsh must assume the existence of a second group which, having heard about but not having witnessed the miracle, reported Jesus to the authorities.

14. So Brown, *John*, I, p. 438. Barrett (*John*, p. 404) maintains that the verse shows not a loose grammatical construction but a Johannine idiom in which a sweeping statement is immediately qualified. The issue is also clouded by Jn 11.45 speaking of those who had come to Mary (with no mention of Martha). This possibly is evidence that the Martha material is a later addition, but at face value it refers to those who came from the house to Mary at the tomb (Jn 11.31) versus from Jerusalem to Martha and Mary at Bethany (Jn 11.19). Thus, the NRSV translates Jn 11.45, 'Many of the Jews therefore, who had come with Mary and had seen what Jesus did, believed in him'.

15. Barrett, *John*, p. 405.

16. A few MSS variously offer ὅσα in both places.

came from Jerusalem to Bethany to console Martha and Mary. When Mary left the house, they followed her to Jesus and to the tomb, where they witnessed him call Lazarus back to life. Many of those who had come to the tomb believed in Jesus when they saw what he did with Lazarus, while others of them who saw what Jesus did with Lazarus disbelieved and reported him to the Pharisees.[17]

A summary of the pertinent exegetical issues yields: (a) Martha and Mary would have gained credibility as witnesses in the eyes of readers familiar with them, but it is impossible to know how many, if any, of the readers were in that position; (b) Martha's expectations in Jn 11.21-22 are hopeful and confident but vague, and certain MSS interpolate ἀλλά to clarify that Martha intimates a belief that Jesus is able to revive Lazarus; (c) Martha's confession in Jn 11.27 is not unmindful of, but rather, builds upon the self-declaration of Jesus in Jn 11.25-26, and $\mathfrak{P}^{66}$ emphasizes this by way of Martha's clear affirmation, πιστεύω, to Jesus' question in Jn 11.26; (d) Mary's physical journey from house to tomb might carry muted symbolic overtones of a faith journey as well, but the textual and grammatical bases for this notion are not firm, and the text makes no mention of her thoughts and hopes as she comes to Jesus; (e) a group of Jews followed Mary from the house to Jesus and to the tomb, where they witnessed his revival of Lazarus, with the result that many of them believed in Jesus while others of them told the Pharisees what he had done.

2. *John 6.1-70: An Interpretative Frame*

Peter's climactic confession of Jesus in the Synoptics (Mk 8.29 and pars.) invites a comparison with that of Martha in John's Gospel (Jn 11.27). That comparison has its proper place but will not be undertaken here, as no assumption is made of Johannine dependence upon the Synoptics or even that John and his readers necessarily knew of them. However, within the boundaries of the John's Gospel itself, Martha's confession of Jesus, uttered at a critical juncture, urges a comparison with that of Peter in Jn 6.69.[18]

17. Morris (*John*, p. 563 n. 89.) perceives that it was the singular event of raising Lazarus that evoked the crowd's belief in Jesus, but he suggests that when some of them reported Jesus to the Pharisees, they may have spoken of other things Jesus had done.

18. The theory that John replaces Peter's Synoptic confession with that of Martha

Within John's literary structure, Martha's confession appears to occupy higher ground than Peter's because it takes place at a climax in Jesus' ministry and within the singularly astonishing event of the raising of Lazarus. However, if the feeding of the multitude is seen as the central episode in a Johannine signs chiasm, then it is the confession of Peter that occupies that higher ground.[19]

The confessions of Peter and Martha occur in settings generally similar in content and pattern. Both contexts include a miraculous sign and an explanatory discourse revealing Jesus as the one who brings life (compare the ἐγώ εἰμι sayings in Jn 6.35; 11.25). The feeding of the five thousand is followed, after the journey to Capernaum, by the discourse on the bread of life, while the discourse on the resurrection and the life is interwoven with the actual events of Lazarus' illness, death and revival. In both instances the miraculous sign is the centre of discussion and division among the participants in terms of knowing and believing in Jesus.

The broad contours of the two stories align as follows.

	Peter		Martha
6.1-4	Description of need	11.1-3	Description of need
6.5-9	Discussion	11.4-16	Discussion
6.10-13	Miracle		
6.14-15	Reaction and response		
6.16-24	Travel interlude	11.17-19	Travel interlude
6.25-59	Discussion and Jesus' self-declaration	11.20-26a	Discussion and Jesus' self-declaration
6.60-66	Division over Jesus		
6.67	Jesus questions the Twelve	11.26b	Jesus questions Martha
6.68-69	Peter confesses	11.27	Martha confesses
6.70	Jesus responds		
		11.28-44	Miracle
		11.45-46	Division over Jesus

In both stories Jesus is in control of the situation throughout, knowing what he intends to do and using the need that has arisen as a vehicle of revelation. In the feeding miracle Jesus' disciples are prominent at the

---

makes assumptions about John's dependence on Synoptic traditions for which there is no hard evidence. Scott (*Sophia*, pp. 202-203) argues such a theory, and I find it curious that in making his argument Scott charts Martha's confession against that of Peter in Mk 8.29 and pars. but not against Peter's confession in Jn 6.69.

19. For this chiasm theory, see M. Girard, 'La composition structurelle des sept signes dans le quatrième évangile', *SR* 9 (1980), pp. 315-24.

outset, give way to the crowds and then regain the focal point at the end. In the resurrection miracle Jesus' disciples are in focus at first, then Martha and Mary, and finally, the Jewish onlookers at the close of the pericope.

The major non-alignment between the two stories is that Peter confesses after the miracle and Martha before it. Some commentators place great import upon the fact that Martha confesses before the miracle occurs (an issue that will need to be addressed later). However, it may be said at this point that Martha did not confess Jesus without prior knowledge of, or belief in, his miraculous abilities. At the very least, Martha (and Mary) believed that Jesus had the power to heal the sick, as Jn 11.3 implies and her words in Jn 11.21 confirm: 'Lord, if you had been here, my brother would not have died' (cf. Jn 11.32).

The focus here will be on the confessions of Peter (P) and Martha (M), which align as follows.

P: κύριε, πρὸς τίνα ἀπελευσόμεθα; ῥήματα ζωῆς αἰωνίου ἔχεις,			
M: κύριε, [πιστεύω] (𝔓⁶⁶)			
P: ἡμεῖς πεπιστεύκαμεν καὶ ἐγνώκαμεν		ὅτι	σὺ εἶ
M: ἐγὼ πεπίστευκα		ὅτι	σὺ εἶ
P:	ὁ ἅγιος	τοῦ θεοῦ.	
M: ὁ χριστὸς ὁ υἱὸς		τοῦ θεοῦ ὁ εἰς τὸν κόσμον ἐρχόμενος.	

a. Peter and Martha both address Jesus, κύριε. Whether translated as 'Sir' or 'Lord', κύριε is a form of address here, and not a part of the confessional formula that follows.

b. The reading of 𝔓⁶⁶ (ναὶ κύριε, πιστεύω, ἐγὼ πεπίστευκα κτλ) I have already discussed, and it is reproduced in the diagram in brackets to remind the reader of its presence. But it may be added that Martha's affirmation, ναί (not given in the comparison), reinforces the idea that her confession is attentive to Jesus' self-declaration in Jn 11.25-26. The words of Peter that immediately precede the substance of his confession are important. 'To whom can we go?' Peter asks Jesus. Whereas the teaching of Jesus has scandalized and repelled others, Peter remains with him (Jn 6.60-68). Peter then says to Jesus, 'You have the words of eternal life', concurring with Jesus' own assessment of his teaching in the preceding discourse: 'The words that I have spoken to you are spirit and life' (Jn 6.63).

c. Both confessions have emphatic personal pronouns, ἡμεῖς and ἐγώ. Thus, the speakers stress their ownership of their confessions. Jesus queries the Twelve, εἶπεν οὖν ὁ Ἰησοῦς τοῖς δώδεκα· μὴ καὶ ὑμεῖς θέλετε ὑπάγειν; (Jn 6.67), and Peter answers on their behalf. Peter expresses faith in Jesus in the name of Twelve, although he is wrong in the case of Judas Iscariot, as Jesus and the narrator hasten to point out (Jn 6.70-71). Peter perhaps is mistaken in projecting his faith onto the Twelve, and if so, his confession should be read as his and his alone. But in any case, on this urgent occasion Peter acts as the spokesperson for the Twelve whom Jesus selected from among the larger circle of disciples.

Jesus queries Martha as an individual: εἶπεν αὐτῇ ὁ Ἰησοῦς... πιστεύεις τοῦτο; (Jn 11.25-26), and she responds as such. If Peter speaks for the Twelve, then perhaps it could be argued, 'Martha appears in this scene as the representative of the believing community responding to the word of Jesus with a full confession of Christian faith. It is a role analogous to Peter's as representative of apostolic faith in Matthew's Gospel.'[20] But since the text of Martha's confession, unlike Peter's, contains nothing to suggest that she is speaking for anyone but herself, this type of argument must rely upon assumptions such as John placing the confession on Martha's lips, or John replacing the Petrine confession of the Synoptics with that of Martha, or John's Gospel reflecting the life of the Johannine church rather than the life of Jesus. Those holding such conjectures take for granted that John's Gospel is unreliable as history and that the Synoptic Gospels form a historical canon for John, but they can offer no evidence that John's ancient audience held such assumptions. If John had felt free to take liberties with the wording of confessions and the identities of their speakers, and if he had intended Martha to speak as the representative of some larger group, why then did he leave her confession, unlike Peter's, in the first person singular? Martha's confession is in no way linked with any of the others present at the raising of Lazarus, neither the disciples, nor Mary, nor the Jews. As far as the narrator is concerned, Martha's confession is hers and hers alone.[21]

20. Schneiders, 'Women', p. 41. Compare the remark of Schüssler Fiorenza (*Memory of Her*, p. 329), 'As a "beloved disciple" of Jesus [Martha] is the spokeswoman for the messianic faith of the community', and that of Scott (*Sophia*, p. 203), 'Martha is not to be accorded a special place of prominence in the community on account of her confession any more than Peter should be, but she *is* representative of the confessing believer within that community'.

21. Schnackenburg (*John*, II, p. 329) rightly insists that the exchanges between

d. Both confessions use the perfect tense, πεπιστεύκαμεν καὶ ἐγνώκαμεν and πεπίστευκα. Commentators note that the perfect tense of πιστεύω indicates a faith which, so to speak, has arrived rather than is in progress. Abbott believes that the most interesting uses of this 'perfect of permanence' in John are to be found with πιστεύω (and ἐλπίζω), expressing '*perfect* conviction'.[22] Nevertheless, that Peter's belief was less than perfect is evidenced by his failure to remain faithful when tested (Jn 18.15-18, 25-27), and that his knowledge (ἐγνώκαμεν) also was imperfect is displayed by his lack of understanding of Jesus' deeds and words (Jn 13.6-11; 18.10-11, 36; 21.20-23).[23]

Martha's faith is tested not, as was Peter's, in the courtyard of the high priest but at the tomb of Lazarus. Martha tells Jesus of her faith in the future resurrection, responding to what may have sounded to her like words of comfort typical of beliefs held by many Jews in first-century Palestine (Jn 11.23-24). When Jesus then challenges her to believe that the future resurrection is present even now in him, Martha responds with a profession of faith in what Jesus has said and who he is (Jn 11.25-27). And yet, almost in the next breath Martha exposes not false sincerity but real doubt. She balks at Jesus' order to remove the stone from Lazarus' tomb, sure that his body has begun to decompose (Jn 11.39). Whatever belief Martha may have arrived at with πεπίστευκα seems either to have evaporated quickly or never to have been as firm as she thought it to be.[24]

In neither case, Peter's nor Martha's, is the sincerity of the confession questioned. Rather, although they had not attained a perfected state of faith in Christ, they may have 'believed perfectly' that Jesus had come from God.[25] Indeed, all disciples know the experience of sincerely believing in Christ and ostensibly understanding him, only to find their faith

---

Jesus and Martha must be interpreted in terms of John's intention as narrator.

22. Abbott, *Johannine Grammar*, §§2474-75.

23. The correlation between faith and knowledge in John's Gospel admits no unqualified generalizations except that the two, while distinct, complete one another and are somewhat synonymous (see Gaffney, 'Believing and Knowing'; Kysar, *Maverick Gospel*, pp. 77-79; Brown, *John*, I, pp. 512-15; Bultmann, *John*, p. 435 n. 4; Schnackenburg, *John*, I, pp. 565-66). However, by appearing in Peter's confession together, πιστεύω and γινώσκω clearly emphasize his conviction.

24. That Jn 11.39 exposes disbelief or misunderstanding in Martha can be disputed. The expectations of Martha and the others will be explored more fully, but for now, I assume that some level of doubt in Martha is shown by Jn 11.39.

25. Abbott, *Johannine Grammar*, §2475.

and knowledge wanting—an experience from which Peter and Martha are not exempt. Painter observes,

> Authentic faith was not a reality during Jesus' ministry, but the Gospel was written for a new situation when such faith had become possible. Descriptions of those who came to partial faith during Jesus' ministry have become examples of the possibility of coming to authentic faith. Thus there is no difference in terminology in the narrative descriptions of partial faith and the descriptions of authentic faith that Jesus uses in his discourses.[26]

e. In both confessions the construction that expresses belief is πιστεύω ὅτι, indicating what the speaker believes about Jesus, the object and content of faith. It is striking that in all the cases where Jesus uses this construction, there is never a title involved, such as those used by Peter and Martha. Rather, Jesus wants people to recognize not messianic titles but his identity with God (Jn 8.24; 13.19), his relationship with the Father (Jn 10.38; 14.10, 11) and his origins in the Father (Jn 11.42; 16.27, 28; 17.8, 21). In fact, it is to convince people that God sent him that Jesus revives Lazarus: ἵνα πιστεύσωσιν ὅτι σύ με ἀπέστειλας (Jn 11.42). Referring to the πιστεύω ὅτι construction, Painter remarks, 'The Gospel paradoxically shows that confessions of faith made in these terms by individuals...were not authentic at the time of making', and Painter puts the confessions of Peter and Martha in that category.[27] If by 'not authentic' Painter means something like 'incomplete' or 'imperfect', then his assessment is correct. Nonetheless, the confessions of both Peter and Martha, as far as they go, are accurate and sincere, even if the confessors themselves are imperfect in faith, knowledge and discipleship.

f. Peter and Martha preface their title(s) for Jesus with σὺ εἶ. Bultmann perceives a correlation between this use of σὺ εἶ and Jesus' use of ἐγώ εἰμι: 'Also in this formulation the character of the confession as answer is preserved: the σὺ εἶ corresponds to the ἐγώ εἰμι, which, whether expressed or unexpressed, sounds through all the sayings of Jesus.'[28] But the correspondence between σὺ εἶ and ἐγώ εἰμι perhaps cannot be pushed as far as Bultmann would like. Although Jesus does make several formal declarations about himself using ἐγώ εἰμι, with only one

26. Painter, *Quest*, p. 332.
27. Painter, *Quest*, p. 331.
28. Bultmann, *John*, pp. 448-49.

exception εἶ is never used apart from σύ in John, whether referring to John the Baptist, Simon Peter, Jesus, Nicodemus or the man born blind.[29] This routine pattern of usage makes it difficult to establish σὺ εἶ, even when applied to Jesus in a confession, as a formula corresponding to Jesus' use of ἐγώ εἰμι.

g. The title(s) for Jesus arrive in the final words of the confessions of Peter (ὁ ἅγιος τοῦ θεοῦ) and Martha (ὁ χριστὸς ὁ υἱὸς τοῦ θεοῦ ὁ εἰς τὸν κόσμον ἐρχόμενος). Neufeld assesses the title ὁ ἅγιος τοῦ θεοῦ used by Peter.

> This is to be taken as a messianic title comparable to, and practically syn-onymous with, ὁ χριστός and ὁ υἱὸς τοῦ θεοῦ, because of its inherent meaning and because of the parallels found in the synoptic gospels. The title is almost without precedent in the Old Testament and is used of Jesus only sparingly in the New Testament. Though the title never attained gen-eral currency in the early church, here it seems clearly to indicate the Holy One promised by God, namely his Son, the Messiah.[30]

Neufeld appraises the Christological titles found in John's Gospel as 'commentaries on the basic Christian *homologia*, Ἰησοῦς ἐστιν ὁ χριστός'.[31] Neufeld also interprets the title in Peter's Johannine confes-sion against the Synoptics and, in so doing, bypasses the genuine insight Peter has within the Johannine context. Bultmann, on the other hand, closely attends to the Johannine context of Peter's confession, emphasiz-ing how the title ὁ ἅγιος τοῦ θεοῦ recognizes that Jesus is the only one who comes from the world beyond and belongs to God, that he repre-sents God in this world as the revealer with the power to judge and to give life, and that he is the one who has consecrated himself as a sacrifice for the world.[32]

It must be seen that Peter's Johannine confession of Jesus shows true discernment of his identity, because it is often argued that his confession

29. The sole exception among the twenty-six occurrences is Jn 19.12, where the Jews say to Pilate: οὐκ εἶ φίλος τοῦ Καίσαρος. Also, many MSS lack σύ at Jn 1.22, but it is present in 𝔓[66c.75].

30. Neufeld, *Christian Confessions*, pp. 77-78. Neufeld (p. 116 n. 1) also states, 'The single occurrence of ὁ ἅγιος τοῦ θεοῦ... may be considered as mes-sianic, although the title in its background cannot be shown to have been so'. Compare Bultmann's opinion (*John*, p. 449) that Peter's title for Jesus is a 'designation which has no recognisable tradition at all as a messianic title'.

31. Neufeld, *Christian Confessions*, p. 79.

32. Bultmann, *John*, pp. 449-50.

is inferior to that of Martha. For example, Schneiders states that by the measure of Jn 20.31, Martha's confession 'is the saving confession of faith, i.e., that Jesus is the Christ, the Son of God, the one coming into the world. (In contrast, Simon Peter's confession in John's Gospel...of Jesus as "the holy one of God" lacks the fullness of Johannine faith).'[33] But the fullness of Johannine faith does not reside in multiplicity or quality of titles alone. It is one thing to acknowledge that Jesus is the Christ, but it is another to perceive how Jesus is the Christ. F.J. Moloney notes that the three phrases of Martha's confession are 'well-worn first-century Jewish expressions', and that Martha's confession is therefore 'not necessarily a full and correct Johannine confession of faith'.[34] That Peter does not call Jesus 'the Christ' in this instance means little. He knows that Jesus is the Christ, for so he was first introduced (Jn 1.41). If anything, the title that Peter uses, 'the Holy One of God', shows a deeper understanding of Jesus' messianic identity as the unique one sent from and consecrated by God (Jn 1.14, 18; 3.16, 18; 10.36; 17.19), thus making it anomalous to contend that Peter's statement of faith is inadequate in Johannine terms.

Neufeld assesses Johannine confessions that use the titles 'Christ' and 'Son of God', of which Martha's is one.

> In the context of the Johannine literature, the *homologia*, 'Jesus is the Christ, the Son of God', frequently bears the characteristics of a Christological formula which was basic in the theology of the church. It appears to be the epitome of correct belief to which every true Christian subscribed, and as such it stands at the beginning of the history of the later established creeds. The function of the *homologia* is suggested by John's use of πιστεύειν with the formula: πιστεύειν ὅτι Ἰησοῦς ἐστιν ὁ χριστὸς ὁ υἱὸς τοῦ θεοῦ.[35]

---

33. Schneiders, 'Women', p. 41. Similarly, Schüssler Fiorenza (*Memory of Her*, p. 329) says that Martha's 'confession parallels that of Peter... but is a Christological confession in the fuller Johannine messianic sense: Jesus is the revealer who has come down from heaven'. Several MSS seem to manifest the belief that Peter's Johannine confession lacked fullness. The variant readings for 'the Holy One of God' at Jn 6.69 include 'the Christ', 'the Christ the Son of God', and 'the Christ the Son of the Living God'.

34. F.J. Moloney, *Woman: First among the Faithful* (London: Darton, Longman & Todd, 1985), p. 79. Notice also that Martha immediately reverts to the more mundane title διδάσκαλος (Jn 11.28).

35. Neufeld, *Christian Confessions*, p. 98.

By any standard, Martha's confession is robust, not only matching the formula used in John's purpose statement (Jn 20.31), but adding the significant clause ὁ εἰς τὸν κόσμον ἐρχόμενος. It could be argued that this addition manifests a lack of understanding because the unperceptive crowd (Jn 6.26), after being miraculously fed, says of Jesus, οὗτός ἐστιν ἀληθῶς ὁ προφήτης ὁ ἐρχόμενος εἰς τὸν κόσμον (Jn 6.14).[36] Martha, however, does not call Jesus, as the one who comes into the world, the prophet, but the Christ, the Son of God. The difference is substantial in that although Jesus nowhere rejects the appellation προφήτης (see Jn 4.44), a firm distinction is drawn between the prophet and the Christ (Jn 1.25; 7.40-41), and, in that προφήτης is an insufficient title for a true estimation of Jesus' deepest identity (Jn 4.19; 7.52; 9.17; cf. 9.35-38). Martha's phrase, ὁ εἰς τὸν κόσμον ἐρχόμενος, added to the titles Christ and Son of God, acts to define and interpret them in a way commensurate with Jesus' self-definition as the one who comes into the world sent from God (Jn 12.46; 16.28; 17.18; 18.37).

Peter's confession lacks manifold titles but has the double assuredness of belief with knowledge, as well as a prominent place at the story's climax. Martha's confession lacks knowledge to complete belief but displays the fullest complement of titles in any Johannine confession, equalling if not surpassing the belief that John covets for readers (Jn 20.31). And so ultimately, the confessions of Peter and Martha can be compared but not made to compete, because the faith expressed in all confessions and by all confessors during Jesus' ministry is inchoate.[37]

If a superlative confession exists in John's Gospel, it has to be that of Thomas who says of Jesus, 'My Lord and my God' (Jn 20.28). But Thomas confesses a risen Jesus and has the advantage of a post-resurrection viewpoint that neither Peter nor Martha enjoyed when they confessed Jesus: 'Faith expressed in the context of Jesus' ministry can only be understood as partial faith. It expresses the attraction of people to Jesus as a miracle worker, teacher, prophet, or Messiah.'[38] True belief

---

36. Notice that the Samaritan woman calls Jesus a prophet and speaks of the coming of the messiah (Jn 4.19, 25). Purvis ('Fourth Gospel', p. 197) maintains that Martha's confession of faith has a messianic view that bears little resemblance to traditional Jewish messianism.

37. Witherington (*Women*, p. 108) sees Martha's confession as the 'least inadequate' to this point in John's narrative. Witherington makes the mistake of ranking the confessions but rightly perceives that all are less than perfect.

38. Painter, *Quest*, p. 343.

involves not only perception, recognition and understanding, but decision, dependence and obedience—things that no one achieves during Jesus' ministry.[39] For John, evidence of true faith and discipleship is supplied not by verb tenses of believing and knowing, or by quality and number of titles for Jesus, but by remaining in his word. This very point is made when the faith of some Jews is exposed by Jesus as ephemeral (Jn 8.45-46) because his word finds no abiding place in them (Jn 8.37), even though John had described them as having come to believe in Jesus (Jn 8.31, note the perfect participle: πρὸς τοὺς πεπιστευκότας αὐτῷ Ἰουδαίους).

The comparison of the confessions of Peter and Martha shows, as would be expected, similarities and differences. Both address Jesus with κύριε, begin with an emphatic personal pronoun (ἡμεῖς/ἐγώ), use πιστεύω in the perfect tense (πεπιστεύκαμεν/πεπίστευκα) plus a ὅτι construction with σὺ εἶ followed by the title(s) (ὁ ἅγιος τοῦ θεοῦ/ὁ χριστὸς ὁ υἱὸς τοῦ θεοῦ ὁ εἰς τὸν κόσμον ἐρχόμενος). As to content, the main difference between the two confessions is that Peter adds knowledge to belief while Martha uses multiple titles for Jesus. Peter and Martha respond as individuals to what Jesus has told them, and neither is parroting his words.

Bultmann states of Peter's confession, 'The *newness* which is proper to every authentic confession is consciously given expression, since the saying of Peter attributes to Jesus a title which has played no role in his own sayings'.[40] Bultmann's observation can be extended to Martha, as her confession says yes to what Jesus has told her and then goes on to make a threefold expression using titles that played no role in his teaching to her. In comparing the confessions of Peter and Martha, what becomes clear is not that one confession is superior to the other, but that their faith statements have similarities and differences that make each one genuine and unique.

3. *Martha and Mary as Witnesses*

The miracle of Lazarus' death and resurrection lies at the heart of the pericope. But while it is Lazarus who undergoes the stupendous experience, he is not the central figure in this episode. That honour, as always, belongs to Jesus. Martha, Mary and those from Jerusalem also eclipse

39. Painter, *Quest*, p. 332.
40. Bultmann, *John*, p. 449.

Lazarus, at least as witnesses, because Lazarus never speaks much less
testifies. Once again in regard to the witnesses, it is necessary to ascer-
tain as closely as possible the level and content of their belief and
testimony.

B. McNeil thinks that the historical question of Lazarus' death and
resurrection is peripheral, even irrelevant.

> The penetrating force and the depth of the insight of this pericope are
> affected in no way by the question of whether the matters it relates are
> 'historical'... The Evangelist employs the language of pictures, and if we
> read his work according to the language of factual reportage, how can we
> hope to grasp his true meaning or intention? No, Jesus is still the resur-
> rection and the life, quite irrespective of whether he brought a particular
> man named Lazarus back from the grave.[41]

McNeil is correct that Jesus' status as the resurrection and the life
does not depend upon the miracle, but wrong that the historicity of the
miracle is of no consequence. It is precisely through the reality of
Lazarus' death and revival that John intends to persuade readers that
Jesus is the resurrection and the life: 'The factuality of the miracles in
John's Gospel is as strongly emphasized as it is because the evangelist is
anxious to show that Christ really is what the deeds of Jesus, as signs,
affirm him to be.'[42] Of course, ancient readers were, and modern readers are, free to think of the miracle as symbolic fiction, and certainly
John shapes the narrative to suit his purposes. But the text itself, even
with its rich symbolism, gives no indication that the death and resurrection of Lazarus are meant to be read simply as myth or allegory. The literary genre of the pericope is neither fable nor parable, and John no
more intends the raising of Lazarus to be read as fiction than he does
the resurrection of Jesus. J.P. Martin writes,

> So strongly does John draw out this 'dependence' of the raising upon
> Jesus' Resurrection that we are forced to conclude that the question, Did
> Lazarus really rise?, is answered by him by affirming the Resurrection of
> Jesus. Modern questions about the historicity of the raising would appear
> misleading to the mind of the author of the Fourth Gospel. It would be
> putting the cart before the horse. *For him it is more important* to know that

41. B. McNeil, 'The Raising of Lazarus', *DRev* 17 (1964), pp. 274-75. Similarly, Kremer (*Lazarus*, p. 35) contends that through its 'Fiktionalität', Jn 11.1-46
clearly differentiates itself from a 'protokollarischen Bericht'.

42. E. Lohse, 'Miracles in the Fourth Gospel', in M. Hooker and C. Hickling
(eds.), *What About the New Testament?* (London: SCM Press, 1975), p. 71.

believers will rise at the Last Day; *consequently*, it is important to know
that Jesus raised Lazarus from the grave during His ministry.[43]

A related argument against the relevance of the historicity question is
that the Lazarus story is John's way of dealing with problems that are
perplexing the Johannine community, specifically, the deaths of believers
in light of Jesus' delayed parousia. Schneiders, for example, maintains
that John is addressing the harsh reality of human death and thus the
question of how the death of believers is to be understood and faced.[44]
Certainly Schneiders is correct. But this makes the historical question
essential rather than irrelevant. What hope, comfort and meaning do a
fictional believer, death and resurrection hold for real believers facing
real death?

The magnitude of the miracles escalates in John, and at the close of
John 9 there would seem to be no room for further crescendo.
Restoring sight to a person born blind is unheard of (Jn 9.32). Yet not
long after, Jesus restores life to a person once dead. The matter of
miracle, first introduced by the change of water to wine at Cana,
becomes acute by the change of death to life at Bethany and sets that
latter event in a class of its own. The pattern by which John confirms
and enhances the fact of the miracles likewise peaks in the raising of
Lazarus. John takes extraordinary pains to stress that Lazarus had not
just fallen asleep or into a swoon. Lazarus truly had died. In forty-four
verses are some nine direct references to the fact of Lazarus' death
(Jn 11.13, 14, 17, 19, 21, 32, 37, 39, 44) as well as four (or five) indirect
ones (Jn 11.31, 34, 38, 41).[45] And these references stem from several
different sources: Jesus, Thomas, Martha, Mary, the sisters' visitors and,
of course, the narrator. Finally, as is so often the case, the events are
precisely located (Jn 11.1, 7, 18).[46]

---

43. J.P. Martin, 'History and Eschatology in the Lazarus Narrative: John 11.1-
44', *SJT* 17 (1964), pp. 342-43.

44. Schneiders, 'Death in the Community', p. 47.

45. In Jn 11.16 Thomas most probably is referring to dying not with Lazarus but
with Jesus, since the disciples had just mentioned the mortal peril should he return to
Judea (Jn 11.8). Nevertheless, the immediate grammatical antecedent of μετ' αὐτοῦ
is Lazarus, and John's penchant for double entendre and misunderstanding allows
readers to think of both Jesus and Lazarus in Thomas' words.

46. Faced with so many allusions to personalities and places, I find it remarkable
that Rochais (*récits de résurrection*, p. 135) can conclude that the identification of
persons and the location of the miracle are of little importance theologically. Factual

John's emphasis on the factuality of the miracle—Lazarus actually was dead and then alive—means that the witnesses of the events are crucial to its credibility. The witnesses (other than Jesus) are the disciples, Martha, Mary and the visitors from Jerusalem.

In Jn 11.14-15 Jesus tells his disciples, Λάζαρος ἀπέθανεν, καὶ χαίρω δι' ὑμᾶς ἵνα πιστεύσητε, ὅτι οὐκ ἤμην ἐκεῖ. The syntax can bear several interpretations. After examining the possibilities, Abbott concludes that Jesus' words signify that

> the Son rejoiced over all the circumstances of the death of Lazarus, as He was ready to rejoice over His own death, and for the same reason—namely that, in both cases, the death would tend to the glory of God by strengthening men's faith in God.[47]

Clearly, Jesus has in mind from the outset that Lazarus' death will, in the end, engender faith (Jn 11.4; cf. 2.11).

However, the disciples vanish from the narrative once Jesus discusses Lazarus' death and asks them to go to him. Jesus' invitation and Thomas' response in Jn 11.15-16 presume the disciples' presence at Bethany, although the narrator never indicates their presence in the scenes with Martha, Mary or at the tomb. This resembles the wine miracle, with the crucial difference that the peroration of that story underlines that it was the disciples who saw Jesus' glory (Jn 2.11) and, by implication, the miracle. Perhaps the disciples might be located in the crowd at the tomb (Jn 11.42), but John never uses ὄχλος for the inner circle of disciples. Just as Jesus' mother gave way to the servants, bridegroom, chief steward and disciples, and just as the Samaritan woman gave way to the villagers, so in the Lazarus episode the disciples are prominent at first but fade into the background as Martha, Mary and their visitors step forward. If the disciples are present at the resurrection of Lazarus, John says nothing of them as witnesses or about the effect of the miracle upon their faith.

Other witnesses are those who come from Jerusalem to console Martha and Mary (Jn 11.18-19). They provide testimony to Lazarus' death by their purpose, presence and questioning of Jesus' ability to have kept Lazarus from dying in the first place (Jn 11.37). These people are identified only as the Ἰουδαῖοι (Jn 11.19, 31, 33, 36, 45) and as the

details are basic to John's theological foundations of true incarnation and valid testimony (Jn 1.14; 19.35; 21.24).

47. Abbott, *Johannine Grammar*, §2102.

ὄχλος (Jn 11.42; 12.17). If both men and women were present in the crowd at Lazarus' tomb, then women were among those who testified in public to the fact of his revival, and persuaded many others to meet Jesus (Jn 12.17-18). Were there women among those witnesses?

The rituals surrounding death and burial provided one of the few specific social functions in the public sphere open to women.[48] Women could be involved in the preparation of the body for burial, and would participate, mainly as keeners, and in the funeral procession, apart from the men. Still, the various rituals for the funeral and interment of the deceased and for comforting the bereaved devolved largely upon men. Archer explains,

> Only the men of the community were placed under the command to escort the dead to the grave and provide comfort for the bereaved at the 'house of mourning'... Although women were not to be denied access to the 'house of mourning', they were, apart from the immediate relatives of the deceased, under no religious obligation to attend.[49]

Thus, the group that comes to comfort Martha and Mary could have been composed of men only, or of both men and women.[50] The latter is most probable, but nothing in the story itself permits any firm conclusion. Those who follow Mary to the grave are said to weep also (Jn 11.33). Visiting the grave to weep was customary, and weeping ordinarily would be the province of women.[51] But Jesus himself weeps (Jn 11.35), and so the weeping of the crowd provides no sure key to its composition. Two factors that certainly confirm the presence of men in the group are the removal of the stone from the aperture of the tomb (Jn 11.41) and that some of them report to the Pharisees (Jn 11.46).

Martha and Mary are prominent figures from the time Jesus arrives in Bethany until the revival of Lazarus. The presence of women in Biblical resurrection stories is distinctive but not surprising. Four of the six Biblical resurrection stories involve the death of a young daughter (Mk 5 and pars.) or son (1 Kgs 17; 2 Kgs 4; Lk. 7).[52] Hence, the presence of

48. The other principal function was a wedding. See Archer, *Her Price*, p. 243.

49. Archer, *Her Price*, p. 280.

50. Wuellner ('Putting Life Back', p. 119) thinks that at least half of the group must have been women, but offers no reason why.

51. Archer, *Her Price*, pp. 281-85.

52. Acts 9 records the death and revival of Tabitha, and Acts 20 that of Eutychus, both of whom would be adults, perhaps young, but in any case, not children. No mention is made of their parents.

the parents, especially the mother as the principal caregiver for children, would be expected; and indeed, the mother is present in each of these four stories.[53] John makes no mention of the parents of Lazarus, and the involvement of Martha and Mary, as his sisters, would be expected.

The question was raised previously of the rationale behind the information John supplies about the family from Bethany. I noted Kremer's view that John assumes that Martha and Mary are known to the readers. Kremer arrives at this conclusion based on the fact that John offers no information about the identity of their parents, their marital status or their social standing.[54] But perhaps that lack of information points elsewhere. Given the manifest concern of John to prove the fact of Lazarus' death (as evidenced by the numerous references to it), the status of the witnesses becomes paramount. If Martha and Mary are to serve as eyewitnesses to this situation, what matters is not their parents, marital status or social position, but their gender and relationship to Lazarus; and in fact, besides their names and place of residence, their relationship to Lazarus is the only other information John gives.

John makes it clear from the outset that Mary and Martha and Lazarus are siblings (Jn 11.1-5). Also, first Martha and then Mary says to Jesus, 'Lord, if you had been here my brother [notice: not 'Lazarus'] would not have died' (Jn 11.21, 32), and Jesus also refers to Lazarus as Martha's brother (Jn 11.23). Most striking is John's reference to Martha as 'the sister of the dead man' (Jn 11.39). This phrase appears redundant after Jn 11.2, 19, 21, 23, and Schnackenburg notes, 'The strictly unnecessary further description of Martha as the dead man's sister...is at most a further indication that the source knew nothing of this and that the evangelist wanted to stress the fact'.[55] What the phrase reveals about John's sources is uncertain, but surely, the presence of 'the sister of the dead man' in Jn 11.39 accentuates yet one more time the finality of Lazarus' death and the identity of Martha as his sister.

I have noted that rabbinic codes allowed exceptions to the wide stricture

---

53. In both 1 Kings 17 and Luke 7 the mother is a widow. In 2 Kings 4 the father plays no active part except to assign care of the son to the mother at the beginning of his illness. In Mark 5 the father fetches Jesus while the mother remains at home with the daughter.

54. Kremer, *Lazarus*, p. 53.

55. Schnackenburg, *John*, II, p. 338 n. 64. The phrase ἡ ἀδελφὴ τοῦ τετελευτηκότος is lacking in some MSS, perhaps a reflection of the fact that that information is, strictly speaking, redundant.

against women as witnesses. The general precept is that women are admitted as competent witnesses in matters within their particular knowledge, and this might include, for example, customs or events involving women only, issues concerning women's purity, purposes of identification (especially of other women) and other matters outside the strictly legal realm.[56] A notable case in point is the testimony of women being sufficient to establish that a particular male was in fact dead: 'Even if a man [only] heard women saying, "Such-a-one is dead", that suffices' (*m. Yeb.* 16.5).[57] The catalogue of women proscribed from witnessing to the death of a woman's husband includes her mother-in-law, mother-in-law's daughter, co-wife, husband's brother's wife and husband's daughter (*m. Yeb.* 15.4).[58] Had Lazarus been married, Martha and Mary, being his sisters, would have been disqualified from testifying to the fact of his death; but as it is, they are perfectly competent witnesses.

In regard to the deceased, two rabbinic rules check and balance one another. Due to bodily decay, 'Evidence [of the identity of a corpse] may be given only during the first three days [after death]' (*m. Yeb.* 16.3). On the other hand, to insure that a person was truly dead, 'Evidence [of a man's death] may be given only after his soul is gone forth, even though he was seen mortally wounded or crucified or being devoured by a wild beast' (*m. Yeb.* 16.3). This accorded with the belief that for the first three days after death, the soul hovers over the body intending to re-enter it but then departs upon seeing that decay has begun (*Gen. Rabbah* 100.7; *Lev. Rabbah* 18.1; cf. *Acts Pil.* 14.3).[59]

56. Cohn, 'Witness', col. 606; cf. Wegner, *Chattel or Person*, p. 121. Note the apocryphal legend (*Prot. Jas* 19.3–20.1) in which a midwife and Salome (the step-sister of Jesus?) act as witnesses at Jesus' birth to the virginity of his mother Mary. Salome says, 'As the Lord my God lives, unless I put (forward) my finger and test her condition, I will not believe that a virgin has brought forth'.

57. When only one witness is present, witness dependability arises, and the testimony of even one woman was upheld (*m. Yeb.* 16.7), although Akiba dissents, wanting to exclude women and close relatives (see Falk, *Jewish Law*, I, p. 115; II, pp. 305-306).

58. That is, the husband's mother, sister, second wife, wife by levirate marriage, and daughter by another wife. These prohibitions protected the woman whose husband was missing but not proven dead from hostile action through false testimony by the husband's close female relatives (Biale, *Women and Jewish Law*, pp. 104-105).

59. Embalming was essentially foreign to Jewish burial customs in first-century Palestine, and so Bultmann (*John*, p. 407 n. 6) is wrong to object that Jn 11.44

Martha is the only eyewitness to state that Lazarus has been dead for four days, that is, that his death is real and final (Jn 11.39; cf. 11.17).[60]

A last issue is the faith of Martha and Mary, on which there is a spectrum of opinions ranging from outright unbelief, to various shades of belief mixed with unbelief, to consummate belief. The sisters make one statement together: 'Lord, he whom you love is ill' (Jn 11.3). This message brings to mind the words of Jesus' mother, 'They have no more wine' (Jn 2.3), but its interpretation is less difficult. By this point Jesus has worked many miracles, and intimates of his like Martha and Mary surely were aware of them. The sisters' message cannot be simply for Jesus' information and must be heard as a request that shows their miracle faith in Jesus by their confidence in his capacity to cure Lazarus.[61] Martha makes five statements alone:

1. 'Lord, if you had been here, my brother would not have died' (Jn 11.21).
2. 'But even now I know that God will give you whatever you ask of him' (Jn 11.22).
3. 'I know that he will rise again in the resurrection on the last day' (Jn 11.24).
4. 'Yes, Lord [I believe], I believe that you are the Messiah, the Son of God, the one coming into the world' (Jn 11.27).
5. 'Lord, already there is a stench because he has been dead four days' (Jn 11.39).

The first of these can be a simple statement without being a reproach, because Martha says, 'If you had been here', not 'If you had arrived in time', or 'If you had come right when we called you'. It underlines the faith, expressed in Jn 11.3, in Jesus' miraculous ability to heal. The

contradicts Jn 11.39. Davies (*Rhetoric and Reference*, p. 311) observes, 'From the evidence available, the Johannine depiction of Jewish burial practice seems to be accurate'.

60. Further reinforcement for the witness of Martha (and Mary) to the death of Lazarus is circumstantial but worth mentioning. Martha and Mary probably would have participated in preparing Lazarus' body for interment, because this task was performed by either men or women for a dead male (only by women for a dead female), and by the relatives and/or friends of the deceased (Archer, *Her Price*, p. 257 n. 3).

61. If the sisters knew of Jesus' powers, it might be asked why they insisted he be present in order to prevent Lazarus' death. Were they incognizant of his ability to heal from afar (see Jn 4.46-54)?

second statement, with its confident expectation, evokes the words of Jesus' mother, 'Do whatever he tells you' (Jn 2.5). It is hard to imagine what else besides resurrection Martha could have in mind for her brother who is unquestionably dead. And yet, her third statement shows that immediate resurrection is not at all what she has in mind, and this is confirmed by her fifth statement in which she protests the opening of the tomb. Her intervening confession, therefore, while still accurate and expressive of sincere faith, simply does not include the idea that in Jesus the future is now: 'Martha represents the follower of Jesus who has yet to grasp that all her expectations and hopes are fulfilled in him.'[62] Mary makes one statement alone: 'Lord, if you had been here, my brother would not have died' (Jn 11.32). This statement is essentially identical to Martha's first statement and voices the same faith in Jesus' miraculous ability to heal.[63] But do Mary's tears make another statement, one about the limits of her faith? Hoskyns reviews the diverse interpretations of Jesus' distress in Jn 11.33-38 and concludes, 'It is the unbelief of the Jews and the half-belief of Martha...and Mary which in the context of the Johannine narrative cause Jesus to burst angrily into tears'.[64]

The failure of Martha and Mary is not that they do not believe in Jesus, but that they do not recognize the νῦν ἐστιν of the hour of the one who was to come into the world from God to bring new life to the dead (Jn 5.25-29; cf. 11.40): 'Like others before, Mary and Martha accept Jesus as a miracle worker and healer and call him to help their brother. Their misunderstanding lies in their failure to relinquish or modify the traditional futuristic eschatology for the Johannine realized eschatology.'[65] Nevertheless, no one present at the tomb that day

---

62. Culpepper, *Anatomy*, p. 163. Marchadour (*Lazare*, p. 122) is mistaken to assert that the narrator has selected Martha to be the 'perfect believer', because there are no such believers in John's Gospel. After making this lofty claim, Marchadour struggles to explain Martha's doubt in Jn 11.39, and resorts to construing it as the narrator's attempt to heighten the suspense of the story. If so, the attempt is ungainly, and one wonders why John would not have used Mary instead of Martha to make the objection at Jn 11.39, since Mary had not been cast as the perfect believer.

63. The two statements have a slightly different emphasis. Martha says, κύριε, εἰ ἧς ὧδε οὐκ ἂν ἀπέθανεν ὁ ἀδελφός μου; Mary says, κύριε, εἰ ἧς ὧδε οὐκ ἂν μου ἀπέθανεν ὁ ἀδελφός.

64. E.C. Hoskyns, *The Fourth Gospel* (ed. F.N. Davey; London: Faber & Faber, rev. edn, 1947), p. 405.

65. Culpepper, *Anatomy*, p. 140; O'Day (*Revelation*, p. 72) makes this same

expected an act of resurrection at that very hour. As a miraculous sign, the raising of Lazarus is, so to speak, off the scale. It truly is the culmination of Jesus' signs and the ultimate revelation during his public ministry.

In terms of the sisters' witness, the issue of their faith and understanding might, after all, be moot. Both Martha and Mary testify to the fact that their brother Lazarus had died, but the text says nothing at all about their response to Jesus bringing him back to life (as is true of the disciples).[66] It is the crowd at the tomb whose responses to the miracle are reported—responses either to believe and thus publicly testify (Jn 11.45; 12.17), or to disbelieve and inform the authorities (Jn 11.46). The authorities believe the report of what happened at the tomb (Jn 11.47). Jewish women were unlikely to have been among those who reported to the Pharisees, and it is virtually certain that these informants were men. The people in Jerusalem for the Passover likewise believe the report of the raising of Lazarus (Jn 12.9, 17), and it can be safely said that women were among those who spread the word of the miracle through the Passover crowds. But again, there is no hard evidence in the text to prove this.

Martha and Mary are eyewitnesses to the crowning sign of Jesus' public ministry. Martha provides the strongest confirmation that her brother Lazarus had not just fallen asleep or into a swoon but was dead, and dead past the three day period during which popular piety held that his life might be expected to return. Martha testifies to the death of Lazarus within the codes and customs whereby a woman might reliably testify to a man's death. Martha also utters the most complete confession, in terms of Christological titles, to be found in John's Gospel. She, like all believers in John, is imperfect in faith and understanding, but her confession is sincere and accurate. It is mistaken to argue on the grounds of Martha's incomplete understanding that her confession itself

point in regard to the Samaritan woman. Both Bultmann (*John*, p. 404) and Witherington (*Women*, p. 106) observe that Martha is blind to the fact that the eternal life of which Jesus speaks is a present reality. Bultmann thinks that this shows Martha's genuine attitude of faith because she, without seeing the life, nevertheless recognizes in Jesus God's eschatological invasion of the world. Witherington, on the other hand, sees Martha's faith as inadequate because her confession does not include the crucial element of belief in Jesus' present power to raise the dead.

66. Although, Jn 11.40 might be taken as a hint that Martha saw the glory of God—that is, the true significance of the miracle—as did the disciples at the Cana wedding (Jn 2.11).

is somehow defective (as is true of Peter's confession as well). To do so misses the point entirely: 'Like Peter, who did not fully understand the Bread of Life discourse, Martha believes not in *what* she understands but in the *one* who has the words of eternal life'.[67] There is no reason to think that in a culture where women could and did make religious confessions that readers would not have valued it as such. Martha's testimony is true.

---

67. Schneiders, 'Death in the Community', p. 53.

CHAPTER 7

Lindars says of the anointing in Jn 12.1-8, 'As simple as the story is, it raises hosts of problems'.[1] These problems revolve mostly around assessing the implications of the similarities and differences of the anointing stories in the four Gospels. References to the Synoptic anointing stories will be necessary, but my purpose and method require that Jn 12.1-8 be interpreted within the context of its own narrative rather than against those of Matthew, Mark and Luke.[2]

The story of the supper and anointing bridges the last action of Jesus' public ministry (the raising of Lazarus in John 11) and the first action of his private ministry (the cleansing of the disciples in John 13). John recalls the raising of Lazarus when introducing the supper (Jn 12.1), and in both incidents the figures are basically the same (Jesus, Lazarus, Martha, Mary, the disciples), as is the location (Bethany). The contrast between the pall of death and the joy of life that comprises the general atmosphere of both stories is created by the dying and rising of Lazarus and, proleptically, of Jesus. This same contrast is detailed in, for example, Mary first shedding tears at Jesus' feet and later pouring scented oil upon them (Jn 11.32-33; 12.3), and the stench of the corpse versus the fragrance of the perfume (Jn 11.39; 12.3). The Bethany supper foreshadows the supper in Jerusalem by way of the meal itself (Jn 12.2;

---

1. Lindars, *John*, p. 412.

2. On the topic of the anointing in the four Gospels, see J.B. Green, *The Death of Jesus: Tradition and Interpretation in the Passion Narrative* (WUNT, 2.33; Tübingen: Mohr [Paul Siebeck], 1988), pp. 106-111; M. Sabbe, 'The Anointing of Jesus in John 12,1-8 and its Synoptic Parallels', in van Segbroeck, *et al.* (eds.), *Four Gospels*, III, pp. 2051-82. Dodd concludes that each Evangelist independently used a separate strand of tradition, and that the strands overlapped (C.H. Dodd, *Historical Tradition in the Fourth Gospel* [Cambridge: Cambridge University Press, 1953], p. 172). J.F. Coakley argues the case for Johannine independence and priority in 'The Anointing at Bethany and the Priority of John', *JBL* 107 (1988), pp. 241-56.

13.2), the moistening and drying of feet (Jn 12.3; 13.5), the corruption of Judas Iscariot (Jn 12.4-6; 13.2, 18, 21-30) and the imminent departure of Jesus (Jn 12.8; 13.1, 3, 33, 36).

1. *John 12.1-8: The Exegetical Issues*

a. Jn 12.7 is the *crux interpretum* for the pouring of oil upon Jesus' feet by Mary. When Judas Iscariot impugns Mary's use of the oil, Jesus answers, ἄφες αὐτήν, ἵνα εἰς τὴν ἡμέραν τοῦ ἐνταφιασμοῦ μου τηρήσῃ αὐτό (𝔓[66] ℵ B D K L Q W Θ Ψ 33. 1241 *al* lat sy[hmg] co), or, ἄφες αὐτήν, εἰς τὴν ἡμέραν τοῦ ἐνταφιασμοῦ μου τετήρηκεν αὐτό (A 065 *f*[1.13] 𝔐 f sy[p.h]). The witnesses for the former reading are decisive, but the variant reading testifies to the difficulty in it, namely, that if Mary had exhausted the oil in anointing Jesus' feet, how can he order that she be allowed to keep it for the day of his burial? There are several ways to translate the verse, some more plausible than others.[3] The alternative translations involve reading τηρήσῃ αὐτό as something like, 'that she might remember this act of anointing'. But John has words for 'remember' (μιμνῄσκομαι, Jn 2.17, 22; 12.16; μνημονεύω, Jn 15.20; 16.4, 21) and never uses τηρέω to mean 'remember'. Also, making αὐτό refer to 'the act of anointing' greatly overtaxes that pronoun while ignoring its obvious referent, τὸ μύρον.[4]

The obscurity in Jn 12.7 does not arise from ἵνα τηρήσῃ, which is clear enough, but from the context, which is much less clear. If the apparent conflict between Mary using all of the oil and keeping some of it could be resolved, the text of the better MSS could be read at face value without having to coerce τηρήσῃ αὐτό to yield something other than its plain meaning. This requires arguing that Mary did not use all of the oil, an argument that Barrett believes misses the spirit of the narrative and ignores the fact that Mary wipes Jesus' feet with her hair.[5] But the spirit of the narrative has to do more with the value of the ointment

3. For reviews of the options, see Daube, *Rabbinic Judaism*, pp. 318-20; Brown, *John*, I, p. 449; Barrett, *John*, pp. 413-14. Barrett finds none of even the best possibilities completely satisfying.

4. A Hellenistic practice was to inter the flask along with the corpse. Thus, it could be argued that αὐτό refers not to the oil but the flask. This hardly works for John's anointing, which is the only one of the four versions not to mention the flask at all (Sabbe, 'Anointing of Jesus', p. 2061 n. 20).

5. Barrett, *John*, p. 414. Barrett rightly dismisses the outlandish proposal of some sort of a miraculously unfailing supply of oil.

than with the amount used, and that it was used on Jesus' feet rather than for some other purpose. Further, how much of the twelve ounces (λίτρα) must Mary pour on Jesus' feet to necessitate that she wipe them with her hair? Certainly, when Mary wipes Jesus' feet with her hair she does not intend to substitute her hair for a towel, but rather, to express her homage and devotion.[6]

Dodd also rejects the idea that Mary retained some of the oil, on the basis of Judas Iscariot's objection, 'Why was this perfume not sold for three hundred denarii and the money given to the poor?' (Jn 12.5).[7] However, it makes better sense to interpret his objection as a protest not against how much of the oil Mary used on Jesus' feet but against it being used for that purpose in the first place. Thus, the reading of 𝔓[66] A B *et al.* is preferable, and to be understood as Jesus saying, 'Let her alone, so that she might keep what oil she has left for the day of my burial'. That Mary never does anoint Jesus' body for burial is a difficulty that cannot be removed other than to say that whatever intentions Jesus may have had for her in that regard, she never fulfills them.[8]

b. A second exegetical issue is comparatively minor but merits brief attention. Jn 12.8, 'You always have the poor with you, but you do not always have me', is absent from some MSS (D it[d] sy[s]), and this absence is difficult to explain.[9] Since Jn 12.8 serves as an apothegm that brings out the point of the story, a subtle shift of emphasis from Judas Iscariot to Mary occurs when the story is read as ending at Jn 12.7. If the absence of Jn 12.8 from Codex D *et al.* is not accidental, then in those MSS Jesus' rejoinder in Jn 12.7 builds solely upon Mary's genuinely

6. This accords with the view of M.E. Glasswell ('ἐκμάσσω', *EDNT*, I, p. 419), that in Jn 12.3 ἐκμάσσω means 'to wipe', while in Jn 13.5, where Jesus uses a towel, it means 'to dry'.

7. Dodd, *Historical Tradition*, p. 168. Even though John says nothing of Mary breaking the flask, Beasley-Murray (*John*, p. 205 n. e) invites the comparison with Mk 14.3, and argues that Jn 12.3, 5 imply that Mary had used all of the ointment. W. Michaelis ('μύρον', *TDNT*, IV, p. 801), however, contends that even the breaking of the flask in Mk 14.3 need not signify the intent to exhaust its contents, but more likely reflects the usual way of opening such containers.

8. Daube (*Rabbinic Judaism*, p. 317) maintains that Jesus' remark in Jn 12.7 must have been taken from the tradition that did include the women's plan to anoint him before burial, and the remark has lost its point in John's Gospel.

9. Other variants here can be attributed to parablepsis. 𝔓[75] 892[s*] *pc* lack part of Jn 12.8, reading simply, τοὺς πτωχοὺς γὰρ πάντοτε ἔχετε. Uncial 0250 lacks Jn 12.7-8 altogether. See *TCGNT*, pp. 236-37.

devout concern for him with no response at all to Judas Iscariot's feigned concern for the poor. The MSS supporting Jn 12.8 are superior, but whether the pericope concludes at Jn 12.7 or Jn 12.8, the overarching theme still remains the imminent death and departure of Jesus. These two brief exegetical points need no recapitulation.

2. *John 13.1-17: An Interpretative Frame*

Because John mentions 'the disciples' and not 'the twelve' at the supper in John 13, it cannot be said categorically that no women attend the event. But that does seem to be the case. Jesus speaks of the dinner companions whose feet he has washed as those 'whom I have chosen', while alluding to the imminent malfeasance of Judas (Jn 13.18). This accords with Jn 6.70-71, where Jesus says, 'Did I not choose you, the twelve? Yet one of you is a devil,' and that one is then identified by the narrator as Judas Iscariot. If any women are present at the supper, no mention is made of them, and the private ministry of Jesus in John 13–16 is directed, at least immediately, to the Twelve.[10] Still, there are links between Mary's anointing of Jesus' feet in John 12 and Jesus' washing of the disciples' feet in John 13 that invite the use of the latter as an interpretative frame for Mary's actions.

The similarities between the anointing in John 12 and the washing in John 13 are apparent. The obvious points of contact are, as already noted, the meal (Jn 12.2; 13.2), the moistening and drying of feet (Jn 12.3; 13.5), the corruption of Judas Iscariot (Jn 12.4-6; 13.2, 18, 21-30), and the imminent departure of Jesus (Jn 12.8; 13.1, 3, 33, 36). A line of interpretation commonly proposed by exegetes runs as follows. Within the context of Jesus' death, Mary anoints his feet and in so doing, anticipates his washing of the disciples' feet and his charge for them to do the same to one another. Thus, Mary 'models what it means to be a disciple: to serve, to love one another, to share in Jesus' death'.[11]

For Mary this involves humbling herself as Jesus will do in washing the disciples' feet. While the task of anointing or washing feet fell upon male or female servants or other women of a Jewish household, wealthier women were able to hire others for such tasks.[12] The ownership of a

10. Note that the remarks directed to Jesus come from Simon Peter (Jn 13.26), Thomas (Jn 14.5), Philip (Jn 14.8) and Judas (Jn 14.22).

11. O'Day, 'John', p. 300. Schneiders ('Women', p. 42) sees Mary as 'a disciple of Jesus in the strict sense of the word'.

12. Archer, *Her Price*, pp. 225-28. The custom of anointing with oil was

house (Jn 11.20, 31), tomb (Jn 11.38) and expensive perfume (Jn 12.3) testifies to the prosperity of the Bethany family, and suggests that they were likely to have had servants.[13] J.C. Thomas observes that in a Jewish setting, 'In cases of deep love or extreme devotion a host or loved one might wash the feet of another. Due to its humble nature, the performance of such an act demonstrates tremendous affection, servitude, or both.'[14] Thus, when Mary anoints Jesus' feet she voluntarily adopts the role of a servant.

The analogy between Mary anointing Jesus' feet in John 12 and Jesus washing the disciples' feet in John 13 has much to commend it, but care must be taken to respect its limits. In anointing Jesus' feet, Mary is demoting herself from host to servant, but unlike Jesus, who washes the feet of subordinates (Jn 13.13), she is not performing the act on an inferior—quite the contrary. Also, two major purposes of Jesus in washing the disciples' feet are to prepare them for service and to cleanse them from sin.[15] These two categories in no way can apply to Mary's anointing of Jesus, because he is commissioned for service by the Father (Jn 1.32-34; 12.44-49), and because Jesus removes the sins of others and is himself without sin (Jn 1.29; 8.46).

In light of Jesus' washing of the disciples' feet, Mary's anointing of his feet shows her personal devotion and the subservient implications of discipleship. To some degree, Mary is the exemplar of how discipleship is to be practiced. But Mary's action, when interpreted with a view to the footwashing in John 13, does not serve to confirm Jesus' identity as the messiah; whether it does so when interpreted within its own context will be examined in the next section.

3. *Martha and Mary as Witnesses*

John marks Martha's presence and action at the supper succinctly: ἡ Μάρθα διηκόνει. Some exegetes look beyond the plain meaning of

associated with wealth (Amos 6.4-7; Mic. 6.12-15).

13. In Jn 11.3 Martha and Mary send a message to Jesus, presumably by way of servants. Also possible is that the sisters hired keeners for Lazarus' funeral (Jn 11.19, 31, 33)—a common practice. Fragment 1 of the *Secret Gospel of Mark* has an incident, strikingly similar to the raising of Lazarus, in which Jesus revives a young man at the request of his sister, and in which the young man is said to be wealthy.

14. J.C. Thomas, *Footwashing in John 13 and the Johannine Community* (JSNTSup, 61; Sheffield: JSOT Press, 1991), p. 42.

15. Thomas, *Footwashing*, pp. 58-60, 115-16.

this phrase (Martha served the meal) for a symbolic meaning (Martha is a paradigm for the Johannine concept of servanthood).

Scott acknowledges the consensus that the Johannine community was not concerned with ecclesiastical offices, but contends that John must have been aware that διακονέω implied more than table service. Scott explains that by the time John's Gospel was compiled, διακονέω and its cognates (διακονία and διάκονος) had taken on a special connotation associated with particular offices of ministry, as is evidenced by some of the Pauline and Pastoral Epistles and by Acts.[16] What Scott fails to demonstrate is that this 'established context' for these words applies to Jn 12.2. A. Weiser notes that only in certain strata of the New Testament do διακονέω and its cognates come to express specific functions in the church, and maintains that διακονέω in Jn 12.2, not being lodged in one of those strata, is an incidental usage.[17] It is insufficient to show that διακονέω and its cognates carried technical meaning in the Pauline and Pastoral Epistles and in Acts, and then assume that διακονέω bears this same meaning in Jn 12.2. The word ἀπόστολος likewise had a special meaning and context among early Christians, but its appearance in Jn 13.16 does not relate to the apostolic office.[18]

Scott also emphasizes that διακονέω appears only three times in John, all in John 12. On the basis of Jn 12.26, Scott asserts that Martha's serving of dinner in Jn 12.2 typifies Jesus' idea of discipleship: 'If it is the *servant* who truly follows, i.e., who is the true disciple, then Martha has already shown that quality, again in advance of any instruction to do so.'[19] But what Jesus has in mind in Jn 12.26—as its immediate context makes abundantly clear—is that the servant who truly follows him does so by dying (Jn 12.24-25). Only by an allegorical *tour de force* could a dying disciple be wrung out of Martha serving dinner.

Schneiders and Schüssler Fiorenza appeal to A. Corell's theory that if any established ministry existed in the Johannine community it was probably that of deacon.[20] Even if Corell's theory be allowed provisionally, the leap that Schüssler Fiorenza makes from διακονέω in Jn 12.2 is

16. Scott, *Sophia*, pp. 212-13.

17. A. Weiser, 'διακονέω', *EDNT*, I, pp. 302, 304.

18. As Schnackenburg (*John*, III, p. 25) notes, ἀπόστολος in Jn 13.16 'has no more than a functional significance... and does not point to the disciples as apostles in any specific sense'.

19. Scott, *Sophia*, p. 213.

20. Schneiders, 'Women', p. 42; Schüssler Fiorenza, *Memory of Her*, p. 330.

precarious: 'If Corell's suggestion is right that the only established office in the Johannine community was that of *diakonos*, then Martha is characterised as fulfilling such a ministry.'[21] To read ἡ Μάρθα διηκόνει as identifying Martha as a διάκονος in the Johannine community requires allegorical exegesis, and such a connotation finds no support in the text itself.[22]

Although Martha surely is Jesus' intimate, follower and servant, there needs to be restraint when reading ἡ Μάρθα διηκόνει in Jn 12.2. If a symbolic meaning is to be found in the phrase, then grammatical, literary and theological grounds demand that one also be sought for ὁ δὲ Λάζαρος εἷς ἦν ἐκ τῶν ἀνακειμένων σὺν αὐτῷ. Yet, it would be equally excessive to rummage for an allegorical meaning behind ἀνάκειμαι in order to construe that phrase as signifying something more than Lazarus dining with Jesus and the other guests. It is Mary rather than Martha or Lazarus who is in focus, and the supplying of narrative details such as Martha serving and Lazarus dining, being typical of John, should not be overinterpreted.[23] In any event, even if Martha's serving does testify to her own devotion and, at some level, to the meaning of discipleship, it does not act as a witness to confirm that Jesus is the messiah.

Mary is more prominent than Martha and Lazarus, and she, along with Judas Iscariot, is a central figure in the story. Unlike Judas Iscariot, however, Mary says nothing, and so the focus is on her actions. Even as Jesus' own witness can be subdivided into words and works, a possibility to be examined is that when Mary silently anoints him she is performing a tacit act of witness.

Anointing was common in the ancient Near East and could signify any number of things depending upon the context: healing, cleansing and purification, exultation and joy, empowerment and commissioning.

21. Schüssler Fiorenza, *Memory of Her*, p. 330. Schüssler Fiorenza (p. 327) uses this same type of symbolic reading to argue that the waiters (διάκονοι) at the Cana wedding betoken the leaders of the Johannine community.

22. Seim ('Roles of Women', p. 72) notes that although 'diakon-terminology' is essential for understanding the role of women in Luke, it is, except for this single reference, absent from John: 'Thus, the servant role is no main gateway for understanding the role(s) of women in the Gospel of John'.

23. Culpepper (*Anatomy*, p. 142) thinks that 'Martha represents the ideal of discerning faith and service, Mary unlimited love and devotion, and Lazarus the hope of resurrection life', but Culpepper confesses to expressing this thought in 'exaggeratedly simple terms, admittedly bordering on allegorization'.

Thus, anointing sometimes was used in legal contexts as a *Rechtsakt*.[24] For my purpose, the crucial distinction to be made is that in ancient Israel anointing was not employed within strictly juridical contexts.

> The main role of symbolic anointment in the ancient Near East... was to ceremonialize an elevation in legal status: the manumission of a slave woman, the transfer of property, the betrothal of a bride, and the deputation of a vassal. In Israel, on the other hand, it was for the inauguration of a king, the consecration of a priest, and the rehabilitation of a leper. The above cases indicate that in Israel symbolic unction took place in the cult but not in legal proceedings.[25]

Thus, if a deeper significance in regard to witness is to be found in Mary's anointing of Jesus, it will be in the religious rather than the forensic realm (as opposed, for example, to the situation in which Martha and Mary testify to the fact of Lazarus' death). However, the life of ancient Israel resists being divided into mutually exclusive legal and religious compartments, and both Derrett and Daube raise legal (perhaps, quasi-legal) issues concerning the anointing.[26]

Building on the idea that in the original tradition the woman was a former prostitute, Derrett argues that she, being legally proscribed from making a cultic offering of the oil in an orthodox way, is able under the law to offer it as a work of charity to prepare a corpse for burial. She does not ask for Jesus' permission before applying the oil, but legally, Jesus could benefit from this anointing without giving consent. Derrett's analysis is useful, but less so for John's version of the anointing. Nothing in John's Gospel hints that Mary of Bethany had an ignominious past, and Derrett must say, 'John, or his source, had evidently forgotten that the woman was an ex-prostitute, so that the point of the story was hardly retrievable'.[27] Further, Derrett sees the woman as being ignorant

---

24. E. Kutsch, *Salbung als Rechtsakt im alten Testament und im alten Orient* (BZAW, 87; Berlin: Alfred Töpelmann, 1963).

25. J. Milgrom and L.I. Rabinowitz, 'Anointing', *EncJud*, III, col. 27.

26. J.D.M. Derrett, 'The Anointing at Bethany', in *Studia Evangelica II* (TU, 87; Berlin: Akademie Verlag, 1964), pp. 174-82; Daube, *Rabbinic Judaism*, pp. 312-24.

27. Derrett, 'Anointing at Bethany', p. 180. K.E. Corley thinks that the phrase 'tax collectors and sinners' may have been a rhetorical slur rather than a literal description, and that 'the accusation that several of the women known to follow Jesus and perhaps frequent his table were "prostitutes" may not have been grounded in social reality and may not tell us anything about their true occupations' (K.E. Corley, 'Were the Women around Jesus Really Prostitutes? Women in the Context of Greco–Roman Meals', in D.J. Lull (ed.), *Society of Biblical Literature*

of the legal dimensions of her act, and that it is Jesus who interprets her
deed in that way: 'Jesus did not therefore accept the gift, but admitted
that her action was lawful in the context he mentioned, but of which she
herself would not have been expected to have knowledge.'[28]

Derrett's analysis raises the legalities involved with burial, an issue
treated in greater depth by Daube. Daube's analysis springs from the
concept of *niwwul* (disgrace), which Daube believes may have been a
major factor in the development of the story of the anointing at
Bethany. Put simply, the Gospel writers are anxious to refute the allegation that Jesus' body was interred improperly, and thus, under a *niwwul*.
For Mark and Matthew, a rebuttal involves upholding that a legitimate
anointing of Jesus was accomplished at Bethany while he was still alive.
This proleptic anointing was perfectly valid as a 'legal fiction'.[29] This
accords with the Synoptic accounts, which make no mention of Joseph
of Arimathea anointing Jesus' body before burial (Mk 15.42-46 and
pars.), and with the reports that the women who had intended to do so
were too late (Mk 16.1; Lk. 23.56). In John, on the other hand, Jesus'
body does receive proper preparation from Joseph of Arimathea and
Nicodemus (Jn 19.38-40), thus discrediting the charge of *niwwul* and
obviating any need for proleptic anointing.[30] Daube concludes that in
John's Gospel no legal fiction is established and that the burial day to
which Jesus refers lies entirely in the future.

Thus, while the analyses made from the legal angle by Derrett and
Daube are valuable, in the case of the Johannine anointing story the legal
context vis-à-vis burial rites dissolves.

Since a legal context for burial is lacking, it is necessary to turn to the
religious context, that is, the act of anointing in regard to commissioning
of prophet, priest or potentate. Elliott comments, 'The original core of
the story of Jesus' anointing...tells of his consecration as king and thus

Seminar Papers, 1989 [Atlanta: Scholars Press, 1989], p. 520).

28. Derrett, 'Anointing at Bethany', p. 179.

29. Daube (*Rabbinic Judaism*, p. 313) defines 'legal fiction' as 'an authoritative
interpretation of facts as something which, but for that interpretation, they would not
be'.

30. Robinson (*Priority of John*, pp. 282-83) argues, however, that what Mary
does to Jesus at supper and what Joseph and Nicodemus do to him at burial are two
different things; hence, Mary's act is not precluded by that of Joseph and
Nicodemus. Compare the remark of Brown (*John*, I, p. 454), 'Since the embalming
at Bethany is only on a figurative level, it does not create an obstacle to a real future
embalming'.

the story is clearly connected with the story of the triumphal entry, in which Jesus is hailed as King-Messiah'.[31] Does Elliott's observation hold true for the anointing according to John? Does Mary, in pouring oil on Jesus' feet, perform an act of testimony to his identity as king or messiah, or for that matter, as prophet or priest?

Lightfoot provides a succinct summary of the three notable contrasts between the Markan and Johannine versions of the anointing.

> In Mk. 14.3-9 the meal at which the anointing occurs is placed *after* the Lord's triumphal entry into Jerusalem, and *an unnamed woman* anoints his *head*. In Jn. 12.1-8, however, the supper takes place the day *before* the Lord's triumphal journey to the capital; and *Mary*, the sister of Martha and Lazarus, anoints the Lord's *feet*, almost at once removing the spikenard, and wiping dry His feet with the tresses of her hair.[32]

Source and redaction analyses are outside the purview of my study, but Lightfoot's summary highlights three relevant issues: the chronology, agent and mode of the anointing.[33]

In contrast to Mark (and Matthew), John narrates the anointing taking place immediately before Jesus enters Jerusalem to the royal acclamation of the people rather than shortly after it, and Barrett finds it 'particularly significant that John reverses the Markan order of these two events. It is as anointed king that Jesus rides into Jerusalem.'[34] The crowd extols Jesus as king after Mary anoints him, and this echoes the sequence of events in the ritual enthronement of a king over Israel in which the people acclaim the king following his anointing. However, in John's Gospel, Jesus is identified as king from the outset of his ministry (Jn 1.41, 49), and so it could be argued that the anointing of Jesus in its Johannine location does not function as it does in the chronologies of Matthew and Mark, that is, to reveal Jesus as king. Still, if Barrett is correct, Mary's act might be seen to affirm Jesus' kingship even if it does not reveal it.

What about Mary as the agent of the anointing? The context of ritual anointing in Israel speaks against construing Mary's action as that of anointing Jesus as king. O.A. Piper notes, 'Ritual anointing, unlike

31. J.K. Elliott, 'The Anointing of Jesus', *ExpTim* 85 (1973–74), p. 106.

32. Lightfoot, *John*, p. 235.

33. Luke and John share significant details that Matthew and Mark do not: the anointing of Jesus' feet, and the woman using her hair (Lk. 7.38). But Luke's chronology, narrative context, theological purpose and anointer differ from those of John.

34. Barrett, *John*, p. 409.

cosmetic anointing, had to be done by a person endowed with special authority in order for the "power" to be conferred to objects or persons'.[35] It thus seems unlikely that an anointing done by a woman could carry ritual messianic or royal overtones. In John's Gospel, however, it is precisely those men in positions of Jewish authority— Pharisees, Sadducees, priests—who fail to recognize Jesus as king (for example, Jn 19.15, 21), let alone the nature of his kingship. John's penchant for irony would be well satisfied by a Jewish woman rather than a Jewish priest anointing Jesus as king, but in this Gospel no human agent anoints or consecrates Jesus. That is the sole province of God (Jn 1.32-33; 10.36; cf. 17.19).[36]

Is there significance in the anointing of Jesus' feet rather than his head? In narrating the event, John repeats the phrase τοὺς πόδας (Jn 12.3). Abbott points out that although John's use of twofold repetition usually manifests itself in events rather than words, it may sometimes be intended to emphasize a disputed or doubtful fact, as in the anointing, where some say that Jesus' head was anointed but John says, 'She anointed *the feet* of Jesus and wiped with her hair *his feet*'.[37] Is John trying to downplay cultic connotations—royal or messianic—of Jesus' head being anointed? Perhaps so, but it cannot be assumed that such connotations are present: 'Whether or not this was a widely practiced custom, it is nonetheless evident that an anointing of the head did not point unambiguously to a royal anointing.'[38] Moreover, John uses ἀλείφω, which refers primarily to physical not cultic anointing. In the LXX ἀλείφω is rarely synonymous with χρίω (for מָשַׁח), the word expressing cultic anointment, and this distinction between ἀλείφω and χρίω is even more rigid in the New Testament.[39] Morris judiciously summarizes the matter.

35. O.A. Piper, 'Messiah', *ISBE*, III, p. 330.

36. Unlike the Synoptists, John describes Jesus' baptism obliquely, emphasizing the Baptist not as the agent of baptism but as a witness to the descent of the Holy Spirit upon Jesus (Jn 1.29-34). The anointing of the king conferred God's Spirit upon him (1 Sam. 16.13-14; Ps. 89.19-21).

37. Abbott, *Johannine Grammar*, §2607. Lk. 7.38 repeats τοὺς πόδας three times.

38. Green, *Death of Jesus*, p. 229. Green (p. 226 n. 15) also argues that whether it was Jesus' head or feet that were anointed, the act itself retains a non-messianic interpretation.

39. W. Brunotte, 'ἀλείφω', *NIDNTT*, I, p. 120; D. Müller, 'χρίω', *NIDNTT*, I, p. 121.

It is a teasing question whether John is making an allusion to messiahship in his story of Mary's anointing of Jesus (12.1-8). Nobody says anything about messiahship, but there is no doubt that John is describing an anointing. It is also a fact that Jesus interprets the anointing in terms of his death (12.7), the heart of his messianic activity. Probably we should take the incident as no more than a social happening of an unusually interesting kind. But at least we can say that the Messiah received an unusual anointing.[40]

Even if the anointing has no messianic or royal overtones, perhaps it can be said of Mary that 'Jesus portrays her as a prophet pointing to and even participating in his burial'.[41] But Jesus is the one who shows the prophetic knowledge; it is Jesus not Mary who marks the anointing as a harbinger of his burial. Nothing in the text signals that Mary intends or is even aware of any deeper implications in her actions, and it may be yet another case of Johannine irony wherein Mary, intending to anoint Jesus as an act of hospitality, unwittingly prepares him for death.[42]

Schneiders writes of John 11–12, 'Throughout this anticipation of the paschal mystery women disciples play the leading positive roles not only as witnesses but as faithful participants'.[43] This statement is surely true but lacks specificity. In what capacity do the women act as witnesses? Martha's serving at supper and Mary's anointing of Jesus form a testimony to what it means to love and serve Jesus. That testimony is true. But although the actions of Martha and Mary at the supper show them to be true followers of Jesus, these actions do not constitute a testimony that declares Jesus' identity as the messiah.

40. Morris, *Jesus Is the Christ*, pp. 71-72.

41. J. Rena, 'Women in the Gospel of John', *EgTh* 17 (1986), p. 142.

42. Many scholars agree that even if Mary's action is freighted with deeper implications, she is unaware of them—for example: Culpepper, *Anatomy*, pp. 141-42; J.R. Michaels, 'John 12.1-11', *Int* 43 (1989), p. 288; Bultmann, *John*, p. 416; Brown, *John*, I, p. 454; Lindars, *John*, p. 419; Schnackenburg, *John*, II, p. 370; Carson, *John*, p. 430.

43. Schneiders, 'Women', p. 43. Schneiders's observation, however, accentuates how conspicuously absent from John's version is Jesus' testimonial to the anointing woman, which is found in one form or another in Matthew, Mark and Luke.

Chapter 8

STANDING NEAR THE CROSS

Jesus' terse statements from the cross in Jn 19.25-27 have loosed a tor-
rent of symbolic interpretations. As a witness to his death, the mother of
Jesus has all but drowned in the flood of putative symbolism that many
exegetes perceive in the relationships between Jesus, his mother and his
Beloved Disciple. Such Marian symbolism was, however, essentially
foreign to John's earliest readers. Collins notes that patristic evidence is
lacking for seeing Mary principally as a symbolic figure, and that patristic exegesis mainly gave a 'private and historicizing interpretation of the
crucifixion scene'.[1] Since my goal is to examine how John's first readers might have reacted to the women as witnesses, what Mary may or
may not symbolize at the cross will be discussed only as pertinent to that
goal.[2]

R.E. Brown sees a tripartite structure in the Johannine passion narrative: (1) arrest and interrogation (Jn 18.1-27), (2) trial (Jn 18.28-19.16a),
(3) crucifixion, death, and burial (Jn 19.16b-42). The second and third of
these three parts each comprises a chiasm of seven episodes, with the
material of interest here, Jn 19.25-27, being the central episode in the
chiasm involving Jesus' crucifixion, death and burial.[3] The location of
Jn 19.25-27 at the centre of a chiasm presumably lends it a measure
of emphasis. Whether John's early readers were conscious of such

1. Collins, 'Mary', p. 107.
2. For reviews and critiques of Marian symbolism, see Collins 'Mary', pp. 130-
41; Räisänen, *Mutter Jesu*, pp. 174-80; Brown *et al.*, *Mary*, pp. 214-18;
Schnackenburg, *John*, III, pp. 277-82. On the symbolism of Mary in Jn 19.25-27,
see A. Dauer, *Die Passionsgeschichte im Johannesevangelium: Eine traditionsgeschichtliche und theologische Untersuchung zu Joh 18,1–19,30* (SANT, 30;
Munich: Kösel, 1972), pp. 323-29. In keeping with my methodology, I will not
explore source and redaction questions which, in any event, are impossible to resolve
with certainty.
3. Brown, *John*, II, pp. 785-86, 859, 911.

structures is uncertain, but they may well have sensed, as does Dodd, that the event of Jn 19.25-27 'breaks the unities of time and place' in a narrative that otherwise focuses unrelentingly upon Jesus' passion.[4] The readers' attention is diverted, at least momentarily, from Golgotha and Jesus in the present, to the home of his Beloved Disciple and mother in the future.

1. *John 19.25-27: The Exegetical Issues*

a. The economy with which John narrates that Jesus was crucified (Jn 19.18) moves Stibbe to remark that John shows less interest in the actual process of the crucifixion than in the conduct of the *dramatis personae* at the cross.[5] This cast includes four Roman soldiers (Jn 19.23), some women (Jn 19.25) and the Beloved Disciple (Jn 19.26). John describes the women at the cross thus: εἰστήκεισαν δὲ παρὰ τῷ σταυρῷ τοῦ Ἰησοῦ ἡ μήτηρ αὐτοῦ καὶ ἡ ἀδελφὴ τῆς μητρὸς αὐτοῦ, Μαρία ἡ τοῦ Κλωπᾶ καὶ Μαρία ἡ Μαγδαληνή (Jn 19.25). But the list of women that John takes pains to furnish still leaves questions about them that can be answered in several ways. How many women are present? Who are they? How are they related to Jesus? What surely was clear to John and probably clear to the first readers is now ambiguous.

If two women are there, they are the mother of Jesus (named Mary of Clopas) and her ἀδελφή (named Mary Magdalene).[6] While this reading has the narratological advantage of introducing only the two women who will participate in the events that follow, it is hard to imagine that Jesus' mother should be called Mary of Clopas.[7] Moreover, that Mary

---

4. Dodd, *Historical Tradition*, pp. 127-28.

5. M.W.G. Stibbe, *John* (Sheffield: JSOT Press, 1993), p. 193.

6. The word ἀδελφή can mean sister, half-sister, stepsister, sister-in-law, or even 'some other family relationship for which modern English would not use the word sister at all' (R. Bauckham, 'Mary of Clopas [John 19.25]', in G.J. Brooke [ed.], *Women in the Biblical Tradition* [SWR, 31; Lampeter: Edwin Mellen, 1992], p. 233).

7. So Bauckham, 'Mary of Clopas', p. 232. Bauckham does not mention the unlikely possibility of Clopas being Mary's brother, but does argue that he could not have been her father, son or husband. Clopas, if he was Joseph's brother (so Hegesippus according to Eusebius, *E.H.* 3.11; 4.22), could have married Mary after Joseph's death as her levir—thus, Μαρία ἡ τοῦ Κλωπᾶ. Legends of Mary's remarriage garner no firm support from John's Gospel (cf. Jn 1.45; 6.42), but in any case, it is most improbable that John would call her Mary here and not in her first

Magdalene was Jesus' aunt (or other near relative) is highly improbable. Finally, if John uses ἀδελφή simply to mean sister (as Jn 11.1, 3, 5, 28, 39 suggest), then Jesus' mother and her sister have the same name, which is unlikely although not impossible.[8] That the text presents two women is grammatically viable but otherwise strained, and few exegetes support it.

If three women are there, they are the mother of Jesus (unnamed), her ἀδελφή (named Mary of Clopas), and Mary Magdalene. The problem with this reading is, again, that it requires two sisters to share one name.[9] However, as was noted, ἀδελφή can carry connotations other than sister, and it is not impossible for Jesus' mother to have had a sister who also was named Mary.

If four women are there, they are the mother of Jesus (unnamed), her ἀδελφή (unnamed), Mary of Clopas and Mary Magdalene. This reading, presenting two pairs of women, the first named and the second unnamed, is the smoothest grammatically and does not raise the problem of two sisters sharing the same name. Although neither the reading of three women nor of four women is secure beyond question, the latter is preferable as it has no potent objections to withstand.

Once it is decided that four women are present, questions linger about the more precise identities of the second and third. The second woman possibly is the same person whom Mark calls Salome (Mk 15.40) and whom Matthew calls the mother of Zebedee's sons (Mt. 27.56).[10] If this is correct, and if the early church traditions are reliable, then this second woman is Jesus' maternal aunt, who stands at the cross with her son, John, the Beloved Disciple, apostle and evangelist. One advantage of this theory is that it fits with the idea that the narrator never mentions any of Jesus' blood relatives by name (in Jn 1.45 Joseph is named by Philip, in Jn 6.42 by the Jews). However, this theory remains speculative, and if ἀδελφή means something other than (blood) sister, another possibility arises. According to McHugh, who reads ἀδελφή as sister-in-law, this second woman is Jesus' father's sister, whom Matthew and

appearance (Jn 2.1), or that John would mention Mary's levirate husband in the very place in which Jesus commends her to the home of the Beloved Disciple.

8.   J. Blinzler provides examples from the ancient Near East (and from his own family!) of siblings with the same name (J. Blinzler, *Die Brüder und Schwestern Jesu* [SBS, 21; Stuttgart: Katholisches Bibelwerk, 1967], p. 116 n. 20).

9.   Bauckham ('Mary of Clopas', pp. 233-34) essays other, less telling objections to the reading of three women.

10.   This view is explored in detail by Robinson, *Priority of John*, pp. 119-22.

Mark identify as Mary, the mother of James and Jose(s/ph) (Mt. 27.56; Mk 15.40).[11]

Two questions flank the third woman, Mary of Clopas. First, is she Clopas's mother, daughter, sister or wife? Second, who is Clopas? After evaluating the evidence (which is too lengthy to rehearse here), Bauckham judges that Mary was Clopas's wife, and that Clopas was Jesus' father's brother, renowned among early Christians as the father of Simon (Symeon), who succeeded Jesus' brother James as leader of the Jerusalem church.[12] Bauckham's conclusions are not the only possible ones, but they make best sense of the data, and no known evidence can be advanced that disproves them.

Blinzler well expresses the uncertainties surrounding the number, identity and relationships of the women in Jn 19.25: 'Possibilities and more possibilities, but we lack the criteria needed to establish which of them is correct.'[13] The many possibilities cannot be resolved beyond all dispute, but in light of the foregoing data, it can be proposed with reasonable confidence that according to John four women stand at the cross: (1) Jesus' mother, (2) his aunt (paternal or maternal), (3) Mary of Clopas (his father's brother's wife), (4) Mary Magdalene. If only the internal evidence of John's Gospel is used, then the name of the second woman remains unknown and her precise relationship to Jesus uncertain: she is either the sister or the sister-in-law of Jesus' mother. But in any case, there would be two unnamed women who are blood relatives of Jesus, one named woman who is a marriage relative and one named woman who is unrelated.[14]

---

11. McHugh, *Mother of Jesus*, pp. 244-45. McHugh (p. 244) remarks, 'I suggest that this hypothesis, and this one alone, explains all the references in the gospels; and that it is confirmed by the testimony of early tradition'.

12. Bauckham, 'Mary of Clopas', pp. 234-43. The Coptic Sahidic identifies Mary as Clopas' daughter (see H.-J. Klauck, 'Die dreifache Maria: Zur Rezeption von Joh 19,25 in EvPhil 32', in van Segbroek *et al.* (eds.), *Four Gospels*, III, pp. 2347-48). E.F.F. Bishop suggests that this identification is supported by Arabic MSS and by the Diatessaron ('Mary (of) Clopas and Her Father', *ExpTim* 73 [1961-62], p. 339).

13. Blinzler, *Brüder und Schwestern*, p. 117.

14. The combined Johannine and Synoptic accounts raise the possibility that all four women could be named Mary. Based upon T. Ilan's statistical study on the names of Jewish women in Palestine in antiquity, Bauckham (*Jude*, p. 43) concludes, 'Every second Palestinian Jewish woman must have been called either Salome or Mary'.

b. In Jn 19.25 the narrator relates that the four women were standing by the cross of Jesus (εἰστήκεισαν δὲ παρὰ τῷ σταυρῷ τοῦ Ἰησοῦ). This statement apparently conflicts with the Synoptic narratives (Mk 15.40 and pars.), which portray the women as watching from a distance (ἀπὸ μακρόθεν).[15] This issue can be addressed by some type of harmonization whereby the women approach and withdraw from Jesus during his time on the cross, or one group stands near the cross and another group farther away. But also, it can be argued that the Synoptic ἀπὸ μακρόθεν need not contradict the Johannine παρὰ τῷ σταυρῷ, because the Synoptic observers had to have been close enough to read the *titulus* and to hear the words spoken by Jesus, his revilers and his co-crucifixants. McHugh contends that the distance from which the Synoptists say that the women watched could not have been great, because Golgotha lies only a few yards west of the wall of Herodian Jerusalem.[16] However, the actual site of Golgotha is not certain.

Some exegetes insist that John is theologizing by placing Jesus' followers near the cross, because the soldiers would have prohibited anyone from getting close, although Stauffer adduces rabbinic evidence to the contrary.[17] But that same charge of theologizing can be directed against the Synoptists, on the grounds that they locate Jesus' relatives and friends at a distance to fulfill Ps. 38.11: 'My friends and companions stand aloof from my affliction, and my neighbours stand far off.' Even if an irresolvable tension exists between the Synoptists and John, there is no compelling reason to prefer their picture to his. Moreover, as Brown notes, 'While the historical question is probably insolvable, we are much more concerned with the import that the episode has for John'.[18] As far as John is concerned, the women are standing nearby the cross.

c. Jesus sees his mother and the Beloved Disciple by the cross, and says to her, 'Woman, here is your son' (Jn 19.26). Is Jesus directing his mother's attention to the Beloved Disciple or to himself? If Jesus is saying, in effect, 'Woman, look at me', it may represent a calculated affirmation by John that Jesus' mother was indeed an eyewitness to his

15. The Synoptists also say nothing of male followers being present at the cross. The presence of the Beloved Disciple there in John will be discussed later.

16. McHugh, *Mother of Jesus*, p. 242.

17. E. Stauffer, *Jesus and His Story* (London: SCM Press, 1960), pp. 111, 179 n. 1. Stauffer's evidence is both challenged (Barrett, *John*, p. 551) and defended (Witherington, *Women*, p. 187 n. 103).

18. Brown, *John*, II, pp. 922-23.

death on the cross. It is possible that in Jn 19.26 Jesus is telling his mother to look at himself, but three aspects of the context make it most unlikely: (1) Jesus' speech being prompted by the presence of the Beloved Disciple as well as that of his mother, (2) the parallel words to the Beloved Disciple by which Jesus unmistakably entrusts his mother to him, (3) the reception of Jesus' mother into the home of the Beloved Disciple. An agraphon from Jn 19.26-30 clearly sees Jesus' words, 'Woman, here is your son', as a reference to the Beloved Disciple and not to himself.

> He says to his mother, 'Don't cry. I am returning to my Father, and to eternal life. Look—your son! This man will take my place'. Then he says to his disciple, 'Look—your mother!' Then, bowing his head, he gave up his spirit.[19]

d. In Jn 19.27 the narrator recounts, 'And from that hour (ἀπ' ἐκείνης τῆς ὥρας) the disciple took her into his own home'. Does the narrator mean that the Beloved Disciple escorts Jesus' mother from the cross to his home at that precise moment, or that at that time she formally passes from Jesus' care into that of the Beloved Disciple? The word ὥρα complicates the matter, since it often acts as a byword for that time when Jesus will be glorified through his exaltation by death on the cross. The question is whether or not ὥρα carries that sense in Jn 19.27.

Besides using ὥρα as a byword for the glorification of Jesus, John uses it more mundanely to designate time, specifically (Jn 1.39; 4.6; 4.52, 53; 19.14) or generally (Jn 5.35). The only other place in John's Gospel where ἐκεῖνος is used with ὥρα is Jn 4.53 (ἔγνω οὖν ὁ πατὴρ ὅτι [ἐν] ἐκείνῃ τῇ ὥρᾳ ἐν ᾗ εἶπεν αὐτῷ ὁ Ἰησοῦς· ὁ υἱός σου ζῇ).[20] The only other place where ἀπό is used with ἐκεῖνος and a unit of time is Jn 11.53 (ἀπ' ἐκείνης οὖν τῆς ἡμέρας ἐβουλεύσαντο ἵνα ἀποκτείνωσιν αὐτόν).[21] Jn 4.53 indicates that at a precise point in

---

19. *Codex evangelii Johannei Templariorum* (text from R.J. Miller (ed.), *The Complete Gospels: Annotated Scholars Version* [Sonoma, CA: Polebridge Press, 1992], p. 424). Compare a second agraphon found after Jn 17.26 in *Codex evangelii Johannei Parisii in sacro Templariorum tabulario asservatus*. During his parting instructions to his disciples, Jesus says, 'But your father will be John, until he comes with me to paradise' (text from R.J. Miller (ed.), *Complete Gospels*, p. 424).

20. Abbott (*Johannine Grammar*, §§2013, 2025-26) notes that this dative construction refers to a precise moment. Compare ἐν ἐκείνῃ τῇ ἡμέρᾳ (Jn 5.9; 14.20; 16.23, 26); τῇ ἡμέρᾳ ἐκείνῃ (Jn 20.19); ἐν ἐκείνῃ τῇ νυκτί (Jn 21.3).

21. Compare ἀπ' ἄρτι (Jn 13.19; 14.7); ἀπ' ἀρχῆς (Jn 8.44; 15.27); also note ἐξ ἀρχῆς (Jn 6.64; 16.4).

time a single event occurred: the official's son was healed at the very same moment in which Jesus declared it. Jn 11.53 indicates that at a more general point in time a process was initiated: the council decided on that day to begin a sustained and systematic effort to put Jesus to death. It would seem that if John had wanted to show the Beloved Disciple taking Jesus' mother from the cross to his home at the very moment in which Jesus so directed, then ἐν ἐκείνῃ τῇ ὥρᾳ or ὥραν ἐκείνην (cf. Jn 4.52) would have been chosen (giving the sense of 'at that hour' rather than 'from that hour'), whereas the choice of ἀπ' ἐκείνης τῆς ὥρας suggests that the ongoing process of the new relationship between the Beloved Disciple and Jesus' mother has begun when Jesus commands it.[22] Further, if John had desired to avoid any allusion to the hour of Jesus' glorification, some type of alternative locution to ὥρα probably would have been chosen (perhaps, for example, the characteristic μετὰ ταῦτα/τοῦτο). Thus, coming during that time when Jesus is elevated on the cross, the ὥρα of Jn 19.27 should not be read prosaically, but as indicating that Jesus' mother, along with the other three women, remains there to witness his death.

Perhaps the strongest argument to be advanced against reading Jn 19.27 as a depiction of the Beloved Disciple and Jesus' mother leaving the cross at that moment is that it would be impossible for him to be present to witness the flux of blood and water from Jesus' side (Jn 19.34). This argument stands, but only if the witness if Jn 19.35 is in fact the Beloved Disciple—something that cannot be presumed and must wait to be addressed.[23]

Reviewing the exegetical issues: (1) four women are at the cross: Jesus' mother, his aunt (paternal or maternal), Mary of Clopas (his father's brother's wife) and Mary Magdalene; (2) the women are close

22. This conclusion perhaps gathers support from Culpepper's (*Anatomy*, pp. 61-62) identification of Jn 19.27 as a mixed completing prolepsis; that is, it tells of an event that begins prior to the ending of the narrative and will continue past its ending, but does not describe that latter part.

23. A. Edersheim explains how the Beloved Disciple could leave Gabbatha, enter the city to tell the four women of what has happened, return alone to witness the crucifixion, leave Golgotha and enter the city and return with the four women, escort Jesus' mother from the cross to his home, and return to Golgotha without her to witness the remaining events (A. Edersheim, *The Life and Times of Jesus the Messiah* [2 vols.; repr., Peabody, MA: Hendrickson, n.d. (1883)], II, pp. 601-603). This type of reading is unfashionable but not impossible. Most telling against it is that John shows no interest in so tracing the movements of the Beloved Disciple.

to the cross; (3) when Jesus says to his mother, 'Woman, here is your son', he is calling her attention not to himself but to the Beloved Disciple; (4) the phrase 'from that hour' does not signal that Mary leaves the cross at that very moment, but that at the time of Jesus' death she passes from his care into that of the Beloved Disciple.

2. *John 2.1-11: An Interpretative Frame*

The mother of Jesus appears only twice in John's Gospel, but does so at the two events that frame Jesus' public ministry: the first of his signs (Jn 2.11) and the end of his work (Jn 19.28). The miracle at Cana and the crucifixion at Golgotha have more in common than just the presence of Jesus' mother. At Cana Jesus' hour has not yet come, while at Golgotha it has arrived; at Cana a group of Jesus' disciples are spotlighted, while at Golgotha his Beloved Disciple stands out; at Cana Jesus changes water into wine, while at Golgotha he drinks sour wine, and blood and water flow from his side; at Cana Jesus begins the unveiling of his glory through a sign, while at Golgotha he consummates it through the cross.

J.A. Grassi analyzes Mary's role at Cana and Golgotha within the context of M. Girard's proposed chiasm of Johannine signs.[24] According to Girard, Jesus' walk on water is not a sign, but his death and the effusion of blood and water are. Thus, there are seven signs, forming a chiasm with the feeding of the five thousand at the centre.

1. The wedding feast at Cana (2.1-12)
2. The restoration of the dying son (4.46-54)
3. The sabbath healing at Bethesda (5.1-16)
4. The multiplication of the loaves (6.1-71)
5. The sabbath healing of the blind man (9.1-41)
6. The restoration of Lazarus to life (11.1-44)
7. The great hour of Jesus: his mother, the cross, and the issue of blood and water from Jesus' side (19.25-37)[25]

24. J.A. Grassi, 'The Role of Jesus' Mother in John's Gospel: A Reappraisal', *CBQ* 48 (1986), pp. 67-80, presented with modifications in *The Hidden Heroes of the Gospel: Female Counterparts of Jesus* (Collegeville, MN: Liturgical Press, 1989), pp. 113-25. The proposal of M. Girard is found in 'La composition structurelle des sept signes dans le quatrième évangile', *SR* 9 (1980), pp. 315-24.

25. Grassi, 'Jesus' Mother', p. 69. H. Saxby also sees Jesus' death as a seventh sign ('The Time-Scheme in the Gospel of John', *ExpTim* 104 [1992], p. 11). Compare Jesus' death as 'the sign of the prophet Jonah' in Mt. 12.38-40.

Girard's plan faces objections. First, although the walk on water is not called a σημεῖον, neither is Jesus' death nor the flux from his side (the other six signs are labeled as such: Jn 2.11; 4.54; 6.2 [cf. 7.21]; 6.14; 9.16; 12.18). Secondly, the death of Jesus does not qualify as a sign because it does not point beyond itself to something else.[26] These objections can be answered with Jn 2.18-22, where Jesus' cryptic words about the destruction and raising of the temple in response to the demand for a sign are explicitly interpreted by the narrator as an allusion to Jesus' death and resurrection. However, Girard's scheme would perhaps be more acceptable if modified to limit the seventh sign to the flow of blood and water itself.[27]

As the central episode, the feeding of the five thousand has links with Cana and Golgotha: Jesus' mother (Jn 2.1; 6.42; 19.25), his hour of glory/death (Jn 2.4; 6.62; 19.27), his blood (Jn 2.9; 6.53-56; 19.34) and the Passover (Jn 2.13; 6.4; 19.14, 29, 31).[28] Grassi notes that Cana and Golgotha shed light on questions about Jesus' mission, humanity and divinity raised at the miraculous feeding, and that Mary plays a key role in that regard. In his article Grassi states that Mary is 'the preeminent witness' of who Jesus is, how he died and the effects of his death. In his book Grassi seems to attenuate that position in saying that she is 'an essential witness' of the reality of Jesus' humanity and divinity. Further, Grassi sees Mary as a co-witness with the Beloved Disciple and a guarantor of his teaching on the reality and meaning of Jesus' death.[29] What follows here is my attempt to resolve some of the issues underlying Grassi's exposition.

26. So Barrett, *John*, p. 78. Nicol (*Sēmeia*, p. 123) takes precisely the opposite view of signs, that they are the realities for which they stand. Dodd (*Interpretation*, p. 439) embraces both views: 'The cross is a sign, but a sign which is also the thing signified'.

27. G. Richter maintains that although the effusion from Jesus' side has been interpreted as a miraculous sign since patristic times, the author did not so intend it ('Blut und Wasser aus der durchbohrten Seite Jesu [Joh 19,34b]', in J. Hainz [ed.], *Studien zum Johannesevangelium* [BU, 13; Regensburg: Friedrich Pustet, 1977], p. 135). Nevertheless, since signs are meant to induce faith (Jn 12.37; 20.30-31), the attestation for the flow of blood and water, being given 'so that you might believe' (Jn 19.35), marks it as a sign.

28. Jn 6.42 is the weak link in Grassi's chain, because there Jesus' mother is mentioned only in passing in an ironic statement from his antagonists, and she is missing entirely from MSS ℵ W b sy[s.c.].

29. See the summaries in 'Jesus' Mother', p. 80; *Hidden Heroes*, p. 122.

First, there is Mary's belief. It is sometimes claimed that from start to finish, at Cana and at Golgotha, John portrays Jesus' mother as 'the prototype and exemplar of faith'.[30] But the range of evaluations on the state of Mary's faith varies wildly, from model belief to outright disbelief. This gamut of assessments is the result of having to interpret Mary's enigmatic words and actions without benefit of a straightforward pronouncement on the matter by John. Such declarations concerning belief and/or knowledge often are provided by the narrator or others (for example, Jn 2.11; 4.39, 42, 53; 6.69; 7.5; 9.38; 11.27). As Gaffney remarks, 'Of every one of the Gospel's major personages, and of most of its minor ones, it is once or oftener affirmed or denied that they believe or know'.[31] Yet, John never articulates the state of Mary's belief or knowledge. This holds true for Cana and Golgotha. Mary's words and actions at Cana show that she most likely possessed at least a miracle faith, but at Golgotha all that is noted is her passive and tacit presence. It is often proposed that the presence of Jesus' mother (and the other three women) contrasts with the unbelief of the four soldiers who carry out his execution, and Dauer maintains that even though the women neither say nor do anything to confirm that they are believers, the simple fact that they are at the cross marks them as such.[32] Perhaps so, but even if Mary's presence at the cross is not an overt statement of faith, it is an overt act of devotion and courage. I agree with Marsh, who perceives that the scant evidence speaks against Mary being a believer, but sensibly concludes that the state of her faith cannot be ascertained.[33]

Secondly, there is Jesus' humanity. From at least as early as the turn of the second century, efforts were being made to combat the views of those who denied the reality of Jesus' humanity, the Docetists. Ignatius, bishop of Antioch, was concerned about the threat to church unity posed by those who promulgated such views of Jesus—μὴ ὁμολογῶν αὐτὸν σαρκοφόρον (*Ign. Smyrn.* 5.2)—and in several letters (ca. 100–110) mentions the mother of Jesus in his apologia.

> There is one physician, who is both flesh and spirit, born and unborn, God in man [v. l. God come in flesh], true life in death, both from Mary and from God, first subject to suffering and then beyond it, Jesus Christ our Lord (*Ign. Eph.* 7.2).

30. So McHugh, *Mother of Jesus*, p. 403.
31. Gaffney, 'Believing and Knowing', p. 224.
32. Dauer, *Passionsgeschichte*, pp. 316-17.
33. Marsh, *John*, p. 616.

> For our God, Jesus the Christ, was conceived by Mary according to God's plan, both from the seed of David and of the Holy Spirit. He was born and baptized in order that by his suffering he might cleanse the water (*Ign. Eph.* 18.2).

> Be deaf, therefore, whenever anyone speaks to you apart from Jesus Christ, who was of the family of David, who was the son of Mary; who was really born, who both ate and drank; who really was persecuted under Pontius Pilate, who was really crucified and died while those in heaven and on earth and under the earth looked on (*Ign. Trall.* 9.1).[34]

If the traditional setting of John's Gospel in Ephesus c. 90–100 has merit, then the book sits squarely within the milieu to which Ignatius writes to combat Docetic ideas, since both Trallia and Smyrna (as well as Magnesia and Philadelphia) lay in the general region of Ephesus.

From the outset of John's Gospel, in Jn 1.14, the humanity of Jesus is established. The debate over whether or not that verse represents a calculated effort by John to refute Docetic ideas has generated a catalogue of opinions. Some exegetes hold that Jn 1.14 belongs to the tradition inherited by John, some that John composed it, and others that it is a redactional insertion.[35] Isolating anti-Docetic fragments in John's Gospel is a complex and uncertain undertaking, but however Jn 1.14 entered the Gospel, and whether intentionally anti-Docetic or not, it was wielded as a weapon against Docetists, as was Jn 19.34, in which the effluence of blood and water from Jesus' side attests the reality of his physical death.[36]

To what extent, if any, does Jesus' mother act as a witness to the reality of his flesh? I noted earlier that under rabbinic regulations, Mary and Martha—women, the sisters of Lazarus—are competent witnesses to the reality and finality of his death. I also showed how John stresses, almost excessively, the reality of Lazarus' death and that Mary and Martha are his sisters. Perhaps in the case of Jesus' mother, the only, or at least the

---

34. See also *Ign. Smyrn.* 1.1; cf. *Epistula Apostolurm* 3. These texts are from J.B. Lightfoot and J.R. Harmer, *The Apostolic Fathers: Greek Texts and English Translations of their Writings* (Grand Rapids: Baker, 2nd edn, 1992).

35. For the various opinions, see U. Schnelle, *Antidocetic Christology in the Gospel of John: An Investigation of the Place of the Fourth Gospel in the Johannine School* (Minneapolis: Fortress Press, 1992), p. 221 n. 78.

36. The notion that human beings are comprised of blood and water was common among ancient Jews and Gentiles. For sources, see E. Schweizer, 'Das johanneische Zeugnis vom Herrenmahl', in *Neotestamentica: Deutsche und englische Aufsätzen 1951–1963* (Zürich: Zwingli-Verlag, 1963), pp. 381-83.

uppermost, concern of John similarly rests in her relationship to Jesus—her motherhood. This would fit with the way Ignatius uses her as a proof of Jesus' human birth, and McHugh goes so far as to contend that the full content of the term 'mother of Jesus' is brought out by the paraphrase 'mother of the Word Incarnate'.[37] But John may have had more mundane motives for not naming her, perhaps simply to avoid confusing her with the three other Marys in the Gospel (cf. Jn 14.22). Also, John could have underlined her motherhood and still named her, just as he named Mary and Martha while accentuating their sisterhood. Further, as I previously noted, with the partial exception of Jesus' human father Joseph, John leaves Jesus' relatives unnamed. Finally, while John is anxious to guarantee Jesus' humanity, he shows no interest, as do Matthew and Luke, in the details of his birth or childhood and, unlike the Synoptists, seems unconcerned to establish Jesus' Davidic lineage, with only one ironic reference to the matter (Jn 7.42).[38] These factors speak against the idea that John wields the locution 'the mother of Jesus' as an anti-Docetic device.

W.A. Bienert lays out the case for thinking that John deploys the mother of Jesus in the battle against Docetists.

> At the beginning stands the wedding at Cana (2.1-12), in which Mary has a hand in preparing for the first manifestation of the Son of God. As his bodily mother she is the guarantor of the real incarnation of the Logos (Jn. 1.14), and her behaviour at the wedding at the same time gives expression to her complete humanity and her earthly limitations. The second time, we find her beneath the cross of Jesus (Jn. 19.25-27). Here too the author's concern is evidently with anti-docetic proof (cf. 19.34) that Jesus on the cross, at the point of death, is a real man who before his death also fulfills the natural obligations of a son towards his mother.[39]

Whether John intended the material with Mary to be anti-Docetic is an open question, but in any case, Jesus' mother well suited the aims of

---

37. McHugh, *Mother of Jesus*, p. 362.

38. This view assumes that the variant 'qui...natus est' in several witnesses at Jn 1.13 is secondary (see *TCGNT*, pp. 196-97). Barrett (*John*, pp. 330-31) comments, 'The birth place of Jesus is a trivial matter in comparison with the question of whether he is ἐκ τῶν ἄνω or ἐκ τῶν κάτω (8.23), whether he is or is not from God'. Notice, however, that while speaking with Pilate of his mission, Jesus testifies (albeit in passing) to his own human birth: 'For this I was born (γεγέννημαι)' (Jn 18.37).

39. W.A. Bienert, 'The Relatives of Jesus', in Hennecke and Schneemelcher, *New Testament Apocrypha*, I, p. 482.

anti-Docetic apologists who happily employed the passages in which she appears for their purposes. Thus, in the final form of John's Gospel, and whether or not John so intended, the presence of Jesus' human mother served as a testimony to early readers of his own humanity.

John 1.14, a key verse used by those keen to refute Docetists, also shows that the revelation of Jesus' glory is programmatic for John. This disclosure of δόξα links the beginning and the ending of Jesus' ministry, Cana and Golgotha. Jesus initially unveils his glory in the water and wine of the miracle at Cana (Jn 2.11), and he supremely unveils it in the blood and water of his death at Golgotha (Jn 12.23-24; compare Peter in Jn 21.19).[40] Thus, Jesus' mother is present not just at the beginning and ending of his ministry but at the incipient and ultimate displays of his glory—the glory that reveals who he is.

At the wedding, the servants know that Jesus produced the wine (Jn 2.9), while the disciples see the sign, behold his glory and believe in him (Jn 2.11). No information like that given about the servants and the disciples is offered about Jesus' mother. If in some way she did share the experience of the servants and the disciples, it is not communicated to the readers. There is strong irony in the fact that except for the Beloved Disciple, those disciples who at Cana beheld Jesus' glory are now absent from Golgotha and its supreme revelation of that glory, while his mother, who had not seen the first unveiling of his glory at the wedding, now stands before its crowning manifestation at the cross. Still, as with the disciples at the wedding, it is someone other than Jesus' mother whom John holds up to readers as the witness to Jesus' death and glory (Jn 19.34-35). Nonetheless, the presence of Jesus' mother at the wedding and the cross bolsters the testimony of Jn 19.35 because she serves as a guarantor of Jesus' humanity, which manifests glory:

> The δόξα is not to be seen *alongside* the σάρξ, nor *through* the σάρξ as through a window; it is to be seen in the σάρξ and nowhere else. If man wishes to see the δόξα, then it is on the σάρξ that he must concentrate his attention.[41]

Jesus' glory is revealed inchoately at Cana and consummately at Golgotha, and the soteriological consequences of this distinction have

---

40. Schnelle (*Antidocetic Christology*, p. 81) observes that for John, δόξα 'means nothing other than Jesus' divinity, which he had before the foundation of the world, now revealed in his earthly activities (especially in the miracles!), and demonstrated in the event of the cross'.

41. Bultmann, *John*, p. 63.

further repercussions for the role of Jesus' mother. Lütgehetmann outlines John's intentions in this regard.

> It is above all in the cross, John wants to say, that Jesus reveals divine glory and thereby his salvific significance for humanity. Thus, the salvation of humanity is not signified equally in both the incarnation and the cross as the beginning and ending of the incarnation of the Word, but pre-eminently in the event of the cross.
>
> John's intention to assert this is perhaps served also by the way in which Jesus' mother is addressed by her son as 'woman'. It therefore might be said that it is not, after all, the incarnation that is decisive for salvation, but only the way of Jesus going to the cross, in which, however, Jesus' mother plays no special part in her role as mother.[42]

Jesus' use of γύναι as a vocative for his mother at the wedding is in fact somewhat stern and distancing. When Jesus calls his mother γύναι as he dies on the cross, the context stands in stark contrast to that of a wedding. At the wedding Jesus had resisted his mother's attempt to encroach upon the course of his ministry because his hour had not yet come; but now his hour has come, and his final act of ministry is to secure her future. It could be argued that Jesus' concern for his mother at the cross proves that γύναι is not, after all, a cold appellation. But on the contrary, within the context of caring compassion γύναι sounds all the more aloof—'indeed, spoken in the hour of death, nothing short of irreverent'.[43] Challenging the 'sentimental presuppositions' about what a dying son may say to his mother, Seim asserts, 'The use of γύναι in 19.26 reflects rather that the distance indicated in 2.4 is still maintained. The Son's unity is with the Father, and it is the will of the Father (and not the mother) that governs and decides the will, the acts and the life of the Son.'[44]

If Jesus rebuffs his mother at the wedding for interfering in the timing of his work, does he now, when his hour has come at the cross, establish a special station for her in his work? The multifarious symbolic interpretations of the new status conferred upon Mary at the cross share one aspect: her motherhood. As the mother of the Beloved Disciple she is variously said to be mother of the new humanity, the new Israel, the church, the Johannine community, the individual believer. Whereas Mary was excluded from Jesus' messianic sign at Cana, it is often

---

42. Lütgehetmann, *Hochzeit von Kana*, p. 336.
43. Dauer, *Passionsgeschichte*, p. 323.
44. Seim, 'Roles of Women', p. 60.

argued, he now installs her as matron of those who believe in him. But such symbolism, whatever allegorical value it may find in post-patristic exegesis, can hardly claim support from the text itself or even to have been in the back of John's mind.

> The difficulty which such speculations come up against consists in the fact that nothing is said by the text about any motherly concern, a right to intercession, nor about any other mediatorial activity. The disciple accepts Mary into his own circle: that is what the evangelist intends, that is the point of what he is saying. The Mariological interpretations can only be justified as a theological foundation and development of Marian piety with a certain support from Church tradition, but not as a Johannine concept.[45]

Further, it cannot be assumed that at the cross Jesus integrates his mother into his work. Just as at Cana Jesus distanced his mother from his work, he can be understood to be doing the same, perhaps even more so, with his work at Golgotha. Buck believes that the material on the mother of Jesus stems from the anti-Marian polemic of a redactor who inserts her into the narrative only to exclude her from Jesus' work.[46] Whether or not the theory of a hostile redactor is plausible, Buck's view of what transpires in Jn 19.25-27 merits attention. Buck asserts that before Jesus dies he denies his mother any participation in his work on the cross:

> The act of redemption must be that of Jesus alone; there is no place for another. In a sense John says that Jesus is no longer his mother's son; he is wholly the son of the Father. So, lest there be misunderstanding, the Mother is denied and sent to her new home.[47]

How does the foregoing discussion speak to Grassi's analysis of the wedding and the cross? Grassi's proposals using the chiastic relationship between the feeding in John 6, the wedding in John 2 and the cross in John 19 are well conceived and explicated. Jesus' identity and origins, humanity and divinity, mission and messiahship are all at issue in the feeding of the five thousand, and the events at Cana and Golgotha shed light on the questions raised at the feeding. The presence of Jesus' mother at Cana and Golgotha and her mention during the discourse following the feeding cannot be a coincidence, and must bear on the aforementioned issues about Jesus. However, to be present and to testify

---

45. Schnackenburg, *John*, III, pp. 280-81.
46. Buck, 'Redactions', p. 174.
47. Buck, 'Redactions', p. 176.

are not the same, and it would seem that the attenuation of Grassi's position, seen in the difference between the summaries of his article and his book, should be carried further. Jesus' mother is not, as Grassi contends in his article, 'the preeminent witness' of who Jesus is, how he died and the effects of his death. If she is, as Grassi has it in his book, 'an essential witness' of the reality of Jesus' humanity and divinity, it is by dint of her existence and presence rather than by anything she says or does.

Summarizing, the mother of Jesus is present at only two events in John's Gospel, both of paramount importance: Jesus' first sign at Cana and his death at Golgotha. At Cana she is verbal and active, at Golgotha she is silent and passive. Estimations of her faith are speculative, as John makes no forthright statement on the matter. Apparently, she has at least a miracle faith at Cana, and her presence at Golgotha surely manifests love and devotion. In that sense, she overcomes the scandal of the cross. She is present when Jesus changes water into wine and when blood and water stream from his side, and early readers may well have seen her as a guarantor of his humanity. And yet, whether or not Jesus' mother perceives his glory—and thus his messianic identity—in the miracle at the wedding and in his death on the cross remains uncertain, perhaps even moot, since John designates not her but others as the witnesses: the disciples at Cana (Jn 2.11) and the witness at Golgotha (Jn 19.35).

3. *The Women at the Cross as Witnesses*

At the heart of early Christian tradition is the death, burial and resurrection of Jesus (1 Cor. 15.3-4). In the Synoptics the women can forge a continuous chain of eyewitness testimony through all three events. This chain is broken in John's Gospel. Joseph of Arimathea and Nicodemus inter Jesus' body apart from any mention of the women whom the Synoptists place firmly at Jesus' burial (Jn 19.38-42; Mk 15.47 and pars.). But it does not necessarily follow that John has no concern for the women at the cross as witnesses to Jesus' death, or, as Seim thinks, that the matter is academic: 'The women and the disciple whom Jesus loved are mentioned before Jesus dies and not after, and there is no point in discussing whether they remained to witness his death or not.'[48] Seim's statement is curious in light of Jn 19.34-35, which contains an

48. Seim, 'Roles of Women', p. 64.

eyewitness asseveration about Jesus' death made in a fashion unparalleled in the New Testament (compare the more general testimony in 1 Jn 1.1). Since Jn 19.27 does not depict the Beloved Disciple ushering Jesus' mother away from the cross at that instant, and since nothing in the text speaks of the other three women departing before Jesus expires, the narrative admits all five as witnesses to his death.

The women at the cross are Jesus' mother, his aunt (maternal or paternal), Mary of Clopas (his father's sister-in-law) and Mary Magdalene. This list represents two unnamed blood relatives, one named marriage relative and one named non-relative. The first thing to notice about this list is its order. Quite often in the New Testament, in both Gospel and Epistle, the order in a list of names will signify rank.[49] In contrast to the Synoptics, in which Mary Magdalene invariably tops lists of women just as Peter does those of men (Mk 15.40, 47 and par.; 16.1 and par.; Lk. 8.2; 24.10), Jn 19.25 places Mary Magdalene last and Jesus' mother first (cf. *Epistula Apostolorum* 9). Hengel attributes the order in Jn 19.25 to a structuring principle whereby the women are listed in order of degree of kinship to Jesus.[50] This accords with my conclusion that the women range from Jesus' closest blood relative (mother), to a more distant blood relative (aunt), to a marriage relative (father's sister-in-law), to a non-relative. Hengel's idea of *Verwandtschaftgrad* for the list in Jn 19.25 is most likely correct, especially because Mary Magdalene was revered by early Christians, many of whom regarded her as the preeminent female disciple of Jesus.[51]

49. See the excursus by M. Hengel ('Die Reihenfolge in Namenlisten als Rangzeichen im N.T.') from 'Maria Magdalena und die Frauen als Zeugen', in O. Betz, *et al.* (eds.), *Abraham unser Vater: Juden und Christen im Gespräch über die Bibel* (AGJU, 5; Leiden: Brill, 1963), pp. 248-50.

50. Hengel, 'Maria Magdalena', p. 250. Hengel points out that in Gal. 2.9 Peter relinquishes his primacy in lists to James the brother of Jesus. Klauck ('dreifache Maria', pp. 2350-51) maintains that although Mary Magdalene is displaced by Jesus' mother from the head of the list, her *Schlußstellung* also carries weight, and that this fits with the macrostructure of John's Gospel.

51. Mary Magdalene received exalted status in Gnostic circles. For example, in *Pistis Sophia* 96 Jesus says, 'But Mary Magdalene and John [note the order], the maiden, will surpass all my disciples and all men who shall receive mysteries in the Ineffable' (she also obtains special revelations in the *Questions of Mary* and the *Apocryphon Johannis*). *Gos. Phil.* 55 states, 'The Saviour loved Mary Magdalene more than all the disciples'. Mary Magdalene later came to be regarded as ἰσαπόστολος by the Greek Fathers.

How can this unique focus by John on Jesus' relatives be understood? The narrative is manifestly concerned with Jesus' family and the ongoing relationships after his departure. Since Jesus' brothers are branded as unbelievers (Jn 7.5), it makes perfect sense for him to entrust his mother to the Beloved Disciple, whose behaviour is the antithesis of unbelief. But also, under Jewish customs Jesus' mother, aunt and father's sister-in-law are competent witnesses to his death. Had Jesus been married, his mother would have been unable to attest his death, whereas his aunt and his father's sister-in-law qualify regardless of his marital status (*m. Yeb.* 15.4). Bultmann contends that John is interested only in Jesus' mother and not in the other women as witnesses of the crucifixion.[52] But it is hard to see why else John would mention Jesus' aunt and father's sister-in-law apart from their capacity as witnesses of Jesus' crucifixion, since this is their only appearance in John's Gospel. They play no other part in the story. It is possible, as is often suggested, that John provides four faithful women to counterpoise the four unbelieving soldiers, but this fails to explain why John outlines their identities and/or their relationships to Jesus (compare the anonymity of the women at the cross in Lk. 23.49).

Stauffer suggests that the Jewish religious leaders who appear at the cross in the Synoptics fulfill a cultic duty as required witnesses to the execution.

> The leaders of the Sanhedrin have arrived as witnesses. Caiaphas has a priestly office here. He is waiting for the pseudo-prophet to confess his guilt, to recant, thus justifying the death sentence of the Great Sanhedrin. Then the Grand Inquisitor may absolve the preacher of apostasy, and he will do so. Thus the crucified man will die the death of a pious man.[53]

Even if Stauffer is correct, John has no interest in Jewish religious leaders as witnesses to Jesus' death, and simply records their protest to Pilate over the inscription 'The King of the Jews' on the *titulus*. However, John is the only Evangelist to locate Jesus' mother and two other female relatives at the cross.[54] The presence of these women serves a rhetorical, even quasi-legal, purpose in the narrative. With the Deuteronomic demand for multiple witnesses in the Johannine atmosphere, the

---

52. Bultmann, *John*, p. 672.
53. Stauffer, *Jesus and His Story*, p. 111.
54. Bauckham (*Jude*, p. 15) concludes that no relatives of Jesus are among the women disciples named by the Synoptists, while on the other hand, the Johannine tradition focuses upon his relatives.

Evangelist advances competent witnesses to the crucifixion who are sympathetic to his case. Along with Jesus' mother, who can confirm the reality of his birth, stand three other women, all four being competent and credible witnesses who can confirm the reality of his death. One of the arguments for seeing Jn 19.25 as listing only two women is that it is hard to see any point in referring to one or two other women who have no narratological or theological function. As witnesses, however, the women have an important narratological and theological function at the cross. Indeed, as P.A. Kerrigan asserts, John regards the women at the cross as official witnesses who guaranteed juridically the events narrated.[55]

Did these women possess the added credibility that would come from being known to the readers? Bauckham offers the following general rule, aware that it has exceptions: 'Where the early Gospel tradition preserves the names of characters in the Gospel story (other than those of public figures such as Pilate and Caiaphas), these named people were Christians well known in the early church. In circles where they ceased to be known, their names often dropped out of the tradition.'[56] Using that guideline, it appears that Mary of Clopas and Mary Magdalene were familiar to readers. But the principle may be turned on its head to argue that they, being unknown to the readers, require naming, while Jesus' mother and aunt need not be named because readers were familiar with them and already knew their names. When this same issue arose previously in relation to the Bethany family, I noted that John does not identify characters consistently. If John does have an identification scheme, it is abstruse.[57] Even the Beloved Disciple, arguably the weightiest figure after Jesus, is introduced as 'one of his disciples...whom Jesus loved'

55. P.A. Kerrigan, 'Jn. 19,25-27 in the Light of Johannine Theology and the Old Testament', *Antonianum* 35 (1960), p. 375.

56. Bauckham, *Jude*, p. 9 n. 14. A. Barr suggests a process in regard to Gospel names: (1) an early stage represented by Mark in which actual names were remembered and used (cf. Mk 15.21), (2) a middle stage represented by Matthew and Luke in which some names were dropped (cf. Mk 15.21 and pars.), (3) a late stage represented by the legendary narratives in which fictional names were invented (cf. *Acts Pil.* 9.4) (A. Barr, 'The Factor of Testimony in the Gospels', *ExpTim* 49 [1937-38], p. 404).

57. After laying out the previously mentioned schema about Gospel names, Barr ('Factor of Testimony', p. 406) notes that John is a writer whose standards are different from the Synoptists. If John's Gospel underwent several revisions over a period of time, it may encompass all three stages of the process Barr describes.

(Jn 13.23) (not, as in many translations, 'one of his disciples...the one whom Jesus loved'), unnamed and apparently not expected to be recognized by the readers. Culpepper cautions, 'It would be precarious to infer any prior knowledge of the women at the cross on the basis of the references to "Mary the wife of Clopas" and "Mary Magdalene" (19.25), but the reader may have heard their names before'.[58] It remains possible that some or all of the four women at the cross were familiar to readers, but there is no way to know for certain.

What can be said about the witness of the women in light of the flow of blood and water from Jesus' side in Jn 19.34? That this flow is singularly important is evidenced in part by the repetition in the verse that attests it (Jn 19.35). I noted previously that John will use twofold repetition in narrative to stress an important fact, for example, 'Mary... anointed Jesus' *feet* and wiped his *feet* with her hair' (Jn 12.3). Abbott explains that Johannine repetitions are unlike anything found in the Synoptics and function within the Jewish canons whereby legal evidence and religious truths are established by double and triple repetition (cf. Deut. 19.15; Ps. 62.11; Jn 1.20).[59] Thus, Jn 19.35 contains a pair of twofold repetitions with minor variations (put somewhat woodenly here in order to bring them out clearly): 'And he who saw has testified (μεμαρτύρηκεν) and true (ἀληθινή) is his testimony (μαρτυρία), and that one knows that he says true things (ἀληθῆ)'. Jn 19.35 frequently is regarded as a gloss, but this is not at all certain. What is certain is that the text as it stands could scarcely be more vehement in defending the factuality of the piercing of Jesus' side and the resulting discharge of blood and water from the wound.

Two questions about Jn 19.35 must be addressed. First, can the eyewitness be identified? Secondly, does the eyewitness or someone else swear to the testimony of the eyewitness?

Although it seems obvious that the Beloved Disciple is the only person who could be 'the one who saw', Lindars, thinking that he leaves Golgotha at Jn 19.27, nominates the soldier who spears Jesus.[60] Putting aside the issue of the Beloved Disciple departing, the soldier makes a good candidate grammatically but a poor one theologically.

---

58. Culpepper, *Anatomy*, p. 216. Culpepper (p. 216) believes that the readers are expected to recognize most of the characters in the story, but he goes on to list several notable exceptions.

59. Abbot, *Johannine Grammar*, §§2587-627.

60. Lindars, *John*, p. 589.

Jesus' enemies stand unequivocally on the side of darkness and deceit, and the only true statements they make about Jesus are those of unwitting irony. The last person John would present in this supremely important moment as a deliberate and positive witness to Jesus is someone who had just participated in his torment and execution.

The Beloved Disciple is the one who sees the blood and water, but is it he or another who affirms what he has seen? The answer to this more difficult question depends whether ἐκεῖνος in Jn 19.35b is understood to resume αὐτοῦ in 19.35a or to designate a second person. If ἐκεῖνος does point to a second person, then a slate of candidates presents itself, including the Father, Jesus and the writer in one form or another (the evangelist, the narrator, the implied author). While ἐκεῖνος is sometimes used to refer to the Father or Jesus, it is used for many other persons as well, and ordinarily the referent is nearby. This leaves the writer, who in a sense is always at hand. But if so, the writer takes an ambiguous, almost contorted, grammatical path to accomplish the simple task of saying, 'I confirm what he saw' (contrast Jn 21.24 in which a second party does use the simpler way: 'We know that his testimony is true'). This leaves the Beloved Disciple, and since he is always spoken of in the third person, it makes best sense that ἐκεῖνος would resume αὐτοῦ.

The Beloved Disciple is the best candidate for both the one who sees and the one who confirms what he has seen. He is at the scene and he is the embodiment of the faithful disciple and ideal witness.[61]

Barr attributes the fervency of expression in the protestation of truth in Jn 19.35 to the fact that although the event is crucial, John has but one witness for it.[62] I have argued that the narrative admits the four women as witnesses to what the Beloved Disciple sees, but Barr's point may be taken up from another angle. Jn 19.35 singles out the flow of blood and water from other crucifixion events as something deserving

---

61. I will make no attempt to determine the precise identity of the Beloved Disciple because understanding the women as witnesses is not contingent upon it. The working hypothesis of Brown *et al.* (*Mary*, p. 211) suffices: the Beloved Disciple was a real albeit now unidentified person who was a companion of Jesus; whether or not he founded the Johannine community, he was its paragon both as the disciple whom Jesus especially loved and as the witness who guaranteed its understanding of Jesus and its status among churches. If, as Culpepper (*Anatomy*, p. 215) believes, the Beloved Disciple probably has no roots in the tradition and is fictionalized to a great degree, it is hard to see how he could function as a persuasive and credible witness.

62. Barr, 'Factor of Testimony', p. 406.

special testimony. The effusion is, according to Abbott, uniquely impressive and requires a combination of more than one witness.[63] I have noted how Abbott found such a combination in the phrasing of Jn 19.35, which attends to the Jewish canons of repetition. But is the requirement for plural attestation not satisfied by the four women—perfectly competent witnesses—standing there? Yes and no. For while the women see Jesus' physical death, when it comes to the deeper significance of the blood and water, clearly symbolizing much more than physical death, it is the Beloved Disciple who sees, and it is his testimony alone that John offers to the readers. The flow of blood and water is a sign, the last and the greatest, for it signifies the new birth and life that the death of Jesus the Messiah brings.[64] As such, it occurs in the presence of the Beloved Disciple, who testifies to it so that the readers might believe (cf. Jn 19.35; 20.30-31). This returns full circle to the Cana wedding and Jesus' first sign. Whatever else Jesus' mother may have seen at the wedding, she is not said to have seen the sign; it is the disciples who do so (Jn 2.11).

It could be argued that Jesus' mother and the Beloved Disciple are equally important in the scene at the cross.[65] But the concept of testimony, so integral to John's Gospel, factors into the scenes where the Beloved Disciple appears, and Dauer marks his preeminence.

> In all other scenes in the Gospel—and this might be the decisive factor—in which this disciple appears, the attention is always focused on him. Time and again the Evangelist returns to him and wants to make an important statement about him always in a new way.
>
> Jn 13.21-30; 20.2-10; 21.7, 20-23 clearly show that when the Beloved Disciple appears, the chief interest of the Evangelist is directed at him and not those named together with him. This observation is also important for the exegesis of 19.26f.[66]

---

63. Abbott, *Johannine Grammar*, §2383.

64. Dauer (*Passionsgeschichte*, p. 332) emphasizes that the witness of the Beloved Disciple is more concerned with the soteriological meaning of Jesus' death than with its factuality. Pancaro (*Law*, p. 197) sees the witness testifying to the 'hidden reality' in the blood and water: Christ is the Lamb of God and the donor of the Spirit. Oddly, Pancaro does not think that the witness testifies to the fact of the blood and water.

65. So Brown *et al.*, *Mary*, p. 210.

66. Dauer, *Passionsgeschichte*, pp. 318, 320.

Thus, while Grassi is correct to say that Jesus' mother is a witness to his humanity and death, and that she can bolster the witness of the Beloved Disciple, he strains the evidence in claiming that she is the Beloved Disciple's joint witness to Jesus' divinity and to the soteriological meaning of the blood and water.[67] On those matters the text is silent in regard to Jesus' mother.

I noted at the start of this chapter that Jesus' mother has been deluged with symbolic interpretation, much of it chimerical. But exotic symbolism is not the only excess visited upon her. Witherington, for example, far outruns any textual evidence when he states, '[Mary] will assume both her old role of motherhood and her new roles as witness, prophetess and proclaimer of God's word in relationship to believers'.[68] Other than the questionable legends about Jesus' mother in the apocryphal corpus, only Acts 1.14 offers any clue as to her involvement in the post-ascension community, and all that is said there is that she participates in communal prayer life. Her activity surely could not have been limited to prayer, but Witherington's projections lack any supporting evidence.

At the cross, Mary Magdalene is afforded precisely the opposite treatment from Jesus' mother, with many exegetes losing sight of her in the shadows cast by Jesus' mother and the Beloved Disciple. This is mirrored in the telling omission Collins makes when saying that 'Mary Magdalene appears in two passages of the Fourth Gospel, John 20, 1-2 and 11-18'.[69] And yet in John's Gospel only Mary Magdalene, along with the Beloved Disciple, can proffer continuous witness between the cross and the empty tomb. She must receive full attention next.

---

67. Grassi, *Hidden Heroes*, pp. 119-20, 122.
68. Witherington, *Women*, p. 95.
69. R.F. Collins, 'The Representative Figures of the Fourth Gospel—II', *DRev* 94 (1976), p. 122.

Chapter 9

MARY MAGDALENE WENT TO THE TOMB

'The Lord truly has risen.' Despite variations in their resurrection accounts, the Evangelists share that *Grundmotiv*, and John is no exception. Neirynck warns that to neglect the Synoptic traditions, sources and texts when interpreting John's account is to work in isolation from current research on John 20.[1] Certainly, explicating the Johannine resurrection narrative with no view at all toward those of the Synoptists puts limits on the analysis. Nevertheless, the Synoptic parallels can be used profitably apart from questions of sources and dependence. The ways in which John's narrative differs from those of the Synoptists bring into relief his individual expression of the resurrection *Grundmotiv* and treatment of the resurrection witnesses.

1. *John 20.1-18: The Exegetical Issues*

a. The theme of seeing and believing is at the heart of John 20, and the chapter contains no less than a dozen references to seeing. What Mary Magdalene sees at the tomb is crucial to her role as a witness. John

---

1. F. Neirynck, 'John and the Synoptics: The Empty Tomb Stories', in *Evangelica II* (BETL, 99; Leuven: Leuven University Press, 1991), pp. 577-78. Neirynck investigates Johannine-Synoptic connections, as do H. Graß, *Ostergeschehen und Osterberichte* (Göttingen: Vandenhoeck & Ruprecht, 3rd edn, 1964), Part I; P. Seidensticker, *Die Auferstehung Jesu in der Botschaft der Evangelisten: Ein traditionsgeschichtlicher Versuch zum Problem der Sicherung der Osterbotschaft in der apostolischen Zeit* (SBS, 26; Stuttgart: Katholisches Bibelwerk, 1967); E.L. Bode, *The First Easter Morning: The Gospel Accounts of the Women's Visit to the Tomb of Jesus* (AnBib, 45; Rome: Biblical Institute Press, 1970), Part I; R. Mahoney, *Two Disciples at the Tomb: The Background and Message of John 20.1-10* (TW, 6; Bern: Herbert Lang; Frankfurt: Peter Lang, 1974). For an attempt to reconcile the events of the narratives, see J. Wenham, *Easter Enigma: Do the Resurrection Stories Contradict One Another?* (Exeter: Paternoster Press, 1984).

recounts how she arrived during darkness (σκοτίας ἔτι οὔσης), while the Synoptists variously indicate that it was light or becoming light (Jn 20.1 and pars.).[2] It is pointless to speculate about the precise level of visibility allowed by the phrase σκοτίας ἔτι οὔσης, but certainly not much light would be required to see that the stone, which was large enough to demand several strong people to move it (cf. Mk 16.3-4; *Gos. Pet.* 12.24), had been dislodged from the mouth of the tomb. Some time will have elapsed while Mary runs to Peter and the Beloved Disciple and they run back to the tomb, allowing the latter two sufficient light at that point to peer into the tomb and see the grave clothes.

Just as important, however, is the metaphor of darkness. Nicodemus's visit to Jesus by night accentuates his imperceptivity (John 3), even as Judas Iscariot's exit from the last supper at night underlines his treachery (John 13). Darkness provides the backdrop for the journey across the lake in which the disciples react with fear to the presence of Jesus (John 6), and their nocturnal fishing expedition is futile until daybreak and Jesus arrive (John 21). Mary's inability to perceive the significance of the empty tomb leaves her metaphorically in the dark, but such a metaphor can make sense only against her accurate visual perception of the empty tomb. The narrative allows that Mary's comprehension is limited but not that her eyes deceive her.

b. The number and identities of witnesses to the empty tomb and to the risen Jesus are crucial. Mary informs Peter and the Beloved Disciple that the Lord has been removed from the tomb and that 'We do not know (οὐκ οἴδαμεν) where they have laid him' (Jn 20.2). But later, she responds to the query of the two angels by saying, 'I do not know (οὐκ οἶδα) where they have laid him' (Jn 20.13). Did Mary come to the tomb alone or with others? The problem is acknowledged in some MSS (notably, sy[s] e), which read οὐκ οἶδα at Jn 20.2, probably to square it with Jn 20.13, but οὐκ οἴδαμεν, the more difficult reading, enjoys far superior attestation.

---

2. Jesus had already been anointed symbolically and literally (Jn 12.1-8; 19.38-42), and John does not give anointing (or anything else) as the reason for Mary going to the tomb (cf. Mk 16.1 and pars.). The *Gospel of Peter* explains that Mary came early in the morning to observe the custom of women lamenting at the grave, which has been made difficult for fear of being seen by irate Jewish leaders (*Gos. Pet.* 12.50-54). Darkness would facilitate a covert visit, but in any event, John is not interested so much in why Mary came to the tomb as in what she experienced there.

The plural οἴδαμεν in Jn 20.2 can be understood as: (1) a Johannine idiom that is not a true plural (cf. Jn 3.2, 11; 9.31), (2) an ancient mode of expression that is not a true plural, (3) a true plural that reflects the presence of other women, (4) a link with or trace of the Synoptic traditions, sources, or Gospels, in which more than one woman goes to the tomb (cf. Mk 16.1 and pars.).

The idea of a Johannine (or other) idiom in which 'we' means 'I' is harder to defend than is often thought.[3] It is not difficult to hear Nicodemus speaking on behalf of others when he says, 'Rabbi, we know that you are a teacher who has come from God; for no one can do these signs that you do apart from the presence of God' (Jn 3.2), because many others in Jerusalem besides Nicodemus had just been moved to some kind of faith (ephemeral or otherwise) in Jesus by his signs (Jn 2.23-25). In Jesus' statement to Nicodemus, 'Very truly, I tell you, we speak of what we know and testify to what we have seen' (Jn 3.11), οἴδαμεν could refer to any number of others, most probably to John the Baptist and/or to Jesus' disciples. When the man born blind says, 'We know that God does not listen to sinners, but he does listen to one who worships him and obeys his will' (Jn 9.31), he speaks for the many others who hold this common Jewish belief (Pss. 66.18; 145.19; Prov. 15.8, 29; Isa. 1.15). These statements of Jesus, Nicodemus and the man born blind show that οἴδαμεν can include people other than the speaker without necessarily enumerating them.

Therefore in Mary's statement, 'We do not know where they have laid him', οἴδαμεν can be read as a true plural in which she speaks on behalf of others (presumably other women), and the singular οἶδα in Jn 20.13 is understood as a normal response to the question, 'Why are *you* crying?' (notice how in Jn 20.13 Mary says 'my Lord' while in Jn 20.2 she had said 'the Lord'). Does Mary's οἴδαμεν provide an example of John's predilection for a sparsely populated centre-stage motivating him to distil several characters into a single representative figure? Probably so.[4] John has no narratological interest in women other than Mary as witnesses. If he had such an interest, he would have

3. Abbott, who in *Johannine Vocabulary* and *Johannine Grammar* exhaustively catalogues such idioms, makes no mention of the οἴδαμεν in Jn 20.2 in that regard.

4. Using the concept of the 'categorical plural' (class for individual), some commentators go in the opposite direction, viewing the appearance of Jesus to the women in Mt. 28.9-10 as that to the one woman, Mary Magdalene, in Jn 20.14-18; Mk 16.9 (see Zerwick, *Biblical Greek*, §7).

catalogued them just as he did the women at the cross. Jn 20.2 allows
that other women saw (or at least knew of) the empty tomb, but John
does not care to advance them as witnesses.[5]

c. A somewhat similar problem arises in Jn 20.8-9. John recounts that
the grave clothes are seen first by Peter and then by the Beloved
Disciple. John then declares that the Beloved Disciple believed, presumably because of the grave clothes, for neither he nor Peter as yet understood the scripture. Bultmann surmises that Peter, ahead of the Beloved
Disciple, had come to faith: 'For if the writer had meant otherwise, and
if the two disciples were set over against each other with respect to their
πιστεῦσαι, it would have had to be expressly stated that Peter did not
believe.'[6] But Bultmann has, in my opinion, misconstrued John's silence
about Peter's reaction. If John had been concerned to avoid giving the
impression that only the Beloved Disciple believed, he would have
expressly stated that Peter did believe. Stauffer writes, '[John] lays the
greatest stress on establishing that...it was he, and he alone, who
regarded the empty tomb not only as the starting point of the Easter
faith, but also as its sufficient basis'.[7]

d. Stauffer's remark introduces the next issue. What did the Beloved
Disciple believe? Did he simply satisfy himself that Mary was correct
about Jesus' body being missing, or, did he also believe that Jesus had
risen from the dead? According to P.S. Minear, the Beloved Disciple
and Peter believe only in Mary's report and join in her confession of
ignorance, 'We don't know where'.[8] Minear adduces three supports for
his opinion: (1) if the Beloved Disciple believed in Jesus' resurrection,
then it makes no sense that he and Peter did not as yet understand the
scripture that says that Jesus must rise from the dead; (2) the subdued

5.   Whether or not Mary speaking for other women in Jn 20.2 reflects some sort
of Synoptic link is uncertain. Brown (*John*, II, p. 984) finds it odd that John would
attempt such a minor and subtle harmonization with the Synoptics while allowing so
many other pronounced differences to stand.

6.   Bultmann, *John*, p. 684.

7.   Stauffer, *Jesus and His Story*, p. 124. Still, it should be kept in mind that
John does not actually say whether Peter believes or not. Mahoney (*Two Disciples*,
p. 260) understands John to think of Peter as not believing, but to gloss over the
matter to avoid the consequences either way.

8.   P.S. Minear, '"We Don't Know Where..." John 20.2', *Int* 30 (1976),
pp. 127-28.

return of Peter and the Beloved Disciple to their homes shows them to be unaware of 'any great sign' or 'radical disclosure from heaven—they act as if nothing had changed; (3) the ensuing episodes are narrated as if they were the first resurrection appearances and the origin of faith. I will take up Minear's three points in reverse order.

First, it is puzzling how Minear can see John's narration of the ensuing episodes as the first Christophanies and the origin of faith somehow to negate the Beloved Disciple's faith in Jesus' resurrection. The Christophanies to Mary, to the gathered disciples and to Thomas are indeed the first ones, as well as being the source of faith for their recipients. But this does not preclude the Beloved Disciple from believing ahead of the others and without a Christophany. Secondly, how should the two disciples be expected to behave? Peter does not believe, and so it is hardly surprising that he returns home with no fanfare (cf. Lk. 24.12). The Beloved Disciple, even though he believes in the risen Jesus, has nothing beyond the grave clothes of which to tell. He has not seen Jesus. His silence in fact is consistent with his behaviour elsewhere, as Culpepper observes: 'The Beloved Disciple's silence about the empty tomb fits the pattern of the last supper scene and his seeing the water and the blood at the cross. He understands but does not bear witness until later.'[9] According to Abbott, the effect of the Greek particles in the passage gives it this sense: 'The two disciples went back to their several homes. One indeed believed. But neither he nor Peter had any message of glad tidings to convey to the Eleven.'[10] Thirdly, the fact that the disciples were ignorant of the scripture not only makes sense following the Beloved Disciple's belief that Jesus is risen, but even emphasizes it. He believes without benefit of the scripture, and unlike Peter, sees the grave clothes as evidence of Jesus' resurrection.[11]

This last point needs further comment. In declaring the Beloved Disciple's faith, the narrator uses ἐπίστευσεν, a 'πιστεύω absolute'. Johannine πιστεύω constructions have come up previously in regard to the Samaritans and Martha, and I noted that a πιστεύω absolute derives its content from its context. All that Mary sees before going to the two

9. Culpepper, *Anatomy*, p. 44.

10. Abbott, *Johannine Grammar*, §2638.

11. The plural ᾔδεισαν in Jn 20.9 seems awkward against the singular ἐπίστευσεν in Jn 20.8. In light of Jn 2.22 it is best understood as showing that all the disciples, not just Peter and the Beloved Disciple, were ignorant of the scripture's meaning.

disciples is that the stone has been moved, for she had not as yet peered into the tomb, and all that she tells them is her surmise of Jesus' body being missing. In between that and the notice of the Beloved Disciple's belief is the detailed narration of his race with Peter to the tomb and the detailed description of the grave clothes. Thus, the Beloved Disciple's faith does not relate to Mary's inference from the stone, because the narrator says that he believed not when he saw the moved stone but when he looked inside the tomb. The ἐπίστευσεν must gather its content from the grave clothes, and so the Beloved Disciple believed either that Jesus' body had been removed or that Jesus himself had risen. Since the whole point of the meticulous description of the undisturbed grave clothes is to affirm that no one had taken Jesus' body, ἐπίστευσεν indicates that the Beloved Disciple concluded from them that Jesus had risen.

e. It is intriguing that the term ῥαββουνί appears only twice in the New Testament: when the blind man asks Jesus to restore his sight (Mk 10.51), and when Mary's eyes are opened in recognition of Jesus (Jn 20.16). Does ῥαββουνί also signal some sort of confession in the risen Jesus to whom it is addressed? Proposals to that effect have been made, from the comparatively modest suggestion of Leidig that Mary's use of ῥαββουνί amounts to a messianic confession, to the more adventurous assertion of Marsh:

> [Rabbouni], as John remarks, means 'teacher'; but, as John does not tell his readers, it was a form of the word 'Rabbi' which was used almost exclusively in address to God. Mary is thus doing more than recognize some quasi-physical identity between the earthly Jesus and the risen Lord; she is giving expression to a new attitude in which Jesus is worshipped as God.[12]

Marsh rightly calls attention to John's rubric, but curiously, he bases his exposition of ῥαββουνί on what John fails to tell readers rather than on what John does tell them. Hoskyns views ῥαββουνί as a declaration of faith corresponding to that of Thomas (Jn 20.28); but as Brown notes, the parallel of Mary's ῥαββουνί with the ῥαββί spoken by the disciples in Jn 1.38 'brings out forcefully the modesty of the title that Magdalene gives to the risen Jesus, a title that is characteristic of the

---

12. Leidig, *Jesu Gespräch*, p. 237; Marsh, *John*, p. 633. Marsh offers no evidence for his claim about ῥαββουνί. E. Lohse contends that ῥαββουνί and ῥαββί do not differ significantly (E. Lohse, 'ῥαββί', *TDNT*, VI, p. 964).

beginning of faith rather than its culmination. Surely it falls far short of Thomas' "My Lord and my God".'[13]

Perhaps the issue is not theological content but differences in the forms of address used by women and men. Lindars comments,

> John is quite correct in supposing that a woman would use [rabbuni], whereas male disciples use the simple *rabbi* (1.38)...It would be quite wrong to build anything on the fact that *rabbuni* is sometimes used in addressing God, for there is no suggestion of an ascription of divinity to Jesus, as the parenthesis *which means teacher* (cf. 1.38) shows.[14]

The context of personal intimacy in which Mary says ῥαββουνί suggests that Lindars is on the right track. As long as Jesus uses the same term of address for Mary as did the angels, γύναι (Jn 20.13, 15), a wall of incognizance remains; but when Jesus calls her Μαριάμ (Jn 20.16), she recognizes her shepherd. Virtually every commentator acknowledges that Jn 20.16 shows Mary to be one of Jesus' sheep whom he calls by name (see Jn 10.1-5). As an intimate of Jesus, she calls him 'Teacher' and 'Lord' (Jn 20.16, 18; cf. 13.13). Thus, ῥαββουνί here implies a close personal bond. Mary Magdalene's use of ῥαββουνί in this context, however, does not constitute a confession of Jesus as the messiah or as God.

f. Jesus' words to Mary in Jn 20.17 present one of the enduring challenges of Johannine interpretation: μή μου ἅπτου, οὕπω γὰρ ἀναβέβηκα πρός τὸν πατέρα. The text of Codex B (μὴ ἅπτου μου) does not affect the issue, and the conjecture of Lepsius (see NA[26] apparatus) that the original text read ἅπτου μου—Jesus ordering Mary to touch him—has no firm basis. Bultmann, convinced that Jesus has already ascended when he meets Mary, thinks that οὕπω refers to Mary's act of touching rather than to Jesus' act of ascending.[15] Thus, the text (presumably) would have this sense: 'Do not touch me yet (or 'any more'?), because I have ascended to my Father'. But if that were John's intent, γάρ would have followed rather than preceded ἀναβέβηκα.

---

13. Hoskyns, *Fourth Gospel*, p. 543; Brown, *John*, II, p. 1010.

14. Lindars, *John*, pp. 606-607.

15. Bultmann, *John*, p. 687. Bultmann (p. 687 n. 1) compiles various proposals that μή μου ἅπτου represents a mistranslated Aramaic original or some other type of error. Suggestions that the text be emended should be received cautiously, as they often look more like attempts to cut the knot rather than untie it.

Interpreting this verse involves at least three things: (1) the definition of ἅπτομαι, (2) the meaning of the present middle imperative μή (μου) ἅπτου, (3) the relation of μή μου ἅπτου to the ensuing clauses in which Jesus speaks to Mary of his ascension and gives her a message for his brothers. Is Mary ordered to refrain from clinging to Jesus, or from touching him at all? Does his command imply that she has already made contact with him, or that he is preempting her from doing so? Is she prohibited from holding Jesus because he has not yet ascended, or because she has a mission to accomplish? Interpretative possibilities abound.[16]

Establishing a precise moment for the ascension is difficult if not impossible because John's thanatopsis for Jesus involves his departure (ὑπάγω), exaltation (ὑψόω), glorification (δοξάζω) and ascension (ἀναβαίνω).[17] Although Jesus ascends at the cross, he still can speak to Mary of his impending ascension even after his resurrection. This leads some commentators to posit that the ascension, in one form or another, occurs after the appearance to Mary and before that to the disciples.[18] It seems odd that something as momentous as Jesus' ascension could go unnarrated and happen, as it were, offstage. However, the same could be said about Jesus' resurrection, which no Evangelist tries to describe (but see *Gos. Pet.* 10.38-42). Still others view the ascension as a process. For example, Graß characterizes Jesus' resurrection appearance to Mary as an *Unterwegserscheinung*, and Carson speaks of Jesus being in the 'process of ascension' until the 'culminating ascension'.[19]

John, it is argued, does not describe two ascensions, but the one ascension under two aspects. The crucifixion–ascension occurs on the spatial plane (below/above), the resurrection–ascension occurs on the

16. Carson (*John*, pp. 642-45) provides a critical review of the most viable options.

17. Early Christians understood Jesus' ascension in various ways: (1) a spiritual ascension preceding the crucifixion, (2) resurrection and ascension in one movement, (3) ascension following resurrection later on the same day, (4) ascension following resurrection after a longer interval. Talbert (*John*, pp. 251-52) cites representative texts.

18. According to Dodd (*Interpretation*, pp. 441-43), Jesus ascends *sub specie aeternitatis* at the crucifixion, but not historically until after the resurrection. Lightfoot (*John*, p. 331) perceives that the ascension occurs between the appearance to Mary and that to the disciples, because they could not receive the Spirit as they did (Jn 20.22) until Jesus had returned to the Father (Jn 15.26).

19. Graß, *Ostergeschehen*, p. 60; Carson, *John*, p. 645.

temporal plane (before/after). This compression of spatial and temporal planes in Jesus' crucifixion, resurrection and ascension defies being decompressed. Thus, it might seem that John, by making both the traditional resurrection appearances and the ascension unfathomable, has left the readers in a conceptual quandary.[20] But is it possible that these difficulties are the result of asking the wrong questions of the text, of looking for it to do that which it has no intention of doing? Schnackenburg insists that because Jesus' hour cannot be dissected into death, resurrection, ascension and glorification, questions about separating resurrection, ascension and glorification, about coming from the tomb and going to the Father, about an intermediate state between resurrection and ascension, are misguided.[21]

Brown attributes much of the difficulty with Jn 20.17 to commentators who erroneously contrast Jesus' injunction against Mary clinging to him with his invitation for Thomas to probe his wounds. According to Brown, the two actions have nothing in common.[22] Brown is correct about the faulty contrast, but he misses that the two actions do have something in common, namely, Jesus' attention to the personal needs of others. C.F.D. Moule writes,

> It is surely much simpler to explain the words to Mary to mean that she need not cling to the Rabbi, for he really is 'with' her and not yet withdrawn from sight. By contrast, then, what Thomas needs is to be met upon his own ground and, since he has resolved to demand tactual evidence, to be offered it—if only to convince him, in the very act, that it may be dispensed with. On this showing, the contrast lies entirely in the needs and circumstances of the two disciples, and not in any difference in the state of the Lord as between the two encounters.[23]

I have pursued this exegetical point at some length because of its difficulty, but also because of its importance to the issue of the witnesses in John 20. If Jesus' ascension occurs in between his appearance to Mary and his appearances to the disciples, it could be argued that Mary's witness of Jesus occupies a lesser plane, that she experiences the resurrected Jesus but not the ascended Jesus. The foregoing discussion shows that this is not so.

20. So Meeks, 'Man from Heaven', p. 66; Ashton, *Fourth Gospel*, p. 508.

21. Schnackenburg, *John*, III, pp. 318-19.

22. Brown, *John*, II, p. 1011

23. C.F.D. Moule, 'The Individualism of the Fourth Gospel', in *Essays in New Testament Interpretation* (Cambridge: Cambridge University Press, 1982), p. 95.

[Jesus] has appeared to her in a form that while it was evidently different from that in which he had been known in the days of his flesh had sufficient elements in it to enable Mary to satisfy herself, and persuade others, of the identity of the Jesus who was, with the Lord who would for evermore be.[24]

The Jesus whom Mary encounters is the same Jesus whom the disciples encounter, and her testimony must be evaluated at the same level.

Summarizing the results of the exegetical issues: (a) the phrase σκοτίας ἔτι οὔσης metaphorically shows Mary Magdalene initially to be in the dark about Jesus' fate, but can do so only if it also allows that she accurately perceives the moved stone; (b) Mary's οὐκ οἴδαμεν reflects that other women also saw that the stone had been moved, but that John is interested in advancing only her as a witness; (c) although Peter and the Beloved Disciple both see the grave clothes, only the latter believes; (d) what the Beloved Disciple believes because of the grave clothes is that Jesus has risen from the dead; (e) Mary's vocative for Jesus, ῥαββουνί, reflects her discipleship and closeness to Jesus, but is not a confession of him as messiah or God; (f) although the death, resurrection and ascension of Jesus cannot be neatly separated chronologically or spatially, it is not the case that Mary meets the resurrected Jesus but the disciples meet the ascended Jesus.

2. *John 20.1-29: An Interpretative Frame*

Mary Magdalene's involvement is best interpreted within the frame of John 20 itself, because the chapter has other episodes that feature either the empty tomb or the risen Christ, and Mary encounters both. The narrative comprises four strands of main characters along with Jesus: Peter and the Beloved Disciple, Mary Magdalene, the disciples, and Thomas. Ashton states that any one of the four episodes featuring these characters could, on its own, effectively close John's Gospel, and he says of the ending of the Mary scene, 'Here we have the quintessence of the early Christian mission: a proclamation, by a witness, that Jesus is risen. Nothing further is required: John could have ended his Gospel here.'[25] But of course, John did not conclude there, and so Mary's part in the drama must be understood within the surrounding material, and the Synoptics can assist in that task also.

24. Marsh, *John*, p. 638.
25. Ashton, *Fourth Gospel*, p. 509.

In John, as in all the Gospels, it is not the male but the female disciples of Jesus who first visit the tomb. But John's narrative immediately differs in certain key elements. No motive is offered for Mary's visit; she does not enter the tomb; no divine agents encounter her straightaway to tell her of Jesus' resurrection and to send her to inform the disciples. Unlike the Synoptic Mary Magdalene, John's Mary departs unenlightened from the tomb. It is perhaps even mistaken to speak of Mary encountering an empty tomb in Jn 20.1. What she encounters is the moved stone. She does not look into the tomb itself at that point, perhaps simply because the darkness will afford her a glimpse of the tomb's huge stone but not of its obscure interior. She sees the stone, assumes the worst and raises the alarm. She has no cause to do otherwise. Literally and figuratively, Mary Magdalene's initial experience at the tomb leaves her in the dark in regard to Jesus' fate.

Mary goes, as it were, straight to the top. She alerts Peter and the Beloved Disciple, who set out to investigate with no delay for discussion or further information. Did the two disciples believe her, disbelieve her, or withhold judgment? John does not say in so many words. Luke leaves no doubt: 'But these words seemed to them an idle tale (λῆρος), and they did not believe them' (Lk. 24.11). Seidensticker concludes from Lk. 24.11 that the apostles reject the *Mittlerschaft* of the women, and Graß that their witness lacks persuasiveness.[26] However, the text does not say that the disciples reject the women's capacity as messengers but the content of the message itself. It cannot be assumed that λῆρος is a term meaning something like 'the prattle of flighty women'. Josephus is challenged as to whether something he said is λῆρος (*War* 3.405). Antiochus brands the beliefs of Eleazar—a priest, lawyer, elder, and foremost man of the assembly—as λῆρος (*4 Macc.* 5.11). Further, if, as scholars increasingly accept, Lk. 24.12 is authentic, then the women did have persuasive power, because Peter at least was not convinced that the women's report was nonsense (cf. Lk. 24.22-24).[27] In the longer ending of Mark, Jesus places the blame for the disciples' unbelief on their stubbornness and not on the women's testimony (Mk 16.14).

According to Graß, John shifts the *Zweifelsmotif* from the disciples as

---

26. Seidensticker, *Auferstehung Jesu*, pp. 121-22; Graß, *Ostergeschehen*, p. 22.
27. Lk. 24.12 is found in 𝔓[75] ℵ B *pm*, but not in Codex D and the Old Latin MSS (see *TCGNT*, pp. 184, 191-93).

a group to Thomas.[28] That may be so, but in Luke, the disciples' doubt does not stem from an intrinsic uncredibility of the women; and in John, Thomas' doubt springs from the resurrection report not of Mary but of his co-disciples. The response of Peter and the Beloved Disciple to Mary Magdalene brings to mind that of the Sychar villagers to the Samaritan woman, whose testimony must have had credibility to elicit the response that it did (Jn 4.29-30). The fact that Peter and the Beloved Disciple hasten to the tomb without delay confirms that they consider Mary's report worth investigating.

When they arrive at the tomb, Peter and the Beloved Disciple see the same thing—the orderly grave clothes—and return home silently. Peter says nothing because he does not believe. The Beloved Disciple is silent because he believes but has seen only the grave clothes and not Jesus himself. When Mary returns to the tomb, John makes it clear that she looks inside for the first time (Jn 20.11).[29] Mary sees two angels. The four Evangelists describe the beings in the tomb differently: one angel (Mt. 28.2), one young man (Mk 16.5), two men (Lk. 24.4), two angels (Jn 20.11). Schnackenburg explains that for the people of John's time, angelic presence was no less real than what is now called evidence, and that John is interested in the angels only in their capacity as witnesses. Similarly, Lindars suggests that the legal requirement for valid witness may explain the angels' presence.[30] Yet, John's angels play the most subdued role of the four resurrection accounts. They are not shown to descend from heaven, move the stone, or dazzle anyone; they provoke no fear, offer no information, assign no mission. All they do is ask Mary why she is weeping. However else the two angels might function in the narrative, they are not active as witnesses, since they inform neither the readers nor Mary of the resurrection. Those tasks are left to the narrator and to Jesus himself.

How do Peter and the Beloved Disciple function in John's version of the empty tomb story? For various reasons, many scholars see Jn 20.2-10 as a later insertion into the Mary Magdalene story. Wink argues that John has inserted Peter and the Beloved Disciple to supersede the

---

28. Graß, *Ostergeschehen*, p. 65.

29. Some MSS show Mary crying inside rather than outside the tomb. The reading is most probably secondary (*TCGNT*, pp. 254-55), but in any event does not change the fact that this is her first glimpse of the tomb's interior.

30. Schnackenburg, *John*, III, pp. 315-16; Lindars, *John*, p. 604.

testimony of Mary which had no credibility in Jewish eyes.[31] Mary's
fitness to testify to the resurrection will be discussed in more detail but
may be addressed here briefly at the literary level. First, it is not at all
certain that Jn 20.2-10 is an insertion.[32] Secondly, the extent of an
insertion, if present, is equally uncertain. Fortna, for example, thinks that
Peter was present in the pre-Johannine source but that the Beloved
Disciple was added later solely to introduce him as Peter's equal and
superior.[33] Such theories are speculative, but in any case, it is difficult to
see how Wink can find that Peter and the Beloved Disciple supplant
Mary's testimony when neither testifies to anything he has seen, and
when the narrator fails to mention the two of them again in regard
either to the incidents at the tomb or the other Christophanies in
John 20.

Ashton isolates themes in the episodes involving Peter and the
Beloved Disciple (faith), Mary Magdalene (recognition), the disciples
without Thomas (mission), and sees the Thomas story as underlining
John's central message.[34] Ashton's scheme has much to commend it,
but should not be absolutized. R.E. Brown, for example, sees John providing in these episodes four different examples of faith.[35] Likewise, the
theme of witness runs through all the material in John 20. Mary, Peter
and the Beloved Disciple can all testify that Jesus' body is not in the
tomb, but what Mary witnesses and what the two disciples witness are
quite different, even discrete. Mary sees the stone, the angels and Jesus,
while the two disciples see the grave clothes. The moved stone, empty
tomb, grave clothes and angels imply but do not prove Jesus' resurrection. In this first resurrection episode it is Mary alone who sees
conclusive proof in the form of Jesus himself.

Mary turns from the angels, sees the figure of Jesus, but does not recognize him. Jesus addresses her as did the angels ('Woman'), repeats
their question ('Why are you weeping?') and adds a second question
('Whom are you looking for?'). Nothing in Jesus' appearance, voice or

31. W. Wink, '"And the Lord Appeared First to Mary": Sexual Politics in the
Resurrection Witness', in D. Hessel (ed.), *Social Themes of the Christian Year*
(Philadelphia: Westminster Press, 1983), pp. 177-82.

32. Neirynck ('John and the Synoptics', p. 595) finds no convincing evidence
that calls for the episode of Peter and the Beloved Disciple to be seen as a later
insertion in a more primitive Mary Magdalene story.

33. Fortna, *Fourth Gospel*, pp. 187-200.

34. Ashton, *Fourth Gospel*, pp. 501-514.

35. Brown, *John*, II, p. 1046.

words causes Mary to recognize him. She assumes that he is the gardener, who might have removed Jesus' body. Jesus then says, 'Mary',
and she responds, 'Rabbouni', recognizing him immediately. Mary's
recognition of Jesus comes not just from the sound of his voice but from
the sound of his voice speaking her name (cf. Jn 10.3-6). The mystery of
Jesus' resurrected state cannot be unravelled, but clearly, John depicts
Jesus as being unrecognizable by appearance and voice alone. This is
true of all the Johannine resurrection appearances. The disciples recognize Jesus not when he appears and speaks, but when he shows them his
hands and side (Jn 20.19-20); Thomas recognizes Jesus only by the sight
of his hands and side (Jn 20.26-29); the disciples do not recognize Jesus
by sight or sound when he appears on the shore and speaks, and it takes
the miraculous catch of fish to evoke recognition in the Beloved Disciple
(Jn 21.4-7).

What can be said, then, of Mary's experience of the risen Jesus?
Abbott thinks that, in a sense, Mary believes without seeing, because
although she sees (Jn 20.1), glances (Jn 20.11) and beholds (Jn 20.12,
14), her faith finally comes by hearing (Jn 20.16).[36] But this lacks precision. Mary's recognition of Jesus, as I have shown, comes not from
hearing Jesus' voice alone but from hearing Jesus call her by name.
Moreover, Jesus' is not a disembodied voice. Mary sees someone, Jesus,
even though at first she does not recognize him, and her report to the
disciples is not, 'I have heard the Lord', but, 'I have seen the Lord'
(Jn 20.18). Abbott states, '"*I have seen* the Lord", implies probably
more than material seeing and perhaps not material seeing at all. It is
very unlikely that the Evangelist supposes that Caiaphas, had he been
standing by the side of Mary, would have seen the Saviour.'[37]

---

36. Abbott, *Johannine Vocabulary*, §§1560-61, 1601-602. Abbott adds that
Mary is denied touching Jesus (Jn 20.17), and is not shown his hands and side
(cf. Jn 20.20, 27).

37. Abbott, *Johannine Vocabulary*, §1599a. Michaelis claims that the resurrection
appearances emphasize the aural over the visual aspect. Michaelis ('ὁράω', p. 359)
characterizes the presence of Jesus as a 'non-visionary reality' beyond categories of
human seeing. Knowing that all the verbs of seeing used in the resurrection appearances must be accounted for, Michaelis (p. 364) suggests that John probably selected
them because 'with their help he could the better emphasise the personal and existen-
tial character of the encounter with Jesus'. This explanation is, in my view, highly
artificial, and projects twentieth-century philosophy onto a first-century text. Surely
John uses verbs of seeing simply to indicate that people really did see (cf. Jn 19.35;
1 Jn 1.1-3).

Speculation about what Caiaphas would or would not have seen is pointless, but Abbott is quite correct that Mary's vision outstrips mere material seeing. Yet, it cannot be true that material seeing is not involved at all. Mary mistakes Jesus for a gardener and calls him 'Teacher', meaning that the resurrection has transformed him in such a way that he, even if not immediately recognizable, is not beyond the pale of material perception.

The appearance to the disciples in Jn 20.19-23 can be contrasted with that to Mary. Whereas Mary recognized Jesus in the calling of her name, the disciples recognize him by the sight of his stigmata. But in any event, both she and they are witnesses to his resurrection. P. Benoit places the appearance to Mary in the category of *apparitions de reconnaissance* in which Jesus at first is not recognized due to his new state but then is made known to individuals; on the other hand, appearances to the apostles normally are reserved for *apparitions de mission*.[38] Such distinctions apply less forcefully to John's resurrection appearances. John uses ἀπόστολος but once (Jn 13.16), and that with only a generic significance. Furthermore, Jesus' mission statement and the gift of the Spirit in Jn 20.21-22 cannot be said to pertain to some sort of apostolic college alone, because although Jn 20.24 suggests that the appearance in Jn 20.19-23 may have been to an inner circle of disciples, Thomas is absent for the commissioning. Thus, even if Mary is the *apostola apostolorum*, it is not only the Twelve (or the Eleven) who are the *apostoli ad mundum*.[39] For John, all believers are sent into the world even as the Father sent Jesus into the world.

The disciples' report to Thomas is identical to that of Mary to them: they have 'seen the Lord' (Jn 20.25). This phrase has the quality of a formula that qualifies the speaker as an official witness to the resurrection (cf. 1 Cor. 9.1; 15.3-8), and places Mary firmly in the same camp as the disciples of Jn 20.19-23. She is not just the apostle to the apostles but an apostle to the readers as well, and as Schneiders points out, her

38. P. Benoit, 'Marie-Madeleine et les Disciples au Tombeau selon Joh 20.1-18', in *Judentum, Urchristentum, Kirche* (BZNW, 26; Berlin: Alfred Töpelmann, 1964), p. 151. According to Ashton (*Fourth Gospel*, p. 509), the mission theme in the Mary episode is compressed to the point of being almost unnoticeable.

39. Against Davies (*Rhetoric and Reference*, p. 335), who is only technically correct to say that Mary is a messenger to the disciples but not included in the commission Jesus gives them. Like Thomas, Mary is absent when the commission is given but not excluded from it.

experience of the risen Christ cannot be trivialized as private, unofficial and without ecclesiastical significance.[40] As noted previously, Thomas doubts the resurrection report of his co-disciples, and this can be contrasted with the response of the disciples to Mary's report. Fortna conjectures that the disciples disbelieved, or certainly misunderstood, Mary's news, because her report to the disciples is not the final episode.[41] Fortna does not explain how the mere presence of more material after Mary's report indicates doubt on the disciples' part. It is easy to see with Fortna that the disciples misunderstand Jesus' ascension message (it still baffles readers), but John gives no hint that the disciples reject what Mary says (cf. Mk 16.11; Lk. 24.11), even if, as Brown maintains, her own faith has not 'detectably penetrated' their group.[42] Indeed, the disciples react to the arrival of Jesus not with surprise but with joy (Jn 20.20; cf. Lk. 24.37), and this lack of surprise may be attributed to Mary's message.

John's formulation of Mary's report is notable: ἔρχεται Μαριὰμ ἡ Μαγδαληνὴ ἀγγέλλουσα τοῖς μαθηταῖς ὅτι ἑώρακα τὸν κύριον, καὶ ταῦτα εἶπεν αὐτῇ (Jn 20.18). This combination of direct and reported speech is awkward, and scribes have sought to smooth it out in various ways (see NA[26] apparatus). Abbott, however, sees in the original text a Johannine technique that emphasizes the first part of Mary's message, ἑώρακα τὸν κύριον.[43] The words that Jesus gives Mary for the disciples in Jn 20.17 need not be repeated for the reader in the very next verse, and so John uses reported speech to show that she delivered Jesus' message: καὶ ταῦτα εἶπεν αὐτῇ. Thus, Mary prefaces Jesus' message to the disciples with the pronouncement, 'I have seen the Lord', which authorizes her mission and guarantees her testimony.

As in all the pericopes studied, the issue of belief arises, and more than anywhere else in John, so also does the relationship between belief and sight. Seeing and believing can neither be divorced nor confused; they are connected and distinct. Abbott observes that Mary of Bethany and Mary Magdalene are almost the only major characters who never use the word 'believe' and are never said to believe in anyone or in anything.[44] Thus, the presence or absence of πιστεύω alone means little,

40. Schneiders, 'Women', pp. 42-43.
41. Fortna, *Fourth Gospel*, p. 189.
42. Brown, *John*, II, p. 1028.
43. Abbott, *Johannine Grammar*, §§1925-26.
44. Abbott, *Johannine Vocabulary*, §1466. Abbott is aware, of course, that John

and the nature of Mary's faith will not be found in the word 'believe' but in the progression of her statements: 'They have taken the Lord... They have taken my Lord... If you have taken him... Rabbouni... I have seen the Lord.'

Mary, in saying three times that Jesus' body has been removed, makes it abundantly clear that she holds no expectations whatsoever of Jesus rising from the dead. But Mary is not alone in that regard, because even Jesus' most explicit resurrection prediction is understood by no one—including the disciples—until after the fact (Jn 2.19-22). She therefore can hardly be cast as a second-rate believer when no one else expects the resurrection. It is more profitable to examine the post-resurrection faith of the characters in the narrative and how they come to that faith.

Bultmann evaluates Mary's response to Jesus in Jn 20.16.

> Mary's address to Jesus, which in a characteristic manner is distinguished from that of Thomas in v. 28, shows meanwhile that she does not yet fully know him, i.e. she does not grasp who he is as the Risen One. She still misunderstands him, insofar as she thinks that he has simply 'come back' from the dead, and that he is again the man she knew as 'Teacher'.[45]

But curiously, Bultmann goes on to say that Mary's use of κύριος in Jn 20.18 is the first time in John's Gospel that the title has its 'genuine *pathos*', and that it is 'wholly suitable for the Risen One' (as in Jn 20.20, 25, 28).[46] So in Jn 20.16 Mary's use of ῥαββουνί shows that she does not perceive Jesus as the Risen One, but in Jn 20.18 her use of κύριος is wholly suitable for the Risen One. Although Bultmann is silent on the matter, the message given to Mary for the disciples in Jn 20.17 apparently effected a quantum change in her understanding of the Jesus she encountered. Bultmann's focus on the titles fails to attend to the context. Mary says ῥαββουνί in response to Jesus saying Μαριάμ. They are both using terms of address that are personal and intimate signs of mutual recognition. Nowhere in John is Ἰησοῦς used as a vocative, and

recognizes different kinds and shades of belief. Recall the observation of Gaffney ('Believing and Knowing', p. 224), 'Of every one the Gospel's major personages, and of most of its minor ones, it is once or oftener affirmed or denied that they believe or know'.

45. Bultmann, *John*, pp. 686-87. Davies (*Rhetoric and Reference*, p. 180), echoing Bultmann's thought, grades Mary's response to the risen Jesus as 'unsatisfactory'.

46. Bultmann, *John*, p. 689 n. 2.

so ῥαββουνί must be the responsive equivalent of Μαριάμ in this particular situation.[47] Both 'Teacher' and 'Lord' are terms used for Jesus
by his disciples (Jn 13.13), including his women disciples (see Martha's
use in Jn 11.27-28). Thus, it is unconvincing to depict Mary's faith in the
risen Jesus as inadequate because she believes that Jesus has merely been
resuscitated to his former state of life. If ῥαββουνί is a title of intimate
recognition, and if κύριος has its genuine *pathos* in Jn 20.18, then Mary
must have the measure of faith and understanding of the ascending Lord
conveyed by the latter title.

If there is one person in John 20 whose belief overshadows that of all
others, most commentators would point to the Beloved Disciple. The
observation of Bode is typical: 'The Beloved Disciple saw the empty
tomb, not the risen Lord, and believed. Thus he comes under the Lord's
final beatitude.'[48] If so, then the Beloved Disciple is the one person alive
during Jesus' ministry who is included among those who later will
believe without having seen (Jn 20.29). But is it accurate to say that the
Beloved Disciple falls under the Lord's final beatitude? He saw the
empty tomb and not the risen Lord. But 'empty tomb' is a misnomer.
The tomb is far from empty. It is curious that so many commentators
place the Beloved Disciple among those who are blessed because they
believe without having seen, when Jn 20.8 says of him, 'He saw and
believed'. Of course, he did not see the risen Jesus, but he did see something, the grave clothes, that led him to believe that Jesus had risen.

Schnackenburg observes of the Beloved Disciple, 'He can, so to say,
read the tracks and signs of his Lord; therein he is the ideal disciple with
the exemplary faith'.[49] As was true with the flow of blood and water
from Jesus' side at the crucifixion, what sets the Beloved Disciple apart
in regard to Jesus' resurrection is not that he believes without seeing but
that he sees beyond what others see: he sees the signs. The immediate
(but not exclusive) point of reference for the 'many other signs' in
Jn 20.30 can be found in the resurrection events of John 20—the grave
clothes and the stigmata. Thus, Seidensticker can speak of the tomb as
'the last sign', perceived in faith by the Beloved Disciple as signifying
the resurrection.[50] The grave clothes are not called a σημεῖον, but they
function as one.

47. Cf. Mk 1.24 and par.; 5.7 and par.; 10.47 and par.; Lk. 17.13; 23.42.
48. Bode, *First Easter*, pp. 79-80.
49. Schnackenburg, *John*, III, p. 312.
50. Seidensticker, *Auferstehung Jesu*, pp. 122-23, 127, 149.

While the Beloved Disciple is exemplary inasmuch as he see signs where others do not, Mary, Peter and Thomas cannot thereby be denigrated as inadequate believers. In particular, Mary Magdalene cannot be singled out as the paradigm of the inadequate believer because the intervention of the risen and ascending Jesus was needed to bring her to faith.[51] The contrast that John draws in the Thomas story is not between seeing and believing but between seeing and not seeing. Thus, the macarism of Jn 20.29—'Blessed are those who have not seen and yet have come to believe'—applies to none of the witnesses in John 20, because none of them came to believe without seeing.

Only two people in John's Gospel are present at both the cross and the tomb: Mary Magdalene and the Beloved Disciple. In both cases, the Beloved Disciple sees signs where others do not: the flow of blood and water, and the grave clothes. However, Mary Magdalene's presence at the cross and the tomb qualifies her as a witness to the events that transpire there and demonstrates her faithfulness even though she does not understand what she experiences until she meets the risen Jesus. In the matter of belief, she stands shoulder to shoulder with all the figures in John 20, because all of them see before they believe. The fact that Jesus blesses those who will believe without seeing what they saw devalues neither the resurrection appearances nor those who witnessed them. In fact, the readers' path to faith leads through their testimony. This topic now must be addressed.

3. *Mary Magdalene as a Witness*

John's claim to provide reliable testimony is nowhere more urgent than in the reality of Jesus' bodily resurrection, and the way he narrates the resurrection lends to John 20 the quality of an affidavit.[52] Barrett insists that modern critics, however they may regard John's resurrection narrative from a modern scientific-historical standpoint, must recognize that John himself takes historical testimony seriously: 'Had John not held the Easter stories to be true (historically and theologically), still more, had he held them to be misleading (whether historically or theologically), he would not have recorded them.'[53]

51. As does, for example, Collins, 'Representative Figures—II', p. 124.
52. Trites (*Concept of Witness*, p. 86) observes, 'The resurrection is of juridical significance in that it constitutes Christ's last and greatest sign'.
53. Barrett, *John*, p. 562.

Bultmann thinks that John does not intend the stories of John 20 to establish genuine Easter faith.[54] That is only partially true. The resurrection stories alone do not establish faith, but the first step toward faith taken by those who have not seen begins with the testimony of those who have (Jn 17.20). It is that testimony which John sets down in John 20. Bultmann marks the resurrection appearances as concessions to the weakness of Jesus' disciples that they should not have needed.[55] However, the appearances occurred not just for the sake of the first disciples but for those who were not eyewitnesses. For them, resurrection appearances are not a concession to their weakness but a consideration of their absence. John writes for the benefit of those who were not present to see for themselves, as Jn 20.29-31 makes clear.

John values the fact of the tomb and the grave clothes even more highly than do the Synoptists. Not only the women, but also Peter and the Beloved Disciple, can testify to the absence of Jesus' body, and those two disciples are eyewitnesses to the disposition of the grave clothes. Polemics directed against Jesus' resurrection did not include the charge that his corpse actually was still in the tomb, but did maintain that it had been removed by his disciples, making the resurrection a hoax. The charge of chicanery against Jesus' followers played a longstanding role (Mt. 28.15), and while the empty tomb does not by itself prove that Jesus rose from the dead, as an essential constituent of the resurrection evidence it had to be defended.

Mary Magdalene's experience is crucial to the resurrection evidence, so much so that she can be viewed as the key to understanding the whole pericope. Mary's thrice repeated statement about Jesus' body having been removed creates an apologetic atmosphere for the passage. There are four components to the resurrection claim about Jesus: (1) his body was not in the tomb; (2) his body had not been removed; (3) his body was not merely resuscitated; (4) his bodily appearances were not phantasms. Each of these pertains to Mary Magdalene's experience.

First, Mary sees only two angels when she looks inside the tomb, and thus can affirm that Jesus' body is not there.

Secondly, Mary sees Jesus himself, confirming that his body was not carried off by human agents (whether they be thought of as Jesus' disciples, the Jewish leaders, the Roman authorities or parties unknown). And there is added apologetic force in the fact that it is one of Jesus'

---

54. Bultmann, *John*, pp. 687-88.
55. Bultmann, *John*, p. 696.

own followers, Mary Magdalene, who first raises the possibility of his body having been stolen.

Thirdly, one argument against resuscitation is the condition of the materials used to wrap Jesus' body for burial. John distinguishes the raising of Jesus from that of Lazarus. Lazarus, restored to his former state of life, needed help to be freed from the winding sheets (Jn 11.44); Jesus, raised to a new state of life, required no such assistance (Jn 20.6-7). The orderly disposition of the wrappings shows that Jesus' body, besides not having been stolen, was not restored to ordinary human life but was raised in a unique way to an indefinable state. Jesus in his resurrection state is recognizable (Jn 20.16, 18, 25, 28) and tangible (Jn 20.17, 27), but can pass through solid materials in order to appear to human senses (Jn 20.6-7, 19, 26). John mentions nothing about Mary seeing the grave clothes, much less scrutinizing them as do Peter and the Beloved Disciple. However, John's reason for advancing Peter and the Beloved Disciple as the witnesses to the grave clothes cannot be that Mary was unable to attest to the resurrected Jesus, because she does meet him in his resurrection state. Rather, John's motive—beyond the resurrection apologetic—is to accent the perceptive faith of the Beloved Disciple, and to that end Peter, not Mary, is the foil.

Fourthly, as with the crucifixion, the matter of Docetism arises. Unlike certain texts in 1 John, it is not clear that the appearances in John 20 were deliberately aimed against Docetic ideas, but certainly, they well suited anti-Docetic apologists who happily adapted John's text for their purposes (for example, *Epistula Apostolorum* 11–12). Schnelle sees a clear anti-Docetic tendency in John's use of the Beloved Disciple, Peter and Thomas to establish the reality of Jesus' bodily resurrection, and Graß discerns anti-Docetic intent behind the appearance to the disciples in Jn 20.19-23.[56] Neither Schnelle nor Graß mentions Jesus' appearance to Mary Magdalene in connection with anti-Docetism. This failure to mention Mary along with Peter, the Beloved Disciple and Thomas is curious because her sensory experience of the risen Jesus is the same as theirs—aural and visual. Further, while all the figures in John 20 are said to see and to hear Jesus, none of them is specifically said to touch him. Mary is forbidden and Thomas invited to touch Jesus, but it is uncertain whether either of them actually does touch him.[57] Perhaps these episodes

---

56. Schnelle, *Antidocetic Christology*, pp. 16-17, 143-44; Graß, *Ostergeschehen*, p. 71.

57. In Jn 20.17 μή μου ἅπτου does not necessarily imply that Mary has already

are intended to demonstrate that Jesus' body is tangible and thus real. But even if that is so, neither Mary nor Thomas is advanced as someone who can testify to that fact because of having touched the risen Jesus.

I have noted previously that Mary Magdalene's experience sets an apologetic tone for the narrative. Beasley-Murray raises the possibility that the apologetic significance of the narrative perhaps is to be found not simply in concerns about Jesus' body:

> In Jewish eyes the testimony of women was unacceptable, hence their report of the empty tomb of small account. That *two men* should verify the evidence was important, since they could fulfill the Jewish requirement of valid testimony according to Deut 19:15.[58]

Beasley-Murray's unqualified generalization concerning the testimony of women is demonstrably incorrect, and in conjunction with his second statement about two men, obscures a crucial fact. Mary is the only person in John 20 whom Jesus visits privately, and so the Deuteronomic statutes would require that her testimony, regardless of her gender, be corroborated by at least one other competent witness.[59] Nevertheless, given that Mary experiences firsthand that Jesus has risen from the dead in a new bodily form, the question remains as to whether or not her testimony to that fact, taken in concert with the testimony of others, would be acceptable.

The idea that Mary's testimony to the resurrected Jesus must be corroborated or supplanted because she is female has been repeated by many commentators over the years.[60] Hengel, noting how Celsus impugns Mary's testimony to the risen Jesus as that of 'a hysterical female', states that from an apologetic perspective the Christophany to

touched Jesus, which some MSS make clear by inserting καὶ προσέδραμεν ἅψασθαι αὐτοῦ before Jn 20.17. Jesus' words about Thomas believing because he sees (versus touches) would indicate that Thomas did not accept Jesus' invitation to touch his wounds.

58. Beasley-Murray, *John*, p. 372.

59. I find it remarkable in light of Mary's experience of the risen Jesus that Dodd (*Interpretation*, p. 430) singles out the Christophany to Thomas as being different from most post-resurrection appearances in that a specific individual is cited as a witness to the facts.

60. For example, from the 1940s through the 1980s: Hoskyns, *Fourth Gospel*, p. 540; Hengel, 'Maria Magdalena', p. 255; Marsh, *John*, p. 631; Bode, *First Easter*, p. 76; F. Porsch, *Johannes-Evangelium* (SKK, 4; Stuttgart: Katholisches Bibelwerk, 1988), p. 210.

Mary is scarcely convincing.[61] According to Origen (*Contra Celsum* 2.55), Celsus's objections run as follows.

> But we must examine this question whether anyone who really died ever rose again with the same body... While [Jesus] was alive he did not help himself, but after death he rose again and showed the marks of his punishment and how his hands had been pierced. But who saw this? A hysterical female, as you say, and perhaps some other one of those who were deluded by the same sorcery.

In his rebuttal, Origen takes two lines of defence. He argues that the resurrection appearance is not an illusion and that the charge of hysteria against Mary is a fabrication for which there is no evidence in the scriptures (*Contra Celsum* 2.60). Origen makes no mention whatsoever of Mary being female when he attacks Celsus' charge that she was hysterical and hallucinating. Origen defends Mary's testimony apart from the issue of her gender. This may be compared with other texts in which resurrection reports from women are doubted or rejected without the gender of the messenger(s) being given as the basis for scepticism (for example, Mk 16.14; Lk. 24.11, 24-25; *Epistula Apostolorum* 10–12). Thus if, as Hengel claims, the appearance to Mary was not persuasive on apologetic grounds, it cannot be assumed that the reason for this was that women were not credible as bearers of resurrection testimony. In fact, Mk 16.14 and Lk. 24.24-25 indicate that the two stumbling blocks to accepting that Jesus rose from the dead are the astounding nature of his resurrection itself and the unwillingness of people to believe, even after a personal experience (Mt. 28.17; Lk. 24.36-43).

Although John's Gospel is the focus here, the list of resurrection witnesses that Paul provides in 1 Cor. 15.3-8 must be discussed because it pertains to Mary Magdalene. How is the conspicuous absence of women—Mary Magdalene in particular—from Paul's list of resurrection witnesses to be explained? The several possibilities are viewed most clearly if presented as options in outline form.

1. Paul's inherited tradition contained stories about the women.
   A. Paul omitted the stories.

2. Paul's inherited tradition lacked stories about the women.
   A. Paul knew the stories but did not add them (or)
   B. Paul did not know the stories (because)
      i. the stories did not exist during his time (or)
      ii. the stories existed but had not been passed on to him.

61. Hengel, 'Maria Magdalena', p. 252.

Of these permutations, only 1.A and 2.A pertain to the present discussion, which seeks to address this question: If Paul either had omitted the women from the traditional list of resurrection witnesses or failed to add them to that list, why would he have done so?

Perhaps Paul sought to give priority to Peter. But this is unlikely given the competition between them (Gal. 2.11-14) and that Paul felt compelled to establish his own authority, particularly against Peter (1 Cor. 9.1-5, note especially Peter's placement in the list in v. 5). In any case, Paul could have placed Peter first in the list without having to drop the women completely.

Perhaps it is unrealistic to expect Paul to include all the witnesses in a short creedal formula. But the desire to be concise would hardly preclude the addition of a few women, especially if they were such important witnesses.

Perhaps Paul is providing a list only of officially commissioned, that is, apostolic witnesses. This of course assumes that women were not or could not have been so commissioned. Although Junia was not a resurrection witness, her example casts strong shadows of doubt over the idea that women apostles did not exist (Rom. 16.7). More telling, however, is the group of more than five hundred that Paul cites as resurrection witnesses. It is difficult to imagine that each person in this large, anonymous, imprecisely numbered group was an officially commissioned apostolic witness.

Perhaps, as Wire suggests, Paul is exerting his authority against that of the women leaders in Corinth whose charismatic prophecies spring from a tradition of resurrection faith that is founded upon women's testimony to the empty tomb and the risen Christ.[62] Just as Paul affixes himself to the traditional list of witnesses, so he expunges the women from it in a bid to keep the women prophets in check. Wire maintains that only this explanation fits the context of Paul's own argument in the letter.

> Paul uses the familiar tradition of Christ's dying and rising to legitimate his claim to be the final member in a select, formally transmitted list of witnesses to Christ's resurrection, witnesses whose reports are said to be the basis of the Corinthians' faith and part of its content. For the women prophets this means that their present experience and communication of the risen Christ are being challenged by another gospel based strictly on the witness of certain male apostles and a single large group.[63]

62. Wire, *Corinthian Women Prophets*, pp. 159-63.
63. Wire, *Corinthian Women Prophets*, p. 163.

Wire's explanation remains in the realm of theory but makes good sense of the context of 1 Cor. 15.3-8. In light of the prophetic ministry conducted by women in Corinth (1 Cor. 11.5), it makes sense that women would enjoy more rather than less credibility as witnesses within that community.[64]

Wire's theory opens up the intriguing possibility that Paul omitted women from the witness list not because they lacked credibility but because they had an even greater measure of it. But still, the most common explanation for Paul's omission of the women from the list is that they lacked standing and credibility as witnesses in Judaism.[65] There is no need to rehearse the evidence disproving the generalization that Jewish women totally lacked witness status, but the principle that allows exceptions to the wide-ranging ban on their testimony needs to be reiterated. Women were permitted to give evidence in certain matters pertaining their knowledge and in some cases where no males could do so. According to John, Jesus appeared to Mary (or perhaps to her with other women) with no male witnesses present. In principle, rabbinical praxis could admit Mary Magdalene's testimony to the appearance of Jesus. But since Mary initially is the lone witness to the risen Jesus, her testimony requires corroboration, which soon arrives in the form of the male disciples who receive two appearances from the risen Jesus (Jn 20.19-29). The corroboration that Mary's testimony receives from the disciples could hardly be any stronger: 'I have seen the Lord... We have seen the Lord' (Jn 20.18, 25).

The two testimonies of Jn 20.18, 25 place Mary Magdalene and the disciples on equal confessional footing, but how does Mary's testimony compare with the declaration made by Thomas: 'My Lord and my God' (Jn 20.28)? Thomas moves beyond historical testimony to the resurrection of Jesus to an interpretative confession of its meaning. The growing awareness of Jesus' identity is seen in the escalation of titles in John 20:

64. Graß (*Ostergeschehen*, p. 111) notes that women's incompetence to testify is unlikely to have deterred Paul from including their stories when it did not prevent the Evangelists from doing so.

65. So, for example, Stauffer, *Jesus and His Story*, p. 124; Hengel, 'Maria Magdalena', pp. 246-47 (although Hengel does state that in the Hellenistic world women's testimony carried greater evidential power); Brown, *John*, II, p. 971; Schnackenburg, *John*, III, p. 321; Wink, 'First to Mary', p. 179; Wenham, *Easter Enigma*, p. 53; C.E.B. Cranfield, 'The Resurrection of Jesus Christ', *ExpTim* 101 (1990), p. 168; P. Perkins, '"I Have Seen the Lord" (John 20.18): Women Witnesses to the Resurrection', *Int* 46 (1992), p. 40.

Rabbouni, Lord, God.[66] Thus, Thomas's declaration is regarded as the 'supreme Christological pronouncement' of John's Gospel.[67] Marsh suggests that 'My Lord' alone would indicate a miracle faith in resuscitation or resurrection, but coupled with 'My God' shows that Thomas sees beyond the miracle to believe that Jesus is one with the Father.[68] On Marsh's principle, Mary Magdalene must be said not to have progressed beyond miracle faith. But that would be true of the other disciples as well, because Thomas' confession is his alone. In any event, the male disciples as a group cannot be set above Mary with whom they share the identical testimony: 'I/we have seen the Lord.'

How, then, does Mary Magdalene stand as a witness? Along with the Beloved Disciple, she is the only person in John's Gospel who can testify to both cross and tomb, to the fact that this same Jesus died and rose. Commentators point out how Mary's repeated insistence that someone had taken Jesus' body shows her unbelief. But no one believed in Jesus' resurrection without first seeing some sort of evidence, either the grave clothes or Jesus himself. Moreover, Mary's repeated fears that Jesus' body had been removed, besides having apologetic value against charges of resurrection hoax, serve another purpose. I have shown before, in regard to the deaths of Lazarus and Jesus, that one important area in which Jewish women were competent to testify was whether a man was dead or alive. When Mary speaks three times of Jesus' body having been removed, she testifies in the most compelling fashion that Jesus was truly dead, and she does this moments before becoming the first person to see him alive.

It is often said that Mary Magdalene is marginalized in John 20, that she is made to serve merely as a courier for the more important personages of the male disciples. This view assumes that the events of John 20 are the author's creation. John's shaping of these events is undeniable, but if their basic pattern has a historical basis, then it makes no sense to speak of Mary being marginalized by John.[69] That Mary is excluded

66. Compare these patterns: Rabbi, Messiah, Son of God, King of Israel (Jn 1); Prophet, Messiah, Saviour of the World (Jn 4); Man, Prophet, Son of Man (Jn 9).

67. Brown, *John*, II, p. 1047. Davies (*Rhetoric and Reference*, pp. 125-26) argues against the notion that Thomas ascribes the title 'God' to Jesus. Davies's case, even if correct, does not change the fact that Thomas' declaration forms the confessional climax of John's Gospel.

68. Marsh, *John*, p. 647.

69. Brown (*Community*, p. 189 n. 335) believes that the tradition of Jesus appearing first to Mary Magdalene has a good chance of being historical.

from Jesus' commission to the disciples (Jn 20.21)—a second idea purported to show Mary's marginalization—is also incorrect. Not only is Thomas also absent during the commissioning, but Jesus, according to John, creates not a college of apostles but a community of witnesses, of which Mary is one. A third formulation of Mary's supposed marginalization is that her testimony is superseded by the ensuing Christophanies to the disciples. But this is precisely the positive pattern of Johannine witness in which a witness's testimony to Jesus is proven to be true, as Scott duly notes.

> As in the case of the Samaritan Woman, Mary Magdalene's witness is only a stage which leads on to a personal encounter with Jesus Sophia and thus to faith in its fullest sense, as we hear in the confession of Thomas (20.28). Thus, the following incidents of 20.19-23 in no way detract from the importance or primacy of her mission in 20.18.[70]

Some scholars gather from John's Gospel that Mary Magdalene held a position of high esteem in the Johannine community and other early Christian communities. It cannot be said with certainty that Mary was a primary apostolic witness, as Schneiders and Schüssler Fiorenza propose, or served a quasi-apostolic function, as Brown suggests.[71] But for John's readers—those who have not seen and must come to believe relying on those who did—Mary Magdalene's testimony to the death and resurrection of Jesus is paramount, and her testimony is true.

70. Scott, *Sophia*, pp. 228-29.
71. Schneiders, 'Women', p. 44; Schüssler Fiorenza, *Memory of Her*, p. 332; Brown, *Community*, p. 189.

Chapter 10

EXCURSUS

1. *John 7.53–8.11: They Stood her in their Midst*

Few conclusions in New Testament study enjoy such wide assent as that which excludes the *Pericope Adulterae* (Jn 7.53–8.11) from the original text of John's Gospel.[1] Occasionally, however, someone is willing to challenge that consensus. J.P. Heil, for example, perceives that the pericope fits well with John's narrative context by virtue of verbal, stylistic and thematic links, and that the story assists rather than obstructs the flow of the narrative. Heil therefore calls for a reassessment of the external evidence and wonders if it is not more likely that the pericope was, after all, an original part of John's Gospel rather than the product of almost impossibly expert shaping by an interpolator.[2] Thematically, the pericope sits comfortably between John 7 and John 8 (cf. Jn 7.24, 51; 8.15, 46) and embodies John's understanding that God sent Jesus not to condemn but to save the world (Jn 3.17). But in my view, the evidence, both internal and external, leads inexorably to the conclusion that the pericope, although an ancient and authentic tradition about Jesus, is not an original part of John's Gospel. Nevertheless, the pericope merits brief attention here because most MSS containing the pericope place it somewhere in John's Gospel (other MSS, notably f^{13}, locate it in Luke), and because its content pertains to my topic.

---

1.   See the discussion by B.F. Westcott and F.J.A. Hort, *Introduction to the New Testament in the Original Greek* (New York: Harper & Brothers, 1882; repr., Peabody, MA: Hendrickson, 1988), pp. 82-88; also, *TCGNT*, pp. 219-22. I use the traditional designation *Pericope Adulterae* for convenience even though it does, as O'Day points out, reflect the interpretive biases that have long dominated study of the passage (G.R. O'Day, 'John 7.53–8.11: A Study in Misreading', *JBL* 111 [1992], pp. 631-40).

2.   J.P. Heil, 'The Story of Jesus and the Adulteress (John 7,53–8,11) Reconsidered', *Bib* 72 (1991), pp. 182-91.

Commentators spare little effort in attempting to reconstruct the circumstances that culminate with the scribes and Pharisees hauling this unnamed woman before Jesus. Is she married or betrothed? Who is the man involved, and where is he? Has she been framed and, if so, why? Is she being led to or from her trial? Is she the recipient of due process or mob justice? Such questions—of which there are many more—are intriguing but cannot be answered with any certainty. Moreover, the narrative itself shows no interest in such questions. The narrator takes for granted that the woman is guilty of adultery (Jn 8.3), and does not discuss background details or address tangential issues.

Were this story to portray a formal trial of the woman, as do, for example, those of Susanna and *The Daughter of Amram*, then her role could be measured profitably against the rules for testimony. But this is hardly a formal trial.[3] The reasons for the woman's passivity and silence therefore can be guessed at but not established. She may have been too terrified to speak, or may not even have had the option of speaking. She may have thought it useless to raise her voice in self-defence, perhaps because of her gender, but perhaps also because the evidence against her was irrefutable: she had been caught in the act. She may have been tried and convicted already, making any protestations futile. But such conjectures are otiose.

This story is of the entrapment type commonly found in the Synoptics (cf. Mk 3.1-6 and pars.; 10.2-12 and par.; 12.13-17 and pars.), and so clearly it is not the woman but Jesus who is on trial: 'They said this to test him, so that they might have some charge to bring against him' (Jn 8.6). Jesus, of course, turns the tables on his adversaries, and in the end it is they who stand trial before him. As for the woman, she enters as the pawn of the scribes and Pharisees, and leaves as a person set free by Jesus; no one has condemned her (Jn 8.11). Her simple statement to that effect is her only testimony, and her testimony is true.

2. *John 9.1-41: They Summoned his Parents*

The importance of Jesus' signs for establishing his identity as the messiah can simply be mentioned again at this point with no need for further discussion. The miraculous sign of restoring sight to the man born blind in John 9 graphically illustrates Jesus' claim in Jn 8.12 to be

---

3. If anything, the episode resembles a lynching. See Derrett's analysis, *Law*, pp. 156-88, especially pp. 166-67.

the light of the world. That claim sparks an acrimonious dispute between Jesus and his antagonists in John 8, whose juridical atmosphere is manifested in the legal parlance used by both sides in the debate over the validity of Jesus' testimony according to the rules for evidence (Jn 8.13-18).

This juridical atmosphere continues throughout John 8 and carries over into John 9, where John shows almost obsessive concern to establish the reality of the miracle. Nearly a dozen times the fact of the man's blindness is stated, and well over a dozen times the fact of his cure. In this forensic environment, and with the proof of the miracle at stake, the witnesses are crucial. The blind man's neighbours make poor witnesses, unable to agree among themselves as to his identity and not fully convinced of his claims (Jn 9.8-12). The authorities likewise remained unconvinced, but the possibility that Jesus has broken their law by healing on the sabbath impels them to launch an official investigation (Jn 9.14, cf. 5.16).[4] In the course of their inquiry they will, obviously, question the man himself. But also, they must interrogate the only witnesses able to establish with certainty both his identity and his congenital blindness, namely, his parents. Ultimately, the proof of the miracle stands on their testimony: 'The parents act as the two witnesses required by the law, to attest that such a miracle has occurred.'[5]

Seeking to avoid the reprisal borne by anyone who acknowledged Jesus as the messiah, the parents are willing to confirm only that the man is their son, that he was indeed blind at birth and that he now can see. The official nature of the investigation is manifested in the words of the parents: αὐτὸν ἐρωτήσατε, ἡλικίαν ἔχει, αὐτὸς περὶ ἑαυτοῦ λαλήσει (Jn 9.21), which Bruce paraphrases, 'You must ask him yourself: he is old enough to bear competent testimony in court'.[6]

E. Stagg and F. Stagg comment on the blind man's parents.

> A woman's witness was not normally accredited in Jewish circles. In this story no priority is given to either parent; the terms 'father' and 'mother' are not employed. Four times in six verses 'the parents' are mentioned;

---

4. Schnackenburg (*John*, II, p. 249) observes that the shift in John's terminology from Pharisees to Jews (cf. Jn 9.13; 9.18) 'certainly intends to indicate the official character of the investigation, since for him "the Jews" quite often function as representatives of the Jewish authorities'. Notice also the formal tenor of the injunction to confess, δὸς δόξαν τῷ θεῷ (Jn 9.24), which the TEV captures well: 'Promise before God that you will tell the truth!' (compare שׂים נא כבוד ליהוה in Josh. 7.19, and similarly, *m. Sanh.* 6.2).

5. Lindars, *John*, p. 346.

6. Bruce, *John*, p. 215.

and the testimony is 'theirs', not 'his' or 'hers'. This stylistic detail may
be without significance; but if it implies anything it is on the side of a
positive attitude toward women.[7]

The stylistic detail most likely is without significance, and in any event
would not imply a 'positive attitude' toward women but rather would
reflect the attitude that permitted women to testify only in those matters
pertaining to their special knowledge. Two examples of such matters in
which both parents participate in the giving of evidence are found in
Deuteronomy. Both parents testify before the elders to the rebelliousness
of their son (Deut. 21.18-21), and both are involved in proving their
daughter's innocence before the elders when her husband accuses her of
not having been a virgin at marriage (Deut. 22.13-21). Thus, it is entirely
normal that the Jewish authorities would interrogate the man's mother
as well as his father, for they, particularly his mother, have the intimate
and authoritative knowledge of his condition at birth. Again, their testimony shrinks from the precipice of confessing Jesus as the messiah, but
the testimony that they do provide is true. It is they—mother as well as
father—who corroborate for both the Jewish authorities and for John's
readers their son's claim to have been cured of the blindness that they
know to have afflicted him from birth.

3. *John 18.12-27: He Spoke to the Doorkeeper*

C.H. Dodd remarks, 'In the account of Peter's threefold denial of his
Master the four Gospels are closely parallel, and introduce identical or
nearly identical words and phrases more often than in any other part of
the Passion narrative'.[8] All the more striking, then, are the differences
between the Johannine and the Synoptic accounts, some of which
involve the people who confront Peter. All four Evangelists agree that
Peter was challenged three times, the first time by a servant woman, ἡ
παιδίσκη. But only John identifies her as the doorkeeper ἡ θυρωρός
(Jn 18.16-17 and pars.), and only John describes her as the agent
through whom the other disciple is able to obtain access to the courtyard for Peter (Jn 18.15-16).[9]

---

7. E. Stagg and F. Stagg, *Woman in the World of Jesus* (Philadelphia:
Westminster Press, 1978), p. 238.

8. Dodd, *Historical Tradition*, p. 83.

9. Other differences in the four accounts are not pertinent for the present purpose, but may be observed in the tables provided by Dodd (*Historical Tradition*,

There is an intriguing relationship between John 10 and John 18 revolving around the figure of the αὐλή, which Stibbe diagrams and labels a 'narrative echo effect'.[10] In John 10 Jesus is the shepherd who secures his sheep in the αὐλή. The doorkeeper opens the door to him, and he leads his sheep in and out, guarding them against thieves, robbers and wolves. Unlike the hired hand who deserts the sheep in a time of danger, Jesus is the good shepherd who lays down his life to protect them. In John 18 Jesus fulfills these functions literally in the walled garden that resembles an αὐλή, exchanging his life for those of his disciples who are imperiled by the thief Judas Iscariot and the wolves who accompany him. Then, in the αὐλή of Annas, the disciple who is known to the high priest assumes the role of the shepherd, Peter that of the hired hand, and the servant woman that of the doorkeeper:

> The implication of these narrative echo effects is that the anonymous disciple functions as the shepherd of the symbolic word-picture in 10.1-5, whilst Peter functions as the hired hand who flees in the hour of danger (though Peter's flight is a metaphorical flight from confession, not a literal desertion).[11]

These 'narrative echo effects', especially those between the parable of the good shepherd and the scene in Annas' courtyard, are much less obvious in the English text than in the Greek text where the words αὐλή, θύρα and θυρωρός appear in both passages. This suggests that John's original audience was much more likely to perceive that the servant woman fulfills the role of the θυρωρός who opens the θύρα of the αυλή to the other disciple and Peter. It can scarcely be coincidence that John is the only Evangelist who marks the servant woman as the θυρωρός, and does so twice.

Unlike the Synoptic versions of Peter's denial, John has the servant woman issuing the first challenge to Peter at the door to the courtyard as he enters rather than once he has established himself in the courtyard proper. Further, she asks Peter not simply if he had been with Jesus, but

---

p. 85) and Brown (*John*, II, pp. 838-39). Bultmann (*John*, p. 645 n. 5.) finds it 'remarkable that a woman keeps watch at the door of the High Priest—and that at night'. But it is not at all extraordinary that Annas should have a woman doorkeeper, nor that she should perform her task at night (LXX 2 Sam. 4.6; Acts 12.6-17). On the theory that in the original story the doorkeeper was a male, see Brown, *John*, II, p. 824; Lindars, *John*, pp. 548-49.

10. Stibbe, *John as Storyteller*, pp. 101-105; *John*, pp. 181-84.
11. Stibbe, *John as Storyteller*, p. 104.

rather, if he is one of Jesus' disciples. In John's context, where the other disciple is known to the high priest and speaks to the doorkeeper, her statement has the sense, 'You are not one of his disciples too, are you— like the man who just spoke to me?'[12] Thus, she sets up the contrast between the other disciple as a shepherd and Peter as a hired hand. She is the first person to force Peter to pass judgment upon his own disciple-ship. The wrenching irony of Peter's encounter with the θυρωρός as he passes through the θύρα and enters the αυλή is that his lie is the truth: his denial of Jesus shows that he is not a disciple of Jesus after all. This servant woman, the doorkeeper, asks Peter, 'You are not also one of this man's disciples, are you?' The Greek phrasing of her question, using μή, indicates that she expects him to answer in the negative. In that sense, her question to Peter is an ironic assessment of his discipleship. Her question is a testimony that is, sadly, all too true.

12. Against Bultmann, *John*, p. 645 n. 7.

Chapter 11

HER TESTIMONY IS TRUE

Any view of women as witnesses in John's Gospel will depend upon how the book itself is viewed. Are the persons and events of John's Gospel real ones from the actual life of Jesus? Are they fictional ones based on the actual life of John's community? Are they vehicles created *ex nihilo* to express John's understanding of Jesus? The women can also be studied as witnesses apart from such questions by looking only at how they function within the narrative itself.

I am disinclined to hear the Gospel of John merely as an echo of the history of the Johannine community. I see little in the content and nothing in the genre of John's Gospel to justify construing it as, so to speak, the Acts of the Johannine Community cloaked in a fictional life of Jesus. If John's Gospel is unreliable as a portrait of Jesus, why should it be any more reliable as a portrait of John's community? If John's Gospel is not what it purports to be, why should it be believed as something it does not purport to be? The source for learning about persons and events in the Johannine church(es) is the Johannine Epistles, which clearly discuss such things. All that we surely have in the Gospel of John is a narrative about Jesus, no doubt shaped by the author's purposes and needs, but still presented by the author as a portrait of Jesus and not as a silhouette of John's community.

It is, in my view, an extremely precarious procedure to read the women in the Gospel of John as statements about the roles, statuses or offices of women in the Johannine church(es), and I will hazard no guesses in that direction.[1] I would rather seek to understand how the women function as witnesses within John's narrative itself and within the

---

1.   Attempts to glean from John's Gospel how women might have functioned in the Johannine community can be found in, among others, Brown, *Community*; Schüssler Fiorenza, *Memory of Her*; Schneiders, 'Women'; de Boer, 'John 4.27'; Scott, *Sophia*.

legal, social and religious realities of first-century Palestine. Thus, there are two questions I wish to pose, one narratological and one historical. First, how are the women presented as witnesses and how does this presentation compare with that of the men? Secondly, how does the testimony of the women align with the cultural constraints on women as witnesses? Responses to these questions should offer a basis for understanding John's presentation of the women as witnesses, and for estimating how the first readers might have responded to them.

1. *Narrative*

Jesus' encounters with individuals comprise one of the most pronounced features of John's narrative. The scenes with Nicodemus, the Samaritan woman, the royal official, the sick man at the pool, the man born blind, Martha and Mary, Pilate, Mary Magdalene and others make indelible impressions upon the reader.

E. Schweizer sees that John's emphasis on the individual pervades his ecclesiology. Unlike Paul's metaphor of the body as interdependent individuals and communities, John's metaphor of the vine and branches stresses the dependence of both the individual believer and the individual church on Jesus.[2] Moule sees John's individualism as the origin of the realized eschatology that is the correlative but not the replacement of futurist eschatology.[3] Collins views John's individualism as the key to understanding the Gospel's meaning, traditions and purpose. Collins perceives that the Evangelist selects figures, probably historical individuals, from the common Gospel tradition or his own tradition and typecasts them as representatives of the various responses to Jesus of belief and unbelief.[4] Culpepper also thinks that John's individualization of characters is noteworthy. Culpepper, unlike Collins, sets aside the question of whether the characters are historically based, but along with Collins he sees that John's characters become 'types' that represent the continuum of responses to Jesus.[5]

As a key component of John's narrative, the focus on individuals

2. E. Schweizer, *Church Order in the New Testament* (London: SCM Press, 1961), pp. 117-24.

3. Moule, 'Individualism', pp. 91-93.

4. R.F. Collins, 'The Representative Figures of the Fourth Gospel—I', *DRev* 94 (1976), p. 31.

5. Culpepper, *Anatomy*, pp. 104-105, 145.

merits the attention it gets from Schweizer, Moule, Collins and Culpepper. But I am convinced that John chose it as a narrative emphasis mostly because it reflects a very real part of Jesus' life—his encounters with individuals—that lends itself particularly well to his rhetorical agenda. From start to finish John seeks to persuade the reader that the messiah is Jesus, and to that end presents an array of individual witnesses. The reader can take refuge in the narrative crowds who are divided over Jesus (Jn 7.40-44), but only temporarily, and eventually must stand alone, confront the individual witnesses, accept or reject their testimonies, and make a decision about Jesus. Is he or is he not the messiah, the Son of God?

Many lines of inquiry could be pursued regarding these witnesses, but the relevant one here is whether John treats the women witnesses as a class or as individuals. In contrast to the Synoptics, John has no villainous women figures such as Herodias and her daughter who successfully conspire to have John the Baptist put to death (Mk 6.17-29 and par.). But if Herodias and her daughter are absent from John, so is Herod himself, ultimately the one responsible for the Baptist's death. Furthermore, there are positive women figures in the Synoptics who are missing in John, for example, the Syrophoenician woman (Mt. 15.21-28 and par.) and the woman with the flow of blood (Mk 5.25-34 and pars.) whose faiths Jesus applauds. There are also the women in Luke's parables: the woman who seeks and finds the lost coin (Lk. 15.8-10) and the widow who persists in her petitions to the obstinate judge (Lk. 18.1-8). Of the several ways to explain why certain traditions are present or lacking in John's Gospel, a most implausible one would be that John's criterion for including or omitting material was how it portrayed women.

Also, except for the man healed at Beth-zatha, there are no negatively portrayed men in John's Gospel who cannot be found in the Synoptics.[6] In John, as in the Synoptics, male Jewish leaders are the targets for Jesus' vituperations, Judas is the betrayer, Peter would prevent Jesus from fulfilling his mission, Pilate is the one who sets the seal on Jesus' fate. Conversely, the Johannine nonpareil of discipleship is a man, the Beloved Disciple, who is not mentioned in the Synoptics.

---

6.   Nicodemus is a partial exception, if one at all. He belongs to the group of Jewish religious authorities who are Jesus' adversaries, and therefore he represents them. But Nicodemus the individual does not oppose Jesus (Jn 7.50-51); rather, he misunderstands him (Jn 3.4, 9), and in John's Gospel this misunderstanding is common to many characters, both male and female.

Finally, John's Jesus is not unswervingly affirming and congenial in his behaviour toward women, as is seen when he upbraids his mother for meddling in the timing of his mission, and when he bluntly exposes the personal life of the Samaritan woman. While it thus can be safely said that there are no major women characters negatively portrayed in John's Gospel, it is insufficient, even misleading, to say that much alone.[7]

It would not be surprising to see John's narrative treating the women witnesses as individuals not as a class, and my exegesis shows this to be the case. Jesus' mother is not put forth as a witness to Jesus' miracle or glory at the wedding, but she is an important witness to his death. The Samaritan woman testifies convincingly to what happened in her meeting at the well with Jesus, but can only offer a tentative suggestion about his identity. At the raising of Lazarus, Martha utters the fullest confession of Jesus' identity in terms of titles, but shows herself to be unaware of the deeper implications of the titles. Mary, unlike Martha, makes no confession of Jesus as the messiah, but along with her sister provides crucial testimony to the fact of their brother's death. At the supper in Bethany, the sisters embody what it means to serve Jesus, but they make no overt testimony to his identity. Along with Jesus' mother, two more of Jesus' relatives, one an aunt by blood and the other an aunt by marriage, witness his death. Mary Magdalene and the Beloved Disciple are the only ones in the narrative who can testify to Jesus' death and to his resurrection. Mary Magdalene's testimony to the disciples, 'I have seen the Lord', is the same as theirs to Thomas, 'We have seen the Lord'. And yet, the narrative advances not Mary Magdalene but the Beloved Disciple as the prime witness to the fact and significance of Jesus' death, and moreover, as the guarantor of the testimony of the narrative itself. If there is a pattern here, it is that there is no pattern, only individuals responding as such to Jesus.

It would not be surprising to see John's narrative treating the men counterparts of the women witnesses in the same way, not as a class but as individuals. And that is the case. John the Baptist, Andrew, Philip, Nathanael, Peter and Thomas offer diversely articulated testimonies to

7.   It might be said that the mother of the man born blind is portrayed negatively, as she cowers from acknowledging that it was Jesus who healed him. However, she is not a major figure, she acts in concert with her husband, and in shrinking from the consequences of publicly confessing Jesus, she is no different than Joseph of Arimathea (Jn 19.38) and Peter (Jn 18.15-18, 25-27).

the identity of Jesus. Nicodemus confesses that Jesus is a teacher come from God, but this teacher of Israel never seems to move beyond the miracles that brought him to that confession. The royal official enters and exits the narrative in a breath, as one born of the Spirit, moving from miracle faith to word faith. The man at the pool of Beth-zatha is never seen to ponder, much less confess, the identity of his healer, and his only testimony is to finger Jesus for the authorities as the man who broke the sabbath laws. The man with congenital blindness testifies both to the miracle and to Jesus, proving himself to have received spiritual as well as physical sight. Lazarus is silent, never uttering a single word of testimony to the most astonishing of all the miracles or to the one who performed it. As with the women, if there is a pattern here, it is that there is no pattern, only individuals responding as such to Jesus.

The observations that in John's narrative there are no villainous women figures and that none of the major women figures is portrayed negatively are not mistaken. What is mistaken is the conclusion, often made, that this betokens a calculated programme by John. John is not trying to present women in a good light, but rather, to do so with individuals who respond positively to Jesus, regardless of their gender. And so John's narrative technique of focusing on individuals is simply that. There is no focus on gender.

In light of this evidence that John is not treating women or men as a class, remarks like this one by Painter are unconvincing: 'It seems probable that the evangelist intends the narrative as a form of comment on the role of women.'[8] It is more accurate to say that John intends the narrative as a form of comment on the positive and negative responses of individuals to testimony to Jesus in the hope of persuading the reader to make a positive response. And this of course is consistent with the focus on individuals that Schweizer, Moule, Collins and Culpepper notice in John's narrative, and with which this part of the discussion began.

It must be kept in mind that the mix of male and female individuals in John's narrative is a well-balanced one. If we conclude that John chose events like the wedding at Cana and the meeting at the well at Sychar to highlight the roles of women, we should also conclude that John chose events like the healings at Beth-zatha and Siloam to highlight the roles of men. But both conclusions are implausible. When John elects to tell a story about an inquisitive woman at a well or a sick man at a pool, surely he does so out of interest in their responses to Jesus and not in

8. Painter, *Quest*, p. 324 n. 35.

their gender. This is also true of the witnesses. John is interested in their testimony not their gender. If individual women witnesses are integral to the events John chose to narrate—and they are—it is not because John wanted to make statements about women, but because he wanted to provide testimonies about Jesus, and these events best suited that purpose.

2. *History*

A strictly literary approach to any of the Gospels is perfectly legitimate, but the limitations must be kept in view. Those who use 'the new criticism' on John's Gospel, methods developed for studying the (modern) novel, sometimes forget that the genre of John's book is not that of the novel but of the gospel—kerygmatic historiography. What often results is the claim that John is concerned not with historical truth but narrative truth. But while the truth value of John's Gospel can be disputed, its truth claim cannot; that is, it is possible to believe that the characters, words and events of the narrative are fictional, but it is mistaken to argue that John presents them as such.

John's narrative is often characterized, particularly by those using literary-critical methods, as being 'realistic' or as having the quality of 'verisimilitude'. How does a modern critic decide whether or not an ancient text is realistic or verisimilar? By comparing the content of the ancient text in question with information garnered from other appropriate ancient texts. Thus, one ancient text is judged to be realistic or not realistic by other ancient texts. But how are these latter texts known to reflect historical reality? The circularity and fallaciousness of this procedure are apparent.

M.C. de Boer wonders why, when the issue in the Samaritan episode in John 4 is not women and men but Samaritans and Jews, Jesus encounters a woman and not a man at the well. De Boer explains,

> Aside from the possibility (perhaps remote) that the narrator is a proto-feminist who thinks it right and good to portray Jesus in conversation with women as well as men, the answer (from a narratological angle) most probably lies in the law of verisimilitude that characterizes realistic narrative (a law that only Jesus himself is allowed to transgress and then only to display his messianic stature and heavenly origin). It is unlikely that Jesus would encounter a man at a well to draw water since that was the work of women in ancient Palestine (Gen. 24.11).[9]

9. De Boer, 'John 4.27', p. 215 n. 21.

How, then, do we know that it was a woman's work to draw water? From another ancient narrative, Genesis. But how do we know that the information about women drawing water in Genesis 24 is not merely 'realistic narrative' as well? Presumably from other ancient texts, and now we are caught up in the verisimilitude circle.

Furthermore, the passage that de Boer has selected comes from a narrative, Genesis, that is questionable for proving his point. It may indeed have been the task of first-century Samaritan village women to draw water, but that can hardly be demonstrated from a text that reflects pastoral life in Mesopotamia some two thousand years earlier. In fact, further along in the same narrative, Jacob encounters shepherds—males (he calls them אחי)—drawing water from a well for their flocks (Gen. 29.3); and when Jacob's cousin Rachel, herself a shepherd, approaches the well to draw water for her father's sheep, Jacob does the job for her (Gen. 29.9-10). It is much more plausible that Jesus simply met a woman at a well than that John felt compelled to concoct a woman in order to maintain verisimilitude in his narrative.

What can be made from all of this? To wade for a moment into the verisimilitude morass, it can be said that John's narrative is just as good a text from which to judge the verisimilitude of other texts as it is a text to be so judged. If the words and deeds of the women in John's narrative plausibly match what is known of John's culture from other texts, then they are just as likely to be real as realistic, to be true as verisimilar.

Exegetes often characterize the activities of the women in the Gospel of John as 'unconventional roles'.[10] The concept of roles for ancient Jewish women is a fragile one, especially when used—as is far too often the case—uncritically: 'The category "position", similar to the categories "status" and "role", does not allow for the variety of Jewish women's experience. Using Judaism as a background often means foreshortening and oversimplifying.'[11]

Do the Johannine women participate in activities unconventional for

10. For instance, Schneiders, 'Women', p. 38; D. Rensberger, *Overcoming the World: Politics and Community in the Gospel of John* (London: SPCK, 1989), p. 130.

11. B. Brooten, 'Jewish Women's History in the Roman Period: A Task for Christian Theology', *HTR* 79 (1986), p. 25. J. Jeremias gives examples that expose the error of making overly rigid generalizations about the constraints on the public life and activities of Jewish women in Jesus' time (*Jerusalem in the Time of Jesus: An Investigation into the Economic and Social Conditions during the New Testament Period* [London: SCM Press, 1969], pp. 361-63).

Jewish and Samaritan women at the time of Jesus? If by unconventional we mean women radically deviating from the religious, social and legal paths prescribed for them, then the answer must be no. They do not debate the Pharisees, teach in the temple, sit on the Sanhedrin, command soldiers or testify at trials. They are involved with weddings, wells, meals, deaths, funerals and burials. They attend to providing refreshments, fetching water, serving dinner, offering hospitality and burying loved ones. In short, the Johannine women do nothing that would justify the thought, 'How astonishing that a Jewish (or Samaritan) woman in first-century Palestine should say this, or do that, or be there'.[12] My exegesis shows that the testimonies of the women according to John are consistent with the conclusion that the women do nothing that could be understood to overstep the religious, legal and social conventions of their culture.

John does not advance Jesus' mother as a witness to the miracle at the wedding, possibly because her relationship to Jesus would render her testimony in such a matter at worst inadmissible and at best suspect. On the other hand, her relationship to Jesus does not debar her from testifying to his death, and indeed, she is found among those who witness the crucifixion, including two aunts of Jesus who likewise are competent to testify to his death and who appear nowhere else in the narrative. The women (including Mary Magdalene) standing near the cross thus comprise an acceptable complement of qualified witnesses to the death of Jesus. Although it is debatable whether or not John had anti-Docetic concerns, it is certain that later authors like Ignatius did have such concerns and that for them Jesus' mother was an invaluable witness to the reality of Jesus' flesh. Only John specifically spells out that Jesus' mother was present at his crucifixion, and the anti-Docetic apologists found in her an ideal witness to and guarantor of the reality of his birth and death.

When the Samaritan woman meets and talks with Jesus at the well, she does nothing that breaches Samaritan etiquette. She entertains the idea that perhaps he is the messiah and, in seeking assistance to make a

---

12. As noted previously, I believe that the disciples' surprise at finding Jesus talking with the woman at the well (Jn 4.27) stems not from the fact that a Jewish man is talking with a (Samaritan) woman, but that Jesus is doing so. Except for the curt exchange with his mother at the wedding, Jesus has had no dealings with women up to that point. But in any event, the disciples are surprised at his behaviour not hers, which, as I have shown, is nothing extraordinary in that context.

determination on that matter, she testifies to her villagers of the miraculous knowledge that Jesus has demonstrated to her. Her testimony has sufficient credibility to be taken seriously, as is seen when the villagers unhesitatingly set out to investigate the man for themselves. My canvass of some Samaritan literature showed that she was very probably a competent witness in her culture, and it also was shown that although some or even many Jews might have viewed her with disdain, she was not an intrinsically incompetent witness under Jewish codes and customs.

Martha and Mary both testify to Lazarus' death. Martha is the only eyewitness to testify that Lazarus has been dead for four days, that is, that his death is real and final. The testimonies of Martha and Mary to Lazarus' death stand within the codes whereby they, women and sisters of the deceased, are competent to so testify. Martha offers the fullest confession, in terms of titles, of Jesus in the Gospel of John, and her confession is in keeping with the Old Testament laws and traditions whereby women can and do make personal confessions of God as well as conduct public proclamations of the same type.

Like the other three women at the cross, Mary Magdalene is a legally competent witness to Jesus' death, and her repeated insistence that Jesus' body has been removed from the tomb serves to confirm the fact of Jesus' death and to refute the allegation of a resurrection hoax. She is the first person to see the resurrected Jesus, and she testifies to the disciples of his resurrection using a phrase that has the quality of a formula that qualifies her as an official witness. Thus along with the Beloved Disciple, who is the witness par excellence in John's Gospel, Mary Magdalene is the only eyewitness to both the death and resurrection of Jesus.

Another example of a woman testifying entirely in accordance with customs and codes whereby a woman gives evidence of something within her particular knowledge is the mother of the blind man whom Jesus heals. In the official investigation into the healing, she and her husband confirm the identity, congenital blindness and healed state of their son. Ultimately, the proof of the healing relies upon their testimony.

It is true that in some cases a woman's testimony is corroborated or surpassed by that of a male. But this does not occur consistently, and in any event does not betoken a calculated programme undertaken by John on the basis of gender. The Samaritan woman's testimony is surpassed by that of Jesus, not because he is a male but because he is the messiah, the Son of God, and as such, his testimony surpasses all human testimony. Martha and Mary are the only ones besides Jesus who testify to the reality of Lazarus's death and, in fact, their testimony corroborates his. Furthermore, while Martha and Mary do not testify to the raising of Lazarus, neither do Jesus' male disciples; it is the crowd that does so. The women at the cross are perfectly competent witnesses to the death of Jesus, and while the Beloved Disciple corroborates and surpasses their testimony, he does so not as a man but as the disciple *par excellence* and guarantor of the book. John advances neither the angels nor a group of women but Mary Magdalene as the first witness to the empty tomb and the risen Jesus. Mary Magdalene's testimony is corroborated by other disciples, but Deuteronomic codes would require an additional one or two witnesses regardless of Mary's gender. In this regard, she is no different from the man cured of blindness, whose testimony undergoes the most intense scrutiny from the authorities who require the corroboration of other witnesses, in this case, his parents.

In no case does John present a woman as a witness in a way that so tramples the religious, social and legal boundaries that readers would feel compelled to reject her. Quite to the contrary, all the women witnesses, regardless of whether their testimonies are limited, corroborated or surpassed, are true and acceptable within the conventions of their culture. Because the behaviour of the women witnesses is not stereotyped, artificial or outside the social, legal and religious walls of their culture, it can be argued with some confidence of each woman witness that her testimony is true; that is, John is reporting actual women's testimonies, surely shaping them to suit his purpose of persuading the reader that the messiah is Jesus, but not fabricating them as part of an agenda to make pronouncements about the roles of women. My exegesis, if correct, adds to the prima facie case for John's reliability as an historian.

3. *Concluding Observations*

I present here a comparison of three comments each from two exegetes, M. Davies and M. Scott, both writing on the women in John, both published in 1992.

> M. Davies: 'The Fourth Gospel recognizes the usefulness of women, but only in their subsidiary function of waiting upon men.'
> M. Scott: 'While I would not contend that the Fourth Gospel sets out to demean the role of the traditional male disciples, it does clearly leave it largely undiscussed and on the margin in comparison with the central position given to the women as exemplary disciples.'

M. Davies: 'Modern commentators fail to notice or discuss the restricted role which the [Fourth] Gospel assigns to women.'
M. Scott: 'The Fourth Gospel allows many of the traditional male figures to be replaced in their function by women.'

M. Davies: 'The Fourth Gospel is one of many texts which has lent its authority to the subordination of women in societies where it has been read.'
M. Scott: '[The Fourth Gospel] may be understood as a perceptive corrective to the dominant stream of the Early Church, which excluded women from positions of authority and leadership.'[13]

It seems almost as if Davies and Scott have read two different Fourth Gospels. Both cannot be right, but both could be, and are, I think, wrong. In my view, the words of Rena place, so to speak, a curse on both their houses:

> There is no one role for women in the Fourth Gospel. They are active but also passive. They are strong but also weak. They listen but also proclaim. Their actions present a colorful and complete denial to any urge to stereotype a female role.[14]

The comparison of Davies's and Scott's remarks indicates how the discussion on women in the Gospel of John has typically proceeded. Both sides construe what the women say and do as evidence of the Evangelist deliberately delineating the place of women, even though they disagree about what that place is. But this is to take a matter of great interest to us and project it onto John as if it were of great interest to him as well. And to do that is to lose all perspective on John's consuming concern, namely Jesus, and that people believe in him.

> The Gospel of John fundamentally contains a single theme: the Person of Jesus. The entire Gospel is concerned with the fact of his presence, the nature of his claim, whence he comes and whither he goes, and how men relate themselves to him. The miracles supply information about Jesus himself; the speeches are concerned with the speaker; the discussions devolve about the person of Jesus.[15]

While John, in my opinion, shows no self-conscious interest whatsoever in the topic of women as such, it cannot be said that his Gospel is

---

13. Davies, *Rhetoric and Reference*, pp. 20, 227, 20; Scott, *Sophia*, pp. 245-246, 238, 238.

14. Rena, 'Women', p. 145.

15. W. Schmithals, 'Introduction', in Bultmann, *John*, p. 5.

so barren of interest in women as individual persons that the topic is not worth discussing. The growing mountain of literature on the subject (including this book) shows this not to be the case, as does, of course, the copious material involving women in the Gospel itself. But the discussion too often subsumes John's overarching concern—persuading readers that the messiah is Jesus—under a topic of comparatively minor interest, thus producing exaggerated and distorted interpretations of the material in which the women appear, and thus, of the Gospel as a whole.

The idea, held by many, that John is manufacturing and/or manipulating women as symbols or paradigms for roles women can and should play rather than presenting them as real examples of how individual persons can and do respond to Jesus is, I think, mistaken. If we so interpret the women in John's Gospel, then on narrative grounds we are obliged to do the same with men. It could be countered that even if the women in John's Gospel are not necessarily symbols or paradigms, that John nevertheless selected an unusually large number of important events involving women. But this is the same argument dressed up in different clothing. The events that John selected best suited his purpose of persuading readers that the messiah is Jesus. That women were present and involved in some or even many of these events is not extraordinary, and does not necessarily mean that John selected them just because of the women. John did not choose material to make statements about women but about Jesus, and about how people, whoever they are, should come to faith in him.

John is by no means oblivious to the concern for justice in community, which is God's eternal passion and which has been shared by many people in all times and places. But John presents no agenda for women, neither to subordinate nor supraordinate them. Rather, John's agenda is for human beings in Jesus Christ, and it is spelled out in the very beginning of his book: 'But to all who received him, who believed on his name, he gave power to become children of God, who were born, not of blood or of the will of the flesh or of the will of man, but of God' (Jn 1.12).

Establishing equality for all persons regardless of their gender (or any other characteristic) is a cause surely born in the heart of God. But the cause of women's equality is not advanced, rather, it is hindered whenever we attempt to force biblical texts to say things we might wish to hear but they do not say. Just as it is dishonest to deny that certain New Testament texts sanctioned slavery, but also fallacious to argue that such texts warrant the sanction of slavery today, it is counterproductive to contend that the Gospel of John is a document that passes edicts for its context and for ours on how women can and should function in the church. That sort of reading amounts to an act of exegetical prestidigitation that in essence admits that those who would use the Bible as a warrant to impose specific patterns of order from ancient communities onto modern ones have a case worthy of being contested. It is to lend dignity to what is actually a frivolous case for the subordination of women.

To help in the effort to advance the cause of equality, not just for women but for all people, God sends a powerful and contemporary Paraclete, the Spirit. John, probably more so than any of the Evangelists, recognizes that while his book is the first step in bringing to faith those who have not seen what his eyewitnesses have seen, it is the Spirit who leads every generation of later believers, including our own, into what the truth of Jesus Christ means for daily living (Jn 16.12-13).

God's will for Christians is not that they rigidly duplicate the life and ministry of Jesus or his first disciples or the Johannine community (as if such a thing were possible), but that they discover, through the Spirit of Christ, the mind of Christ for each community in its own time and place. It is possible to discover God's will for any contemporary context by Spirit-led exegetical and hermeneutical study of John's Gospel, but not by projecting contemporary contexts back onto it. Any exegesis is strained that has the Gospel of John setting out roles for people on the basis of gender or any other category, and is in fact contrary to John's teaching that all believers are God's children who, born of the Spirit, move in ways that defy human delineation (Jn 1.12-13; 3.5-8).

The witnessing disciple responsible for the inscription of John's Gospel defines the book as a μαρτυρία, a testimony, and his testimony is vouched to be true (Jn 21.24). Are the testimonies of the women that this disciple reports also guaranteed to be true? Is her testimony true just as his testimony is true? It depends, then as now, not upon the gender but upon the faith of the witness who is born of the Spirit as a child of God. Their testimony is true who truly believe that the messiah, the Son of God, is Jesus.

BIBLIOGRAPHY

Abbott, E.A., *Johannine Vocabulary: A Comparison of the Words of the Fourth Gospel with Those of the Three* (London: A. & C. Black, 1905).

—*Johannine Grammar* (London: A. & C. Black, 1906).

Archer, L.A., *Her Price Is beyond Rubies: The Jewish Woman in Graeco–Roman Palestine* (JSOTSup, 60; Sheffield: JSOT Press, 1990).

Ashton, J., *Understanding the Fourth Gospel* (Oxford: Clarendon Press, 1991).

Aune, D.E., *The New Testament in its Literary Environment* (Philadelphia: Westminster Press, 1987).

Balz, H., and G. Schneider (eds.), *Exegetical Dictionary of the New Testament* (3 vols.; Grand Rapids: Eerdmans, 1990–93).

Barr, A., 'The Factor of Testimony in the Gospels', *ExpTim* 49 (1937-38), pp. 401-408.

Barrett, C.K., *The Gospel according to St John: An Introduction with Commentary and Notes on the Greek Text* (Philadelphia: Westminster Press, 2nd edn, 1978).

Barth, K., *Erklärung des Johannes-Evangeliums: Kapitel 1–8* (Zürich: Theologischer Verlag, 1976).

Bassler, J.M., 'I Corinthians', in C.A. Newsom and S.H. Ringe (eds.), *The Women's Bible Commentary* (London: SPCK, 1992), pp. 321-29.

Bauckham, R., *Jude and the Relatives of Jesus in the Early Church* (Edinburgh: T. & T. Clark, 1990).

—'Mary of Clopas (John 19.25)', in G.J. Brooke (ed.), *Women in the Biblical Tradition* (SWR, 31; Lampeter: Edwin Mellen, 1992), pp. 231-55.

Baumgarten, J.M., *Studies in Qumran Law* (SJLA, 24; Leiden: Brill, 1977).

Beasley-Murray, G.R., *John* (WBC, 36; Waco, TX: Word Books, 1987).

Benoit, P., 'Marie-Madeleine et les disciples au tombeau selon Joh 20.1-18', in *Judentum, Urchristentum, Kirche* (BZNW, 26; Berlin: Alfred Töpelmann, 1964), pp. 141-52.

Bernard, J.H., *Critical and Exegetical Commentary on the Gospel of St. John* (ICC; 2 vols.; Edinburgh: T. & T. Clark, 1928).

Beutler, J., *Martyria: Traditionsgeschichtliche Untersuchungen zum Zeugnisthema bei Johannes* (FTS, 10; Frankfurt: Josef Knecht, 1972).

Biale, R., *Women and Jewish Law: An Exploration of Women's Issues in Halakhic Sources* (New York: Schocken Books, 1984).

Bienert, W.A., 'The Relatives of Jesus', in E. Hennecke and W. Schneemelcher, *New Testament Apocrypha* (2 vols.; Cambridge: James Clarke, rev. edn, 1991), I, pp. 470-88.

Bishop, E.F.F., 'Mary (of) Clopas and Her Father', *ExpTim* 73 (1961–62), p. 339.

Bittner, W.J., *Jesu Zeichen im Johannesevangelium: Die Messias-Erkenntnis im Johannesevangelium vor ihrem jüdischen Hintergrund* (WUNT, 2.26; Tübingen: Mohr [Paul Siebeck], 1987).

Bligh, J., 'Jesus in Samaria', *HeyJ* (1962), pp. 329-46.

Blinzler, J., *Die Brüder und Schwestern Jesu* (SBS, 21; Stuttgart: Katholisches Bibelwerk, 1967).

Bode, E.L., *The First Easter Morning: The Gospel Accounts of the Women's Visit to the Tomb of Jesus* (AnBib, 45; Rome: Biblical Institute Press, 1970).

Boecker, H.J., *Law and the Administration of Justice in the Old Testament and Ancient East* (London: SPCK, 1980).

Boers, H., *Neither on this Mountain nor in Jerusalem: A Study of John 4* (SBLMS, 35; Atlanta: Scholars Press, 1988).

Boice, J.M., *Witness and Revelation in the Gospel of John* (Exeter: Paternoster Press, 1970).

Boling, R.G., and G.E. Wright, *Joshua* (AB, 6; Garden City, NY: Doubleday, 1982).

Borgen, P., 'God's Agent in the Fourth Gospel', in J. Neusner (ed.), *Religions in Antiquity* (NumenSup, 14; Leiden: Brill, 1968), pp. 137-48.

Botha, J.E., *Jesus and the Samaritan Woman: A Speech Act Reading of John 4.1-42* (NovTSup, 65; Leiden: Brill, 1991).

Bowman, J., 'Samaritan Studies', *BJRL* 40 (1958), pp. 298-327.

—*Samaritan Documents Relating to their History, Religion and Life* (POTTS, 2; Pittsburgh: Pickwick Press, 1977).

Brenner, A., *The Israelite Woman: Social Role and Literary Type in Biblical Narrative* (Sheffield: JSOT Press, 1985).

Brooten, B., 'Jewish Women's History in the Roman Period: A Task for Christian Theology', *HTR* 79 (1986), pp. 22-30.

Brown, C.A., *No Longer Be Silent: First Century Jewish Portraits of Biblical Women* (GBT; Louisville: Westminster/John Knox Press, 1992).

Brown, R.E., *The Gospel according to John* (2 vols.; AB 29, 29a; New York: Doubleday, 1966).

—'The Paraclete in the Fourth Gospel', *NTS* 13 (1966–67), pp. 113-32.

—*The Community of the Beloved Disciple: The Lives, Loves, and Hates of an Individual Church in New Testament Times* (London: Geoffrey Chapman, 1979).

Brown, R.E., *et al.* (eds.), *Mary in the New Testament* (Philadelphia: Fortress Press, 1978).

Brox, N., *Zeuge und Märtyrer: Untersuchungen zur frühchristliche Zeugnis-Terminologie* (SANT, 5; München: Kösel, 1961).

Bruce, F.F., *The Acts of the Apostles: The Greek Text with Introduction and Commentary* (Grand Rapids: Eerdmans, 1953).

—*The Gospel of John: Introduction, Exposition and Notes* (Grand Rapids: Eerdmans, 1983).

Brunotte, W., 'ἀλείφω', *NIDNTT*, I, pp. 119-21.

Buck, H.M., 'Redactions of the Fourth Gospel and the Mother of Jesus', in D.E. Aune (ed.), *Studies in the New Testament and Early Christian Literature* (NovTSup, 33; Leiden: Brill, 1972), pp. 170-80.

Buis, P., and J. Leclerq, *Le Deutéronome* (Paris: Gabalda, 1963).

Bultmann, R., *The Gospel of John: A Commentary* (Philadelphia: Westminster Press, 1971).

—'γινώσκω', *TDNT*, I, pp. 689-719.

Burge, G.M., *The Anointed Community: The Holy Spirit in the Johannine Tradition* (Grand Rapids: Eerdmans, 1987).

Cameron, A., *Christianity and the Rhetoric of Empire:The Development of Christian Discourse* (Berkeley: University of California Press, 1991).

Campbell, E.F., *Ruth* (AB, 7; Garden City, NY: Doubleday, 1975).

Campbell, K.M., 'Rahab's Covenant', *VT* 22 (1972), pp. 243-44.

Carson, D.A., 'The Purpose of the Fourth Gospel: John 20.31 Reconsidered', *JBL* 106 (1987), pp. 639-51.

—*The Gospel according to John* (Grand Rapids: Eerdmans, 1991).

Chesnutt, R.D., 'Revelatory Experiences Attributed to Biblical Women', in A.-J. Levine (ed.), *Women Like This: New Perspectives on Jewish Women in the Greco–Roman World* (SBLEJL, 1; Atlanta: Scholars Press, 1991), pp. 107-125.

Coakley, J.F., 'The Anointing at Bethany and the Priority of John', *JBL* 107 (1988), pp. 241-56.

Cohen, B., *Jewish and Roman Law: A Comparative Study* (2 vols.; New York: Jewish Theological Seminary of America, 1966).

Cohn, H.H., 'Oath', *PJL*, cols. 615-21.

—'Rebellious Son', *PJL*, cols. 491-92.

—'Witness', *PJL*, cols. 605-12.

Collins, R.F., 'Mary in the Fourth Gospel: A Decade of Johannine Studies', *LS* 3 (1970), pp. 99-142.

—'The Representative Figures of the Fourth Gospel—I', *DRev* 94 (1976), pp. 26-46.

—'The Representative Figures of the Fourth Gospel—II', *DRev* 94 (1976), pp. 118-32.

—*John and His Witness* (ZNST; Collegeville, MN: Liturgical Press, 1991).

Corley, K.E., 'Were the Women around Jesus Really Prostitutes? Women in the Context of Greco–Roman Meals', in D.J. Lull (ed.), *Society of Biblical Literature Seminar Papers 1989* (Atlanta: Scholars Press, 1989), pp. 487-521.

Cranfield, C.E.B., 'The Resurrection of Jesus Christ', *ExpTim* 101 (1990), pp. 167-72.

Culpepper, R.A., *Anatomy of the Fourth Gospel: A Study in Literary Design* (FFNT, 1; Philadelphia: Fortress Press, 1983).

Dahl, N.A., 'The Johannine Church and History', in W. Klassen and G.F. Snyder (eds.), *Current Issues in New Testament Interpretation* (London: SCM Press, 1962), pp. 124-42.

Daube, D., *The New Testament and Rabbinic Judaism* (London: Athlone Press, 1956).

—*Witnesses in Bible and Talmud* (OCP; Oxford: Centre for Postgraduate Hebrew Studies, 1986).

Dauer, A., *Die Passionsgeschichte im Johannesevangelium: Eine traditionsgeschichtliche und theologische Untersuchung zu Joh 18,1–19,30* (SANT, 30; Munich: Kösel, 1972).

Davies, M., *Rhetoric and Reference in the Fourth Gospel* (JSNTSup, 69; Sheffield: JSOT Press, 1992).

Davies, W.D., and D.C. Allison, *A Critical and Exegetical Commentary on the Gospel according to Saint Matthew* (ICC; 2 vols. [vol. 3 forthcoming]; Edinburgh: T. & T. Clark, 1988–91).

de Boer, M.C., 'Narrative Criticism, Historical Criticism, and the Gospel of John', *JSNT* 47 (1992), pp. 35-48.

—'John 4.27—Women (and Men) in the Gospel and Community of John', in G.J. Brooke (ed.), *Women in the Biblical Tradition* (SWR, 31; Lampeter: Edwin Mellen, 1992), pp. 208-230.

de Jonge, M., 'Jewish Expectations about the "Messiah" according to the Fourth Gospel', *NTS* 19 (1972-73), pp. 246-70.

Delling, G., 'λαμβάνω', *TDNT*, IV, pp. 5-15.

Derrett, J.D.M., 'The Anointing at Bethany', in *Studia Evangelica II* (TU, 87; Berlin: Akademie Verlag, 1964), pp. 174-82.

—*Law in the New Testament* (London: Darton, Longman & Todd, 1970).

—'Ananias, Sapphira, and the Right of Property', *DRev* 89 (1971), pp. 225-32.

—'The Samaritan Woman's Purity (John 4.4-52)', *EvQ* 60 (1988), pp. 291-98.

Dodd, C.H., *The Interpretation of the Fourth Gospel* (Cambridge: Cambridge University Press, 1953).

—*Historical Tradition in the Fourth Gospel* (Cambridge: Cambridge University Press, 1963).

Dollar, S.E., 'The Significance of Women in the Fourth Gospel' (ThD dissertation, New Orleans Baptist Theological Seminary, 1983).

Domeris, W.R., 'The Johannine Drama', *JTSA* 42 (1983), pp. 29-35.

Duke, P.R., *Irony in the Fourth Gospel* (Atlanta: John Knox Press, 1985).

du Rand, J.A., 'Die Evangelie van Johannes as getuigende vertelling', *NGTT* 24 (1983), pp. 383-97.

Elliott, J.K., 'The Anointing of Jesus', *ExpTim* 85 (1973–74), pp. 105-107.

—'The Two Forms of the Third Declension Comparative Adjectives in the New Testament', *NovT* 19 (1977), pp. 234-39.

Elon, M. (ed.), *The Principles of Jewish Law* (Jerusalem: Keter Publishing House, 1975).

Endes, J.C., *Biblical Interpretation in the Book of Jubilees* (CBQMS, 18; Washington: Catholic Biblical Association of America, 1987).

Engel, H., *Die Susanna Erzählung: Einleitung, Übersetzung und Kommentar zum Septuaginta-Text und zur Theodotion-Bearbeitung* (OBO, 61; Göttingen: Vandenhoeck & Ruprecht, 1985).

Falk, Z.W., *Introduction to Jewish Law of the Second Commonwealth* (AGJU, 11; 2 vols.; Leiden: Brill, 1972).

Fee, G.D., 'On the Text and Meaning of John 20,30-31', in F. van Segbroeck, *et al.* (eds.), *The Four Gospels 1992* (BETL, 100; 3 vols.; Leuven: Leuven University Press, 1992), III, pp. 2193-2205.

Feldman, E., *Biblical and Post-Biblical Defilement and Mourning: Law as Theology* (New York: Yeshiva University, 1977).

Fitzmeyer, J.A., *The Genesis Apocryphon of Qumran Cave 1: A Commentary* (BibOr, 18; Rome: Biblical Institute Press, 1966).

Foerster, W., 'σῳζω', *TDNT*, VII, pp. 965-69.

Fortna, R.T., *The Gospel of Signs: A Reconstruction of the Narrative Source Underlying the Fourth Gospel* (SNTMS, 11; Cambridge: Cambridge University Press, 1977).

—*The Fourth Gospel and its Predecessor: From Narrative Source to Present Gospel* (Philadelphia: Fortress Press, 1988).

Fossum, J., 'Sects and Movements', in A.D. Crown (ed.), *The Samaritans* (Tübingen: Mohr [Paul Siebeck], 1989), pp. 293-389.

Gaffney, J., 'Believing and Knowing in the Fourth Gospel', *TS* 26 (1965), pp. 215-41.

Gaster, M., *The Samaritans: Their History, Doctrines and Literature* (London: Humphrey Milford and Oxford University Press, 1925).

—*Studies and Texts in Folklore, Magic, Mediaeval Romance, Hebrew Apocrypha, and Samaritan Archaeology* (2 vols.; New York: Ktav, 1971).

Gemser, B., 'The *RÎB* or Controversy-Pattern in Hebrew Mentality', in M. Noth and D.W. Thomas (eds.), *Wisdom in Israel and in the Ancient Near East* (VTSup, 3; Leiden: Brill, 1955), pp. 120-37.

Giblin, C.H., 'Suggestion, Negative Response, and Positive Action in St John's Portrayal of Jesus (John 2.1-11.; 4.46-54.; 7.2-14.; 11.1-44.)', *NTS* 26 (1980), pp. 197-211.

Giesen, H., 'ὥρα', *EDNT*, III, pp. 506-508.

Ginzburg, L., *The Legends of the Jews* (7 vols.; Philadelphia: Jewish Publication Society of America, 1968).

Girard, M., 'La composition structurelle des sept signes dans le quatrième évangile', *SR* 9 (1980), pp. 315-24.

Glasswell, M.E., 'ἐκμάσσω', *EDNT*, I, p. 419.

Goldin, H.E., *Hebrew Criminal Law and Procedure* (New York: Twayne, 1952).

Goodenough, E.R., *Jewish Symbols in the Greco–Roman Period* (12 vols.; New York: Bollingen, 1953–65).

Gordis, R., *The Song of Songs and Lamentations: A Study, Modern Translation and Commentary* (New York: Ktav, rev. edn, 1974).

Graß, H., *Ostergeschehen und Osterberichte* (Göttingen: Vandenhoeck & Ruprecht, 3rd edn, 1964).

Grassi, J.A., 'The Role of Jesus' Mother in John's Gospel: A Reappraisal', *CBQ* 48 (1986), pp. 67-80.

—*The Hidden Heroes of the Gospels: Female Counterparts of Jesus* (Collegeville, MN: Liturgical Press, 1989).

Green, J.B., *The Death of Jesus: Tradition and Interpretation in the Passion Narrative* (WUNT, 2.33; Tübingen: Mohr [Paul Siebeck], 1988).

Haenchen, E., *The Acts of the Apostles* (Philadelphia: Westminster Press, 1971).

—*Das Johannesevangelium: Ein Kommentar* (Tübingen: Mohr [Paul Siebeck], 1980).

Hall, R.G., *Revealed Histories: Techniques for Ancient Jewish and Christian Historiography* (JSPSup, 6; Sheffield: JSOT Press, 1991).

Hanson, A.T., *The Prophetic Gospel: A Study of John and the Old Testament* (Edinburgh: T. & T. Clark, 1991).

Harvey, A.E., *Jesus on Trial* (London: SPCK, 1976).

Heil, J.P., 'The Story of Jesus and the Adulteress (John 7,53–8,11) Reconsidered', *Bib* 72 (1991), pp. 182-91.

Heiligenthal, R., 'ἔργον', *EDNT*, II, pp. 49-51.

Hengel, M., 'Maria Magdalena und die Frauen als Zeugen', in O. Betz, *et al.* (eds.), *Abraham unser Vater: Juden und Christen im Gespräch über die Bibel* (AGJU, 5; Leiden: Brill, 1963), pp. 243-56.

—'The Interpretation of the Wine Miracle at Cana: John 2.1-11', in L.D. Hurst and N.T. Wright (eds.), *The Glory of Christ in the New Testament* (Oxford: Clarendon Press, 1987), pp. 83-122.

Hindley, J.C., 'Witness in the Fourth Gospel', *SJT* 18 (1965), pp. 319-37.

Hoskyns, E.C., *The Fourth Gospel* (ed. F.N. Davey; London: Faber & Faber, rev. edn, 1947).

Isser, S.J., *The Dositheans: A Samaritan Sect in Late Antiquity* (SJLA, 17; Leiden: Brill, 1976).

Janzen, J.G., 'Song of Moses, Song of Miriam: Who Is Seconding Whom?', *CBQ* 54 (1992), pp. 211-20.

Jeremias, J., *Jerusalem in the Time of Jesus: An Investigation into the Economic and Social Conditions during the New Testament Period* (London: SCM Press, 1969).

Judge, P.J., 'A Note on Jn 20,29', in van Segbroeck, *et al.* (eds.), *The Four Gospels 1992*, III, pp. 2184-92.

Kaufman, M., *The Woman in Jewish Law and Tradition* (Northvale, NJ: Jason Aronson, 1993).

Keenan, B., *An Evil Cradling* (London: Arrow, 1993).

Kennedy, G.A., *Classical Rhetoric and its Christian and Secular Tradition from Ancient to Modern Times* (London: Croom Helm, 1980).

—*New Testament Interpretation through Rhetorical Criticism* (Chapel Hill: University of North Carolina Press, 1984).

Kerrigan, P.A., 'Jn. 19,25-27 in the Light of Johannine Theology and the Old Testament', *Antonianum* 35 (1960), pp. 369-416.

Kilpatrick, G.D., 'John iv 41 ΠΛΕΙΟΝ or ΠΛΕΙΟΥΣ', *NovT* 18 (1976), pp. 31-32.

Kittel, G., 'λέγω', *TDNT*, IV, pp. 100-43.

Klauck, H.-J., 'Die dreifache Maria: Zur Rezeption von Joh 19,25 in EvPhil 32', in van Segbroeck, *et al.* (eds.), *The Four Gospels 1992*, III, pp. 2343-58.

Kleinknecht, H., 'λέγω', *TDNT*, IV, pp. 77-91.

Koester, C.R., ' "The Saviour of the World" (John 4.42)', *JBL* 109 (1990), pp. 665-80.

Kremer, J., *Lazarus, die Geschichte einer Auferstehung: Text, Wirkungsgeschichte, und Botschaft von Joh 11,1-46* (Stuttgart: Katholisches Bibelwerk, 1985).

Kutsch, E., *Salbung als Rechtsakt im alten Testament und im alten Orient* (BZAW, 87; Berlin: Alfred Töpelmann, 1963).

Kysar, R., *John, the Maverick Gospel* (Atlanta: John Knox Press, 1976).

La Potterie, I. de, 'Jésus roi et juge d'après Jn 19,13', *Bib* 41 (1960), pp. 217-47.

—*La vérité dans saint Jean* (2 vols.; AnBib, 73, 74; Rome: Biblical Institute Press, 1977).

Lees, E.K., *The Religious Thought of St John* (London: SPCK, 1950).

Leidig, E., *Jesu Gespräch mit der Samaritanerin und weitere Gespräche im Johannesevangelium* (Basel: Friedrich Pustet, 1981).

Leivestad, R., *Christ the Conqueror* (London: SPCK, 1954).

Léon-Dufour, X., 'Towards a Symbolic Reading of the Fourth Gospel', *NTS* 27 (1981), pp. 439-56.

Levison, J.R., 'Did the Spirit Inspire Rhetoric? An Exploration of George Kennedy's Definition of Early Christian Rhetoric', in D.F. Watson (ed.), *Persuasive Artistry* (JSOTSup, 50; Sheffield: JSOT Press, 1991), pp. 25-40.

Lightfoot, R.H., *St John's Gospel: A Commentary* (Oxford: Clarendon Press, 1956).

Limbeck, M., 'ἀθετέω', *EDNT*, I, p. 35.

Lindars, B., *The Gospel of John* (NCB; London: Marshall, Morgan & Scott, 1972).

Lindboe, I.M., 'Recent Literature: Development and Perspectives in New Testament Research on Women', *ST* 43 (1989), pp. 153-63.

Lindner, H., and E. von Eicken, 'ἀποστέλλω', *NIDNTT*, I, pp. 126-28.

Loewe, R., *The Position of Women in Judaism* (London: SPCK, 1966).

Loewenstamm, A., 'Samaritans', *EncJud*, XIV, cols. 725-58.

Lohse, E., 'Miracles in the Fourth Gospel', in M. Hooker and C. Hickling (eds.), *What about the New Testament?* (London: SCM Press, 1975), pp. 64-75.

—'ῥαββί', *TDNT*, VI, pp. 961-65.

Louw, J.P., and E.A. Nida (eds.), *Greek–English Lexicon of the New Testament according to Semantic Domains* (2 vols; London: United Bible Societies, 1988).

Lowy, S., *The Principles of Samaritan Bible Exegesis* (SPB, 28; Leiden: Brill, 1977).

Lütgehetmann, W., *Die Hochzeit von Kana (Joh 2,1-11): Zu Ursprung und Deutung einer Wundererzählung im Rahmen johanneischer Redaktionsgeschichte* (BU, 20; Regensburg: Friedrich Pustet, 1990).

MacDonald, E.M., *The Position of Women as Reflected in Semitic Codes of Law* (Toronto: University of Toronto, 1931).

Macdonald, J., *The Theology of the Samaritans* (London: SCM Press, 1964).

Mack, B., *Rhetoric and the New Testament* (Minneapolis: Fortress Press, 1990).

Mahoney, R., *Two Disciples at the Tomb: The Background and Message of John 20.1-10* (TW, 6; Bern: Herbert Lang; Frankfurt: Peter Lang, 1974).

Malatesta, E., *St John's Gospel 1920–1965: A Cumulative and Classified Bibliography of Books and Periodical Literature on the Fourth Gospel* (AnBib, 32; Rome: Biblical Institute Press, 1967).

Marchadour, A., *Lazare: Histoire d'un récit, récits d'une histoire* (LD, 132; Paris: Cerf, 1988).

Marsh, J., *The Gospel of St John* (Philadelphia: Westminster Press, 1968).

Marshall, I.H., *The Gospel of Luke: A Commentary on the Greek Text* (NIGTC; Grand Rapids: Eerdmans, 1978).

—*The Acts of the Apostles* (TNTC; Grand Rapids: Eerdmans, 1980).

Martin, J.P., 'History and Eschatology in the Lazarus Narrative: John 11.1-44', *SJT* 17 (1964), pp. 332-43.

Martyn, J.L., *History and Theology in the Fourth Gospel* (New York: Harper & Row, 1968).

McHugh, J., *The Mother of Jesus in the New Testament* (London: Darton, Longman & Todd, 1975).

McNeil, B., 'The Raising of Lazarus', *DRev* 17 (1964), pp. 269-75.

Meeks, W.A., *The Prophet King: Moses Traditions and the Johannine Christology* (NovTSup, 14; Leiden: Brill, 1967).

—'The Man from Heaven in Johannine Sectarianism', *JBL* 91 (1972), pp. 44-72.

Meiselman, M., *Jewish Woman in Jewish Law* (LJLE, 6; New York: Ktav, 1978).

Metzger, B.M., *A Textual Commentary on the Greek New Testament: A Companion Volume to the United Bible Societies' Greek New Testament* (New York: United Bible Societies, 1971).

Michaelis, W., 'μύρον', *TDNT*, IV, pp. 800-801.

—'ὁράω', *TDNT*, V, pp. 315-82.

Michaels, J.R., 'John 12.1-11', *Int* 43 (1989), pp. 287-91.

Milgrom, J., and L.I. Rabinowitz, 'Anointing', *EncJud*, III, cols. 27-31.

Minear, P.S., ' "We Don't Know Where..." John 20.2', *Int* 30 (1976), pp. 125-39.

—*John: The Martyr's Gospel* (New York: Pilgrim Press, 1984).

Mlakuzhyil, G., *The Christocentric Literary Structure of the Fourth Gospel* (AnBib, 117; Rome: Biblical Institute Press, 1987).

Moloney, F.J., 'From Cana to Cana (Jn 2.1–4.54) and the Fourth Evangelist's Concept of Correct (and Incorrect) Faith', in E.A. Livingstone (ed.), *Studia Biblica 1978*

    II: *Papers on the Gospels* (JSNTSup, 2; Sheffield: JSOT Press, 1980), pp. 185-213.

—*Woman: First among the Faithful* (London: Darton, Longman & Todd, 1985).

Montgomery, J.A., *The Samaritans, the Earliest Jewish Sect: Their History, Theology and Literature* (repr., New York: Ktav, 1968 [1907]).

Moore, C.A., *Daniel, Esther, and Jeremiah: The Additions* (AB, 44; Garden City, NY: Doubleday, 1977).

Morris, L., *The Gospel according to John* (NICNT; Grand Rapids: Eerdmans, 1971).

—*Jesus Is the Christ: Studies in the Theology of John* (Grand Rapids: Eerdmans, 1989).

Moule, C.F.D., 'The Individualism of the Fourth Gospel', in *Essays in New Testament Interpretation* (Cambridge: Cambridge University Press, 1982), pp. 91-109.

Moulton, J.H., and G. Milligan, *The Vocabulary of the Greek New Testament Illustrated from the Papyri and other Non-Literary Sources* (repr., London: Hodder & Stoughton, 1949 [1930]).

Mowinckel, S., *He That Cometh* (Oxford: Basil Blackwell, 1956).

Müller, D., 'χρίω', *NIDNTT*, I, pp. 121-24.

Murphy, C., 'Women and the Bible', *The Atlantic Monthly* (August, 1993), pp. 39-64.

Neirynck, F., 'John and the Synoptics: The Empty Tomb Stories', in *Evangelica II* (BETL, 99; Leuven: Leuven University Press, 1991), pp. 571-600.

Neufeld, V., *The Earliest Christian Confessions* (NTTS, 5; Leiden: Brill, 1963).

Nicol, R., *The Sēmeia in the Fourth Gospel: Tradition and Redaction* (NovTSup, 32; Leiden: Brill, 1972).

Nörr, D., 'Problems of Legal History in the Gospels', in H.J. Schultz (ed.), *Jesus in his Time* (Philadelphia: Fortress Press, 1971), pp 115-23.

O'Brien, M.A., *The Deuteronomic History Hypothesis: A Reassessment* (OBO, 92; Göttingen: Vandenhoeck & Ruprecht, 1989).

Ò'Cearbhalláin, S., 'What to me . . . ?', *TA* 2 (1987–88), pp. 145-54.

O'Day, G.R., *Revelation in the Fourth Gospel: Narrative Mode and Theological Claim* (Philadelphia: Fortress Press, 1986).

—'John 7.53–8.11: A Study in Misreading', *JBL* 111 (1992), pp. 631-40.

—'John', in Newsom and Ringe (eds.), *The Women's Bible Commentary*, pp. 293-304.

Okure, T., *The Johannine Approach to Mission: A Contextual Study of John 4.1-42* (WUNT, 2.31; Tübingen: Mohr [Paul Siebeck], 1988).

Olsson, B., *Structure and Meaning in the Fourth Gospel: A Text-Linguistic Analysis of John 2.1-11 and 4.1-42* (ConBNT, 6; Lund: Gleerup, 1974).

Painter, J., *John: Witness and Theologian* (London: SPCK, 1975).

—*The Quest for the Messiah: The History, Literature and Theology of the Johannine Community* (Edinburgh: T. & T. Clark, 1991).

Pamment, M., 'Is there Convincing Evidence of Samaritan Influence on the Fourth Gospel?', *ZNW* 73 (1982), pp. 221-30.

Pancaro, S., *The Law in the Fourth Gospel: The Torah and the Gospel, Moses and Jesus, Judaism and Christianity according to John* (NovTSup, 42; Leiden: Brill, 1975).

Patrick, D., and A. Scult, *Rhetoric and Biblical Interpretation* (JSOTSup, 82; Sheffield: Almond Press, 1990).

Perkins, P., '"I Have Seen the Lord" (John 20.18): Women Witnesses to the Resurrection', *Int* 46 (1992), pp. 31-41.

Pervo, R.I., 'Aseneth and her Sisters: Women in Jewish Narrative and in the Greek

Novels', in A.-J. Levine (ed.), *Women Like This: New Perspectives on Jewish Women in the Greco–Roman World* (SBLEJL, 1; Atlanta: Scholars Press, 1991), pp. 145-60.

Pesch, W., 'ὀργή', *EDNT*, II, pp. 529-30.

Piper, O.A., 'Messiah', *ISBE*, III, pp. 330-38.

Porsch, F., *Johannes-Evangelium* (SKK, 4; Stuttgart: Katholisches Bibelwerk, 1988).

Preiss, T., *Life in Christ* (London: SCM Press, 1954).

Procksch, O., 'λέγω', *TDNT*, IV, pp. 91-100.

Pummer, R., *The Samaritans* (IR 23.5; Leiden: Brill, 1987).

—'Samaritan Rituals and Customs', in A.D. Crown (ed.), *The Samaritans* (Tübingen: Mohr [Paul Siebeck], 1989), pp. 650-90.

Purvis, J.D., 'The Fourth Gospel and the Samaritans', *NT* 17 (1975), pp 161-98.

—'The Samaritans and Judaism', in R.A. Kraft and G.W.E. Nickelsburg (eds.), *Early Judaism and its Modern Interpreters* (SBLCP; Philadelphia: Fortress Press; Atlanta: Scholars Press, 1986), pp. 81-98.

Rad, G. von, *Deuteronomy* (London: SCM Press, 1966).

Räisänen, H., *Die Mutter Jesu im Neuen Testament* (AASF, B.47; Helsinki: Suomalainen Tiedeakatemia, 2nd edn, 1989).

Reim, G., *Studien zum alttestamentlichen Hintergrund des Johannesevangeliums* (SNTSMS, 22; Cambridge: Cambridge University Press, 1974).

Rena, J., 'Women in the Gospel of John', *EgTh* 17 (1986), pp. 131-47.

Rengstorf, K.H., 'ἀποστέλλω', *TDNT*, I, pp. 398-447.

Rensberger, D., *Overcoming the World: Politics and Community in the Gospel of John* (London: SPCK, 1989).

Richardson, H.N., 'Some Notes on 1QSa', *JBL* 76 (1957), pp. 108-22.

Richter, G., 'Blut und Wasser aus der durchbohrten Seite Jesu (Joh 19,34b)', in J. Hainz (ed.), *Studien zum Johannesevangelium* (BU, 13; Regensburg: Friedrich Pustet, 1977), pp. 120-42.

Riesenfeld, H., 'Zu den johannischer ἵνα-Sätzen', *ST* 19 (1965), pp. 213-20.

Riga, P., 'Signs of Glory: The Use of "Semeion" in St John's Gospel', *Int* 17 (1963), pp. 402-24.

Roberts, C., 'John 20.30-31 and 21.24-25', *JTS* 38 (1987), pp. 409-10.

Robertson, A.T., *A Grammar of the Greek New Testament in the Light of Historical Research* (London: Hodder & Stoughton, 1914).

Robinson, J.A.T., 'The "Others" of John 4.38: A Test of Exegetical Method', in *Twelve New Testament Studies* (SBT, 34; London: SCM Press, 1962), pp. 61-66.

—*The Priority of John* (London: SCM Press, 1985).

Rochais, G., *Les récits de résurrection des morts dans le Nouveau Testament* (SNTSMS, 40; Cambridge: Cambridge University Press, 1981).

Roth, C. (ed.), *Encyclopaedia Judaica* (16 vols; Jerusalem: Keter Publishing House, 1972).

Sabbe, M., 'The Anointing of Jesus in John 12,1-8 and its Synoptic Parallels', in van Segbroeck, *et al.* (eds.), *The Four Gospels 1992*, III, pp. 2051-82.

Sasson, J.M., *Ruth: A New Translation with a Philological Commentary and a Formalist-Folklorist Interpretation* (Sheffield: JSOT Press, 2nd edn, 1989).

Schmithals, W., 'Introduction', in R. Bultmann, *The Gospel of John: A Commentary* (Philadelphia: Westminster Press, 1971), pp. 3-12.

Schnackenburg, R., *The Gospel according to St John* (repr., 3 vols.; New York: Crossroad, 1990 [1979]).

Schneiders, S.M., 'Women in the Fourth Gospel and the Role of Women in the Contemporary Church', *BTB* 12 (1982), pp. 35-45.

—'Death in the Community of Eternal Life: History, Theology, and Spirituality in John 11', *Int* 41 (1987), pp. 44-56.

Schnelle, U., *Antidocetic Christology in the Gospel of John: An Investigation of the Place of the Fourth Gospel in the Johannine School* (Minneapolis: Fortress Press, 1992).

Schottroff, L., *Der Glaubende und die feindliche Welt: Beobachtungen zum gnostischen Dualismus und seiner Bedeutung für Paulus und das Johannesevangelium* (WMANT, 37; Neukirchen: Neukirchener Verlag, 1970).

Schüssler Fiorenza, E. (ed.), *Aspects of Religious Propaganda in Judaism and Early Christianity* (South Bend: University of Notre Dame Press, 1976).

—*In Memory of Her: A Feminist Theological Reconstruction of Christian Origins* (London: SCM Press, 1983).

Schweizer, E., *Church Order in the New Testament* (London: SCM Press, 1961).

—'Das johanneische Zeugnis von Herrenmahl', in *Neotestamentica: Deutsche und englische Aufsätzen 1951–1963* (Zürich: Zwingli-Verlag, 1963).

Scott, M., *Sophia and the Johannine Jesus* (JSNTSup, 71; Sheffield: JSOT Press, 1992).

Seidensticker, P., *Der Auferstehung Jesu in der Botschaft der Evangelisten: Ein traditionsgeschichtlicher Versuch zum Problem der Sicherung der Osterbotschaft in der apostolischen Zeit* (SBS, 26; Stuttgart: Katholisches Bibelwerk, 1967).

Seim, T.K., 'Roles of Women in the Gospel of John', in L. Hartmann and B. Olsson (eds.), *Aspects on the Johannine Literature* (ConBNT, 18; Uppsala: Uppsala University Press, 1987), pp. 56-73.

Setel, D.O., 'Exodus', in Newsom and Ringe (eds.), *The Women's Bible Commentary*, pp. 26-35.

Sly, D., *Philo's Perception of Women* (BJS, 209; Atlanta: Scholars Press, 1990).

Smalley, S.S., *John: Evangelist and Interpreter* (Exeter: Paternoster Press, 1978).

Smith, G.V., 'Prophet', *ISBE*, III, pp. 986-1004.

Stagg, E., and F. Stagg, *Woman in the World of Jesus* (Philadelphia: Westminster Press, 1978).

Staley, J.L., *The Print's First Kiss: A Rhetorical Investigation of the Implied Reader in the Fourth Gospel* (SBLDS, 82; Atlanta: Scholars Press, 1988).

Stauffer, E., *Jesus and His Story* (London: SCM Press, 1960).

Stenhouse, P., 'Samaritan Chronicles', in A.D. Crown (ed.), *The Samaritans* (Tübingen: Mohr [Paul Siebeck], 1989), pp. 218-65.

Stibbe, M.W.G., *John as Storyteller: Narrative Criticism and the Fourth Gospel* (SNTSMS, 73; Cambridge: Cambridge University Press, 1992).

—*John* (Sheffield: JSOT Press, 1993).

Swidler, L., *Women in Judaism: The Status of Women in Formative Judaism* (Metuchen, NJ: Scarecrow Press, 1976).

Talbert, C.H., *Reading John: A Literary and Theological Commentary on the Fourth Gospel and the Johannine Epistles* (London: SPCK, 1992).

Tenney, M.C., 'The Meaning of "Witness" in John', *BSac* 132 (1975), pp. 229-41.

Thomas, J.C., *Footwashing in John 13 and the Johannine Community* (JSNTSup, 61; Sheffield: JSOT Press, 1991).

Townsend, H.C., 'The Gospel of Evidence', *Expositor* 8.25 (1923), pp. 312-20.

Trites, A.A., *The New Testament Concept of Witness* (SNTSMS, 31; Cambridge: Cambridge University Press, 1977).

Van Belle, G., *Johannine Bibliography 1966–1985: A Cumulative Bibliography on the Fourth Gospel* (BETL, 82; Leuven: Leuven University Press, 1988).

Wahlde, U.C. von, 'The Witnesses to Jesus in John 5.31-40 and Belief in the Fourth Gospel', *CBQ* 43 (1981), pp. 385-404.

Walker, R., 'Jüngerwort und Herrenwort: Zur Auslegung von Joh 4.39-42', *ZNW* 57 (1966), pp. 49-54

Warner, M., 'The Fourth Gospel's Art of Rational Persuasion', in *idem* (ed.), *The Bible as Rhetoric* (London: Routledge & Kegan Paul, 1990), pp. 153-77.

Wegner, J.R., *Chattel or Person? The Status of Women in the Mishnah* (New York: Oxford University Press, 1988).

Weinfeld, M., *Deuteronomy and the Deuteronomic School* (Oxford: Clarendon Press, 1972).

Weinfeld, M.W., *The Organizational Pattern and the Penal Code of the Qumran Sect* (NTOA, 2; Göttingen: Vandenhoeck & Ruprecht, 1986).

Weiser, A., 'διακονέω', *EDNT*, I, pp. 302-304.

Wenham, J., *Easter Enigma: Do the Resurrection Stories Contradict One Another?* (Exeter: Paternoster Press, 1984).

Westcott, B.F., *The Gospel according to St John: The Greek Text with Introduction and Notes* (2 vols.; London: John Murray, 1908).

Westcott, B.F., and F.J.A. Hort, *Introduction to the New Testament in the Original Greek* (repr., Peabody, MA: Hendrickson, 1988 [1882]).

Wilder, A.N., *Early Christian Rhetoric* (Cambridge, MA: Harvard University Press, 1971).

Wilton, M.R., 'Witness as a Theme in the Fourth Gospel' (PhD dissertation, New Orleans Baptist Theological Seminary, 1992).

Wink, W., ' "And the Lord Appeared First to Mary": Sexual Politics in the Resurrection Witness', in D. Hessel (ed.), *Social Themes of the Christian Year* (Philadelphia: Westminster Press, 1983), pp. 177-82.

Winter, B.W., 'Civil Litigation in Secular Corinth and the Church: The Forensic Background to 1 Corinthians 6.1-8', *NTS* 37 (1991), pp. 559-72.

Wire, A.C., *The Corinthian Women Prophets: A Reconstruction through Paul's Rhetoric* (Minneapolis: Fortress Press, 1990).

Witherington, B., *Women in the Ministry of Jesus* (SNTSMS, 51; Cambridge: Cambridge University Press, 1984).

Wuellner, W., 'Where Is Rhetorical Criticism Taking Us?', *CBQ* 49 (1987), pp. 448-63.

—'Putting Life Back into the Lazarus Story and its Reading: The Narrative Rhetoric of John 11 as the Narration of Faith', *Semeia* 53 (1991), pp. 113-32.

Zerwick, M., *Biblical Greek Illustrated by Examples* (SPIB, 114; Rome: Biblical Institute Press, 1963).

INDEXES

INDEX OF REFERENCES

OLD TESTAMENT

NEW TESTAMENT

OTHER ANCIENT REFERENCES

JOURNAL FOR THE STUDY OF THE NEW TESTAMENT
SUPPLEMENT SERIES